English

Class 06

Authors
Srishti Agarwal
Chetansi Sharma

ARIHANT PRAKASHAN
(School Division Series)

ADMINISTRATIVE & PRODUCTION OFFICES
Regd. Office
'Ramchhaya' 4577/15, Agarwal Road, Darya Ganj, New Delhi -110002
Tele: 011- 47630600, 43518550; Fax: 011- 23280316

Head Office
Kalindi, TP Nagar, Meerut (UP) - 250002, Tel: 0121-7156203, 7156204

SALES & SUPPORT OFFICES
Agra, Ahmedabad, Bengaluru, Bareilly, Chennai, Delhi, Guwahati, Hyderabad, Jaipur, Jhansi, Kolkata, Lucknow, Nagpur & Pune.

PO No. : TXT-59-T070643-4-26

Published By Arihant Publications (India) Ltd.

For further information about the books published by Arihant, log on to www.arihantbooks.com or e-mail at info@arihantbooks.com

Follow us on    

PRICE ₹ 290.00

PRODUCTION TEAM

Publishing Managers
Mahendra Singh Rawat &
Keshav Mohan

Project Head
Karishma Yadav

Project Coordinator
Manju

Cover Designer
Bilal Hashmi

Inner Designer
Ankit Prajapati

Page Layouting
Sundar Bisht

Proof Readers
Harsh Agarwal
Sumit Bharti

Inside the Book

SECTION A : READING SKILLS

CHAPTER 1

Unseen Passages

Let's REVISE

Unseen Passage or Reading Comprehension is a language activity that involves a thorough understanding of a given passage or poem consisting of one or more paragraphs. It tests the understanding powers and analytical skills of a student with questions that evaluate the reader's ability to

- find the main idea or a suitable title for the text.
- find information directly specified in the passage.
- draw conclusions from the given passage.
- determine the meaning of words used in the passage.
- determine the author's style, mood or point of view.

Types of Passages

There are many types of passages from which questions can be asked. However, in Class VI, we focus on three types of passages.

They are

1. **Factual Passages** These passages include a set of facts and descriptions which are provided in a clear and straightforward manner.
2. **Discursive Passages** These passages include opinions, thoughts and comments that reader interprets to form his/her own opinions.
3. **Poetry** These include poems written by poets from all over the world.

Types of Questions

Two types of questions are asked from a reading comprehension

1. Multiple Choice Questions
2. Subjective Short Answer Type Questions

For a better understanding of the type of questions, we have divided the passages into these two categories.

Points to be Kept in Mind

- Read the passage carefully and thoroughly to understand its contents.
- Read all the questions given.
- Now, read the passage for the second time and underline the words, phrases and sentences which can be answers to the questions asked
- **For Subjective Type Questions**
  (i) Write the answers in one or two sentences. Word count should not be more than 20 words.
  (ii) Write your answers in the same tense in which the questions are asked
  (iii) Answer should be to-the-point and in your own words.
- **For MCQs**
  (i) Read all the four options carefully.
  (ii) Choose the answer that best connects with the question as per the passage.
- Underline the words you don't understand and try to guess their meaning from the meaning of the sentence. It will help you in answering vocabulary related questions.
- Read the passage again to counter check your answers and write your answers briefly and to the point.

SAMPLE PASSAGES

PASSAGE 1

Read the following passage and answer the questions that follow.

The Ganges is 2525 km long river which originates in the western Himalayas in India's Uttarakhand state and flows South and East through the Gangetic plain of North India to Bangladesh. It ends into the Bay of Bengal. There are many rivers in India but the Ganges is the most sacred river for the Hindus. Every year, the Hindus celebrate the descent of the Ganges from heaven to the Earth. They celebrate it as Ganga Dussehra. A dip in the Ganges on this day is said to rid the person of ten sins.

It is also important historically, with many former provinces and capitals (such as Pataliputra, Kannauj, Kara, Kashi, Allahabad, Murshidabad, Munger, Baharampur, Kampilya and Kolkata) located on its banks. The Ganges was ranked as the fifth most polluted river of the world in 2007. Pollution threatens not only humans but also over 140 fish species and the endangered Ganges river dolphin.

Many environmental initiatives were taken up by the Central and State Governments to clean it up. But they failed due to lack of technical expertise, poor environmental planning and lack of support from religious authorities.

The river suffers from extreme pollution levels, which affect the 400 million people who live close to the river. Sewage from many cities along the river's course, industrial waste and religious offerings wrapped in non-degradable plastics add large amounts of pollutants to the river as it flows through densely populated areas. The river water is neither fit for drinking nor for taking bath. It is said that 80% of all illnesses in India and one-third of deaths can be attributed to water-borne diseases. The polluted water can also cause allergy and skin problems.

Questions

1. Where does the Ganges river originate?

2. Complete the following sentence

The Ganges river flows through the Gangetic plain of North India to ....

3. Complete the following analogy

Ganges : Sacred River :: .... : Endangered Species

4. What does the writer mean by the following word 'Non-degradable plastics'?

5. Which of the following cities is not located on the banks of the Ganges?

(a) Pataliputra (b) Kannauj
(c) Mumbai (d) Kolkata

6. The Ganges river was ranked as the .... most polluted, river in the world in 2007.

(a) first (b) third
(c) fifth (d) seventh

Answers

1. The Ganges River originates in the Western Himalayas in Uttarakhand, India.
2. Bangladesh
3. Ganges River Dolphin
4. Non-degradable plastics are plastics that do not break down naturally in the environment.
5. (c) Mumbai 6. (c) fifth

PASSAGE 2

Read the following passage and answer the questions that follow by choosing the correct option.

The Group of Twenty (G20) is the global forum for international economic cooperation. The G20's work is divided into two tracks : The Finance Track and the Sherpa Track.

The Group of Twenty (G20) comprises 19 countries (Argentina, Australia, Brazil, Canada, China, France, Germany, India, Indonesia, Italy, Japan, Republic of Korea, Mexico, Russia, Saudi Arabia, South Africa, Turkey, United Kingdom and United States) and the European Union. The G20 members represent around 85% of the global GDP, over 75% of the global trade, and about two-thirds of the world population. The G20 Summit is held annually. The First G20 Summit was held in 2008 in Washington DC, USA.

On 9th and 10th September, the G20 2023 Summit was held in New Delhi, India with the nation having G20 Presidency. At the G20 Summit, under the theme of "One Earth, One Family, One Future," important issues such as food security, climate and energy, development, health and digitalisation were discussed.

In the 'One Earth' session, participants discussed such issues as the world economy, food security, climate and energy, and environment. In the 'One Family' session, participants discussed inclusive growth, the SDGs, health and other issues. G20 members confirmed the importance of reducing poverty, inequality and preparing for pandemic. In the 'One Future' session, the leaders discussed the international reforms, digital and other issues.

Questions

1. Where was the first G20 Summit held?
2. Complete the following sentence
   The G20 members represent around 85% of the global GDP, over 75% of the global trade, and about .... of the world population.
3. Complete the following analogy
   G20 : International Economic Cooperation :: SDGs: ....
4. What does the writer mean by 'Sherpa Track'?
5. Which of the following issues was discussed in the 'One Earth' session at the G20 2023 Summit?
   (a) Inclusive growth (b) Digitalisation
   (c) Climate and energy (d) International reforms
6. What does the word 'inclusive' most likely mean in the context of the passage?
   (a) Exclusive
   (b) Comprehensive
   (c) Limited
   (d) Partial

Answers

1. The first G20 Summit held in. Washington DC, USA
2. two-third
3. Sustainable Development Goals
4. The Sherpa Track refers to the part of the G20's work that deals with non-financial issues, such as political engagement, development, and social policies.
5. (c) Climate and energy
6. (b) Comprehensive

PRACTICE PASSAGES

Including All Types of Passages

PASSAGE 1

Read the passages given below carefully and answer the questions that follow. Practice

When we enter New York harbour, the first thing we see is the Statue of Liberty. What impresses us the most is its size and magnificence. But have you ever wondered how it came to be there?

The Statue of Liberty was a gift from the people of France to mark the one hundred year anniversary of American Independence. In 1869, sculptor Frederic Auguste Bartholdi began to plan his concept for the monument. Bartholdi chose the look of classic Greek and Roman figures. He envisioned Liberty as a strong and proud figure, one who personified not only the majestic Greek goddesses of the past, but also the working men and women of the present. Finally, in 1884 the work was finished and Liberty was packed into 214 crates and sent to New York City.

Now, only one problem stood in the way. While the French had raised a lot of funds to build the statue, New York had not secured the funds to build its foundation. It was not until a New York newspaper implored people for donations that money became available. Finally, on 28th October 1886 Americans celebrated the unveiling of the Statue of Liberty.

Questions

1. Who gifted the Statue of Liberty to the United States?
2. Complete the following sentence
   The Statue of Liberty was a gift from the people of France to mark the .... anniversary of American Independence.
3. Complete the following analogy
   Frederic Auguste Bartholdi : Sculptor :: Liberty : ....
4. What does the writer mean by 'Implored'?
5. What characteristics did Bartholdi want his figure to have?
   (a) Strong, proud and hard-working
   (b) Dedication and sincerity
   (c) Greek and Roman qualities
   (d) Egoistic and grand
6. How many years did it take for Bartholdi to complete his sculpture?
   (a) 14 years (b) 15 years
   (c) 20 years (d) 17 years

PASSAGE 2

Read the following passage and answer the questions that follow by choosing the correct option.

The importance of learning is to help a child grow in life. Education makes a child a right thinker and a good decision-maker. He gains knowledge from what is going on in the world. Good learning teaches him to question and makes him aware about history so that he can be a better judge of the present.

A well-educated man is a better citizen and helps others to grow. He tries to bring overall development of people around him. Such person becomes pride for his family and brings honour to his country. A nation becomes prosperous if there are more number of literate people. Education brings three-fold development of a child's physical, mental and spiritual level. Therefore, a child needs a perfect system which can inculcate such things.

His institute must do full justice to develop him physically, mentally and spiritually. Parents should make the right choice while selecting schools for their children.

School education is very important as it lays the foundation stone for development of a child. Therefore, for the past few years, the demand for good schools has grown by leaps and bounds. Everybody from the poorest of the poor to the well-off knows the value of selecting a good school.

School Education System in India has been changed and is divided into four parts: Foundational, Preparatory, Middle, Secondary. Schooling in India follows the '5+3+3+4 pattern'.

The government started Sarva Shiksha Abhiyaan to ensure universal elementary education for all children aged from 6 to 14 years. On 1st April, 2010, India reached a milestone in country's struggle for children's Right To Education (RTE).

The Constitution has made elementary education a fundamental right. The Right of Children to Free and Compulsory Education (RTE) Act 2009, came into force. It is based on three-fold development of a child.

Questions

1. What is the main purpose of education according to the passage?
2. Complete the following sentence

   Education brings three-fold development of a child's physical, mental and .... level.
3. Complete the following analogy

   Well-educated man : Better citizen :: Literate people : ....
4. What does the writer mean by the 'Leaps and bounds'?
5. What is the Right of Children to Free and Compulsory Education (RTE) Act, 2009 based on?
   (a) Two-fold development of a child
   (b) Three-fold development of a child
   (c) Four-fold development of a child
   (d) Five-fold development of a child
6. What should parents consider when selecting schools for their children?
   (a) The school's location
   (b) The school's reputation
   (c) The school's ability to develop a child physically, mentally, and spiritually
   (d) The school's extracurricular activites

PASSAGE 3

Read the following passage and answer the questions that follow by choosing the correct option.

It was known that Sonia was the best speller in Class VI. She could spell difficult words like 'handkerchief' and 'modification' very easily. She was loved by her teacher as she used to get good scores in each weekly spelling test.

A new English teacher came in the class and his name was Sanjeev Srivastava.

He introduced a rule for spelling tests that those students who do not score at least 60% in the spelling tests would have to copy each word seventy-five times for next week's spelling test. Seema, who sat next to Sonia, always struggled in writing spellings. Last time, she scored only 48% in the test which meant copying each word seventy-five times.

Sonia was confident that her spelling abilities are good and decided not to study for her next spelling test.

The test began the next day. Srivastava pronounced each word and then repeated it. Everything was fine until he spoke 'Czechoslovakia'. Sonia scribbled c-z-e-c-h-o-s-l-o-v-a... now what? Whether it will be 'kia or kiya'. She wondered.

The teacher started pronouncing the next word.

Sonia thought that Seema knew the spelling as she has written it many times. Sonia rolled her eyes to the right to see Seema's paper. Sonia saw the word in Seema's paper and finished the word with the letters 'kia'.

Sonia was nervous because she cheated for the first time in her life. She thought, "Is it the way to keep my unmatched record-by being a cheater?" She decided to erase it and write what she knew. She wrote the wrong answer.

She wrote 'kiya'. She was happy and sighed with relief. She thought, "What if I don't get perfect scores? At least I am honest."

Questions

1. Why did Sonia not study for the spelling test?
2. Complete the following sentence

   Sonia could spell difficult words like 'handkerchief' and '..........' very easily.
3. Complete the following analogy

   Sonia : Best speller :: Seema : ....
4. What does the writer mean by 'Scribbled'?
5. Which quality would you attach to Sonia?

   (a) Happy (b) Courageous

   (c) Jealous (d) Honest
6. What was the consequence for students who did not score at least 60% in the spelling tests?

   (a) They had to stay after school

   (b) They had to copy each word seventy-five times

   (c) They had to take a retest

   (d) They had to write an essay

PASSAGE 4

Read the following passage and answer the questions that follow by choosing the correct option.

The civilisation is growing faster and our need for energy is increasing day-by-day. We use energy in the form of petrol, diesel and natural gas. These are likely to be exhausted in due course of time as they are fossil fuels and people are continuously using it. People are using energy in home, office, hospitals, industries and through transportation.

Electricity is also a form of energy and depends on availability of petrol and water resources.

Everybody is facing the problem of energy shortage. We can suppress our demand and minimise non-essential consumption. Industry can also reduce wastage by using materials requiring lower energy. It should curtail heat loss to the environment and can save energy by adopting quality control measures. Power cut can save energy or conserve it for better usage.

Energy conservation is possible through modernisation of plant and equipment. Electronics item like the television, radio and computer can be used carefully. Wasteful usage of lights can be avoided. People should travel in bus and railways while commuting to save energy. Animals can be used for transportation for short distances. Energy shortage is a global problem and needs to be solved as our future generation needs it.

Questions

1. What are the forms of energy mentioned in the passage?
2. Complete the following sentence

   Energy conservation is possible through modernisation of ....
3. Complete the following analogy

   Petrol, diesel and natural gas : Fossil fuels :: Electricity : ....
4. What does the writer mean by 'Energy conservation'?
5. Which of the following is not mentioned as a way to save energy in the passage?

   (a) Using materials requiring lower energy

   (b) Travelling by bus and railways

   (c) Using animals for transportation for short distances

   (d) Increasing the use of air conditioning
6. Why is energy conservation important according to the passage?

   (a) To reduce electricity bills

   (b) To ensure availability for future generations

   (c) To improve industrial efficiency

   (d) To promote technological advancements

PASSAGE 5

Read the following passage and answer the questions that follow by choosing the correct option.

Honesty is a virtue. People say we should always speak the truth as we don't have to remember what we said. Honest people are respected and trusted everywhere as they stand by the truth. But people might find themselves in a situation that requires them to tell one or two lies to avoid trouble. This can provide a temporary solution, not a final breakthrough. Being honest is not easy. Those who speak the truth face difficulty in the beginning but later things become simple.

Honesty is the best policy because no matter how good you are at telling lies, the truth will always come out. Honesty helps to steer us in the right direction in life and helps us avoid criminal activities. An honest person always lives a satisfied life because his conscience is clear. Such a person does not have to worry about being caught.

People who constantly lie not only lose their friends but also their reputation since no one would like to associate with a dishonest person. Even when a dishonest person tries to speak the truth, nobody believes him. A dishonest person loses self-confidence in life. Sometimes, people lie again and again to escape problems. They make their life more complicated.

People who are dishonest have a tendency to cheat others. They will be involved in corrupt activities. They fool people to fulfill their selfish ends. Therefore, it is important to be honest as this leads to a good and free life.

People are rewarded later in life if they follow the path of truth. Always live an honest life and stand up to right things. Keep in mind that you are solely responsible for what you say or do. Be honest and everything will turn good for you.

Questions

1. What is the main virtue discussed in the passage?
2. Complete the following sentence

   Honest people are respected and trusted everywhere because they ....
3. Complete the following analogy

   Honest people : Respected :: Dishonest people : ....
4. What does the writer mean by 'Temporary solution' in the context of telling lies?
5. According to the passage, what happens to people who constantly lie?

   (a) They gain more friends
   (b) They lose their reputation
   (c) They live a satisfied life
   (d) They are always believed
6. What is the meaning of the word 'conscience' as used in the passage?

   (a) A person's moral sense of right and wrong
   (b) A person's physical health
   (c) A person's intelligence
   (d) A person's social status

PASSAGE 6

Read the following passage and answer the questions that follow by choosing the correct option.

Though fast foods are easy to prepare and liked by almost all people, they are very harmful for human beings. Many researchers have proved that these food items are not good for health. They are fried in oil which can have ill-effects on health. This can make us obese. Especially, cholesterol is very harmful for heart. Obesity can further lead to diabetes and high blood pressure. Such foods don't have good nutrition value for body.

Children who eat too much of fast food will suffer from lifestyle diseases. Their growth will be affected as compared to those who eat nutritious food. Children are not able to control themselves when it comes to eating fast food. It takes less time to prepare and is convenient to eat. People find it delicious and they are easily available. They prefer to eat burgers, pizza, noodles, etc.

People are imitating Western culture and preferring fast food over home-made food. It is one of the ill-effects of adopting the Western culture. Change in lifestyle has taught people to alter their eating habits. People are working for long hours.

They don't have time to shop for kitchen and prepare food. People have started working so who will prepare meals. The standard of living has increased and people can spend more on such fast food. Eating it is considered to be fashion, so youth prefers it.

Fast food culture has also resulted in ending the family tradition of eating together. Children rarely eat together which gives them less opportunity to talk to their parents and elders.

The foreign companies which prepare fast food promote it by giving discounts in such a way that children get attracted towards it. Advertising of fast food is promoting its sale across the world. The companies are making profits at the cost of children's health.

Questions

1. What is one of the main health issues caused by fast food?
2. Complete the following sentence

   Children who eat too much fast food will suffer from ....
3. Complete the following analogy

   Fast food : Obesity :: Nutritious food : ....
4. What does the writer mean by 'Lifestyle diseases' in the context of eating fast food?
5. According to the passage, why do people prefer fast food over home-made food?

   (a) It is more nutritious
   (b) It is cheaper
   (c) It is convenient and takes less time to prepare
   (d) It is healthier
6. What is the meaning of the word 'imitating' as used in the passage?

   (a) Ignoring (b) Copying
   (c) Criticising (d) Avoiding

PASSAGE 7

Read the following passage and answer the questions that follow.

ChatGPT is an artificial intelligence programme that generates dialogue. Created by open AI, this highly-capable chatbot uses machine learning algorithms to process and analyse large amounts of data to generate responses to user inquiries. This language processing programme is able to understand human language as it is spoken and written, allowing it to understand ChatGPT spits back out an easily understandable answer in a variety of formats with precise stipulations.

For example, you can ask the question, 'Explain how climate change affects endangered species.' You can tell it, 'Write me a poem', and when it does, say, 'Now make it more exciting.'

One of the key features of ChatGPT is its ability to generate responses like humans in real time. It can give natural answers to questions in a conversational tone and can generate stories, essays, and poems. Moreover, ChatGPT can : answer questions, solve math equations, translate between languages, debug and fix code, write a story/poem and classify things.

Perhaps more amazing is the ease at which ChatGPT produces these responses. Students could potentially spend hours researching and drafting an essay on quantum mechanics, whereas ChatGPT can produce a well-written alternative in seconds. There are some limitations of ChatGPT. Due to its infancy, the chatbot may generate incorrect information or have a limited understanding of a topic because answers are based on data that is limited to 2020 and prior.

Questions

1. What is ChatGPT?
2. Complete the following sentence

   ChatGPT can generate responses in a variety of formats with ....
3. Who created ChatGPT?
4. What does the writer mean by 'Machine learning algorithms'?
5. What is one of the key features of ChatGPT?
   (a) It can only answer questions
   (b) It can generate responses like humans in real time
   (c) It can only solve math equations
   (d) It can only translate between languages
6. What does the word 'infancy' mean in the context of the passage?
   (a) Advanced stage (b) Early stage
   (c) Middle stage (d) Final stage

PASSAGE 8

Read the following passage and answer the questions that follow.

Chandrayaan-3 is India's ambitious and successful lunar mission. Chandrayaan-3 lander stands about 2 meters tall and has a mass of just over 1,700 kg. Following in the footsteps of its predecessors, Chandrayaan-1 and Chandrayaan-2, Chandrayaan-3 mission was launched on 14th July 2023 from India's main space port Satish Dhawan Space Centre Second Launch Pad in Andhra Pradesh. After circulating around the orbit of Earth, it transferred to a lunar orbit and emerged as a focus of national pride and global interest. The spacecraft entered lunar orbit on 5th August, 2023 and lander touched down near the lunar South Pole on 23rd August, 2023.

Chandrayaan-3 is expected to remain functional for two weeks, running a series of experiments to study the mineral composition of the South Pole of the lunar surface. The lunar South Pole is a region with water ice, or frozen water that could be a source of oxygen, fuel and water.

Questions

1. When was Chandrayaan-3 launched?
2. Complete the following sentence

   Chandrayaan-3 lander stands about .... tall and has a mass of just over ....
3. Complete the following analogy

   Chandrayaan-1 : Predecessor :: Chandrayaan-3 : ....
4. What does the writer mean by 'Lunar South Pole'?
5. What does the word 'ambitious' mean in the context of the passage?
   (a) Unimportant (b) Modest
   (c) Aspiring (d) Simple
6. What is the primary purpose of Chandrayaan-3's experiments?
   (a) To study the atmosphere of the moon
   (b) To study the mineral composition of the lunar South Pole
   (c) To communicate with aliens
   (d) To explore the entire lunar surface

PASSAGE 9

Read the following passage and answer the questions that follow.

Health is as valuable as money and without it you would not enjoy anything in life. Without good health, neither people will work efficiently nor will students study properly. Hence, everyone needs to be healthy.

There are various ways by which people can live a good and healthy life. Many people do not get enough time for physical exercise. Thus, they become obese, suffer from hypertension and diabetes. Even children like to sit in front of their computers and avoid outdoor games and activities.

People should visit a gym or go for morning walk or work out so that they can burn fat deposited in their body. Children should play outside rather than sitting and playing video-games at their houses.

They should drink plenty of water, it keeps our skin healthy and burns body fat. Proper sleep is also important as our body needs to relax and reduce stress. We should eat proper balanced diet. Eat more fruits, vegetables and avoid fatty foods. Quit unhealthy habits like smoking, drinking alcohol and chewing tobacco.

Questions

1. Why is health considered as valuable as money?

2. Complete the following sentence

Without good health, neither people will work efficiently nor will ....

3. Complete the following analogy

Physical exercise : Obesity prevention :: Proper sleep : ....

4. What does the writer mean by 'Balanced diet'?

5. According to the passage, what should children do instead of playing video games?

(a) Watch TV (b) Play outside
(c) Read books (d) Sleep more

6. What does the word 'obese' mean in the context of the passage?

(a) Underweight (b) Overweight
(c) Healthy (d) Fit

PASSAGE 10

Read the following passage and answer the questions that follow.

In a village, a boy lived with his father and mother.
The parents were depressed due to their son's bad temper. The boy used to get angry very soon. He scolded neighbours and even his friends due to anger. They started avoiding him. His parents counseled him but unfortunately all their attempts failed. Finally, the boy's father came up with an idea. His father gave him a bag of nails. He asked his son to hammer one nail to the fence every time he gets angry. The little boy found it strange and accepted it.

He hammered 30 nails in the fence on the first day. Every time he lost his temper, he hammered a nail. In the next few days, the number of nails hammered was reduced to half. He found it difficult to hammer nails and decided to control his temper. Gradually, the number of nails reduced and a day arrived when no nail was hammered.

The boy did not lose his temper. He told his father about the same. His father told him to remove the nails every day as he had controlled his anger. The boy was able to pull out most of the nails except some nails. He told his father about it. The father appreciated him and asked him pointing towards the hole, 'What do you see there?'

He replied, 'A hole in the fence!' The father said, 'The nails were your bad temper and they were hammered on people. You can remove the nails but still see holes in the fence. You cannot pull out a few nails. You can stab a man but the wound will remain there. Your bad temper and anger were like that. Words are more painful than physical abuse. Use words for good.'

Questions

1. Why were the boy's parents depressed?

2. Complete the following sentence

The boy hammered 30 nails in the fence on the first day because ....

3. State whether the following statement is True or False.

The parents wanted their son to stop being angry.

4. What does the writer mean by the following phrase?

'Words are more painful than physical abuse.'

5. What did the boy's father ask him to do every time he got angry?

(a) Go for a walk
(b) Hammer a nail into the fence
(c) Write in a journal
(d) Talk to a friend

6. What does the word 'counselled' mean in the context of the passage?

(a) Ignored
(b) Advised
(c) Punished
(d) Praised

PASSAGE 11

Read the passage given below to answer the questions that follow.

Peer pressure is a phenomenon wherein we tend to get influenced by the lifestyle and the ways of thinking of our peers. Peer pressure can prove beneficial but it is most often observed to have negative effects.

The thought, behaviour and taste in fashion, music, television and other walks of life of the masses are often seen to have a deep impact on society. We tend to get influenced by the lifestyle of our peer group. The changing ways of life of our peers often force us to change our ways of looking at life and leading it. It's a human tendency to do what the crowd does. Few have the courage to resist peer pressure and be their own selves rather than being one among the lot.

Peer pressure is bound to affect most of us both positively and negatively. The distinction between positive and negative peer pressure lies in a thoughtful analysis of the views of the masses. Following your peers blindly leaves a negative impact on your life while an analytical approach to looking at peer behaviour can help you act positively.

Peer pressure is not always bad. It can help you analyse yourself and contemplate your ways of life. Some of the practices that the masses follow may actually teach you the way of living. You may be able to change yourself for the better. Looking at what others do can help you bring about a positive change in your way of thinking. If you can pick selectively, peer pressure can actually result in a positive change in your way of life.

Questions

1. What is peer pressure?
2. Complete the sentence appropriately

   The people around you are bound to influence you because ....
3. State True or False.

   Peer pressure can prove beneficial but it is most often observed to have negative effects.
4. What does the writer mean by 'Analytical approach'?
5. According to the passage, what is a negative effect of following your peers blindly?
   - (a) It helps you learn new things
   - (b) It leaves a negative impact on your life
   - (c) It makes you more popular
   - (d) It improves your decision-making skills
6. What does the word 'contemplate' mean in the context of the passage?
   - (a) Ignore
   - (b) Consider
   - (c) Forget
   - (d) Reject

PASSAGE 12

Read the passage given below to answer the questions that follow.

Today's woman is a highly self-directed person, alive to the sense of her dignity and the importance of her functions in the private domestic domain and the public domain of the world of work. Women are rational in approach, careful in handling situations and want to do things as best as possible. The Fourth World Conference of Women held in Beijing in September 1995 had emphasised that no enduring solution of society's most threatening social, economic and political problems could be found without the participation and empowerment of women. The 1995 World Summit for Social Development had also emphasised the pivotal role of women in eradicating poverty and mending the social fabric.

The Constitution of India has conferred upon women equal rights and opportunities – political, social, educational and of employment—as men. Because of oppressive traditions, superstitions, exploitation and corruption, a majority of women are not allowed to enjoy the rights and opportunities bestowed upon them. One of the major reasons for this state of affairs is the lack of literacy and awareness among women. Education is the main instrument through which we can narrow down the prevailing inequality and accelerate the process of economic and political change in the status of women.

The role of women in a society is very important. Women's education is the key to a better life in the future. A recent World Bank study says that educating girls is not a charity, it is good economics and if developing nations are to eradicate poverty, they must educate the girls. Society would progress only if the status of women is respected and the presence of an educated woman in the family would ensure education of the family itself.

Questions

1. What did the Fourth World Conference of Women emphasise?
2. Complete the following sentence

   The Constitution of India has conferred upon women equal rights and opportunities in ....

3. According to the passage, what is one of the major reasons women are not allowed to enjoy their rights and opportunities?
(a) Lack of interest
(b) Lack of literacy and awareness
(c) Lack of resources
(d) Lack of support from men

4. What does the word 'eradicate' mean in the context of the passage?
(a) Increase (b) Eliminate
(c) Support (d) Ignore

5. What does the writer mean by 'The way of living'?

6. Which word from the passage means the same as 'friends'?

PASSAGE 13

Read the following poem and answer the questions that follow by choosing the correct option.

If you've tried and have not won,
Never stop for crying;
All that's good and great is done
Just by patient trying.
Though young birds, in flying, fell,
Still their wings grow stronger,
And the next time they can keep
Up a little longer.
Though the sturdy oak has known
Many a wind that bowed her,
She has risen again and grown
Loftier and prouder.
If by easy work you beat,
Who the more will prize you?
Gaining victory from defeat,
That's the test that tries you.

Questions

1. How can one succeed in life?

2. Complete the following sentence
The young birds' wings grow stronger and the next time ....

3. Complete the following analogy
Young birds : Flying :: Sturdy oak : ....

4. 'Oak' mentioned in the poem is the name of a/an ....
(a) insect (b) animal
(c) place (d) tree

5. Which is the pair of antonym present in the poem?
(a) Stop-won (b) Great-good
(c) Patient-stronger (d) Victory-defeat

6. What does the writer mean by 'patient trying'?

PASSAGE 14

Read the following poem and answer the questions that follow by choosing the correct option.

The mountain and the squirrel
Had a quarrel,
And the former called the latter
"Little prig."
Bun replied,
"You are doubtless very big;
But all sorts of things and weather
Must be taken in together
To make up a year
And a sphere.
And I think it no disgrace
To occupy my place.
If I'm not so large as you,
You are not so small as I,
And not half so spry:
I'll not deny you make
A very pretty squirrel track.
Talents differ; all is well and wisely put;
If I cannot carry forests on my back,
Neither can you crack a nut."

Questions

1. Why did the mountain and the squirrel quarrel with each other?

2. Complete the following sentence
The squirrel thinks it is no disgrace to ....

3. Complete the following analogy
Mountain : Big :: Squirrel : ....

4. Give synonym for the word 'disgrace'.
(a) Shame
(b) Track
(c) Grace
(d) Beauty

5. Who cannot crack a nut in the poem?
(a) The mountain (b) Forest
(c) Squirrel (d) Track

6. What does the writer mean by 'Talents differ'?

PASSAGE 15

Read the following poem and answer the questions that follow.

We are friends
I got your back
You got mine,
I'll help you out
Anytime!
To see you hurt
To see you cry
Makes me weep
And want to die
And if you agree
To never fight
It wouldn't matter
Who's wrong or right
If a broken heart
Needs a mend
I'll be right there
Till the end
If your cheeks are wet
From drops of tears
Don't worry
Let go of your fears
Hand in hand
Love is sent,
We'll be friends
Till the end!

Questions

1. What does the speaker promise to do if their friend is hurt?
2. Complete the following sentence
   The speaker says they will be friends till the ....
3. The word ...... in the poem is a synonym of 'repair'.
4. What does the writer mean by 'Hand in hand'?
5. According to the poem, what does the speaker want to do when they see their friend cry?
   (a) Laugh (b) Ignore
   (c) Weep and want to die (d) Smile
6. What does the word 'mend' mean in the context of the poem?
   (a) Break (b) Fix
   (c) Ignore (d) Create

PASSAGE 16

Read the following poem and answer the questions that follow.

A habit is a sticky thing;
Much good or evil it can bring;
It binds a victim, holds him fast,
And keeps him in a vice-like grasp.
Bad habits grow with extra speed,
Much like a healthy, growing weed.
The roots grow deep, the stem grows stout;
How difficult to pull it out!
Good habits are a little slow;
They need a lot of care to grow;
If tended well, they grow more fair
Than any bloom a plant can bear.
Good habits help us all through life;
Bad habits bring us pain and strife;
Our habits, whether right or wrong,
Each day will grow more firm and strong

Questions

1. Why is habit a sticky thing?
2. What does the writer mean by 'Vice-like grasp'?
3. The word .... from the poem means the same as 'sufferer'.
4. State whether the following statement is True or False.
   Bad habits grow slowly as compared to good habits.
5. According to the poem, what do good habits feed to grow?
   (a) Extra speed (b) A lot of care
   (c) Neglect (d) Pain and strife
6. What does the word 'stout' mean in the context of the poem?
   (a) Weak (b) Thin
   (c) Strong (d) Fragile

ANSWERS (REVIEW EXERCISE)

Passage 1

1. The Statue of Liberty was gifted to the United States by the people of France.
2. one hundred year
3. Statue
4. The word 'implored' means begged or earnestly asked for.
5. (a) Strong, proud and hard-working
6. (b) 15 years

Passage 2

1. According to the passage, the main purpose of education is to help a child grow in life, become a right thinker, and a good decision-maker.
2. spiritual
3. Prosperous nation
4. The phrase 'leaps and bounds' means rapid and significant progress or improvement.
5. (b) Three-fold development of a child
6. (c) The school's ability to develop a child physically, mentally and spiritually

Passage 3

1. Sonia did not study for the spelling test because she was confident in her spelling abilities and believed she didn't need to prepare.
2. 'modification'
3. Struggled with spellings
4. The word 'scribbled' means to write or draw something quickly and carelessly.
5. (d) Honest
6. (b) They had to copy each word seventy-five times

Passage 4

1. The passage mentions several forms of energy
   - Petrol
   - Diesel
   - Natural gas
   - Electricity
2. plant and equipment
3. Water resources
4. The writer uses the phrase 'energy conservation' to refer to the practice of reducing energy consumption and minimising waste.
5. (d) Increasing the use of air conditioning
6. (b) To ensure availability for future generations

Passage 5

1. The main virtue discussed in the passage is honesty.
2. stand by the truth
3. Distrusted
4. In the context of telling lies, the writer means that a 'temporary solution' is a short-term fix that might help avoid immediate trouble but does not provide a lasting resolution.
5. (b) They lose their reputation
6. (a) A person's moral sense of right and wrong

Passage 6

1. One of the main health issues caused by fast food is obesity.
2. lifestyle diseases
3. Healthy growth
4. 'Lifestyle diseases' refer to health problems such as obesity, diabetes and high blood pressure that are caused by unhealthy eating habits and lack of physical activity.
5. (c) It is convenient and takes less time to prepare
6. (b) Copying

Passage 7

1. ChatGPT is an artificial intelligence program that generates dialogue.
2. precise stipulations
3. ChatGPT was created by OpenAI.
4. The writer means that these are complex computational methods used by ChatGPT to process and analyse large amounts of data to generate responses.
5. (b) It can generate responses like humans in real time
6. (b) Early stage

Passage 8

1. Chandrayaan-3 was launched on 14th July, 2023.
2. 2 meters, 1,700 kg
3. Successor
4. The writer refers to the Southern region of the moon, which is significant for its potential water ice deposits.
5. (c) Aspiring
6. (b) To study the mineral composition of the lunar South Pole

Passage 9

1. Health is considered as valuable as money because without it, you would not enjoy anything in life.
2. students study properly
3. Stress reduction
4. Balanced diet means eating a variety of foods in the right proportions, including more fruits and vegetables and avoiding fatty foods.
5. (b) Play outside
6. (b) Overweight

Passage 10

1. The boy's parents were depressed because of their son's bad temper.
2. he lost his temper frequently
3. True
4. By the phrase, the writer means that harsh words can leave lasting emotional scars, similar to how physical wounds leave marks.
5. (b) Hammer a nail into the fence
6. (b) Advised

Passage 11

1. Peer pressure is a phenomenon wherein we tend to get influenced by the lifestyle and ways of thinking of our peers.
2. it is a human tendency to do what the crowd does
3. True
4. The writer means thoughtfully examining and evaluating the views and behaviours of peers to determine whether to follow them.
5. (b) It leaves a negative impact on your life
6. (b) Consider

Passage 12

1. The Fourth World Conference of Women emphasised that no enduring solution to society's most threatening social, economic and political problems could be found without the participation and empowerment of women.
2. Political, social, educational and employment domains.
3. (b) Lack of literacy and awareness
4. (b) Eliminate
5. The writer means the habits, customs and lifestyle that a person or group of people typically follow.
   It encompasses how they live their daily lives, including their behaviours, routines and values.
6. The word from the passage that means the same as 'friends' is 'peers'.

Passage 13

1. According to the poem, one can succeed in life by patient trying.
2. they can keep up a little longer.
3. Wind
4. (d) tree
5. (d) Victory-defeat
6. The writer means that 'patient trying' refers to the act of persistently and calmly continuing to make efforts towards a goal, even when faced with difficulties or failures.

Passage 14

1. The mountain and the squirrel quarreled because the mountain called the squirrel a 'little prig,' which offended the squirrel.
2. occupy its place
3. Small
4. (a) Shame
5. (a) The mountain
6. The phrase 'Talents differ' means that everyone has unique abilities and strengths.

Passage 15

1. The speaker promises to help their friend anytime and be there for them till the end.
2. end
3. mend
4. The writer means being together and supporting each other closely.
5. (c) Weep and want to die
6. (b) Fix

Passage 16

1. A habit is described as a 'sticky thing' because it tends to cling to a person and is difficult to change or break.
2. By the phrase, the writer means that habits can hold a person very tightly and are difficult to break free from, similar to how a vice grips an object firmly.
3. victim
4. False
5. (b) A lot of care
6. (c) Strong

Passage 9

1. Health is considered as valuable as money because without it, you would not enjoy anything in life.
2. students study properly
3. Stress reduction
4. Balanced diet means eating a variety of foods in the right proportions, including more fruits and vegetables and avoiding fatty foods.
5. (b) Play outside
6. (b) Overweight

Passage 10

1. The boy's parents were depressed because of their son's bad temper.
2. he lost his temper frequently
3. True
4. By the phrase, the writer means that harsh words can leave lasting emotional scars, similar to how physical wounds leave marks.
5. (b) Hammer a nail into the fence
6. (b) Advised

Passage 11

1. Peer pressure is a phenomenon wherein we tend to get influenced by the lifestyle and ways of thinking of our peers.
2. it is a human tendency to do what the crowd does
3. True
4. The writer means thoughtfully examining and evaluating the views and behaviours of peers to determine whether to follow them.
5. (b) It leaves a negative impact on your life
6. (b) Consider

Passage 12

1. The Fourth World Conference of Women emphasised that no enduring solution to society's most threatening social, economic and political problems could be found without the participation and empowerment of women.
2. Political, social, educational and employment domains.
3. (b) Lack of literacy and awareness
4. (b) Eliminate
5. The writer means the habits, customs and lifestyle that a person or group of people typically follow. It encompasses how they live their daily lives, including their behaviours, routines and values.
6. The word from the passage that means the same as 'friends' is 'peers'.

Passage 13

1. According to the poem, one can succeed in life by patient trying.
2. they can keep up a little longer
3. Wind
4. (d) tree
5. (d) Victory defeat
6. The writer means that 'patient trying' refers to the act of persistently and calmly continuing to make efforts towards a goal, even when faced with difficulties or failures.

Passage 14

1. The mountain and the squirrel quarreled because the mountain called the squirrel a 'little prig', which offended the squirrel.
2. occupy its place
3. Small
4. (a) Shame
5. (a) The mountain
6. The phrase 'Talents differ' means that everyone has unique abilities and strengths.

Passage 15

1. The speaker promises to help their friend anytime and be there for them till the end.
2. end
3. mend
4. The writer means being together and supporting each other closely.
5. (c) Weep and want to die
6. (b) Fix

Passage 16

1. A habit is described as a 'sticky thing' because it tends to cling to a person and is difficult to change or break.
2. By the phrase, the writer means that habits can hold a person very tightly and are difficult to break free from, similar to how a vice grips an object firmly.
3. victim
4. fake
5. (b) A lot of care
6. (c) Strong

SECTION B : WRITING

CHAPTER 1

Notice Writing

A notice is a short piece of written communication issued by individual, groups, institutions or organisations to convey some important information to a large group of people. It is a formal announcement about functions, events and occasions. It is also used to make announcement about something that has happened or is about to happen. It is written in 40-50 words.

Types of Notice

There are many types of notices that we write. They include

- Announcement of a competition or event
- Lost and found
- Call for submissions
- Announcement regarding upcoming tours or trips
- Information regarding meetings, etc.

However, in Class VI we will focus only on notices written for Announcement of a Competition or Event and Lost and Found.

Points to be Kept in Mind

- Always put the notice in a box.
- The language used must be simple and clear.
- Do not exceed the word limit, if given in the question.
- A notice should/must include some value points (necessary details) in order to make it precise and effective.
- The notice should be written in third person, i.e., pronouns like I, me, you, mine, your, etc., should not be used except in Lost/Found notices.
- Remember to read your notice to make sure that you have not made any mistake in it.

Format of a Notice

You are Vanita, the Cultural Secretary of your school. Draft a notice for an Inter School Dramatics Competition Auditions to be held in your school.

Name of the Organisation issuing the notice	**Sulekha Memorial Public School, Delhi**
The word 'NOTICE' to be written in capital letter	**NOTICE**
Date of issuing the notice on the left side	27th January, 20XX
Subject of the Notice in Bold	**Inter School Dramatics Competition Auditions**
Content of the notice	This is to inform the students of Class VI and VII that our school is organising an Inter School Dramatics Competition on 12th February at Tagore Theatre. Those willing to take part in the competition as a part of the school team are invited to the auditions for the selection of our school's Dramatics Team on 1st February, 20XX at 12:30 pm in the Assembly Hall. For any further details, contact Ms. Shah.
Name & Designation of the person issuing the notice	Vanita (Cultural Secretary)

SAMPLE NOTICES

Notice for Competition/Events

A notice written for competitions give us all the details required by the interested students. These include

- Name of the competition or event
- Date
- Time
- Day
- Venue
- Eligibility (if any)
- For further details, contact info

1. Draft a notice in about 50 words urging students of Classes VI to XII to participate in a three-week Leadership Camp to be held in your school. Mention the date, time and venue of the camp. You are Ravi/Ravina, Head Boy/Girl.

Ans.

XYZ Public School

NOTICE

25th May, 20XX

Leadership Camp

This is to inform the students of Classes VI to XII that our school is organising a three-week leadership camp. The details of the camp are as follows

Dates 3rd June, 20XX to 24th June, 20XX

Time 9:00 am to 12:00 pm

Venue School Playground

Interested students can give their names to Mrs. Roshni in Sports Room by 1st June, 20XX. For further details, contact Rohan (Student Coordinator) in Room 205.

Ravi/Ravina
(Head Boy/Girl)

2. Your school is organising Paris Olympics Live Video Screening in school premises. Draft a notice on behalf of the school Principal asking for participation of students.

Ans.

XYZ Public School

NOTICE

5th August, 20XX

Invitation to Paris Olympics Live Video Screening

This is to inform the students of Classes VI to XII that our school will be hosting live video screenings of the 2024 Paris Olympics right here on our school premises. The details of the screening are given below

Date Sunday, 7th August, 2024

Time 10:00 am

Venue School Auditorium

All students are cordially invited to join us for this thrilling event.

Rohan

(Head boy)

3. Your school is going to celebrate Sports Day in the school premises. As a Sports Captain, write a notice inviting names of interested students for various games. Mention dates of selection of students. You are Rohit, Sports Captain.

Ans.

XYZ Public School

NOTICE

4th October, 20XX

Sports Day Celebration

This is to inform all students that our school will celebrate Sports Day on 15th December, 20XX in the school premises. As our games and sports teacher has instructed, interested students may give their names for different races and other events to the undersigned by 18th October, 20XX. Selected students will be informed about their participation by 1st December, 20XX. For the detailed list of events, contact Manish, Sports Secretary.

Rohit

(Sports Captain)

4. You are Rohan, Activity Secretary of your school. Write a notice of about 50 words inviting students of Classes VI and VII to attend a Story-Telling Session which is to be held in the school auditorium. Mention the necessary details.

Ans.

XYZ Public School

NOTICE

10th October, 20XX

Story-Telling Session

This is to inform the students of Class VI and VII that our school will be having a Story-Telling Session on 15th of October, 20XX in the school auditorium. The Chief Guest and story-teller of the session will be respected Mrs. Roy. All the students of the mentioned classes are requested to assemble in front of the auditorium at 9 am sharp. For further details, contact your respective class teachers.

Rohan

(Activity Secretary)

5. Write a notice to be put on your school's notice board about a Charity Show in Aid of Cancer Patients. You are Amar/Amrita, Secretary of Cultural Club.

Ans.

Aryamba Public School, Kochi

NOTICE

12th June, 20XX

Charity Show for Cancer Patients

This is to inform the students that a charity show will be organised by the Cultural Club of the school in aid of cancer patients. The details are as follows

Date 20th November, 20XX

Venue School Cultural Hall

Time 3:00 pm to 6:00 pm

All the interested students may give their names to their respective class teachers latest by 15th November, 20XX. Kindly cooperate and participate to make this show a great success. For any other details, you may contact the undersigned.

Amar

(Secretary, Cultural Club)

Notice for Lost and Found

A notice for Lost and Found includes details that would help the owner of the thing or the finder of the thing to recognise the lost/found item. The details include

- The location where the thing was lost or found
- A very clear description of the thing
- Contact information of the person who has lost/found the thing
- Mention of a reward for finders of the lost thing

6. You are a student of Class VI in Bal Bharti School, Bikaner. You have lost your Science book in the school playground. Write a notice for the school notice board so that the finder may help you.

Ans.

Bal Bharti School, Bikaner

NOTICE

25th February, 20XX

Lost Science Book

This is to inform all that I, Ira Mehta, of Class VI lost my Science book in the school playground during lunchtime. The book is blue in colour and titled 'Living Science' Class VI. Anybody who finds it is requested to give it to me in Class VI or to the Reception. The person finding it and handing it over will be rewarded.

Ira Mehta
(Class VI)

7. You have found an expensive Milton Water Bottle in the school playground. Draft a notice in not more than 50 words for the school notice board. You are Rani, Class VI, Angel School, Faridabad.

Ans.

Angel School, Faridabad

NOTICE

31st October, 20XX

Found a Milton Water Bottle

This is to inform all that I, Rani, of Class VI, have found a red-coloured Milton Water bottle in the school playground during the 7th period yesterday. The bottle has an Iron Man logo on it with the initials AW carved on its bottom. Owner may please contact the undersigned in her class between the 6th and the 7th period.

Rani
(Class VI-C)

8. You are Mohit/Madhuri Shaw of Class VI of RPB Public School, Jaipur. You Lost your Geometry Box in the school playground last Tuesday. Draft a notice in not more than 50 words for your school notice board informing the students about the loss of your geometry box.

Ans.

RPB Public School, Jaipur

NOTICE

11th May, 20XX

Lost Geometry Box

All the students of our school are hereby informed that a geometry box is lost in our school playground last Tuesday. It was a simple blue-coloured box having 2 pens, 2 pencils, a steel scale, a sharpener and an eraser inside the box. Whoever finds the box, please collect it and return it to me in my class. Finder will be rewarded with a treat in the school canteen.

Mohit Shaw
(Class VI)

9. You have found a school bag in the playground. Write a notice for the school notice board in about 50 words. You can imagine the necessary details.

Ans.

XYZ School

NOTICE

7th August, 20XX

Found a Bag

This is to inform all the students of our school that a blue-coloured school bag has been found on the school premises. The bag contains some books, a lunchbox, a water bottle and a few other items. If anyone has lost their school bag, they can come to the school office and describe what was in your bag so that it can be returned to you.

Rohan Saxena
(School Head)

PRACTICE QUESTIONS

1. You lost your Titan wrist-watch in your school. Draft a notice, in not more than 50 words, to be placed on your school notice board. You are Rani of Ahalya Devi Senior Secondary School, Gwalior.
2. Your school is planning to organise a Water Conservation Awareness Programme for the students. As school captain of SLV Public School, Lucknow, draft a notice in about 50 words informing the students about the programme mentioning day, date, time and venue. You are Sanjay/Sanjana.
3. You are Puneet/Puneeta, the Headboy/Headgirl of Dronacharya Public School, Gurgaon. Write a notice for the school notice board informing students about 'Cleanliness Drive' in school. Mention date and time.
4. Tarun Niketan Senior Secondary School has decided to organise Diwali Mela in the school premises. Draft a notice on behalf of the school Principal asking for participation of students and parents. Parents can put up stalls and can give their names for the occasion latest by 20th October.
5. You are Praveen Garg, Activity Incharge of your school. Write a notice about Inter-House Group Song Competition to be held on the Independence Day. Mention necessary details.
6. The Debating Society of your school is organising an inter-school debate. The last date for submitting names for the audition is Friday, 17th March. There will be on-the-spot trials. Draft a notice in about 50 words informing students about the team selection time, date, and venue.
7. While walking in a park in your neighbourhood you found a small plastic bag containing some documents and some cash. Write a notice in about 50 words to be put on the park notice board asking the owner to identify and collect it from you. You are Amar/Amrita.
8. You are Bhavya of St. Peter's School, Noida. You have lost your I-card in the school premises. Draft a notice for the school notice board for the same.
9. You have found an expensive Geometry Box in the School Canteen. Draft a notice for the school notice board for the same.
10. You are Mayank/Manisha. You have lost your Hindi book during the lunch break. Draft a notice for the school notice board for the same.

Message Writing

A message is a short, informal piece of writing conveying important information received over the telephone. It is written when the person to whom the message is to be given is not available to take the message. In such a case, the message is given to the person who picks up the telephone.
This person, then writes the message in clear and to-the-point manner. Hence, it is very important to know how to write a message properly.

Points to be Kept in Mind

- Make a note of the message carefully in a box.
- Use simple and clear language in your message.
- Do not give unnecessary information in the message.
- Always include the name of the caller in the message.
- Your message should not be in more than 50 words.
- Remember to read your message to make sure that you have not made any mistake in it.

Format of a Message

Read the following conversation between Mrs. Shobha and Dr. Chetan.

Dr. Chetan Hello! Is it Mrs. Poonam?

Mrs. Shobha Yes, may I know who am I talking to?

Dr. Chetan I am Dr. Chetan. May I talk to Mrs. Poonam, Vice-Principal of XYZ School?

Mrs. Shobha Good morning Doctor! I am Shobha, Poonam's mother. She has gone to meet a colleague of hers and left her phone here. Can I do anything for you?

Dr. Chetan Yes, please. In fact, she wanted me to confirm my visit to her school for a health talk for students on the coming Monday. Please tell her I shall come as per schedule.

Mrs. Shobha Ok Doctor, I shall convey your message to her.

Dr. Chetan Thank you Mrs. Shobha.

As Mrs. Reema is going for a meeting, she writes the message for Arpita. Write her a message.

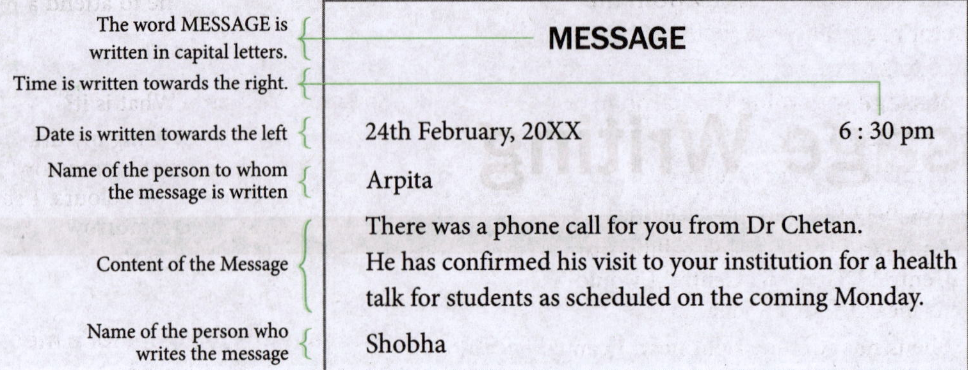

SAMPLE MESSAGES

1. Read the following conversation between Ragini and Prateek about Parth, Ragini's brother. Ragini has to go for her tuitions so she leaves the message for Parth. Write her a message.

Prateek Hello! Can I speak to Parth?

Ragini May I please know who is on the line?

Prateek I am Prateek, Parth's friend.

Ragini Sorry Prateek, he has just gone to a stationery shop. I am Ragini, his sister. I can take the message for him.

Prateek Yes please. Actually, it being Sunday tomorrow, I, along with two friends are going to see the newly released movie XYZ at Utsav Cinema. An extra ticket can be arranged for Parth if he could join us. He should let me know today by 7:00 pm.

Ragini Ok, I shall convey the message to him.

Prateek Thank you.

Ragini You're welcome!

Ans.

MESSAGE

11th April, 20XX 5 : 00 pm

Parth

Prateek, your friend called up when you were away at the stationery shop. He is going to see the newly released movie XYZ at Utsav Cinema tomorrow with friends. They can arrange a ticket for you if you wish to join them. You have to tell him about it today by 7:00 pm.

Ragini

2. Read the telephonic conversation between Rohit and Vishal. Vishal is going for his tuition class so he leaves a message for Manav. Write his message in not more than 50 words.

Rohit Hello! Could I speak to Manav?

Vishal He is not at home. May I know who is on the line?

Rohit I am Rohit, your neighbour.

Vishal Rohit, I am Manav's elder brother, Vishal. How are you?

Rohit I am fine. Could you take my message for him?

Vishal Yes, sure.

Rohit Please tell him that I need my Social Studies book that he took yesterday as soon as possible. I have to make a school project. Also please tell him that I'll need his help for the project when he comes back.

Vishal Ok, I will convey your message.

Rohit Thank you, Bye.

Ans.

MESSAGE

17th July, 20XX 6 : 00 pm

Manav

Rohit, our neighbour and your friend called up when you were away. He has called to ask you to return his Social Studies book that you took yesterday as he has to make a school project. He also wants your help in the project. Kindly talk to him.

Vishal

3. You are Rita. Your mother had recently gone for a health checkup. You received a call from the Assistant Doctor regarding the result of her reports. Since you have to go out, you leave a message for her. Draft a message regarding the same in not more than 50 words.

Dr. Kaushik Is this A/24, Geeta Colony?

Rita Yes, may I know who is calling?

Dr. Kaushik I am Dr. Priya Kaushik calling from Central Diagnostic Centre. I would like to speak to Mrs. Sneha.

Rita She is not at home right now. I can take the message for her.

Dr. Kaushik Could you please tell her that I have seen all her test reports. They do not show any serious problems and if there would be no improvement, we might take some more tests. I advise her to continue the same set of medicines for a week and I have fixed her appointment with the cardiologist for four o'clock at the Christ Hospital. She must reach there on time with all her reports.

Rita Thank you, Doctor. I will convey her the same.

Ans.

MESSAGE

17th September, 20XX 5 : 00 pm

Mom

Dr. Priya Kaushik from Central Diagnostic Centre called to inform you that she has seen your test reports and they are fine. There is no serious problem. However, she has informed that if there is no improvement, she might take some more tests. She has advised you to continue the same set of medicines for a week. She has also fixed your appointment with the cardiologist for 4 pm at the Christ Hospital. You have to be there by 4 pm with your reports.

Rita

4. Manav wants Simran to bring his drawing and sketch book to school along with a set of oil colours. He calls her but finds out from Sonam that she is not at home. Read the telephonic conversation between Manav and Sonam. Manav leaves a message for Simran.

Manav Hello, may I speak to Simran?

Sonam I am sorry. She is not at home.

Manav Why didn't she come to school today?

Sonam She has gone to attend a marriage with her mother.

Manav Will you please convey my message to her?

Sonam Yes, sure. What is it?

Manav Tell her to bring my drawing and sketch book to school tomorrow. She should also get a set of oil colours. I shall meet her at the school tomorrow.

Sonam Ok, I will tell her.

Manav Thanks

As Sonam was to go out for a meeting, she wrote the message for Simran.

Ans.

MESSAGE

23rd September, 20XX 6 : 00 pm

Simran

Manav rang up to tell you that you should take his drawing and sketch book to school tomorrow. He has requested you to carry a set of oil colours too. He shall meet you in the school.

Sonam

5. Read the telephonic conversation between Aradhya and Aman and write a short message left by Aman for his mother in about 50 words.

Aradhya Hello, Aman. Can I speak to Mom?

Aman Mom is not at home. She has gone to a neighbour's house.

Aradhya I have been selected for Inter-State Debate Competition to be held in New Delhi. I have to leave for Delhi tomorrow at 05:30 am. Please ask mother to do my packing for this programme as I will be back home late tonight from the college library.

Aman Congratulations on your selection. And I will let Mom know about it.

Ans.

MESSAGE

23rd September, 20XX 5 : 00 pm

Dear Mom

Aradhya rang up in your absence to inform that she has been selected for Inter-State Debate Competition to be held in New Delhi. She shall be leaving tomorrow at 5:30 am. Please pack her bags for this programme as she will be home late tonight from the library.

Aman

PRACTICE QUESTIONS

1. Read the following conversation carefully.

Rajeev Hello! Am I speaking to Mr. Sunil?

Vijay I am his son Vijay speaking. Father is not present here at the moment.

Rajeev Ok Vijay, I'm Rajeev, Secretary of Modern Club. Tell your father that the meeting of the club officials has been postponed till the next week. Exact date, time and venue will be intimated to him well in time.

Vijay Ok uncle, I will give the message.

Vijay goes for evening games and wants to leave the message for his father. Write the message for Vijay.

2. You are Simran. Your brother is not at home. You received a call from his friend regarding the cancellation of dance class. Since you have to go out, you will leave a message for him. Draft a message about the same in not more than 50 words.

Raj Hello! Is this 25-A/12, Kamla Nagar?

Simran Yes, may I know who's calling?

Raj I am Raj, Samar's friend. Can I talk to him?

Simran He has gone to the market with mom and forgot his mobile here. Can I pass a message?

Raj Sure, I called to tell him that today's class is suspended as our teacher had to go for a family emergency. The cancelled class will be held on Sunday. Please inform him of the same.

Simran Oh! Sure. I will. Thank you

Raj You're welcome. Bye

3. You receive a phone call from your Dad's office in his absence and have the following conversation with the speaker. Draft a message for your father.

Mr. Sharma Hello, Mr. Anand?

You Hello, Dad is not at home, may I know who is calling?

Mr. Sharma I am Ramesh Sharma, your Father's assistant at his office.

You Hello, Mr. Sharma. He is not at home. Do you have a message for him?

Mr. Sharma Yes, please inform him that the 10 am meeting in the morning has been rescheduled to 12pm.

You Okay, uncle. I will tell Dad once he comes back.

4. Read the following telephonic conversation between Nidhi and Pulkit. Nidhi wants Pulkit to convey a message to Madhu that her interview was postponed by one day and she needs to bring necessary documents along with her. Pulkit leaves a message for Madhu. Write the message in about 50 words.

Nidhi Sharma Hello! Is it 20xxxx10?

Pulkit Yes. May I know who is calling?

Nidhi Sharma This is Nidhi Sharma. Can I speak to Madhu?

Pulkit No, sorry, she has gone to the library.

Nidhi Sharma Please tell her that her interview scheduled today at 12:30 pm for job at BSNL office has been postponed by one day. It will be held tomorrow at 11.00 am sharp at the same place. She should reach BSNL office in time and also bring her original certificates along with two sets of photocopies. Don't forget it's important.

Pulkit Sure, I will convey the message.

Nidhi Sharma Thanks

5. Read the telephonic conversation between Karan and Supriya and write a short message left by Supriya for Prem in about 50 words.

Karan Hello Supriya, where is Prem?

Supriya He has gone to the market.

Karan Please tell him that I am going out for two days so I will not be joining him for daily practice sessions in the evening.

Supriya Fine. Is there anything else I need to tell him?

Karan Yes, tell him to inform Shagun and Raman also about the schedule.

Supriya Ok

Karan Ok, Bye.

CHAPTER 3

E-Mail Writing

In the present world, with improvement in internet and technology, e-mail has emerged as the easiest, fastest and important means of communication. It allows us to send, receive, store and forward messages to a number of persons simultaneously.

E-mails can be both formal and informal. However, they are most commonly used in formal communication. In Class VI, we will cover writing informal e-mails and e-mail to school authorities only.

Parts of an E-mail

An e-mail generally comprises many parts. They are

1. **Recipient's/Receiver's Address** The first thing you need to enter when composing an e-mail is the recipient's address. An example of e-mail address is : sakshiwrites@gmail.com. When sending a message to multiple recipients, be sure to separate all addresses with a comma.
2. **Cc and Bcc** Another option when sending a message to multiple recipients is to use the Cc, or carbon copy, and Bcc or blind carbon copy. When using the Cc feature, all recipients can see the e-mail addresses of all people to whom the message was sent. If you want your communication to be more private, choose the Bcc option and the identities of the other recipients will not be visible to anyone.
3. **Subject Line** The subject line is the first part of your e-mail that the recipient will see. So, when entering the subject line write precisely what the e-mail is about.
4. **Starting Salutation** Always write the name of the receiver of the mail before writing your message.
5. **Body** The body is where you actually write the message that you want to send.
6. **Attachments** If you have files that you want to share with your recipients, you can include them as attachments in an e-mail.
7. **Ending Salutation** You should always end your e-mail with a note of thanks and your name.

Points to be Kept in Mind

- Receiver's address should be properly and clearly written.
- The Subject of the e-mail should be short and concise.
- Do not use SMS language in an e-mail.
- Always write an e-mail in not more than 100 words.
- Use clear and easy language to write your message.
- Remember to re-read your e-mail to make sure that you have not made any error in it.

Format of an E-mail

Write an e-mail to the Principal of your school requesting him to grant you five-days leave to attend your sister's marriage.

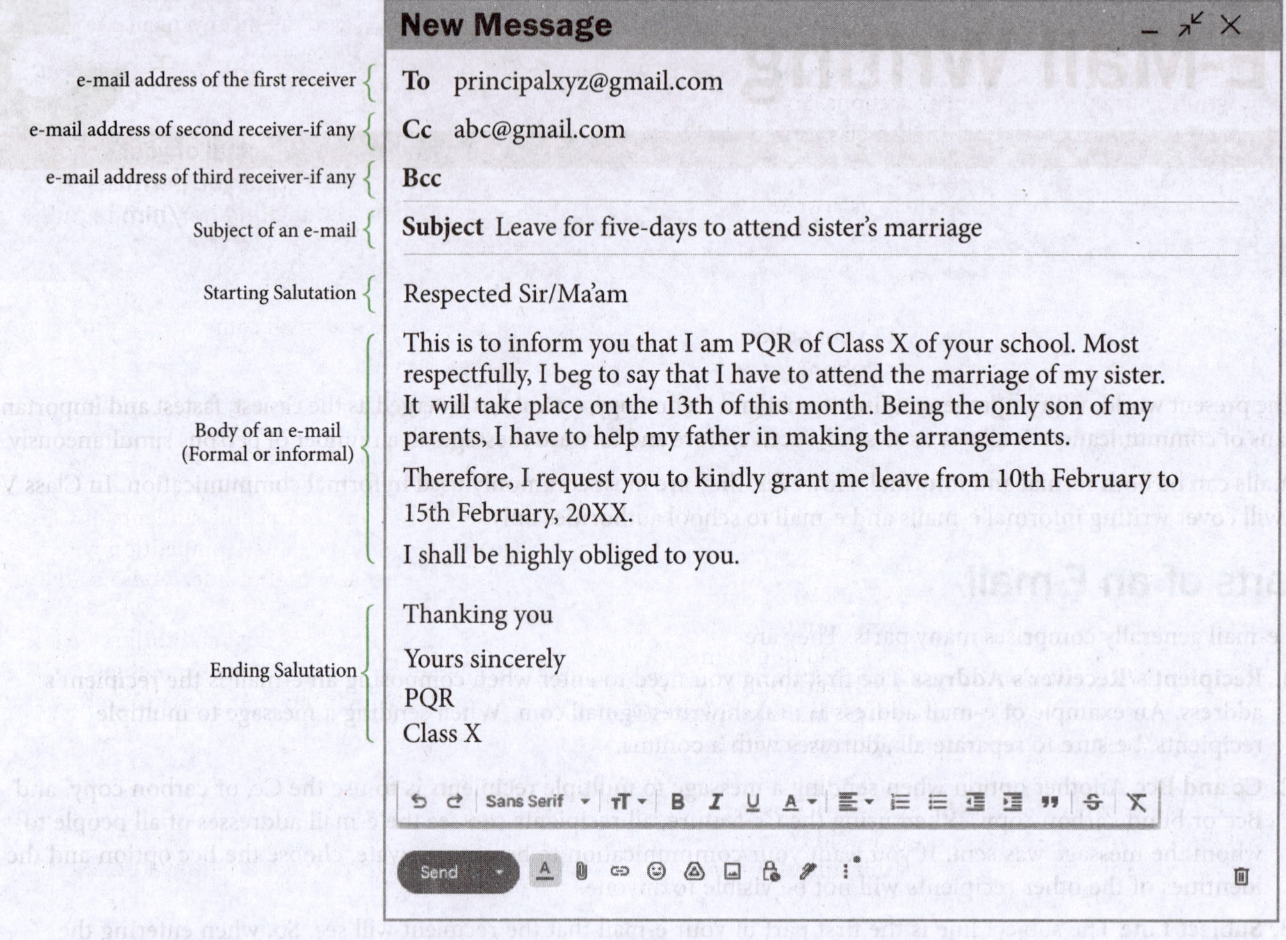

New Message

e-mail address of the first receiver — **To** principalxyz@gmail.com

e-mail address of second receiver-if any — **Cc** abc@gmail.com

e-mail address of third receiver-if any — **Bcc**

Subject of an e-mail — **Subject** Leave for five-days to attend sister's marriage

Starting Salutation — Respected Sir/Ma'am

Body of an e-mail (Formal or informal) —

This is to inform you that I am PQR of Class X of your school. Most respectfully, I beg to say that I have to attend the marriage of my sister. It will take place on the 13th of this month. Being the only son of my parents, I have to help my father in making the arrangements.

Therefore, I request you to kindly grant me leave from 10th February to 15th February, 20XX.

I shall be highly obliged to you.

Ending Salutation —

Thanking you

Yours sincerely

PQR

Class X

Note it This is a page that you will see when you are writing an e-mail from you mail account. However, while writing an e-mail in answer, you follow a different format. We include the sender's e-mail in our format while writing Cc and Bcc becomes optional.

SAMPLE E-MAILS

1. Write an e-mail to the Principal of your school requesting him to make arrangement for some more furniture for your classroom. Also give reason for your demand.

Ans. From students@gmail.com

To principalxyz@gmail.com

Cc

Subject Arrangement for more furniture

Respected Sir/Ma'am

This is to inform you that we, the students of Class VI B, have written this mail to inform you that there is a lack of proper furniture in our classroom. We are a class of sixty students. However, there are only forty seats in this class to sit on. Thus, 20 seats are short. Because of this reason, many students have to stand daily which makes us tired and we are unable to focus on our studies.

So, you are requested to make arrangement for 20 more seats. We shall be highly obliged to you.

Thanking you

Students of Class VI B

2. Write an e-mail to the school Principal requesting him/her to arrange special classes in English.

Ans. From students@gmail.com

To principalxyz@gmail.com

Cc abc@gmail.com

Subject Request for arranging special classes in English

Respected Sir/Ma'am

This is to inform you that we, the students of Class VI, have written this mail to request you to arrange special classes in English as our result of English in the test examination is not satisfactory. We are very weak in writing, unseen and grammar sections. So, we request you to arrange three English classes in a week in the month of January 20XX.

Please look into this matter and help us at your earliest.

Thanking you

Students of Class VI

3. Write an e-mail to the Principal of your school requesting him for concession in school fees.

Ans. From students@gmail.com

To principalxyz@gmail.com

Cc abc@gmail.com

Subject Request for fee-concession

Respected Sir/Ma'am

This is to inform you that I, PQR of Class VI of your school, have written this mail to request you to grant me a full fee-concession. The financial condition of my family is not good. My father is the only earning member in the family and he is admitted in the hospital due to an illness. So, I am unable to pay my school fees. I am a good student and also among the toppers of the class. I also participate in many extracurricular activities. I assure you that nothing would change in my performance. Kindly grant me full concession in school fees. I will be highly obliged to you.

Thanking you

PQR

4. Write an e-mail to the Principal of your school complaining against insufficient supply of water in your school.

Ans. From students@gmail.com

To principalxyz@gmail.com

Cc abc@gmail.com

Subject Insufficient water supply

Respected Sir/Ma'am

This is to inform you that I, PQR of Class VI of your school, am writing this mail on behalf of all the students to bring to your kind consideration the problem of insufficient water supply in our school.

As you know, summer has started and temperature is soaring up. In such temperatures, all of us require water in large amounts. However, whenever we go to the water coolers, either the cooler is not working or the pressure of tap is so low that it takes almost 15 minutes to fill our water bottles. The result is that we all mostly remain thirsty for the fear of missing out important details in our classes.

We, therefore, request you to kindly order a booster pump installation to end the inconvenience to all of us.

Thanking you

PQR

5. Write an e-mail to the Principal of your school requesting him/her to grant you permission to conduct an event and inviting her/him to judge the competition.

Ans. From students@gmail.com

To principalxyz@gmail.com

Cc abc@gmail.com

Subject Invitation to judge the dance competition of our school

Respected Sir/Ma'am

This is to inform you that we, the students of Class VI to XII, have organised a dance competition with the help of our teacher as a part of inter-house activity. The event will take place on 15th May, 20XX from 12:00 pm onwards in the school auditorium. We would be honoured to have you as our chief guest and judge. We look forward to your presence in the event.

We hope for a positive reply.

Thanking you

XYZ

6. Write an e-mail to your friend Vinaya describing your birthday party.

Ans. From suresh@gmail.com

To vinaya@gmail.com

Cc

Subject My amazing birthday party

Dear Vinaya

How are you? I am fine here and wish the same for you. Thank you for the good-wishes and that amazing card on my birthday. The card was really beautiful. However, I missed you. All our friends and my family members were present at the party and it was a great celebration.

Everybody liked the birthday cake and food. We all danced to amazing songs and played many games. We enjoyed ourselves till late in the evening. My uncle from England gave us a surprise visit. My parents were very happy about it. My uncle brought with him a special gift from London.

I will show you the same when you come here.

With love

Suresh

7. Your father has sent you a watch as a present on your birthday but it is not keeping correct time. Write an e-mail informing him of this fact and requesting him to tell you the procedure to get it replaced.

Ans. From abc@gmail.com

To shah@gmail.com

Cc xyz@gmail.com

Subject Problems with the watch

Dear Father

How are you? I am fine here and wish the same for you. Thank you very much for sending the beautiful wrist-watch on my birthday. However, the watch has some defect. It loses about five minutes in every twenty-four hours.

I remember you telling me that the watch has one year's guarantee. So, I want to get it replaced. Please tell me how to do so. I shall wait for your reply.

With regards

ABC

8. Your friend, Kunal is fond of reading good books. Write a letter to him inviting him to visit the Book Fair which is going to be held in your city in December. You are Rajiv Mittal.

Ans. From rajiv@gmail.com

To kunal@gmail.com

Cc

Subject Invite to Book Fair

Dear Kunal

How are you? I am fine here and wish the same for you. I have written this mail to tell you that our city is organising a Book Fair in the third week of December. All the major publishers of the country and from abroad are taking part. It is an opportunity for book-lovers. You are very fond of reading good books. So, I invite you to visit this Book Fair so that we can enjoy looking at and buying the books that we want and spend some time together. Please let me know about your plans.

Waiting for a positive reply.

With regards

Rajiv

PRACTICE QUESTIONS

1. Write an e-mail to the Principal of your school requesting him to grant you leave of four days as you have to visit your father who is getting treatment in hospital.
2. Write an e-mail to the Principal of your school requesting him to make arrangement of foreign language classes.
3. Write an e-mail to the Principal of your school, requesting her or him to ask students to participate in the charity drive.
4. Write an e-mail to the Principal of your school requesting him to make arrangement for some extracurricular activities for your classroom.
5. Write an e-mail to the school Principal requesting him/her for construction of a Cycle-shed.
6. Write an e-mail to the school Principal requesting him/her to set up a canteen.
7. Write an e-mail to your younger sibling telling him the importance of being hard-working and punctual to gain success.
8. Your friend has received a prize in an inter-school debate competition. Send an e-mail congratulating her on her achievement. You are Nisha and your friend is Neha.
9. Write an e-mail to your friend Divya telling her about how you spent your summer vacations.
10. Write an e-mail to your friend inviting him/her to your birthday party.

CHAPTER 4

Paragraph Writing

A paragraph is a short composition wherein a group of sentences are related to a single idea. In a paragraph, sentences related to a topic are organised in a proper manner to give information. There is no specific rule regarding the format or the length of a paragraph. However, a paragraph must contain a heading which tells us its topic/theme and the entire paragraph revolves around it.

Points to be Kept in Mind

- All sentences of the paragraph should relate to the main idea/topic.
- Use simple and clear language.
- Follow the word limit, if given.
- Remember to re-read your paragraph to make sure that you have not made any mistake in it.

SAMPLE PARAGRAPHS

1. You have visited a bookstore which was established in the same year India got its independence. Describe the many books you have encountered there and the feeling of visiting such a place.

Ans. A Visit to a Bookstore

On my way to school, I always come across a bookstore which looks old but lively. I was fascinated by its environment whenever I saw it from the window of the school bus. So, I decided to visit the bookstore on a Sunday morning. The name of the bookstore is Bibiliophile's Heaven and it has been a favourite place for booklovers since the time of India's Independence. Inside the bookstore, I saw people of various ages picking, choosing and buying books. When I went through the various bookshelves, I found books of many genres such as fiction, classic, comic, horror and children's story books. I spent around 2 hours inside the bookstore and bought 5 books. I also got a membership which would allow me to borrow books from the store. I really enjoyed my whole time there. I plan to go to the bookstore frequently.

2. Write a paragraph on one of the best gifts that you have received.

Ans. The Best Gift I have ever Received

One of the best gifts I have ever received was given to me by my uncle. I got a laptop which I desperately needed for the school studies. It is in black colour with a 16-inch display. It weighs less than a kilo and I can easily carry it in my bag. I often use it in my bed as well as on my study table. The laptop has all the applications that I would need. It has a great graphic card and good processor to support my graphic designing learning. It also has an in-built camera that allows me to attend some of my classes online. A good thing about my laptop is that it allows me to watch movies online without leaving the comfort of my home. Further, it has a really good sound quality which brings me joy as

I love listening to music. Moreover, the laptop is quite handy for me. I can search the internet, get help for my studies and learn many new things from my laptop. According to me, it has proved as a very useful device for many years.

3. Write a paragraph on 'The Season I Like the Most'.

Ans. The Season I Like the Most

There are 5 seasons that we know of. Each of these seasons come with their own characteristics which make us like or dislike it. Hence, I also have a season that I adore and that is my favourite season.
My favourite season is the rainy season or the Monsoons. In India, it is a very important season. Agriculture in India depends largely on the water given by the rains. For me, it is the most colourful of all the seasons. One can see a lot of greenery around oneself. The dark clouds are a great blessing and are eagerly awaited after the scorching summer heat. You can see many birds, animals and insects coming out of their homes to enjoy the cold rain. Not to forget the steaming pakoras and tea along with the paper boats that we can float in puddles. The best part of the season is that one gets a lot of unexpected holidays and off from school due to the rains. It is a pleasure to go out in the rains and get wet in the water.

4. Write a short paragraph on 'An Annual Function'. You may take help of the following questions

(i) When was it held this year?

(ii) Who was the Chief Guest?

(iii) Which cultural programmes were presented?

(iv) What prize did you get?

Ans. An Annual Function

Every year our school celebrates an Annual Function to remember our achievements of the year. This year's annual day was held in my school on 21st February, 20XX. It was held at the school auditorium and the preparations for it began in December. Just like every year, this year also we had a Chief Guest- Ms. Rupa Mishra, the District Collector. The function began with 'Saraswati Vandana'. Then, the Principal welcomed the Chief Guest and the other guests with garlands. Next, a Ghoomer dance was presented by the girls of various classes. The physical movements of the dancers attracted everyone. Afterward, *Maa Tujhe Salaam*, an action patriotic group song was displayed. The actions of the singers charmed the viewers. Further, a drama on the benefits of the modern technology was staged. Viewers were excited to watch it. Later, the prizes were given away to the students. I got a trophy for being an all rounder in my class.

5. Write a paragraph of about 100 words on 'My Hobby'. Use the following words: gardening, morning, grow, flowers, vegetables, fresh air, fresh and free vegetables, neighbours, temple, happy.

Ans. My Hobby

Hobbies give pleasure to everyone. Whenever you have free time, you enjoy participating in your hobby. It brings you joy, relaxes you and takes away all the tiredness of the day. My hobby is gardening. I love sitting in nature, planting seeds and watching life take form in front of me because of my efforts. My hobby is very useful for my family. There is a piece of land behind my house which is my mini garden. There I grow flowers which my elders use for pooja. I also grow various vegetables and herbs. Till now, I have planted tomato, coriander, green chillis, oregano, ginger, oranges and strawberry. Not just this, my garden helps in keeping me healthy. I get up early in the morning and work in the garden. In this way, I get fresh air and light exercise. I feel happy to see my garden.

PRACTICE QUESTIONS

1. Write a paragraph on 'My Favourite teacher'.
2. Write a paragraph on 'If I were a Bird....' in about 150 words.
3. Write a paragraph on 'My Visit to a Museum'.
4. Write a paragraph on 'A Day I Would Like to Forget'.
5. Write a paragraph on 'The Scene at the Market'.
6. Write a paragraph on 'My Visit to the Golden Temple'.
7. Write a paragraph on 'My Favourite Book'.
8. Write a paragraph on 'If I Knew About My Future...'

CHAPTER 5

Biographical Sketches

A Biographical Sketch is a short summary of a person's life. It is an overview of the life and work of a person, including information such as their childhood, education and achievements. It is generally used to introduce someone or to describe their extraordinary accomplishments and work done for the country or in any other field.

A biographical sketch should include the following information

- Who the person is, what they are known for
- What was their early life like
- Their major accomplishments
- When and where they were born
- Their education and career
- What they are doing now

Points to be kept in Mind

- Bio-sketch are written on the basis of an outline provided. Hence, stick to the outline.
- Keep your bio-sketch small and use simple language.
- Be sure to include the person's name at the beginning of the biography.
- Include only those details that are significant to the person's life.
- Always use the third person pronoun–he, she and they to write the bio-sketch.
- Do not include your personal opinion in the bio-sketch.
- Remember to re-read your bio-sketch to make sure that you have not made any mistake in it.

SAMPLE BIOGRAPHICAL SKETCHES

1. Using the information given below, write the biographical sketch of Virat Kohli in about 100 words.

Clues

- **Date of birth** 5th November, 1988, New Delhi
- **Trained under** Delhi Cricket Academy in 1998
- **Debut matches**
  - Cricket debut in October 2002 with the Delhi Under-15 team
  - ODI debut in 2008
  - T20 debut in 2010
- India's Test Captain from 2014 to 2022
- **Teams** Indian National Cricket Team, Royal Challengers Bangalore (Indian Premier League)
- **Achievements**
  - First player in ICC cricket history to win all 3 ICC awards in a single year
  - Arjuna Award
  - Padma Shri
  - Rajiv Gandhi Khel Ratna Award

Ans. **Virat Kohli**

Virat Kohli is an Indian cricket player who has made a name for himself in the world of cricket. Born on 5th November, 1988 in New Delhi, Virat Kohli started playing cricket in 1998 under the guidance of Delhi Cricket Academy. He made his official debut in October, 2002 with Delhi Under-15 team. He first played for ODI in 2008 and T20 in 2010 with Team

India. Virat led the Indian National Cricket Team as Test Captain from 2014 to 2022. In November, 2023 Kohli scored his 50th ODI century to surpass Tendulkar's record and became the first player to score 50 centuries in ODI cricket. He is known as the first player in ICC cricket history who bagged all the 3 ICC awards in a single year. He has also received the revered Arjuna Award, Padma Shri and Rajiv Gandhi Khel Ratna Award. Apart from the national team, Virat also played for Royal Challengers Bangalore (Indian Premier League). Virat Kohli is known as one of the best batsmen in the world.

2. Using the information given below, write the biographical sketch of Manu Bhaker in about 100 words.

Clues

- **Date of birth** 18th February 2002, Goria village, Jhajjar district, Haryana
- Played other sports such as tennis, skating and boxing in school and also participated in a form of martial arts called 'thang ta'
- **Achievements**
  - Olympic Medals (2024 Summer Olympics, Paris)
  - Bronze in the women's 10-meter air pistol event (first Indian female shooter to win an Olympic medal).
  - Bronze in the mixed 10-meter air pistol team event (first Indian woman to win two Olympic medals).
- **Other Notable Achievements**
  - Gold medal at the 2022 Asian Games in the women's 25m pistol team event.
  - Individual gold medal at the 2018 Commonwealth Games in the women's 10meter air pistol event (set a new Commonwealth Games record).
  - Youngest Indian to win a gold at the ISSF World Cup in 2018 (achieved at the age of 16).

Ans. Manu Bhaker is an Indian Sport Shooter and Olympic medalist. She was born on February 18, 2002, in Jhajjar, Haryana, a state known for its boxers and wrestlers. As a school going students, Bhaker played many sports like tennis, skating and boxing in school and also participated in a form of martial arts called 'thang ta'. Today, she is one of the most acclaimed athletes with two bronze medals at the 2024 Summer Olympics in Paris. She secured a bronze in the women's 10 metre air pistol event, becoming the first female shooter from India to win a medal at any Olympics. She has made India proud in many events. She won a gold medal at the 2022 Asian Games in the women's 25m pistol team event and another individual gold medal which she won at the 2018 Commonwealth Games in the women's 10m air pistol event. In fact, she set a new Commonwealth Games record. Further, she is also the youngest Indian to win a gold at the ISSF World Cup in 2018 (achieved at the age of 16). Manu Bhaker has become the most successful Indian woman shooter in history at a very young age.

3. Using the following clues, write a bio-sketch of Elon Musk.

Clues

- **Born** 28th June, 1971, Pretoria, South Africa
- **Nationality/Citizenship** American
- **Occupation** Entrepreneur
- **Education** Bachelor's degrees in Physics and Economics in 1997 from University of Pennsylvania
- **Known for**
  - Electronic payment firm PayPal, co-founder
  - SpaceX, maker of launch vehicles and spacecraft
  - Owns X (formerly known as Twitter)
  - Major investor of Tesla
- Current richest man

Ans. Elon Musk, born on 28th June, 1971, is a famous Entrepreneur. Although he was born in Pretoria, South Africa, he has acquired an American citizenship. He graduated in 1997 with his bachelor degree from University of Pennsylvania in the field of Physics and Economics. He has always had a talent for computers so he co-founded the electronic payment company, Paypal which is famous worldwide. The biggest achievement of Elon Musk is the founding of SpaceX, a firm which makes launch vehicles and spacecraft products. He is also the owner of X which was formerly Twitter and is a major investor in the Tesla Company. Elon Musk is currently one of the richest men in the world.

4. Write a biographical sketch of Vishwanathan Anand – Grandmaster, a world Chess Champion in your own words. Clues have been given.

Clues

- **Born** 11th December, 1969 in Tamil Nadu
- **Nationality** Indian
- **Hobbies** Listening to music, swimming and reading
- **Instructor** Learnt chess from mother at the age of 6
- **Marital status** Married
- **Children** A son
- **Known for** Undisputed Title of World Chess Champion from 2007 to 2013
- **Achievements**
  - First Asian at 17 to win the World Chess title at the FIDE World Junior Championship, 1987.
  - Published his collection of games under the title 'Vishy Anand: My Best Games of Chess'.
  - Padma Shri at the age of 18
  - Rajiv Gandhi Khel Ratna
  - Padma Vibhushan
  - Arjun Award
  - Chess Oscar

Ans. Vishwanathan Anand was born on 11th December, 1969 in Tamil Nadu. He is an Indian chess player who held the undisputed title of World Chess Champion from 2007 to 2013. He learnt to play chess from his mother at the age of 6 and became the first Asian at the age of 17 to win the world chess title at the FIDE World Junior Championship in the year 1987. He has published his collection of games under the title 'Vishy Anand: My Best Games of Chess.' Anand is fond of listening to music, swimming and reading. He is married to Aruna Anand and has a son. Viswanathan was awarded the Padma Shri at a young age of 18 years. Besides that, he has also bagged the Rajiv Gandhi Khel Ratna, Padma Vibhushan, Arjuna Award and Chess Oscar.

5. On the basis of the following points write a short biography of Swami Vivekananda.

Clues

- **Birth** 12th January, 1863, in Simla in Calcutta.
- **Parents** Biswanath Dutta and Bhubaneswari Devi
- **Names** Narendranath; Pet name-Bile
- **Childhood** Naughty and restless; early education at home; Metropolitan School; Presidency College and General Assemblies Institution
- **Education** Monastic Life: Met Sri Ramakrishna and became his disciple; known as Swami Vivekananda
- **Achievements**
  - Participation in the Parliament of Religions at Chicago in 1893
  - Founded Ramakrishna Math
  - Misson at Belur, in 1898
- **Death** 4th July, 1902

Ans. Swami Vivekananda, the popular Hindu monk of India, was born on 12th January, 1863, in Simla in Calcutta. His parents- Biswanath Dutta and Bhubaneswari Devi named him Narendranath but lovingly called him Bile. Bile was very naughty and restless but very bold and brave in his childhood. He had his early education at home and school education at the Metropolitan School. Then, he was admitted to the Presidency College and later to the General Assemblies Institution. At this time, young Narendranath heard about Sri Ramakrishna and was tremendously influenced by him. Soon, he became his great student and came to be known as Swami Vivekananda. Then, he went to America to join the Parliament of Religions held in Chicago in 1893. Later, he founded the Ramakrishna Math and Mission at Belur in 1898 for the service of suffering humanity. This great patriot of India died on 4th July, 1902.

PRACTICE QUESTIONS

1. Write the biography of Narendra Damodardas Modi, the current Prime Minister of India in your own words. Clues have been given.

- **Born** 17th September, 1950, Vadnagar, Gujarat
- **Education** MA degree (Political Science) from Gujarat University
- **Organisations**
  - Former member of pro-Hindu group, Rashtriya Swayamsevak Sangh (RSS) in 1970s
  - Bharatiya Janata Party (BJP), political party
- **Known for**
  - Current Prime Minister of India, 2014–Present
  - Former Chief Minister of Gujarat, 2001–2014
- **Achievements/successful projects**
  - Demonetisation in India
  - Successful G20 summit 2023
  - GST bill
  - India's position in the global scenario

2. Using the information given below, write the bio-sketch of Dr. APJ Abdul Kalam, the 11th President of India.

- **Name** Avul Pakir Jainulabdeen Abdul Kalam (APJ Abdul Kalam) **Nickname** Missile Man
- **Born** 15th October, 1931
- **Place of Birth** Dhanushkodi, Rameshwaram, Tamil Nadu, India
- **Occupation** Engineer, Scientist, Author, Professor, Politician
- **Died** 27th July, 2015
- **Place of Death** Shillong, Meghalaya, India
- **Famous as** Dr. APJ Abdul Kalam, President from 2002 to 2007

3. Write the bio-sketch of the given famous personality by using the clues given below.

- **Full name** Lionel Andres Messi
- **Born** 24th June, 1987, Rosario, Argentina
- **Early football career** Youth team of Newell's Old Boys, 1995
- **Known as** One of the greatest football players of all time
- **Position** Forward
- **Teams** Argentina National Team, FC Barcelona and PSG (Paris St.-Germain), Inter Miami
- **Achievements**
  - Olympic gold, Beijing 2008
  - Eight Ballon d'Or awards
  - FIFA's World Cup Champion, 2022

4. Write the bio-sketch of Albert Einstein by using the clues given below.

- **Full name** Albert Einstein
- **Born** 14th March, 1879, Ulm, Wurttemberg, Germany
- **Died** 18th April, 1955 (aged 76)
- **Ethnicity** German Jewish
- **Citizenship** United States (from 1940 onwards)
- **Known for** Theory of Relativity [$E = mc^2$], Unified Field Theory
- **Awards** Nobel Prize in Physics (1921), Person of the Century by Time Magazine.

5. Using the information given below, write a bio-sketch of JK Rowling, a famous author.

- **Full name** Joanne Kathleen Rowling
- **Born** 31st July, 1965, Yate, England
- **Early life**
  - First book called 'Rabbit' at the age of six
  - First novel about seven cursed diamonds and the people who owned them, at age of 11
- **Education** University of Exeter in 1986
- **Known for** Harry Potter Series
- **Achievements**
  - Officer of the Order of the British Empire (OBE)
  - French Legion of Honour
  - First Recipient of the Hans Christian Andersen Award

6. Given below are the details of the famous singer, S.P. Balasubrahmanyam.

- **Full name** Sripathi Panditaradhyula Balasubrahmanyam
- **Date of Birth** 4th June, 1946
- **Place of Birth** Konetammapeta, Nellore District
- **State** Andhra Pradesh
- **Educational qualifications** Engineering course (A.M.I.E)
- **Entry into film field** 1966
- **First Film** Sri Sri Sri Maryada Ramanna
- **Entry into Bollywood** 1980
- **Total number of songs sung** About 40,000
- **Awards**
  - National Film Award for best male playback singer
  - National Award from Government of Andhra Pradesh - 25 times
  - State Award from Tamil Nadu
  - State Award from Karnataka
  - Padma Shri
  - Padma Bhushan

Based on the above information, write a biographical sketch of S.P. Balasubrahmanyam.

CHAPTER 6

Diary Entry

Diary entry is a piece of informal writing wherein you write your feelings and opinions regarding some event that happened during the day. It is usually written at the end of the day. A diary acts like a friend with whom you share your innermost emotions without any fear.

Points to be Kept in Mind

- Use the first person pronoun-'I' to write your diary.
- Use simple and clear language in your diary.
- Always include what you feel in your diary entry.
- Remember to re-read your diary after writing it to make sure that it does not contain any error.

Format of a Diary Entry

You are Saurabh. You took part to enact a scene at the school stage from the story of Satyawadi Harishchandra on the 'Annual Day' of your school. Your role and acting was widely admired by the audience and the Chief Guest gave you a special prize for your best performance playing the character of Harishchandra. Write a diary entry expressing your joy.

Day and Date / Time	Wednesday, 19th November, 20XX 9:00 pm
Greeting	Dear Diary
Body of the Diary	Today was one of the happiest day for me. What a great feeling! Cheers from the audience! Applause from everyone. I had not imagined that I would get such a wonderful feeling when I performed on the stage. You remember that I told you that our teacher had given me a chance to play the character of Satyawadi Harishchandra in a dramatic scene for the 'Annual Day' celebration of our school. Guess what, it was fantastic! I was the centre of attention and everyone loved it. At the end, the Chief Guest himself hugged me amidst cheers from the audience. He announced a special prize for me for the best actor award. My joy knew no bounds. I noticed a gleam in the eyes of my parents in the audience. I was extremely happy.
Signature/Name of the Writer	Saurabh

SAMPLE DIARY ENTRIES

1. You have participated in a yoga session on International Yoga Day at Jawaharlal National (JNL) Stadium. The yoga teacher was very kind and gentle and he taught everyone patiently. You were in a good mood after attending the session. Write a diary entry expressing your happiness. You are Jiya.

Ans. Sunday, 21st June, 20XX 10:00 pm

Dear Diary

I had a superb day today! I was a little unwilling to attend the yoga session but my mother insisted that we should go so, I just went along with her. There were around 100 people and 5 yoga instructors gathered in the yoga area in JNL Stadium. Yoga mats were also arranged in a proper manner. We started with breathing exercises then went on to do body movements and meditation in a slow and steady way. The instructors were very gentle people and were guiding everyone patiently. I felt so light and my mood became so much better. I'm glad that I decided to go.

Jiya

2. One of your best friends took you to a restaurant for a treat. You saw there a child of your age sadly engaged in scrubbing utensils in the cold water in winters. You were upset and felt sad for the child. Write a diary entry expressing your grief.

Ans. Thursday, 19th March, 20xx 9:00 pm

Dear Diary

Can the elders be so cruel to a child of 12-13 years to force him to wash utensils with cold tap water in winters? Alas! I saw it today. When I went with a friend to a restaurant, the poor child was scrubbing and washing utensils at the entrance. For a moment, we did not feel like going in and eating. This was the saddest view of child labour. One wonders when our authorities and system would implement the laws against child labour and send the kids of poor parents to school to learn and enjoy the golden period of life.

Satish

3. You have travelled from train many times but the journey that you had made today ended horribly. Imagining the thing that went wrong in your train journey, write a dairy entry.

Ans. 24th April, 20XX, Friday 7:00 pm

Dear Diary

Life is so unpredictable. I was in high spirits when I boarded the Rajdhani Express from Bhopal to Delhi. After all, I had travelled from trains many times and always looked forward to train journeys. I expected the same this time as I found my seat in the compartment. It was quite comfortable and near the window. The journey was nice and so were my co-passengers. I had a nice sleep. But when I got up in the morning, the train was near Delhi. I got up to wear my shoes. They were not there. I looked for them under the seats but they were missing. My bag was missing too. Certainly, they were stolen. All my documents and cash were in the bag. I did not know what to do. It was a horrible feeling to be helpless. However, as I got off the train, I saw a man running away with my shoes and bag. I screamed and some people ran after him but could not catch him. I had started crying and had to call my father telling him about the stolen things. I got a scolding and decided to never travel by train again.

Ankit

4. You went to see the India International Trade Fair held at Pragati Maidan, New Delhi. Using the hints given below together with your ideas on the subject, make a diary entry of what you saw and experienced there.

Hints – As usual IITF was held at Pragati maidan – All leading countries participated – Chinese dominated the show – All states of India – Cultural programmes – Food Courts – High prices dampened the spirit

Ans. 16th June, 20XX, Thursday 8:00 pm

Dear Diary

A visit to the Indian International Trade Fair at Pragati Maidan has always been a rewarding experience for me. It was the same this year too. I went to this year's trade fair with my parents. It was a different world over there. To be precise, it was a fairyland. The sections of Germany, Canada, the USA, China and Great Britain attracted a large crowd. However, China dominated the show.

India was represented by almost all states and establishments like the Indian Railways, Indian Tourism, LIC, Tatas and what not. The 'Food Courts' served all tastes from Pizzas to Choley Bhaturey. We bought pairs of shoes, mobiles and garments. The fair provided opportunities for a lot of fun and entertainment but it was quite expensive. Film show, folk dances and puppet shows drew huge crowds. Anyway, it was a very pleasant and rewarding experience.

Neha

5. Write a diary entry entailing the short account of how you played a prank on your mother.

Ans. 1st, April 2023, Saturday 9:00 pm

Dear Diary

I had a lot of fun pulling a prank on my mom today. My mom was boiling milk in the evening. While it was boiling, she went to the bedroom to fold some clothes for a few minutes. When the milk was ready, I poured it into a container, placed it in the refrigerator and put the pan on the rack. When mom arrived a short while later she noticed the burner was empty. She was really puzzled. She then started to boil a second pack of milk. This time she went to attend a telephone call when I played my trick again on her. After returning to the kitchen, she discovered that the milk was again missing. This time she yelled in horror. She believed that the house was haunted. I yelled 'pranked you' and laughed so hard. I told dad the story when he got home. Even he laughed heartily. I'll be writing soon again. Now is the time for me to go to bed.

Tanya

PRACTICE QUESTIONS

1. Your school Principal one day called you on the stage in the morning assembly. He unexpectedly gave you a big white and pink-coloured rose flower, praising you for being the most disciplined and punctual student on the basis of your class teacher's report. Share your joy with your diary entry. You are Ranjan.
2. You had been shortlisted for the selection of the head girl of your school. Finally, with the help of senior teachers, the Principal found you to be the most suitable candidate for this position when you cleared the difficult interview. Next day you will be given the proud badge in a function. Write a diary entry expressing your happiness.
3. You quarrelled with a friend in a street and even used bad language for a very small matter. Your friend kept cool throughtout. Later, you felt guilty. Write a diary entry expressing your regret.
4. You were waiting for the school bus at the pick-up point. Suddenly, you heard a loud thud at some distance. You turned back and saw an old man had slipped and fallen. The poor fellow was looking for the spectacles which had fallen away. You rushed and helped the man who thanked you and blessed you. Write a diary entry about how nice you felt for helping him.
5. Your father announced in the family that the whole family is going to spend a part of the summer vacation in Shimla. You felt excited and happy. Write a diary entry about how you wish to enjoy during your stay at Shimla.
6. You won a free trip to Malaysia; Write a diary entry about what all things you would carry there and what all you wish to buy from there.
7. On your way to a school trip you saw tourists throwing garbage on the site of a tourist spot. You felt angry and wanted to tell them to properly throw the garbage in the dustbin. But as you were on your way and inside the bus, you couldn't say anything. Write a diary entry expressing your frustration. You are Andrea.
8. You have been selected as the main singer for a big stage. Express your excitement and nervousness in a diary entry. You are Niloy.
9. You went to watch a movie in 5D for the first time with your school. It was an amazing experience as you could feel that you were a part of the movie. Write a diary entry about this experience.
10. On your trip to Amritsar you went to the nearby science museum where you saw many life-sized figures of dinosaurs. You also saw many short documentaries about human life. Write about your visit to the museum in your diary.

CHAPTER 7

Story Writing

Story is a record of an event which can be true or imaginary. The purpose of the story is to impart a moral, capture a moment, event or to inculcate values and just to entertain the readers. Story Writing is a language skill that tests the student's creativity and writing skills.

Main Elements of a Short Story

1. **Theme** It is the main idea or message of the story.
2. **Plot** It is the logical connection among all parts of the story. A proper beginning, a middle and an end are essential components of a good plot.
3. **Setting** It is the time and location of the story.
4. **Characters** The people, animals or other living creatures of the story are its characters. A short story has one main character and very few minor characters to support the plot.

Points to be Kept in Mind

- Read the clue/outline carefully given in the question.
- Think about the possible plot and the characters.
- Start the story as instructed in the question.
- Starting or beginning should be brief and interesting.
- Build the plot by using dialogues and interesting points.
- End the story appropriately by giving a climax.
- A proper conclusion or moral can be given at the end of the story (if possible).
- Always give a title to the story.
- Re-read the story to make sure you have not made any mistakes in it.

SAMPLE STORIES

Type I : Based on Verbal Inputs

1. Write a story with the help of outlines given. Give the story a title and write down the moral of the story.

Ant and grasshopper lived in a grassy meadow..........summer time.........plenty of food......ant worked hard collecting grains but grasshopper lazed arounu...........grasshopper mocked ant for working...........ant told grasshopper to save food for winter but it didn't follow the advice.........winter came and grasshopper hungry and helpless.........asked ant for help but ant denied the request.........grasshopper realised his mistake.

Ans. The Ant and the Grasshopper

Once, in a tall grassy meadow, there lived an ant and a grasshopper. In the summer when there was no scarcity of food, the ant worked hard day and night. It was collecting grains from the nearby farms. The whole time the grasshopper was not working at all. He was lying lazily while watching the ant. He even mocked the ant saying that the ant was working unnecessarily. The ant was worried for the grasshopper and told him to start collecting food.

However, the grasshopper just laughed it off as a joke. When winter came, the grasshopper couldn't find any food and was getting very hungry. He thought of asking the ant for food since the ant had stored food. But the ant scolded him for not taking the advice and asked him to go away. The grasshopper regretted not working when he still had time.

Moral of the story Always be prepared for the expected future.

2. Write a story with the help of the outlines given. Add title and moral of the story.

A farmer bought a well from a wicked man............the wicked man refused to give water saying he sold only the well.........farmer went to king......king called for the wicked man......asked him why he denied access to well water.....king asked wicked man to take away all the water since well is farmer's.......wicked man defeated and apologised.

Ans. The Farmer, the Well and the Wicked Man

Once upon a time, there lived a farmer who worked very hard for his fields. He needed water for his farm so he bought a well from a man. When the farmer went to fetch water, the man told him that he was not permitted to take water from the well as he only sold the well and not the water inside the well. The farmer understood the wickedness of the man.

He was frustrated and went to seek help from the king. The king called the wicked man to the court to explain the reason behind his action towards the farmer. The king thought for a while and came up with a solution. The king told the wicked man that since the well now belonged to the farmer he was not allowed to keep his water inside the well. He ordered the wicked man to either pay the farmer for using his well or take out all the water from the well. The wicked man realised that his plan has failed. He apologised to the king as well as the farmer and took back his words.

Moral of the story Cheating never goes unpunished.

3. Read the outlines below and develop a story by using them and your own ideas.

A man and his wife........their goose laid golden egg everyday......... . They wished to become rich fast .... thought bird has gold inside.........killed it.........lost even an egg everyday.

Ans. The Goose that Laid the Golden Eggs

Once upon a time, a man and his wife wanted to buy cows and a goose for their farm. They went to the market and bought three cows and a goose for a small amount of money. They did not like how the goose looked but needed its eggs. The next day when they went to collect the goose's egg, they found that she had laid a golden egg. The man and his wife sold the egg for a huge price. This became a daily routine for them as the goose laid one golden egg everyday.

Soon the man and his wife became rich. However, even then, they felt that they were not rich enough. They had become greedy and wanted to be rich fast. They imagined that the bird must have a good store of gold inside it. So, they killed the bird to get the whole gold at once.

However, after killing the bird they found it as ordinary as any other goose. Thus, they neither got any gold nor could they enjoy having a golden egg daily since the goose had been killed.

Moral of the story Greed can lead to one's downfall.

4. Read the outlines given below and develop a story based on the outlines. Provide a title and mention the lesson/moral provided by the story.

Mother dog and puppies lived in a farm.........naughty puppies........mother told kids not to go near well........one pup got curious and went.........pup looked down the well.......saw his reflection.......mistook it for another pup......jumped down to fight.........started to drown.........the farmer saved him.

Ans. The Curious Puppy

Once in a big farm, there lived a mother dog and her puppies. Since the puppies were little and always playing around, the mother told the pups to not go near the well. She tried to warn them of the trouble of going there as her pups were naughty. However, one of the pups got curious and thought of visiting the well. On one fine day the pup sneaked out and went beside the well. When he looked down the well, to his surprise, he saw another pup reflected on the water surface.

He thought it was a different pup and wanted to fight it. He jumped down the well but unfortunately, there was only water. As a result, he was drowning helplessly. He cried for help. Hearing the sound of a pup crying, a farmer came running and picked up the pup. The pup was ashamed of his action and promised to never disobey his mother again.

Moral of the story Always listen to the advice of your elders.

5. Read outlines of a story given below. Develop them in a complete story.

A man had four sons......quarrelling with each other.......father was worried.....tried to make them realise their folly......bundle of sticks.....each to break it............but failed......untied the bundle.......... each stick broken. .... united they would be stronger.

Ans. Father and his Quarrelling Sons

A man had four sons who were always quarrelling with each other. They always had one topic or another to fight. Their quarrels increased so much that they hated the sight of each other and so, started living separately. This made the man worried. He wanted to make them realise their folly and unite them. So, one day he called them and asked them to tie a few sticks in a bundle.

Then, he asked each son in turn to break it across his knee. Each tried and failed. The father asked them to untie the bundle and break the individual sticks. Now, each of them easily broke those sticks.

The man then said to his sons, "If you are united like sticks in a bundle you will be strong and your enemy cannot harm you. But if you quarrel like this you will be weak and you can be attacked by any one."

Moral of the story Unity is strength.

Type II : Based on Visual Inputs

6. Write a story with the help of the visual given below. Give a title also.

Ans. The Wolf and the Crane

Once upon a time in a green dense jungle, there lived a wolf and a crane. Both the wolf and the crane hated each other and did not talk kindly to each other. The reason behind their hatred is their first meeting. The wolf and the crane met a few years ago. The wolf was greedily eating the deer it had hunted. While eating, he was not careful and a bone got stuck in his throat. He tried to cough it so that it could come out but nothing happened.

Then, he approached the crane and requested her to pull it out with the help of her long beak.

"I will pay you for it", he added. The crane pulled out the bone easily hoping to become the wolf's friend. However, after she took out the small piece of bone the wolf thanked her rudely and started leaving. The crane cried "Where is my fee?" 'Well', retorted the wolf quickly showing his teeth, "Go and tell your friends proudly that you put your head into a wolf's mouth and did not get it bitten off."

7. Look at the given image and write a story titled 'Hidden Treasure'.

Ans. **Hidden Treasure**

Once upon a time there was an old farmer. He had four sons who were very lazy. They did not do anything for the entire day. They would sit in their rooms and order people around to do things for them. The old man was fed up with his sons and tried to explain the value of work to them but to no avail. Once the farmer fell very ill.

He thought of a plan. He called his sons together and told them that there was a treasure hidden in the field. They need to dig the field to get the treasure. After saying this the farmer died. His sons dug the field.

However, they did not find the treasure. Their neighbour advised the sons to sow seeds in the field. They did so and the crop was very good. Then they understood what their father wanted them to do. They worked hard in life and became very rich. They were happy.

Moral of the story Work is worship.

8. Look at the given image and write a story titled 'Bad Company'.

Ans. **Bad Company**

Once a rich man had only one son. As a result, the boy was very pampered. He had everything he wanted and lived a very luxurious life. However, as he grew up he fell into bad company. He used to spend his entire day outside roaming in the street doing nothing but eating junk food and spending money.

His father advised him to leave the bad company but he did not leave. So, the father thought of a plan. One day, he brought some fresh apples and a rotten apple. He asked his son to put all the apples in a basket. After two days, all the apples were rotten. His father told him that one rotten apple had made all the apples bad, so one bad boy would make all the boys bad. The boy learnt a lesson. He left the bad company. His father was very happy.

Moral of the story Better alone than in a bad company.

PRACTICE QUESTIONS

1. Write a story with the help of verbal clues given in the box. Give it a suitable title.

All the mice together....discussed protection from the cat....suggestion from an experienced mouse ....fasten a bell round the neck of cat/an old mouse reacted.......who will bell the enemy, the cat.

2. Here is the beginning of a story. Complete it by giving a new ending. Name of the story is 'The Crow and the Fox'.

One day a crow was sitting on a branch of a tree with a piece of cheese in her beak. A fox noticed it and thought of some way of getting the cheese.

3. Read the following outlines and develop them in a story. The title of the story may be 'The Boy Bathing'.

A boy was bathing in a river....in danger of being drowned....a man heard his cries for help....the man came and began to scold for being careless.... the boy requested to help first.

4. Write a story with the help of the following outlines. Title of the story may be 'The Mischievous Dog.'

Once there was a dog....bit people without provocations....nuisance to visitors to master's house ....a bell round his neck.....the dog proud of tinkling it ....an old dog reminded of the punishment.

5. Develop the following outlines in a story, 'The Wolf in Sheep's Clothing.'

A wolf disguised himself to prey upon sheep....in sheep skin he slipped among sheep....deceived the shepherd....was shut in with the flock....supply of mutton....shepherd mistook for sheep.......killed the wolf.

6. Read the outlines below and develop them in a story. Give the story a suitable title also.

A hare was making fun of a tortoise for he was slow....the tortoise challenged him for a race....a fox was the judge....they started off....the hare thought to rest and slept........the tortoise kept going.......the hare woke up and started fast .... tortoise had already reached the goal.

7. Look at the given image and write a story titled 'The Greedy Dog'.

8. Look at the given image and write a story titled 'The Donkey and the Load of Salt'.

9. Look at the given image and write an appropriate story for it.

10. Look at the given image and write an appropriate story for it.

Article Writing

An article is a piece of writing that is written to inform, to persuade or to entertain the reader about something. It has several paragraphs containing a distinct beginning, a middle and a conclusion.

Writing an article is a very challenging task for anyone. It requires a high level of creativity, a good vocabulary and a great knowledge of the subject. Hence, knowing the elements and the format of an article is very important.

Elements of an Article

1. **Title/Heading** The title should be thought-provoking and catchy and should highlight the theme. It may comprise a single word, a phrase or a sentence of 4-6 words.
2. **Name of the writer** Write your name immediately after the heading in the form of a byline.
3. **Introduction** Keep the topic in perspective; specify it keeping the reader's interest intact by providing some surprising information or interesting facts related to the context.
4. **Description of the topic** Highlight various facets of the topic like the causes and effects, advantages and disadvantages, etc.
5. **Ending** Wind up your article with your own views-criticism, suggestions, etc.
6. **Conclusion** End the article with a desire, an appeal or a warning.

Points to be Kept in Mind

- Understand carefully the hints/information given in the verbal or visual input.
- Arrange all the hints/information in an order in which you want them to develop.
- Divide your article into several paragraphs when necessary. All the sentences in the paragraphs should be related to the main ideas of the topic.
- Use simple and straightforward language.
- Avoid the use of personal pronouns.
- Remember to re-read your article to make sure that there are no grammatical or punctuation mistake in it.

Format of an Article

Compulsory value-based education is the only remedy for inculcating values among the future citizens of the country. This will also help in the prevention of crime in the country. Write an article on the need of compulsory value-based education. Use the following clues to frame your article.

An approach to teaching and learning- develops relationships and promotes positive human values- qualitative improvement in attitude and behaviour- help the students think about positive universal values- inclusive school philosophy

Ans.

Title/Heading — **Value-Based Education**

Byline (Writer's name) — by XYZ

Introductory Paragraph:

Value-based education is an educational philosophy, an approach to teaching and learning that develops relationships and promotes positive human values. Schools that adopt such an approach state that there is a qualitative improvement in students' attitude and behaviour. The purpose of value-based education is to help the students think about positive universal values and practical consequences of expressing them.

Main body:

Value-based education also supports schools in promoting an inclusive school philosophy. It helps students to raise their self-esteem and take responsibility for their own behaviour and learning. It also enables students to examine the kind of life that is worth living and to consider what kind of life they want for themselves. Value-based education involves an agreed set of principles, deeply held convictions that are important to all aspects of school life and work. The process is holistic and developmental, demanding a greater deal from the school's community. Value-based education is thus a philosophy for developing and supporting schools of excellence.

SAMPLE ARTICLES

1. In today's competitive age, the students' main focus is on academics and coaching classes for entrance examinations, so they tend to neglect participation in outdoor games. Lack of open spaces is another reason for avoiding athletics and sports. Write an article on 'Poor Physical Fitness of School Students'.

Ans. Poor Physical Fitness of School Students

by XYZ

Being physically active and fit holds utmost importance especially among today's younger generation who isn't active. In today's competitive age, a student's main focus is on academics and coaching classes for entrance examinations; so they tend to neglect participation in outdoor games. Students have jam-packed schedules with their entire focus on academics.

Due to non-involvement of physical activities and sports in student life, health of the students is negatively affected. Being young, students have a lot of potential to develop a hobby that keeps their fitness regulated for the lifetime. A healthy and fit person is capable of living life to the fullest without any major medical or physical issues. Being healthy to a large extent is related to the physical well-being of a person.

Being physically fit adds to your personality. It lets you perform physical activities without being tired or restless. Being physically fit also ensures you being mentally fit and stress free. One has to include regular exercises in one's daily routine to remain healthy and maintain physical fitness. So, a student has to lead a healthy life style to experience happiness, peace and to enjoy energetic and enthusiastic lifestyle.

2. Scarcity of water is felt by people everywhere in villages, in towns and in big cities. Global warming has affected rainfall and snowfall. Our population is increasing and demand for water is on the rise. Rainwater harvesting, conservation of water along with control on its wastage shall help us meet our water needs in future. Write an article on the topic, 'Water Problem' using the clues given above.

Ans. **Water Problem**

by Ankita

The Earth is called the Blue Planet, and for reasons known well to all of us. About 97% of the Earth is made of water and yet the amount of water available for use to man is alarming. India suffers from water shortage for cultivation and drinking despite the fact that many big rivers flow through some parts of India.

The cause of this scarcity is global warming which has led to irregularities in rainfall and snowfall and depletion of underground water resources. Further, rapid urbanisation, industrialisation and the ever increasing population has led to an increase in demand of everything. As a result, all of the underground water is lost due to overexploitation. And now it is estimated that by 2020 several Indian cities like Delhi and Bengaluru will have lost their groundwater supply completely.

India is blessed with rainfall in several regions which can be harvested properly to meet our growing needs. Schemes that promote proper town planning and water harvesting need to be launched on a big scale. Eco clubs should be established in all the schools of the country to spread awareness among the students about the need to stop the reckless use of water and water conservation. Only then we can ensure a safe future for our coming generations otherwise, the day is not far when we may witness another world-war not for land, but for water.

3. Teachers are regarded as nation builders. They are responsible for developing the character of students and transforming them into responsible citizens. Write an article on the topic, 'Role of Teacher in the Society'.

Ans. **Role of Teacher in the Society**

by XYZ

Teachers play a key role in the growth of the society. Teachers are regarded as nation builders. They are responsible for not only educating the children but also for developing their character and transforming them into responsible citizens.

The children of today are the leaders of tomorrow and teachers are those significant individuals that make a child ready for their future. Teachers act as a support system that is lacking elsewhere in students' lives. They help them shape opinions and form ideas about societies, life and personal goals. This expands students' limits and pushes their creativity.

Teacher's role in society is both valuable and significant. They are the ultimate role models for students. They are able to see each child's strengths and weaknesses and provide better guidance. They are the gurus who build our character while inculcating discipline in students. Teachers have a major contribution to society's development and upliftment. They teach the students the right values of life and the difference between right and wrong. Thus, teachers are truly a backbone of the society who make the students realise the best of their abilities.

4. As sports captain of your school, write an article for your school magazine emphasising the need of adventure sports in youngsters' lives. Such sports help us in being strong, both in body and mind. There is a lot of geographical diversity (mountains, hills, rivers, beaches, etc.) in our country. There is a great scope for such sports. These sports prepare us to face the future challenges of life.

Ans. **Need of Adventure Sports in Youngsters' Lives**

by XYZ

The craze of adventurous and exciting sports among youngsters is skyrocketing like never before. Experiencing life outdoors and exploring unexplored regions by participating in trekking, water rafting, canoeing, scuba diving, rock climbing and more gives an adrenaline rush. Adventure sport is a term given to all those sports that involve speed, height, a high level of physical exertion along with a highly specialised gear required under high risk or danger. Games like mountain biking, skiing, and skateboarding, etc. are great not only to get the real feel of excitement and enjoyment but also because it has a positive impact on the mind and the body.

Adventure sports have been important in increasing confidence and physical abilities while preparing an individual to face any challenge of life. And so many parents even encourage their children to take part in some sports to keep them healthy and fit as these sports do involve lots of physical exercise.

There is great scope for such sports in India. India offers immense opportunity for adventure lovers throughout its length and breadth with its geographical diversity of mountains, hills, rivers, and beaches. Today, adventure sports are known to teach self-reliance, teamwork and result in improved self-esteem. The emotional and physical benefits of adventure sports are impressive and numerous.

5. You are Rahul of Class VI B. Information technology has brought about a global revolution in all fields. Computer aided education is fast becoming the order of the day. The market is flooded with educational CDs and online learning is a new phenomenon. Write an article on 'Computers Replace Classroom Teaching' for your school magazine.

Clues

- Advent of technology
- Anywhere and at anytime
- Lecture recorded
- Audio-visual method
- Combined theory and practical

Ans. **Computers Replace Classroom Teaching**

by Rahul, Class VI B

Education earlier used to have two main constituents that are classroom teaching and learning. But with the advent of information technology, it appears that the process of teaching is about to change in a big way. With changing habits, timelines and expectations, a variety of new technologies have come into picture. Now online teaching is very prevalent. One can view CDs, multimedia presentations and online video lectures anywhere, anytime at one's convenience. Even lectures by teachers are recorded and uploaded on the internet where students, after watching the video, can leave their questions to which they get replies via. e-mail.

One major benefit of using IT as an educational aid is that it is easier for students to learn from audio-visual media. It has efficiently combined theory and practical classes at one place. Students have the convenience of re-playing any lecture that they do not understand. Because of its time saving and comprehensive nature, IT has become a major tool for education.

PRACTICE QUESTIONS

1. India is a tourist's dream destination. Give your views on the tourism potential of India in an article.

   Clues
   - Places of worship–religious tourism
   - Foreigners–places of historical interest
   - The rich–hill stations during summers
   - The Sun-kissed beaches in winters
   - Leisure tourism
   - Medical tourism–world class hospitals.

2. The number of private vehicles is increasing in the cities. It leads to traffic jams and a rise in air pollution levels. The only solution seems to be that people start using public transport. Write an article on the topic 'Importance of Public Transport'.

3. Make in India is an initiative by Government of India. It intends to create employment for the youth of India and help bring best practices to Indian business. Write an article for a business magazine on its impact to create employment for the youth of India. You can use the following clues.

   Clues
   - To give more incentive to business
   - To lure businessmen
   - Create employment opportunities
   - Attract capital and technological investment
   - Results already visible
   - Suggestions for improvement

4. Hard-work and punctuality are essential for a happy and successful life. They help in meeting the desired targets of our lives. You are Kavya/Kanha. Write an article highlighting the importance of hard-work and punctuality in a student's life.

5. You are Ram/Rajani. You feel that in India, with its rich and varied heritage, linguistic and cultural diversity is essential to live in harmony which alone will lead to prosperity and peace. Write an article on the topic 'Unity in Diversity', specifying the advantages of unity and how we can promote it in spite of our diversity in religion, culture and language.

6. Write an article to be published in a newspaper on the importance of following the 'Rules of the Road' in about 80-100 words.

7. We cannot imagine life without our mobile phones, TV sets and other modern gadgets. Write an article on 'Role of Modern Gadgets'. You are Rashi/Rishi. You can take help from the given clues.
   - What are gadgets?
   - Importance of gadgets in everyday life
   - Disadvantages of using gadgets
   - Step to ensure proper usage of gadgets

8. You are Reena/Rithik, the Environment Secretary of Sunshine Public School. Write an article for your school magazine on how we, as individuals, can contribute to save our planet based on the clues given below.
   - Relentless burning of fossil fuels has led to an increase in the atmospheric temperature
   - We must follow the 3R's of survival—Reduce, Reuse and Recycle.
   - We should reduce our daily consumption of resources and avoid wastage.

CHAPTER 9

Speech Writing

A speech is an effective way of communicating a message to a large audience. It is one of the ways of spreading awareness regarding social issues or giving information regarding other important issues.

Components of a Speech

1. **Introduction** It begins with greeting the chief guest / principal / teachers and other listeners. It may include a striking statement, a saying or anything else which will immediately make the audience interested.
2. **Elaboration of the topic** It will include a sequence of ideas to build up to the summing up and conclusion. You may include examples, evidence or data to support the ideas.
3. **Summing up** Summarise the most important points in your speech but do not repeat them.
4. **Conclusion** Depending on the purpose of your speech, conclude with a call for an action, an appeal, a warning, a request and an expression of thanks.

Points to be Kept in Mind

- Do not forget to write the introduction to the speech with a formal address to the audience.
- Use simple and clear language to make the speech understandable.
- Remember to end the speech with a 'thank you'.
- Always re-read your speech to make sure that there is no grammatical or punctuation error in it.

Format of a Speech

Air pollution in the city of Delhi has been alarming for the past few years. With this concern, prepare a speech of about 100-120 words on the topic of increasing air pollution to be delivered in the morning assembly.

Formal address	Good morning respected Principal, teachers and my dear friends.
Main body	I am Rohit of Class VI-A. Today, I'll be presenting my speech on the topic of 'Air Pollution'. Air is essential for living beings to survive. As the saying goes, 'Breathe healthy and be healthy', it is important to breathe in clean air to keep fit. Do you know that the air quality index is in the extreme level in our city Delhi? It means that the air quality is very poor and impure. This is the case in a lot of major cities of the world. We should be alarmed of such drastic change in the air quality as it will affect our health greatly. We can ask how it has come down to this situation. It is mostly because of the smoke from vehicles and factories. Due to the mass deforestation, there are fewer trees to purify the polluted air in the environment. It is high time that we all come together to find a solution to this issue. We can start with small steps like planting a tree in our surrounding areas.
Formal thanks to audience	Thank you!

SAMPLE SPEECHES

1. Power shortage has become a norm even in the metropolitan cities. One way to face this situation is by preventing the wastage of power. Write a speech on the importance of power in our daily life and how to save power at school and at home. Imagine that you are the Principal of your school.

Ans. Good morning teachers and my dear students.

Today I stand before you to speak about the importance of power in our daily life and how to save it. Power or electricity lights up our homes and all household appliances. From fans, TVs, lights, geysers, phones, etc. everything works with electricity. And the electricity we use comes from the quickly disappearing natural resources such as coal, gas and oil. We are using these resources at a much faster pace than they can be renewed. So, the need of the hour is to save power. Though electricity can be generated, it is not easy to do so and this fact needs to be recognised at the earliest.

It is high time that we started saving power. Saving electricity will save fossil fuels too. As children, you too can do your bit in saving power. You must make sure that lights, fans and all other electrical appliances are turned off when not in use. We are also planning to start an 'Energy club' in our school. Remember, power needs to be utilised efficiently for future. Wasting power is going to leave us powerless and I am sure no one would like that. So children, make it a habit to save electricity. Set an example for others in doing so and lead the country to a brighter future.

Thank you!

2. You have always been proud of being a citizen of the country which shows love and care for elders. However, now this value is found to be disappearing. Write a speech on 'Difficulties Faced by Senior Citizens'.

Ans. We have always been proud citizens of a country which shows love, compassion and care for elders. But is it true even today?

Good morning everyone, I have come before you all to talk about the 'Difficulties Faced by Senior Citizens.' Deteriorating health, malnutrition, lack of shelter, loneliness, etc. are some of the most common problems that senior citizens face. Combine these with rejection by family and immoral attitude of their children and we all will feel bad for them. In today's world, where everyone is over-busy, it becomes too much if senior citizens expect their family members to attend to their requirements or even spend some part of their day with them.

The love and respect that our ancestors showed to our elderly have been lost. They are uncared for and often live alone all on their own. Their physically weak bodies and mentally weak minds are often neglected. The problems faced by senior citizens need to be handled with care. By paying attention to caring for them, we can show our elders that we have not forgotten about them. They need to be shown love, care and respect by all. Moreover, awareness needs to be created so that they can lead productive and independent lives. With a view to ensure the well-being of senior citizens we need to strengthen their place in society. Let us not forget home is the best place for elderly.

Thank you!

3. Write a speech on the topic, 'Library Plays an Important Role at School'. It is to be delivered in the morning assembly. You are Karuna/Karan, Head Girl/Head Boy.

Ans. The school library is central to learning and plays a key role in encouraging innovation and problem-solving.

Good morning respected Principal Sir, teachers and my dear friends. I have come before you all to speak on the topic, 'Library Plays an Important Role at School'.

Libraries make a difference to students' understanding and achievement. They provide support to both students and teachers. The presence of the school library ensures that each student has equal access to academic resources, books, and reading material. It also provides teachers full access to relevant curriculum, books, reference material, etc. The library not only promotes learning but also builds knowledge and confidence in students. It is a fundamental resource for supporting students' learning and encourages collaborative learning and sharing of ideas.

Students who regularly visit a library develop questioning skills and become creative thinkers. It is in the library where students become active seekers and users of information. The school library thus aims to give every student the opportunity to learn, to enjoy reading and to enhance their knowledge and understanding.

Thank you!

4. Write a speech on the topic 'Grow More Trees to Reduce Pollution.'

Ans. "A single tree can absorb approximately 1 tonne of carbon dioxide during its lifetime."

Good morning respected Principal Sir, teachers and my dear friends. I have come before you all to speak on the topic, 'Grow More Trees to Reduce Pollution'.

This statement in itself describes the role that trees play to maintain the cycle and process that supports different life forms on Earth. Trees, in the presence of sunlight and water, absorb carbon dioxide from the atmosphere and release oxygen to the atmosphere. They clean the air making it breathable and are good for the diversity of flora and fauna. They give us food, shelter and many more things. They provide shade during Sun and rain. Besides, they also help in preventing soil erosion, for their roots bind the soil tightly. The trees are able to muffle the city noises there by reducing noise pollution. The streets and surroundings inhabited by large numbers of trees are quite cooler compared to the places that don't have many trees. The trees slow down the rate of water evaporation thus helping in water conservation and increasing atmospheric moisture. They also help to replenish the level of groundwater. Hence, there is a need to grow more trees to reduce pollution.

Thank you!

5. Write a speech on 'Healthy Habits makes life Happy' to be spoken in your school assembly.

Ans. Good morning teachers and fellow students, today I want to talk about something that is the key to a happy life – healthy habits. As Class 6 students, we are at an age where developing good habits can set us on a path of lifelong well-being.

Healthy habits encompass a range of practices, from eating nutritious foods and staying physically active to getting enough sleep and managing stress. When we adopt these habits, we not only feel better physically but also mentally and emotionally. Regular exercise keeps our bodies strong and energetic while nutritious meals fuel our minds for better learning and focus. Adequate sleep allows us to rejuvenate and be more productive during the day. Taking care of ourselves also includes taking care of our surroundings and the environment. Let's remember to keep our surroundings clean and minimise waste.

By cultivating healthy habits from a young age, we are laying a strong foundation for a happier and fulfilling life ahead. So, let's pledge to prioritise our health and well-being and inspire others to do the same.

Thank you!

6. Write a speech on the topic, 'The Significance of Sports in Schools'. It is to be delivered in the morning assembly. You are Karuna/Karan, Head Girl/Head Boy.

Ans. Good morning esteemed Principal, respected teachers, and dear friends

As Karuna/Karan, the Head Girl/Head Boy, I stand before you to emphasise the vital role that sports play in our school community. Beyond the classroom, sports contribute significantly to our overall development.

Contrary to the belief that sports distract from academics, physically active students often perform better in their studies. Regular exercise enhances cognitive abilities, concentration, and memory, leading to improved grades. A positive sports culture within our institution can boost our school's ranking and admission rates. When we actively participate in sports, it reflects positively on our school's reputation and overall appeal.

Engaging in sports promotes physical fitness, reduces stress, and contributes to overall well-being. Healthy students are better equipped to learn and excel in all aspects of life. Through sports, we learn teamwork, discipline, resilience, and time management. These skills extend beyond the field and prepare us for future challenges.

So, it is high time. Let us recognise the importance of sports, not just as a recreational activity, but as an integral part of our holistic education.

Thank you!

PRACTICE QUESTIONS

1. India is known as a diverse country. Write a speech of about 100-120 words on the topic of 'Unity in Diversity' which is to be presented at the morning school assembly.
2. The quote 'Health is Wealth' is heard very often. Write a speech of about 100-120 words on the topic 'Health is Wealth' which is to be delivered at the morning assembly.
3. You're Ravi of Class VI-A. Write a speech of about 100-120 words on the topic 'Importance of Sports and Games' for a speech competition.
4. Write a speech of about 100-120 words on the topic 'Swachh Bharat' to be delivered during the morning school assembly.
5. Water is an essential part of human life. Write a speech of about 100-120 words on the topic 'Conservation of Water' for a speech competition.
6. Write a speech of about 100-120 words on the topic 'Punctuality' to be presented at the morning school assembly.
7. Mobile phone of today is no longer a mere means of communication. Music lovers are so glued to it that they don't pay attention even to the traffic while crossing the roads. This leads to accidents, sometimes even fatal ones. Write a speech to be delivered in the morning assembly advising the students to be careful in the use of this otherwise very useful gadget. Imagine you are Principal of your school.
8. Write a speech on the topic 'Power of Imagination' for the Principal of your school.
9. Junk food can be very appealing to children, but they cause more harm to them than they can imagine. Prepare a speech to be delivered in the school assembly on the 'Harmful Effects of Junk Food on School Children'. Use the hints given below.

   Hints
   - Proves to be harmful
   - Addictive
   - Obesity, chronic illness, low self-esteem, depression
   - Decreases concentration level
   - High calorie, fats, carbohydrates and added sugars
   - Creates deficiency of nutrients
   - Diabetes, blood pressure, stroke
   - Slow poison
10. Social media sites are very popular among teenagers. They spend majority of their free time on these sites socialising with their friends. Prepare a speech to be delivered in the morning assembly on the topic- 'Social Media-Good or Bad for Children'? Use the following hints.

    Hints
    - Has positive aspects, but one has to be cautious of bullying and victimisation
    - Can break a person
    - Fake facebook accounts
    - Valuable time wasted on social media sites
    - Can affect the future

Letter Writing

Letter writing is one of the most effective ways of communication. Today, although telephone, fax and e-mail have replaced personal (informal) letters, formal letters are still used. Trade, official correspondence, public representation, complaints and other dealings, transactions and communication with people are still conducted through formal letters. Therefore, one must learn the art and skill of letter writing. Different kinds of letters follow different conventions.

Types of Letters

We write two kinds of letters which are discussed below

1. **Informal Letters** An informal letter is a letter that we usually use to write to our friends, family or relatives. These letters are personal letters that are not used for official purposes. Hence, they use a very informal and simple language.
2. **Formal Letters** These letters are generally written to officials regarding serious issues. They have set patterns and are written using a crisp and clear language in a matter-of-fact style. The language should be kept simple without including any unnecessary expressions.

   There are many kinds of formal letters. However, in Class VI we will focus on

   - Letter to the Editor
   - Application to the Principal

Main Elements of a Letter

- **Sender's Address** According to the latest format, sender's address is written at the top along with the pin code. Do not write sender's name with the address.

  e.g. K-127, Ashok Nagar
  New Delhi-110092

- **Date** It appears directly below the sender's address after leaving a one line space. It is advisable to always write the full date in the following format.

  e.g. 25th December, 20XX

- **Receiver's Address** It appears directly below the date and comprises the receiver's name, designation and the complete address.

  e.g. The Editor
  The Hindustan Times
  47/1567, Daryaganj
  Delhi-110002

Note it While writing the address (both sender's and receiver's), one must not use 'comma' at the end of each line. If the address is not provided in the question, then you may create a fictitious address but writing an address is mandatory. We write sender's address only in formal letters.

- **Subject** Subject is written in a formal letter. It can be written after the receiver's address or after the salutation. It should be short and to the point.

e.g. **Subject** Application for the post of Content Writer

- **Salutation** This consists of words of greeting and is written on the left hand side of the page just below the date after leaving a line. The form of greeting depends upon your relation to the person to whom the letter is being written.

– In case of informal letters, you use Dear Rohan, Dear Mummy, etc.

– In case of formal letters, you use only Sir/Ma'am.

- **The body** The body is the main part of any letter. This is written in response to the given topic in a simple and direct language.

The body includes three main parts

(i) **Introductory paragraph/sentence** States the purpose of writing the letter.

(ii) **Informative paragraphs** Details about the subject of the letter. It includes arguments related to the theme of the letter written in a simple and organised manner.

(iii) **Concluding paragraph/sentence** The closure of the letter/conclusion stating hope, request or comment.

- **Complimentary Close** It is a courteous way of ending the letter. The expression used must match the salutation.

– In case of informal letter, we use Yours friendly/Yours lovingly.

– In case of formal letter, we use Yours sincerely/Yours faithfully.

- **Signature, Name and Position** It is written just below the 'complimentary close' and includes the sender's name and designation (if applicable).

e.g. Ankita Chakravarti
Editor

Points to be Kept in Mind

- The subject line should match with what is asked in the question. It should be short and to-the-point.
- Get right to the purpose of the letter in polite language.
- Be clear, concise and to-the-point. Stick to the word limit of 100-120 words.
- Use simple language so that the letter is easy to understand. Do not use long-winded sentences.
- Re-read your letter to check the format and to make sure that there are no grammatical errors in it.

1. Informal Letters

Write a letter to your cousin enquiring about his/her first ever trip to Europe. You are Ravi/Komal of 24, Park Street, Delhi. (100-150 words)

Sender's address	24, Park Street, Delhi
Date	24th September, 20XX
Salutation	Dear Manu/Kanika
Body of the letter	How are you? I am fine here. I was so glad to hear from my mother that you are back home after the trip. Hope you had a safe and enjoyable trip. I have been waiting to hear all about it from you. Since this was the first time you have been to a foreign land, I guess every little bit of the trip was as exciting as you expected it to be. I have heard from my friends residing there that the place is extremely beautiful and that the people there are very endearing. However, I was worried when I got to know that you had some mishaps during your stay there. Hope all of you there were safe. I hope everything else was fine except for this. I had spoken to your mother earlier and she told me that you would be coming home after two weeks. I can't wait to meet you and hear all your stories. Waiting eagerly for your reply!
Complimentary Closing	Yours lovingly
Name and Signature	Ravi/Komal

SAMPLE LETTERS

1. Write a letter to your friend congratulating her/him for topping the board examinations.

Ans. 96, Green park
Rohini, New Delhi

16th January, 20XX

Dear Khushi

I am so excited to know that you have topped your board examinations. It's been a long time since we met. I wish I could congratulate you in person.

Your result has proved how much effort, hard-work and dedication you have given to your exams. I am not shocked by this news because I have known you since we were in class 2. You have always been a sincere and hardworking girl. I knew that you were a bit nervous but then I was sure that you will score brilliantly. The only thing I regret is that I couldn't be there with you at the celebration party because I was having my exams then.

Hope to meet you as soon as possible. My parents and grandparents have also congratulated you on your success!

With lots of love

Yours lovingly

Anaya

2. Write a letter to your friend Rama/Raman requesting him/her to spend the summer holidays with you.

Ans. 100, Old Lake Town
Kolkata- 26

16th March, 20XX

Dear Rama

It's been a long time since we met. How are you? I hope you are doing well and hope this letter finds you in good health.

As you know that summer vacation has already started, I was thinking of spending the vacations together in Mumbai. I want to take you out on a city tour as well as introduce my friends and family to you. I would love to go out and have street food with you. We can enjoy some time near Marine Drive. We can also visit Goa and Pune while here. I am just excited at the thought of me and you spending the vacations together. I just hope that you share your response with me and let me know if it will be possible for you to come to my place.

With lots of love

Yours lovingly

Sakshi

3. Write a letter to your brother wishing him a speedy recovery from an accident.

Ans. 106, Nilambar Apartment
Bosebihar Avenue, Kolkata- 26

16th January, 20XX

Dear Mahesh

I hope this letter finds you in good health. Last week I got to know about your accident and I was highly depressed.

Thank God that he saved you from something very serious. Everything is going to be ok. I had a word with the doctor yesterday and he told me that there is nothing to worry about for the time being. Just a few more days in the hospital and you will be back home! I also had a talk with mom and she was very upset with whatever has happened. But now she is happy that you are recovering.

I have good news for you. Our entire family and friends have decided to celebrate once you come back. We all are praying for your speedy recovery. Hope to see you soon and in good health!

Lots of Love

Yours truly
Aditya

4. Write a letter to your friend expressing your appreciation for his recently published book.

Ans. 62, Regency block,
Raipur

3rd April, 20XX

Dear Ratula

How are you doing? I hope all is well. I just read the novel which you wrote last week in Kolkata. How can someone write so beautifully? Amazing! My father has also appreciated your work and has asked me to tell you that you are doing an incredible job.

I really appreciate the words that you have used and the tone. The best part of your novel is that your work is absolutely real and derived from real-life experiences. It shows your writing skills and how much effort you have given to your writings. You have done absolute justice and I am proud of the way you have handled it.

Ratula, it has been two years since we drifted apart because of our higher studies and career. I hope to meet you soon. Go ahead! The sky is the limit!

With best wishes

Yours lovingly
Soniya

2. Formal Letters

Write a letter to the editor of a local newspaper expressing your concern about the problems the neglect of the parks has created and suggest measures to reclaim the parks for children. You are Gautam/Gauri 2, Gobind Enclave, Meerut.

Sender's address	2, Gobind Enclave, Meerut
Date	12th March, 20XX
Receiver's address	The Editor The Jagran Times Meerut
Subject of the letter	**Subject** Neglect of parks
Salutation	Sir/Ma'am
Body of the letter	Through the columns of your esteemed newspaper, I would like to draw the attention of the authorities to the problems created due to the neglect of the parks in Gobind Enclave. It is unfortunate that the parks of the area are neglected. As a result, some undesirable elements have taken over them. The grass has grown very big and looks unkempt. The gates of the park are broken allowing the entry to anyone and everyone. This poses an issue of security. Further, there is no proper walking space or area for the children to play. All in all the park is in utter ruin. The parks have turned squalid that even the residents have stopped going there. The pathetic condition of the park has made them look like a big pit of garbage. Thus, it is no more safe for the children to go and play there. It is time that the authorities take immediate action to restore the park. We hope that the concerned authorities will take immediate steps to reclaim these parks for children.
Complimentary Close	Thanking you
Name and Signaure	Yours truly Gautam/Gauri (Concerned Citizen)

SOLVED EXAMPLES

Letter to the Editor

1. Write a letter to the editor of a local daily urging people to use public transport and to have patience while driving.

Ans. 4, Raja Road
Karnal

5th July, 20XX

The Editor
The Hindustan
Karnal

Subject Use of Public Transport

Respected Sir/Ma'am

Kindly allow me to make an appeal to the public through the columns of your esteemed newspaper about the advantages of public transport usage.

Everybody can observe easily that the increase in the number of private vehicles on the road is the major cause of air pollution as well as noise pollution. More vehicles mean more congestion and traffic jams. Everybody tries to move first and fast which not only increases the chance of accidents but also causes a lot of pollution.

An easy and quick solution of the problem is that we should make more use of public transport. It will prove more beneficial as it will save our energy, money and time and we can use that energy elsewhere. Moreover, I want to make an appeal to the vehicle-owners to practice patience while driving because our life is very precious. It is better to reach late than never.

This is a matter of grave concern and I hope you'll publish my opinion in your esteemed newspaper.

Thanking you

Yours sincerely
XYZ

2. You are Shubha/Krushna Mohanty, residing in Subhadra Apartments, Bhubaneswar, Orissa. You have observed, with increasing concern, that garbage collection continues to be done without segregation in your neighbourhood. Write a letter to the Editor of The Real Times, Bhubaneswar, explaining your concern along with the rationale behind the importance of garbage segregation.

Ans. Subhadra Apartments
Bhubaneswar, Orissa

11th December, 20XX

The Editor
The Real Times
Bhubaneswar
Orissa

Subject Non-segregation of garbage by residents

Respected Sir/Ma'am

Through the columns of your esteemed newspaper, I would like to draw the attention of the concerned authorities to the issue of non-segregation of garbage by the residents of my area JP Nagar, Bhubaneswar. Despite promotion by the municipal body and the media on the benefits of garbage segregation, the residents in our area continue to resort to their old practice of garbage dumping.

Most of the residents in the area do not segregate their waste. For the ones who are practicing this religiously, their efforts go in vain as the garbage collector puts all the waste in one bag. The Resident Welfare Association (RWA) in the area should promote the benefits of garbage segregation by pasting posters, playing audio message on the collection vans, etc. The people who practice segregation should be awarded a certificate.

The authority should also watch the CCTV footage to penalise the residents who are not doing this.

I sincerely hope that all this would help in making this initiative a success.

Thanking you

Yours truly
Shubha/Krushna Mohanty

3. You are Ram/Rajani, a resident of Nagpur. You feel students should use the Internet mostly for gaining knowledge rather than wasting away time merely on entertainment. Write a letter to the Editor, 'The Harbinger', 9, Bund Marg, Hyderabad, pointing out how schools can control students' net surfing at school and enable them to use internet fruitfully.

Ans. E-114, Nandanvan Colony
Nagpur

31st January, 20XX

The Editor
The Harbinger
9, Bund Marg
Hyderabad

Subject Control net surfing at school

Respected Sir/Ma'am

Through the columns of your esteemed newspaper, I would like to draw the attention of the concerned authorities to the students who are wasting away their precious time on the internet merely for entertainment.

Our public schools have modernised their libraries to provide internet surfing facilities to senior students so that they can complete their assignments better and also gain knowledge necessary to be well-informed and do well in their exams.

However, the schools have not introduced much control on the net surfing by students resulting in the students wasting their time in entertaining themselves by playing interactive games available on various sites or watching videos and other prohibited material. Students should use the internet to gain knowledge rather than wasting away their time merely on entertainment.

In this regard, schools must ensure that they install suitable software which will block content like interactive games and other sites which are prohibited. Unless this is done effectively, the whole purpose of providing the net facility will be defeated. So, the schools should control students' net surfing at school and enable them to use the Internet fruitfully.

Thanking you

Yours sincerely

Rajani

4. You are Abhinav, a sports lover. Write a letter to the Editor of a Local Daily expressing your views on improving facilities for sportsmen. You can use the following clues.

Clues

- Facilities provided are pathetic
- No facility of international standards
- Poor performance in overseas tournaments
- Need of action for improvement

Ans. 32/4, Sector-4
Rohini, New Delhi-110088

6th December, 20XX

The Editor
Local Daily
Delhi

Subject The state of sports facilities in India

Respected Sir/Ma'am

Through the columns of your esteemed newspaper, I would like to draw the attention of the concerned authorities towards the pathetic condition of sports facilities in India.

If we look at the state of the sports facilities, we will know the shocking condition of the location as well as the equipment of all the sports except cricket. Given that most of our sportspersons practice in these facilities and then go on to represent our nation on the international platform, the facility do not even stand close to the international standards. There are no artificial grass surfaces, the shooting range is not maintained and there is a shortage of equipments. All this results in the poor overall performance of our athletes in overseas games. It is time for the government and all the concerned authorities to take actions to improve this condition.

Thanking you

Yours truly

Abhinav

Application to the Principal

1. Write an application to the Principal of your college stating that college library is lacking in function.

Ans. The Principal
Moonlight School
Lucknow

6th October, 20XX

Subject Need for Improvement in the Working of the Library

Respected Sir/Ma'am

I take the liberty to draw your kind attention to the need for improvement in the working of our school library. Our school library is really in a bad shape. It is housed in a small stuffy room. There is no proper arrangement of the lights and half of the fans are out of order. Our school has well over a thousand students but there is seating arrangement for only fifty students in the library. No proper attention is given to keep the library neat and clean.

The non-availability of books is another factor. It causes inconvenience to the students. Most of the books exist in the catalogue only.

I hope you will take personal interest in the matter and do the needful to improve the situation.

Thanking you

Yours faithfully

Dinkar Aggarwal
Class Representative

2. Write an application to the Principal of your school requesting him to grant you five-days leave to attend your sister's marriage.

Ans. The Principal
MM International School
Ghaziabad

5th February, 20XX

Subject Leave for five-days to attend Sister's Marriage

Respected Sir/Ma'am

This is to inform you that I am XYZ, a student of class VI of your school. I have written this letter to request you to grant me leave. I have to attend the marriage of my sister which will take place on the 13th of this month. Being the only son of my parents, I have to help my father in making the arrangements. Therefore, I request you to kindly grant me leave from 10th February to 15th February, 20XX.

I would be highly obliged to you.

Thanking you

Yours obediently
XYZ

3. Write an application to the Principal of your school requesting him to issue your Transfer Certificate and Character Certificate as your father has been transferred to another city and you have to go along and join another institution.

Ans. The Principal
Kisan School
Mathura, UP

16th August, 20XX

Subject Issuing Transfer Certificate and Character Certificate

Respected Sir/Ma'am

This is to inform you that I am XYZ, a student of class VI of your school. I have written this letter to request you to issue my Transfer Certificate and Character Certificate. I have to leave the school because my father has been transferred to Allahabad. So, to join any other school in Allahabad I need to have my Transfer Certificate and Character Certificate.

I may also bring to your notice that I joined this institution in 20XX. I have always secured first position and have had good conduct too. I have always participated actively in school events and have won many of them.

So, I request you to kindly issue me these certificates.

Thanking you

Yours obediently
XYZ

4. Write an application to the Principal of your school requesting him to make regular arrangement for evening games.

Ans. The Principal
SD International School
Ghaziabad, UP

8th November, 20XX

Subject Request for Better Arrangements for Games and Sports

Respected Sir/Ma'am

On behalf of all the students, I wish to bring to your notice that many students want to play cricket and football in the school ground in the evenings. But there is no such arrangement in our school. Therefore, I request you to grant us permission to play and make some arrangements for regular evening games so that students may stay back and play after school.

Thanking you

Yours sincerely
PQR

PRACTICE QUESTIONS

1. Write a letter of condolence to a friend who has lost his father and mother in car accident.
2. Write a letter to a friend inviting her over for lunch.
3. Write a letter to your father requesting him to increase your pocket money.
4. Write a letter to a friend asking him to spend a holiday with you in some hill station.
5. Write a letter to your cousin telling him about your recovery from illness.
6. You are Kavita/Kailash staying at B-101, Yamuna Vihar, Delhi. You find it disturbing that despite a ban on the use of polythene bags its use is rampant in the city. Write a letter to the Editor of a national daily expressing your concern about the apathy of people towards environmental degradation. Also suggest ways to mobilise city dwellers for the cause of safe environment with the help of school children.
7. A book fair was organised in your city Bhopal. Thousands of people including a large number of students visited the fair. It aroused a great interest in reading and buying books. You want that such book fairs are held in other cities of the state also to promote the habit of reading. Write a letter to the Editor of a local newspaper giving your views. You are Navtej/Navita, F-112 Malviya Nagar, Bhopal.
8. Write an application to the Principal requesting him to take your class to a picnic spot.
9. Write an application to your class teacher requesting him to put a zero period for your class.

I would be highly obliged to you.

Thanking you

Yours obediently

XYZ

3. Write an application to the Principal of your school requesting him to issue your Transfer Certificate and Character Certificate as your father has been transferred to another city and you have to go along and join another institution.

Ans. The Principal

Kesari School

Mathura, UP

14th August, 20XX

Subject: Issuing Transfer Certificate and Character Certificate

Respected Sir/Madam

This is to inform you that I am XYZ, a student of class VI of your school. I have written this letter to request you to issue my Transfer Certificate and Character Certificate. I have to leave the school because my father has been transferred to Allahabad. So, to join any other school in Allahabad I need to have my Transfer Certificate and Character Certificate.

I may also bring to your notice that I joined this institution in 20XX. I have always secured first position and have had good conduct too. I have always participated actively in school events and have won many of them.

So, I request you to kindly issue me these certificates.

Thanking you

Yours obediently

XYZ

4. Write an application to the Principal of your school requesting him to make regular arrangement for evening games.

Ans. The Principal

SD International School

Ghaziabad, UP

8th November, 20XX

Subject: Request for Better Arrangements for Games and Sports

Respected Sir/Madam

On behalf of all the students, I wish to bring to your notice that many students want to play cricket and football in the school ground in the evening. But there is no such arrangement in our school. Therefore I request you to grant us permission to play and make some arrangements for regular evening games so that students may stay back and play after school.

Thanking you

Yours sincerely

PQR

PRACTICE QUESTIONS

1. Write a letter of condolence to a friend who has lost his father and mother in car accident.
2. Write a letter to a friend inviting her over for lunch.
3. Write a letter to your father requesting him to increase your pocket money.
4. Write a letter to a friend asking him to spend a holiday with you at some hill station.
5. Write a letter to your cousin telling him about your recovery from illness.
6. You are Kavita, Kailash staying at B-101, Vardhman Vihar, Delhi. You find it disturbing that despite a ban on the use of polythene bags, its use is rampant in the city. Write a letter to the editor of a national daily expressing your concern about the apathy of people towards environmental degradation. Also suggest ways to mobilise city dwellers for the cause of safe environment with the help of school children.
7. A book fair was organised in your city Bhopal. Thousands of people including a large number of students visited the fair. It roused a great interest in reading and buying books. You want that such book fairs are held in other cities of the state also to promote the habit of reading. Write a letter to the Editor of a local newspaper giving your views. You are Navin/Navita, F-112 Indira Nagar, Bhopal.
8. Write an application to the Principal requesting him to take your class to a picnic spot.
9. Write an application to your class teacher requesting him to put a zero period for your class.

SECTION C : GRAMMAR

Sentence

CHAPTER 1

1.1 Definition of Sentence

A sentence can be defined as a group of words which is meaningful and makes complete sense in itself.

All sentences begin with a capital letter and end with a question mark (?), an exclamation mark (!) or a full stop (.).

e.g. • I love my country.
• Don't you like this weather?
• What a pleasant weather!

Parts of a Sentence

A sentence can be divided into two parts – a subject and a predicate.

(i) **Subject** It is the part of a sentence that contains the noun or pronoun performing the action in the sentence.

e.g. • **Jaipur** is also known as the Pink City.
• **Shreya** drives a car to work every day.
• **Preeti** is writing a poem.

(ii) **Predicate** It is the part of a sentence that tells us something about the subject. It tells about the action that is being performed by the subject.

e.g. • All the food **was eaten by the puppy**.
• Shreya **drives a car to work every day**.
• Jaipur **is also known as the Pink City**.

1.2 Kinds of Sentences

Sentences can be classified into following types

Assertive/Declarative Sentences

Sentences that are used to state a general statement, a fact, or an opinion are called Assertive or Declarative Sentences. These sentences always end with a full stop (.).

e.g. • The Earth revolves around the Sun. (Fact)
• I enjoy reading sci-fi novels. (Opinion)

Assertive sentences can further be divided into two types

(i) **Positive or affirmative sentences** are statements that express a fact, an opinion, or an action in a positive manner.

e.g. • The flowers in the garden are blooming.
• I enjoy playing the guitar.

(ii) **Negative sentences**, on the other hand, express an action by negating a fact, opinion, or action.

e.g. • I do not like spicy food.
• They never miss an opportunity to learn.

Interrogative Sentences

Sentences that are used to ask questions are called Interrogative Sentences. These sentences always end with a question mark (?).

These are of three types

(i) **Yes/No questions** are questions that can be answered with 'yes' or 'no.' They generally begin with a helping verb followed by the subject and the main verb.

e.g. • Did you finish your homework?
• Are you going to the party?

(ii) **Wh-questions** are questions that begin with a wh-word (who, what, when, where, why, which, how).

e.g. • Where did you go on vacation?
• How did you solve the problem?

(iii) **Question tags** are short questions added to the end of a statement. They are used to confirm information or seek agreement. Question tags are a way of turning a statement into a question.

e.g. • She doesn't like coffee, does she?
• He's finished his work, hasn't he?

Imperative Sentences

Sentences that are used to give command, advice, suggestion, request or warning are called Imperative Sentences. They generally end with a full stop (.)

e.g.
- Close the door quietly. (command)
- Eat a balanced diet for better health. (advice)
- Could you help me with this assignment? (request)
- Let's go for a walk in the park. (suggestion)
- Be cautious while crossing the street. (warning)

Exclamatory Sentences

Sentences that are used to express a strong emotion or feeling are called Exclamatory Sentences. These sentences always end with an exclamation mark (!).

e.g.
- What a pleasant day it is!
- That birthday cake was so good!

PRACTICE EXERCISE

Objective and Subjective Questions

1. Fill in the blank with the correct question tags.

(i) She is a doctor, ...?
(a) isn't she (b) doesn't she
(c) is she (d) does she

(ii) You have never been to Paris, ...?
(a) don't you (b) have you
(c) aren't you (d) do you

(iii) He can swim, ...?
(a) can he (b) can't he (c) does he (d) doesn't he

(iv) They won't be late, ...?
(a) will they (b) won't they
(c) do they (d) don't they

(v) She didn't finish her homework, ...?
(a) did she (b) didn't she
(c) does she (d) doesn't she

(vi) It's a beautiful day, ...?
(a) is it (b) it is (c) isn't it (d) does it

(vii) They had a great time at the party, ...?
(a) do they (b) hadn't they
(c) didn't they (d) did they

(viii) He has visited London before, ...?
(a) hasn't he (b) has he (c) didn't he (d) does he

(ix) You won't forget to call, ...?
(a) will you (b) won't you
(c) do you (d) don't you

(x) She likes playing the guitar, ...?
(a) does she (b) doesn't she
(c) is she (d) isn't she

2. Identify the subject in the given sentences.

(i) In the garden, colourful flowers bloom during spring.
(a) Garden (b) Colourful flowers
(c) Bloom (d) During spring

(ii) The students eagerly awaited the announcement of the exam results.
(a) The students (b) Eagerly awaited
(c) Announcement (d) Exam results

(iii) During the storm, the old oak tree withstood the strong winds.
(a) During the storm (b) The old oak tree
(c) Withstood (d) Strong winds

(iv) To enhance your writing skills, practice is essential.
(a) To enhance your writing skills
(b) Practice
(c) Is
(d) Essential

(v) The mysterious figure vanished into the darkness of the alley.
(a) The mysterious figure (b) Vanished
(c) Darkness of the alley (d) Into the darkness

(vi) During the meeting, the team presented their innovative ideas.
(a) During the meeting (b) The team
(c) Presented (d) Innovative ideas

(vii) In the distance, a majestic mountain range adorned the horizon.
(a) In the distance (b) A majestic mountain range
(c) Adorned (d) The horizon

(viii) The energetic puppy enthusiastically chased its own tail in the backyard.
(a) The energetic puppy (b) Enthusiastically chased
(c) Its own tail (d) In the backyard

(ix) Despite the challenges, she persevered and achieved her goals.
(a) Despite the challenges (b) She
(c) Persevered (d) Achieved her goals

(x) **Amidst the chaos, a single rose bloomed in the neglected garden.**

(a) Amidst the chaos

(b) A single rose

(c) Bloomed

(d) In the neglected garden

3. Identify the type of the given sentences. Write Assertive, Interrogative, Exclamatory or Imperative in the space next to the sentence.

(i) "A merry Christmas, uncle! God save you!" cried a cheerful voice.

(ii) Oh dear, what nonsense I'm talking about!"

(iii) Here are 10 more sentences for you to identify their types.

(iv) The old library contains a vast collection of rare books.

(v) What a stunning view from the mountaintop!

(vi) Could you please lend me your pen for a moment?

(vii) Despite the rain, the children played joyfully in the puddles.

(viii) Read the instructions carefully before assembling the furniture.

(ix) How exciting it is to explore new cultures and traditions!

(x) The thunderstorm last night was truly frightening.

(xi) Is it possible to learn a new language in just one month?

(xii) Examine the evidence thoroughly before drawing any conclusions.

(xiii) Oh, what a surprise to see you here!

4. Arrange these jumbled words to form meaningful sentences. The kind of sentence to be formed is written in brackets.

(i) the was delicious dinner homemade. (Assertive)

(ii) quietly library students the studied in. (Imperative)

(iii) the to happy park go the family did. (Interrogative)

(iv) for her performance outstanding classmates applauded. (Exclamatory)

(v) carefully your project review before submitting. (Imperative)

(vi) what with happened your backpack? (Interrogative)

(vii) the new exploring city enjoy the tourists. (Assertive)

(viii) don't touch the please artwork. (Imperative)

(ix) It What a surprise beautiful was! (Exclamatory)

(x) playing video the games enjoyed boys. (Assertive)

ANSWERS

1. (i) (a) isn't she (ii) (b) have you

(iii) (b) can't he (iv) (a) will they

(v) (a) did she (vi) (c) isn't it

(vii) (b) hadn't they (viii) (a) hasn't he

(ix) (a) will you (x) (b) doesn't she

2. (i) (b) Colourful flowers

(ii) (a) The students

(iii) (b) The old oak tree

(iv) (b) Practice

(v) (a) The mysterious figure

(vi) (b) The team

(vii) (b) A majestic mountain range

(viii) (a) The energetic puppy

(ix) (b) She

(x) (b) A single rose

3. (i) Exclamatory (ii) Exclamatory

(iii) Assertive (iv) Assertive

(v) Exclamatory (vi) Imperative

(vii) Assertive (viii) Imperative

(ix) Exclamatory (x) Assertive

(xi) Interrogative (xii) Imperative

(xiii) Exclamatory

4. (i) The homemade dinner was delicious. (Assertive)

(ii) Students studied in the library quiety. (Assertive)

(iii) Did the family go to the park? (Interrogative)

(iv) Outstanding performance! Classmates applauded for her. (Exclamatory)

(v) Review your project carefully before submitting. (Imperative)

(vi) What happened with your backpack? (Interrogative)

(vii) The tourists enjoy exploring the new city. (Assertive)

(viii) Please don't touch the artwork. (Imperative)

(ix) What a beautiful surprise it was! (Exclamatory)

(x) The boys enjoyed playing video games. (Assertive)

Noun

2.1 Definition of Noun

Noun is the name of a person, place, animal, thing, organisation, feeling or idea. In other words, noun is a naming word.

e.g.
- The **girls** are singing songs.
- **Ridhi** is playing with **ball.**
- **China** is the most populous **country.**
- **Honesty** is the best policy.

2.2 Kinds of Noun

Noun can be classified into following kinds

Common Noun

Common noun is the name given in common to every person animal or thing.

e.g.
- The **boys** are playing in ground.
- That **mall** is very big.
- The **kitten** is playing with a ball.

Common nouns are not capitalised unless they appear at the beginning of a sentence.

Proper Noun

Proper noun is the name of a particular person, place, animal, bird, thing or organisation.

e.g.
- **Draupadi Murmu** is the President of **India.**
- **Indira Gandhi International Airport** is in Delhi.
- **Samsung** is a very successful **Korean** company.

Proper nouns always begin with a capital letter no matter where they appear in a sentence.

Collective Noun

Collective noun is the name given to a group of people, animals, birds or things. Such a group is generally treated as a singular unit.

e.g.
- The **jury** was against him.
- Riti has a **deck** of cards.
- The school **choir** is melodious.

Some Collective Noun

- A **flock** of birds
- A **council** of ministers
- A ship **crew**
- A **troupe** of performers
- A **swarm** of bees
- A **murder** of crows
- The school **staff**
- A **panel** of experts
- A **shoal** of fish
- A **colony** of ants

Abstract Noun

Abstract Noun is the name given to an idea, emotion or quality. Abstract nouns can only be felt or experienced; one cannot touch or see it.

e.g.
- The **moonlight** made the room brighter. (idea)
- Joy was filled with **happiness** at her success. (emotion)
- Rani Laxmi Bai is remembered for her **bravery.** (quality)
- There is greatness in **simplicity.** (quality)

Material Noun

Material noun is the name given to non-living substances around us from which things are made.

e.g.
- This bangle is made of **gold.**
- The car toy is made of **plastic**
- The bed is made of **wood.**

PRACTICE EXERCISE

Objective and Subjective Questions

1. Fill in the blank with an appropriate noun.

(i) If I had a ...., things would have been easier.

(a) car (b) time machine
(c) rainbow (d) pizza

(ii) I wish the .... were a little clearer.

(a) refrigerator (b) toothpaste
(c) weather (d) road signals

(iii) Do not worry, I will take care of your ....

(a) quarrel (b) party
(c) pet unicorn (d) documents

(iv) He felt that he was cheated by the ....

(a) talking parrot (b) street vendor
(c) robot (d) chocolate factory

(v) He visited many ...., before he returned ....

(a) countries, home
(b) museums, pool
(c) mansions, haunted
(d) shops, poor

(vi) He was at the dance with ....

(a) a penguin (b) Mohan
(c) robot (d) feet

(vii) The minister delivered a long ....

(a) lullaby (b) song
(c) order (d) speech

(viii) Have you ever been to .... ?

(a) India (a) Metaverse
(a) evening (a) multiverse

2. Choose the most appropriate option of a collective noun to fill in the blank.

(i) The .... of scouts went on an adventurous trip.

(a) troop (b) fleet
(c) bunch (d) hive

(ii) Nobody is as hardworking as a .... of ants.

(a) herd (b) group
(c) swarm (d) colony

(iii) The shepherd drove the .... of cattle into the barn.

(a) den (b) herd (c) pack (d) swarm

(iv) A .... of volleyball players have just arrived for the Annual Sports Meet.

(a) cluster (b) squad
(c) team (d) band

(v) A .... of worshippers gathered for Holika Dahan.

(a) choir (b) congregation
(c) arrangement (d) bunch

(vi) The chief guest was presented with a .... of flowers.

(a) bouquet (b) bunch
(c) basket (d) pack

(vii) A ...... of wolves roamed the streets.

(a) pack (b) group
(c) den (d) herd

(viii) The .... of whales is a majestic sight to witness.

(a) shoal (b) crew (c) band (d) pod

(ix) We have a .... of mango trees in our village backyard.

(a) cluster (b) collection
(c) pack (d) garden

(x) There was a massive .... of traders and tourists at the Delhi Art Fair.

(a) group (b) grove
(c) caravan (d) assembly

3. In the following sentences, identify the words that are nouns, and write down what type of nouns they are. One sentence may have more than one noun in it.

(i) The farmer returned home late in the evening.
(ii) The students have to make projects on pollution control.
(iii) Sumidha was invited to join the troupe of dancers.
(iv) She loves platinum jewellery.
(v) Rajeev paints with charcoal and Vidushi uses glitter.
(vi) The park resounded with children's laughter.
(vii) Dussehra is a festival celebrated all over India.
(viii) There are five principles in Islam.
(ix) Raju asked for some money from his father.
(x) The President is the first citizen of our country.

4. Fill in the blank with abstract nouns of your choice to make the sentences meaningful.

(i) Sweet is the taste of ....
(ii) We should respect each other's .... and ....
(iii) Our choice defines who we are far more than our ....
(iv) .... and Ahimsa were Gandhiji's tools.

(v) The crowd's .... could be felt through the TV screen.

(vi) The Queen's sword was a .... of ..... and courage.

(vii) .... is in the eyes of the beholder.

(viii) Being .... is a virtue.

(ix) .... is the stepping stone to success.

(x) Dr. APJ Abdul Kalam is an .... to the young minds of the country.

5. Make abstract nouns from the words given below. Hint: Abstract nouns generally end with -ness, -ity etc.

(i) Pure (ii) Generous
(iii) Strong (iv) Free
(v) Clean (vi) Slip
(vii) Care (viii) Friend
(ix) Discover (x) Lonely

ANSWERS

1. (i) (a) car (ii) (c) weather
(iii) (d) documents (iv) (b) street vendor
(v) (a) countries, home (vi) (b) Mohan
(vii) (d) speech (viii) (a) India

2. (i) (a) troop (ii) (d) colony
(iii) (b) herd (iv) (c) team
(v) (b) congregation (vi) (a) bouquet
(vii) (a) pack (viii) (d) pod
(ix) (a) cluster (x) (c) caravan

3. (i) Farmer → Common noun
Evening → Common noun
(ii) Students → Common noun
Project → Common noun
Pollution → Abstract noun
(iii) Sumidha → Proper noun
Troupe → Collective noun
Dancers → Common noun
(iv) Platinum → Material noun
Jewellery → Common noun
(v) Rajeev → Proper noun
Charcoal → Material noun
Vidushi → Proper noun
Glitter → Material noun
(vi) Park → Common noun
Children → Common noun
Laughter → Abstract noun
(vii) Dussehra → Proper noun
Festival → Common noun
India → Proper noun
(viii) Principles → Abstract noun
Islam → Proper noun
(ix) Raju → Proper noun
Money → Material noun
Father → Common noun
(x) The President → Proper noun
Citizen → Common noun
Country → Common noun

4. (i) justice (ii) culture, language
(iii) abilities (iv) Truth
(v) enthusiasm (vi) symbol, freedom
(vii) Beauty (viii) truthful
(ix) Failure (x) inspiration

5. (i) Pure - Purity
(ii) Generous - Generosity
(iii) Strong - Strength
(iv) Free - Freedom
(v) Clean - Cleanliness
(vi) Slip - Slipperiness
(vi) Care - Carefulness
(viii) Friend - Friendship
(ix) Discover - Discovery
(x) Lonely - Loneliness

Noun : Number

3.1 Kinds of Number Noun

On the basis of number, noun can be classified into the following types

Countable Nouns

Nouns that can be counted are called countable nouns. Countable noun answers the question 'how many'.

e.g.
- Sheila bought **seven oranges.**
- He went home after **six months.**
- He owns **many watches.**

Uncountable Nouns

Nouns that cannot be counted are called uncountable nouns. An uncountable noun answers the question 'how much'.

e.g.
- There is only **a little salt** left in the jar.
- My shoes are filled with **sand.**
- There is **too little light** in this room.

Singular and Plural Nouns

Countable nouns can be Singular and Plural

- **Singular Nouns** Nouns that refer to only one person, place, animal, thing or organisation are called singular nouns.

  e.g.
  - Can you please move that **table**?
  - The **room** is occupied.

- **Plural Nouns** Nouns that refer to more than one person, place, animal, thing or organisation are called plural nouns.

  e.g.
  - Arrange the **chairs** neatly.
  - The **students** are going on a school trip.

Forming Plural Forms

We follow the rules given below to convert singular nouns into plural nouns.

(i) By simply adding '-s' at the end of nouns.

	Singular		Plural
e.g.	• Rat	–	rats
	• Ship	–	ships
	• Flower	–	flowers
	• Door	–	doors

(ii) By Adding '-es' to the nouns which end in 's', 'ss', 'sh', 'ch', 'x', 'z'.

	Singular		Plural
e.g.	• Dress	–	dresses
	• Wish	–	wishes
	• Witch	–	witches
	• Fox	–	foxes
	• Quiz	–	quizzes
	• Glass	–	glasses

(iii) When the word ends with '-y', replace the '-y' with '-ies'.

	Singular		Plural
e.g.	• Baby	–	babies
	• Sky	–	skies
	• Lorry	–	lorries

(iv) Most nouns ending in '-o' form the plural by adding '-s' or '-es', depending on the word.

	Singular		Plural
e.g.	• Studio	–	studios
	• Potato	–	potatoes
	• Piano	–	pianos
	• Hero	–	heroes
	• Logo	–	logos
	• Volcano	–	volcanoes

(v) Singular nouns ending in 'f' or 'fe' are converted to plural form by replacing it with 'ves'.

	Singular		Plural
e.g.	• Knife	–	knives
	• Thief	–	thieves
	• Shelf	–	shelves

Exception

Singular	Plural
Brief	Briefs
Roof	Roofs
Giraffe	Giraffes

(vi) Some nouns are converted to their plural forms by changing the vowels.

e.g. • Man — men
• Thesis — theses
• Tooth — teeth
• Datum — data
• Fungus — fungi

(vii) Plural of Compound Nouns.

Compound nouns are nouns formed by combining two or more words to create a single, more specific term.

e.g. • Runner-up — runners-up
• Sister-in-law — sisters-in-law
• Passer-by — passers-by
• Milk-man — milk-men

PRACTICE EXERCISE

Objective and Subjective Questions

1. Choose the plural form of the following words from the options given.

(i) Crisis
(a) Crisises (b) Crises (c) Crisisies (d) Cris

(ii) Baby
(a) Babys (b) Babies (c) Babes (d) Babys'

(iii) Half
(a) Halves (b) Halfs (c) Halfe (d) Halvies

(iv) Country
(a) Countries (b) Countrys (c) Countryes (d) Countrie

(v) Toy
(a) Toys (b) Toyes (c) Toyen (d) Toyees

(vi) Piano
(a) Pianoes (b) Pianos (c) Pianis (d) Pianas

(vii) Mouse
(a) Mouses (b) Mice (c) Mices (d) Mousen

(viii) Toothbrush
(a) Toothbrushes (b) Teethbrush
(c) Teethbrushes (d) Toothbrushies

2. From the following list of words, separate the countable and uncountable nouns. Write them down in separate lists.

Puzzle	Syrup	Grass	Cream
Cookie	Pizza	Goggles	Confetti
Telescope	Stars	Parrot	Cupcake
Rice	Book	Homework	Fruit
Slime	Sandwich		

3. Change the following sentences from singular to plural. One has been done for your reference.

• The company is expanding its office. (Singular)
• The companies are expanding their officers. (Plural)

(i) The child is playing in the park.

....

(ii) The toy is on the shelf.

....

(iii) The medium used for this arkwork is charcoal.

....

(iv) The chef is preparing a delicious meal.

....

(v) The diagnosis of a rare disease can be challenging.

....

(vi) The syllabus for this course is difficult.

....

(vii) The world is deep in crisis.

....

(viii) The goose crossed the road to the lake.

....

(ix) Her sister-in-law wears saree.

....

(x) The sheep was grazing the green grass.

....

ANSWERS

1. (i) (b) Crises (ii) (b) Babies
(iii) (a) Halves (iv) (a) Countries
(v) (a) Toys (vi) (b) Pianos
(vii) (b) Mice (viii) (a) Toothbrushes

2. Countable Nouns
(i) Puzzle (ii) Cookie
(iii) Goggles (iv) Fruit
(v) Telescope (vi) Parrot
(vii) Cupcake (viii) Book
(ix) Homework (x) Sandwich
(xi) Pizza

Uncountable Nouns
(i) Syrup (ii) Grass
(iii) Cream (iv) Rice
(v) Slime (vi) Confetti

Please note that some words can be used as both countable and uncountable nouns depending on the context. For example, 'fruit' can refer to a single fruit (countable) or fruit in general (uncountable).

3. (i) The children are playing in the park.
(ii) The toys are on the shelf.
(iii) The media used for this artwork is charcoal.
(iv) The chefs are preparing delicious meals.
(v) The diagnoses of rare diseases can be challenging.
(vi) The syllabi for these courses are difficult.
(vii) The world is deep in crises.
(viii) The geese crossed the road to the lake.
(ix) Her sisters-in-law wear sarees.
(x) The sheep were grazing the green grass.

CHAPTER 4

Nouns : Gender

4.1 Gender

Nouns may be divided as masculine, feminine, neuter or common gender.

Masculine Gender

A noun that refers to a male person or animal is called masculine gender.

e.g. Peacock, Man, Husband

Feminine Gender

A noun that refers to a female person or animal is called feminine gender.

e.g. Peahen, Woman, Wife

Common Gender

A noun that refers to either male or female person or animal is called common gender. It is a gender neutral noun.

e.g. Cousin, Chairperson, Athlete, Scientist etc.

Neuter Gender

A noun that refers to non-living things or a noun that is neither male nor female is called neuter gender.

e.g. Pencil, Space, Gold etc.

4.2 Rules for Changing Masculine into Feminine

(i) Masculine can be changed into feminine by adding 'ess'.

Masculine	Feminine
Lion	Lioness
Host	Hostess
Giant	Giantess
God	Goddess

(ii) In some nouns ending in 'r', Masculine can be changed into feminine by removing the vowel before the last letter and adding -ress

Masculine	Feminine
Tiger	Tigress
Monitor	Monitress
Actor	Actress
Editor	Editress

(iii) Masculine can be changed into feminine by using a completely different word.

Masculine	Feminine
King	Queen
Hero	Heroine
Uncle	Aunt
Husband	Wife

(iv) Feminine of the compound nouns are made by changing the masculine word of the compound noun.

Masculine	Feminine
Bull-calf	Cow-calf
Son-in-law	Daughter-in-law
Milkman	Milkmaid
Peacock	Peahen

(v) Feminine of some masculine nouns are made by removing the last vowel and consonant and then by adding '-ess'.

Masculine	Feminine
Governor	Governess
Murderer	Murderess

PRACTICE EXERCISE

Objective and Subjective Questions

1. What is the gender of the underlined word in the following sentences?

(i) The entrepreneur successfully launched his startup, revolutionising the tech industry.
(a) Feminine (b) Masculine (c) Neuter (d) Common

(ii) The architect designed the innovative skyscraper, incorporating sustainability into her plans.
(a) Feminine (b) Masculine
(c) Neuter (d) Common

(iii) The doctor examined the patient and prescribed some medication.
(a) Feminine (b) Masculine (c) Neuter (d) Common

(iv) The mechanic repaired the intricate engine, demonstrating her expertise in automotive engineering.
(a) Feminine (b) Masculine
(c) Neuter (d) Common

(v) Spectacles are a pair of lenses that are worn to correct vision or protect the eyes.
(a) Feminine (b) Masculine (c) Neuter (d) Common

(vi) Do not sit on the chair, it is broken.
(a) Feminine (b) Masculine
(c) Neuter (d) Common

(vii) The Duchess is visiting Scotland this summer.
(a) Feminine (b) Masculine
(c) Neuter (d) Common

(viii) The navigators are experts of the sea route.
(a) Feminine (b) Masculine
(c) Neuter (d) Common

2. The underlined words are nouns based on gender. Identify which type of noun they are.

Write M for Masculine gender
F for Feminine gender
C for Common gender
N for Neuter gender

(i) Mountain (ii) Flower
(iii) Sibling (iv) Nephew
(v) Neighbour (vi) Rooster
(vii) Poet (viii) Drake
(ix) River (x) Moon
(xi) Raven (xii) Doe
(xiii) Beach (xiv) Author
(xv) Duck (xvi) Cousin
(xvii) Ram

ANSWERS

1. (i) (b) masculine (ii) (a) Feminine
(iii) (d) Common (iv) (a) Feminine
(v) (c) Neuter (vi) (c) Neuter
(vii) (a) Feminine (viii) (d) Common

2. (i) Mountain: N (Neuter Gender)
(ii) Flower: N (Neuter Gender)
(iii) Sibling: C (Common Gender)
(iv) Nephew: M (Masculine Gender)
(v) Neighbour: C (Common Gender)
(vi) Rooster: M (Masculine Gender)
(vii) Poet: C (Common Gender)
(viii) Drake: M (Masculine Gender)
(ix) River: N (Neuter Gender)
(x) Moon: N (Neuter Gender)
(xi) Raven: C (Common Gender)
(xii) Doe: F (Feminine Gender)
(xiii) Beach: N (Neuter Gender)
(xiv) Author: C (Common Gender)
(xv) Duck: F (Feminine Gender)
(xvi) Cousin: C (Common Gender)
(xvii) Ram: M (Masculine Gender)

Pronouns

5.1 Definition of Pronouns

A pronoun is a word that is used in place of a noun in a sentence.

e.g.
- The **lawyer** sat immovable before **his** table and read the New Testament.
- **Aunt Madina** looks more Indian with **her** dark, beautiful Asian eyes.
- The **cat** is wagging **its** tail.

In the sentences given above, bold words are pronouns which are used in place of nouns which are underlined in the sentences.

5.2 Kinds of Pronouns

Pronouns can be classified into following kinds.

Personal Pronouns

Personal pronouns are used in place of the names of people and things. It must agree with the gender and the number of the noun it replaces.

(i) **I** was talking about Prachi's dog.
(ii) **You** need to read the book.
(iii) **He** went to the gym.

These pronouns are typically categorised into three different persons and it can be singular or plural.

This table lists the personal pronouns

Person	Singular Form	Plural Form
1st Person (the speaker)	I, me	We, us
2nd Person (the person being addressed)	You	You
3rd Person (the person being discussed)	He, him (Masculine) She, her (Feminine) It (For singular things)	They, them (For all genders)

Possessive Pronouns

Possessive pronouns are used to show ownership or possession.

e.g.
- These are **his** glasses.
- These orchards are **theirs.**
- The pleasure of hosting you is **ours.**

Possessive pronoun has different forms depending on their number and person. Study the table given below

Person	Singular Form	Plural Form
1st Person (the speaker)	Mine	Ours
2nd Person (the person being addressed)	Yours	Yours
3rd Person (the person being discussed)	His (Masculine) Hers (Feminine) Its (For singular things)	Theirs (For all genders, as well as things)

Note it Apostrophes are not used in Possessive Pronouns.
Yours — correct
Your's — incorrect

Demonstrative Pronouns

Demonstrative pronouns are used to indicate a specific person, place or thing. It tells whether the noun is near or far.

There are four demonstrative pronouns

- This, That (Singular)
- These, Those (Plural)

'This' and 'These' are used to refer to people or things that are close to the speaker.

e.g.
- Can you **pass** this bottle please?
- **These** are the paintings I recently bought.

'That' and 'Those' are used to refer to people or things that are farther away from the speaker.

e.g.
- I am excited to visit **that** Church.
- **Those** Mussoorie roads can never be forgotten.

Relative Pronouns

Relative pronouns are those that refer to a noun previously mentioned in the sentence.

There are five relative pronouns, Who, Whom, Whose, Which, That

e.g.
- Do you see the dog **that** is playing outside?
- Marie Curie is the scientist **who** discovered radium.

Reflexive Pronouns

Reflexive pronouns are those that are used to refer back to a person or thing.

Some reflexive pronouns are Myself, Ourselves, Yourself, Yourselves, Itself, Himself, Herself, Themselves.

e.g.
- John said he would go shopping **himself.**
- I have to wash the car **myself.**
- The cat hurt **itself.**

In the sentences given above himself, myself and itself are referring to he, I and cat respectively.

Emphatic Pronouns

Emphatic pronouns are used to emphasise the subject of the sentence.

e.g.
- I **myself** completed the project.
- Ruskin Bond **himself** signed this book for me.

Indefinite Pronouns

Indefinite pronouns are words that indicate persons or things in a general way and not a particular person or thing.

Some indefinite pronouns are

Anybody, Somebody, Nobody, Everybody, One, None, Many, Few etc.

e.g.
- The collage was made by **everybody.**
- **Somebody** has accepted the job, the vacancy is filled.

PRACTICE EXERCISE

Objective and Subjective Questions

1. Choose the best alternative to complete the sentences

(i) The cat with soft fur belonged to ....

(a) he (b) him
(c) his (d) its

(ii) I was surprised by the size of .... new house.

(a) their (b) them
(c) they (d) there

(iii) The painting on the wall is not ....

(a) my (b) mine
(c) me (d) your

(iv) The task was challenging, but .... finished it quickly.

(a) their (b) we
(c) us (d) her

(v) The antique clock belonged to .... great-grandparents.

(a) our (b) ours
(c) mine (d) them

(vi) The robot lost .... grip on the object and it fell.

(a) its (b) it
(c) it's (d) his

(vii) Bobby is a cousin of ....

(a) me (b) us
(c) mine (d) our

(viii) .... and my brother are best friends.

(a) He (b) Him
(c) His (d) I

(ix) .... were talking about ....

(a) We, her (b) Us, she
(c) We, she (d) She, us

(x) ...... called to see if we could join them for dinner.

(a) Her (b) Hers
(c) She (d) His

2. Choose the best alternative

(i) Which of the following is a demonstrative pronoun?

(a) He (b) She
(c) Whose (d) That

(ii) Choose the correct demonstrative pronoun to complete the sentence:
"............ is my favourite book."

(a) This (b) Her
(c) It's (d) Many

(iii) Identify the pronoun in the sentence. "What are you saying right at this moment?"

(a) Are (b) Moment
(c) What (d) This

(iv) In the sentence, "I can't believe you ate .... entire cake!" What demonstrative pronoun correctly fills in the blank?

(a) this (b) many
(c) those (d) some

(v) Choose the correct pronoun to complete the sentence. "Each student must bring .... own lunch to school."

(a) they (b) their
(c) his or her (d) it

(vi) Which part of the sentence has an error?

(a) All the (b) students
(c) completed (d) there assignments

(vii) Please don't blame .... for your injury.

(a) yourself (b) yourselves
(c) me (d) myself

(viii) Identify the word used as an emphatic pronoun in the following sentence. I believe he himself suggested that we should not invite him.

(a) He (b) Himself
(c) We (d) I

(ix) She rarely takes her phone with .... when she is going to bed.

(a) herself (b) her
(c) hers (d) she

(x) Satyam and I .... confident that we will get into Harvard.

(a) am (b) will
(c) is (d) are

3. Rewrite the sentences by joining them using the most appropriate relative pronoun.

(i) This is the head prefect. She is honest.
(ii) This is the couple. Their photo appeared in the newspaper yesterday.
(iii) Here is the pen. You lost it yesterday.
(iv She is my sister. She got the award.
(v) Ramesh is a brilliant student. He won the Rhodes scholarship.
(vi) The dog is asleep. The dog is mine.

(vii) I studied in this school. It is big.

(viii) My friends like my yellow dress. I bought it from Chandni Chowk.

(ix) I admire my grandma. She is very kind.

(x) They play basketball. These students are athletic.

4. Identify the type of pronoun of the underlined word.

(i) Radhika enjoyed reading her book in the park.

(ii) We went to he market to buy some groceries.

(iii) The car, which belongs to Arjun, is parked in the garage.

(iv) I myself completed the project on time.

(v) They are planning to visit their family next weekend.

(vi) What are you doing later tonight?

(vii) These are chocolate cookies.

(viii) That is a beautiful painting on the wall.

(ix) She was talking to herself in the mirror.

(x) Rohit and his brother went to the store to buy their groceries.

5. Identify whether the underlined pronouns are emphatic or reflexive.

(i) She herself cooked dinner.

(ii) They cleaned the room themselves.

(iii) He is going to fix the car himself.

(iv) We can finish the project ourselves.

(v) You should be proud of yourself.

(vi) I myself will take care of the issue.

(vii) The cat washes itself.

(viii) They congratulated themselves for their achievement.

(ix) She herself baked the cake.

(x) He built the treehouse himself.

(xi) We believe in ourselves.

(xii) You yourself should be able to do it.

(xiii) I myself prepared the presentation.

ANSWERS

1. (i) (b) him (ii) (a) their
(iii) (b) mine (iv) (b) we
(v) (a) our (vi) (a) its
(vii) (c) mine (viii) (a) He
(ix) (a) We, her (x) (c) She

2. (i) (d) That (ii) (a) this
(iii) (c) What (iv) (a) this
(v) (c) his or her (vi) (d) there assignments
(vii) (c) me (viii) (b) himself
(ix) (b) her (x) (d) are

3. (i) This girl, who is the head prefect, is honest. Or, This is the head prefect who is honest.

(ii) This is the couple whose photo appeared in the newspaper yesterday.

(iii) Here is the pen that you lost yesterday.

(iv) The girl who got the award is my sister.

(v) Ramesh, who won the Rhodes scholarship, is a brilliant student.

(vi) The dog that is asleep is mine.

(vii) That school in which I studied is big.

(viii) My friends like the yellow dress which I bought from Chandni Chowk.

(ix) My grandma is a kind lady whom I admire. Or, I admire my grandma, who is very kind.

(x) The students who/ that play basketball are athletic.

4. (i) Possessive pronoun ('her')
(ii) Personal pronoun ('We')
(iii) Relative pronoun ('which')
(iv) Emphatic pronoun ('myself')
(v) Personal pronoun ('They')
(vi) Personal pronoun ('You')
(vii) Demonstrative pronoun ('These')
(viii) Demonstrative pronoun ('That')
(ix) Reflective pronoun ('herself')
(x) Personal pronoun ('their')

5. (i) Emphatic (ii) Reflexive
(iii) Reflexive (iv) Reflexive
(v) Reflexive (vi) Emphatic
(vii) Reflexive (viii) Reflexive
(ix) Emphatic (x) Reflexive
(xi) Reflexive
(xii) Emphatic
(xiii) Emphatic

CHAPTER 6

Adjectives

6.1 Definition of Adjectives

An adjective is a word that modifies or describes a noun or pronoun.

e.g. • My puppy has **brown** eyes.
• The school building is **huge.**
• The G-20 celebration was **grand.**
• Everybody wore **pink** clothes for the Barbie movie.

In the sentences given above, brown, huge, grand and pink are adjectives that describe the nouns 'eyes' 'school', 'building' 'G-20 celebration' and 'clothes'.

6.2 Kinds of Adjectives

Adjectives can be classified into the following types

Adjectives of Quality

An adjective of quality describes the quality of the noun or pronoun. These are also called descriptive adjectives.
It answers the question 'what kind'?

e.g. • Princess Diana had an **elegant** demeanour.
• The firefighters are a **courageous** bunch.

Adjectives of Quantity

An adjective of quantity specifies the quantity or amount of noun or pronoun. It is generally used with uncountable nouns. They answer the question 'how much'?

e.g. • I'll have **some** ice cream for dessert.
• Do we have **enough** food for the party?

Adjectives of Number

An adjective of number is used to indicate the exact or specific number of a noun or a pronoun. It is used with countable nouns. It answers the question 'how many'?

e.g. • There are **seven** days in a week.
• We bought a **dozen** roses for the anniversary.

Demonstrative Adjective

A demonstrative adjective is used to indicate or demonstrate which specific noun is being referred to.

It answers the question 'which?'

In English, there are four demonstrative adjectives—this, that, these and those.

'This' and 'These' are used to denote a thing nearby, or an event that is nearby, or has happened recently.

e.g. • What's in **this** box?
• Please pick up **these** toys from the floor.

'That' and 'those' are used to refer to objects that are farther away, or to events that have happened further in the past, or are scheduled at a later time in the future.

e.g. • I remember **that** vacation we took last year.
• Who are **those** people waiting at the bus stop?"

Interrogative Adjective

An interrogative adjective is used to ask questions about a noun. It comes before the noun they qualify.

There are only three interrogative adjectives- What, Which and Whose.

e.g. • **What** time is the meeting?
• **Which** colour do you prefer?
• **Whose** car is parked in the driveway?

Possessive Adjective

A possessive adjective shows ownership or possession.

Some possessive adjectives are my, your, his, her, its, our, and their.

e.g. • They painted **their** house blue.
• The dog wagged **its** tail.

Proper Adjective

A proper adjective is an adjective that is formed using a proper noun. The first letter of a proper adjective is always capitalised.

e.g. • She has a **British** accent.

6.3 Degrees of Comparison

Adjectives are used to make comparison between two or more nouns. When we use an adjective to compare the qualities of two or more nouns, we use degrees of comparison.

e.g. • Raghav is a **strong** boy. (Positive degree)
- Raghav is **stronger** than Vaibhav. (Comparative degree)
- Prem is the **strongest** boy in the class. (Superlative degree)

6.4 Forms of Degree of Comparison

Positive Degree of Comparison

The simple or base form of the adjective is called the positive degree.

e.g. • Neeta is a **tall** girl.
- He is a **good** student.

Comparative Degree of Comparison

A comparative degree of an adjective is used to compare the quality of two nouns.

e.g. • Neeta is **taller** than her friend.
- He is a **better** student than the class montior.

Superlative Degree of Comparison

A superlative degree of an adjective is used to compare the quality of more than two nouns.

e.g. • Neeta is the **tallest** girl in her class.
- He is the **best** student in the whole school.

Rules to form Comparative and Superlative Degrees of Adjectives

1. In most adjectives, we add '– er' at the end of a positive degree of an adjective to make it comparative. We add '– est' at the end of a positive degree of an adjective to make it superlative.

Positive Degree	Comparative Degree	Superlative Degree
Fast	Faster	Fastest
Small	Smaller	Smallest
Warm	Warmer	Warmest
Thick	Thicker	Thickest
Bright	Brighter	Brightest

2. If an adjective ends with 'y' and has a consonant just before 'y', we remove it and add 'ier' at the end to make it comparative. We add '-iest' at the end to make it superlative.

Positive Degree	Comparative	Superlative
Funny	Funnier	Funniest
Busy	Busier	Busiest
Easy	Easier	Easiest
Dirty	Dirtier	Dirtiest
Happy	Happier	Happiest

3. Sometimes the last letter of the positive adjective is doubled before adding '-er' for comparative and '-est' for Superlative.

Positive Degree	Comparative	Superlative
Big	Bigger	Biggest
Sad	Sadder	Saddest
Hot	Hotter	Hottest
Slim	Slimmer	Slimmest
Wet	Wetter	Wettest

4. In adjectives containing two syllables, we add 'more' before the adjective to make it comparative. Similarly, we add 'most' before the adjective to make it superlative.

Positive Degree	Comparative	Superlative
Modern	More modern	Most modern
Polite	More polite	Most polite
Famous	More famous	Most famous
Active	More active	Most active
Generous	More generous	Most generous

5. Some adjectives have completely different words as their comparatives and superlatives. They do not follow any of the rules given above.

Positive Degree	Comparative	Superlative
Good	Better	Best
Bad	Worse	Worst
Far	Farther/Further	Farthest/Furthest
Little	Less	Least
Many/Much	More	Most

Note it The words 'elder', 'older', 'eldest' and 'oldest' do not have a positive degree. They are used to compare the age of people.

PRACTICE EXERCISE

Objective and Subjective Questions

1. Fill in the blanks with the correct degree of adjective.

(i) This is the .... solution to the problem.
(a) logical (b) logically
(c) more logical (d) most logical

(ii) She is the .... student in her class.
(a) intelligent (b) more intelligent
(c) most intelligent (d) intelligenter

(iii) The garden looks .... since you tidied it up.
(a) better (b) good (c) best (d) dirty

(iv) He is .... than his classmates.
(a) smart (b) smarter
(c) smartest (d) more smarter

(v) On a .... day like this, I love taking long walks.
(a) nice (b) nicer
(c) nicest (d) most nice

(vi) The flowers in the garden are ....
(a) beautiful (b) beautifully
(c) more beautiful (d) most beautiful

(vii) The new software is .... to use than the old one.
(a) easy (b) easier
(c) easiest (d) more easier

(viii) The city is .... during rush hour.
(a) busy (b) most busy
(c) busier (d) more busier

(ix) That bakery is known for serving the .... pastries in town.
(a) more delicious
(b) delicious
(c) deliciousest
(d) most delicious

(x) This library has the .... collection of rare books.
(a) biggest (b) largest
(c) expensive (d) mostly

2. Identify which part of the sentence contains an error.

(i) More people have at least seven dreams a night.
(a) More people (b) Have
(c) at least seven dreams (d) a night.

(ii) All birds have wings and much (but not all) can fly.
(a) All birds have (b) wings, and
(c) much (but not all) (d) can fly.

(iii) The sea otter is the most smallest sea mammal.
(a) The sea otter (b) is the
(c) most smallest (d) sea mammal

(iv) Two men investigate farther on why the road is blocked.
(a) Two men (b) investigate farther
(c) on why (d) the road is blocked.

(v) When the nucleus of an atom is split, it releases a more amount of energy.
(a) When the nucleus
(b) of an atom is split,
(c) it releases a more amount
(d) of energy.

(vi) Diamond is the hard substance on Earth.
(a) Diamond is (b) the hard
(c) substance (d) on Earth

(vii) Dolphins are wonderfully creatures.
(a) Dolphins (b) are
(c) wonderfully (d) creatures

(viii) **The elephant is the most large land mammal on Earth.**

(a) The elephant is (b) the most large
(c) land mammal (d) on Earth.

(ix) **Much historians are working in this area.**

(a) Much historians (b) are working
(c) in (d) this area

(x) **Ashoka is known for his large compassion.**

(a) Ashoka is (b) known
(c) for his (d) large compassion

3. Identify what type of adjectives are the underlined words.

(i) Whose jacket is this?
(ii) She wore an elegant and sparkling evening gown
(iii) She makes us write all our essays as simply as possible.
(iv) Sachin stood for several minutes outside the door.
(v) He is always the first student to reach the class.
(vi) I have two sisters.
(vii) Bhumika loves French perfume.
(viii) Taylor Swift is the most successful artist of the year.
(ix) We went to the movies this Saturday.
(x) Which hotel do you want to book?

4. Identify which word(s) in the sentence is an adjective.

(i) Hermit crabs are curious creatures found near the coasts of Europe.
(ii) Tsunamis are among the most destructive of natural disasters.
(iii) Kanchana was allowed to leave her room for fifteen minutes every eight hours.
(iv) Julius Caesar brought the first giraffe ever seen in the West to Rome.
(v) Macbeth had enough power, but no integrity.
(vi) 'Rhythm' is the longest English word without a vowel.
(vii) Human thigh bones are stronger than concrete.
(viii) Earth is the only planet not named after a God.
(ix) A Russian man who wore a beard during the time of Peter the Great had to pay a special tax.
(x) Enough paper is recycled in the USA every day.

ANSWERS

1. (i) (d) most logical
(ii) (c) most intelligent
(iii) (a) better
(iv) (b) smarter
(v) (a) nice
(vi) (a) beautiful
(vii) (b) easier
(viii) (c) busier
(ix) (d) most delicious
(x) (b) largest

2. (i) (a) **Most** people have at least seven dreams a night.
(ii) (c) All birds have wings and **many/most** (but not all) can fly.
(iii) (c) The sea otter is **the smallest** sea mammal.
(iv) (b) Two men investigate **further** on why the road is blocked.
(v) (c) When the nucleus of an atom is split, it releases a **huge/ large/ big** amount of energy.
(vi) (b) Diamond is a **hard/ the hardest** substance on Earth.
(vii) (c) Dolphins are **wonderful** creatures.
(viii) (b) The elephant is **the largest** land mammal on Earth.
(ix) (a) **Many historians** are working in this area.
(x) (d) Ashoka is known for his **great** compassion.

3. (i) Interrogative Adjective
(ii) Adjective of Quality
(iii) Possessive Adjective
(iv) Adjective of Quantity
(v) Adjective of Number
(vi) Adjective of Number
(vii) Proper Adjective
(viii) Adjective of Quality
(ix) Demonstrative Adjective
(x) Interrogative Adjective

4. (i) Hermit, curious
(ii) Destructive, natural
(iii) Fifteen, eight
(iv) First
(v) Enough, no
(vi) Longest, English
(vii) Stronger
(viii) Only
(ix) Russian, special
(x) Enough

CHAPTER 7

Articles

7.1 Definition of Article

Articles are used to point out the noun that is being referred to in a sentence. The words 'A', 'An' and 'The' are called articles.

e.g.
- Mrs. Rabbit took **a** basket and her umbrella.
- Priyal went through **the** woods to the baker's.
- **An** old mouse was running in and out over the stone doorstep.

7.2 Types of Article

Articles are classified into two types

(1) Indefinite Article (2) Definite Article

Definite Article

'The' is the only definite article. It is used to refer to a particular noun. It can be used with both singular and plural nouns.

e.g.
- Our friends who had always lived in **the** city, came to visit us.
- Charles Babbage is considered as **the** father of computer.

Uses of the Definite Article 'the'

1. The article 'the' is used when a noun is being used for the second time.

   e.g.
   - Shalini was talking to **a** girl. **The** girl was crying.
   - John found **a** book at the library. **The** book was about space exploration.

2. When a singular noun is meant to represent a whole class.

   e.g.
   - **The** cow is a useful animal.
   - **The** rose is a symbol of love.

3. It is used before some proper names

   (i) Oceans and seas, such as the Pacific, the Black Sea

   e.g. • **The** Pacific Ocean is **the** largest and deepest ocean on Earth.

   (ii) Rivers, such as the Ganga, the Nile

   e.g. • **The** Ganga is a sacred river in India, considered holy by millions of people.

   (iii) Canals, such as the Suez Canal

   e.g. • **The** Suez Canal connects the Mediterranean Sea to the Red Sea.

   (iv) Deserts, such as the Sahara

   e.g. • **The** Sahara is the world's largest hot desert, covering much of North Africa.

   (v) Group of islands, such as the West Indies, the Philippines

   e.g. • **The** Philippines is an island nation known for its stunning beaches.

   (vi) Mountain ranges, such as the Himalayas, the Alps

   e.g. • **The** Himalayas, with their majestic peaks, span several countries including India, Nepal, and Bhutan.

   (vii) A very few names of countries that refer to a group of states such as the USA, the Philippines, the Netherlands etc.

   e.g. • **The** Netherlands is known for its tulip fields.

   (viii) Names of newspapers and journals such as The Times of India, the Time Magazine etc.

   e.g. • I enjoy reading articles on current events in **The** Times of India.

   (ix) It is used before the names of well-known monuments, stadiums, theatres, auditoriums, universities, etc. such as the Qutub Minar, the Sydney Opera House etc.

   e.g. • A large number of visitors visit **the** Qutub Minar every year.

   (x) Before the names of certain books (epics, religious or holy books) such as the Bible, the Mahabharata etc.

   e.g. • Many find solace in the teachings of **the** Bible.

4. It is used with the Superlative degree of adjectives.

   e.g. • The Valley of Flowers is **the** most beautiful garden I have seen.

5. It is used with ordinal numbers (first, second, third, fourth etc.)

   e.g. • India became **the** second team to win the Men's Cricket World Cup in 1983.

6. It is used with things that are unique like the Sun, the Earth, the moon, the sky etc.

   e.g. • **The** moon is the only natural satellite of **the** Earth.

7. It is used before the adjectives that are used as a noun.

   e.g. • **The** brave were felicitated by **the** nation.
   - **The** rich are getting richer and **the** poor are getting poorer.

Indefinite Article

The words 'A' and 'An' are indefinite articles.

They refer to a singular countable common noun.

e.g. (i) I have **an** umbrella with me.

(ii) Can I have a glass of water?

Use of the Article 'A'

1. It is used before singular countable nouns that start with a consonant sound.

   e.g. 'a boy', 'a bag', 'a dog' etc.

2. The article 'a' is used before words that start with vowels that have a consonant sound.

   e.g. a unique style, a unit, a utensil etc.

3. To make a common noun of a proper noun.

   e.g. There is a Gandhi within all of us.

Use of the Article 'An'

1. The article 'an' is used before singular countable nouns that start with a vowel sound.

   e.g. **an** actor, **an** egg, **an** elephant, etc.

2. In some cases, article 'an' is used before the words that are starting with a consonant. The consonant sound is silent in these words or have a vowel sound.

   e.g. **an** honour, an hour etc.

Omission of Articles

1. It is omitted before the proper and material nouns.

   e.g. • Mohnish is a hardworking boy. (Proper Noun)
   - I am going to Paris. (Proper Noun)
   - Gold is a precious metal. (Material Noun)

2. It is not used before the abstract nouns when used in a general manner.

   e.g. **Honesty** and **gratitude** will take you a long way in life.

3. It is not used before an uncountable noun.

   e.g. I would like to have **some** water.

4. It is not used before the plural nouns referring to the entire class or species.

   e.g. • **Dogs** are known for their loyalty to humans.
   - **Mountains** cover a significant part of the Earth's surface.

5. It is not used before the names of languages and academic subjects.

   e.g. • **Maths** is my favourite subject.
   - I am learning **German**.

6. It is not used before the names of games.

   e.g. **Cricket** is the national sport of England.

7. It is not used before the names of continents, countries or cities.

   e.g. • I am planning a trip to **Europe**.
   - **France** is a beautiful country.
   - I come from the city of **Bhagalpur**, in **Bihar**.

8. It is not used before the names of days, months, festivals and seasons.

   e.g. • My birthday is in **December**.
   - **Saturday** is the most awaited day of the week.
   - **Diwali** is my favourite festival.

9. Before names of relations, like father, mother, aunt, etc.

   e.g. We are going to visit **grandma**.

PRACTICE EXERCISE

Objective and Subjective Questions

1. Fill in the blanks with the correct options.

(i) "Sally Carrol," he said with .... curious intensity, "don't you like us?"
(a) a (b) an (c) the (d) No article

(ii) Marylyn Wade and Joe Ewing appeared in .... doorway.
(a) a (b) an (c) the (d) No article

(iii) He remembered .... story of .... man, caught in a storm, who killed .... animal.
(a) the, a, an (b) a, a, a
(c) a, the, an (d) the, the, an

(iv) .... large piece of a wet plant fell on .... little fire.
(a) The, the (b) A, the
(c) A, no article (d) No article

(v) There was nothing .... clear about them.
(a) a (b) an (c) the (d) No article

(vi) I could not say, "I'm .... scared and I don't want to be alone."
(a) a (b) an (c) the (d) No article

(vii) .... rumours you have heard are true.
(a) A (b) An (c) The (d) No article

(viii) He surprised even himself, at his boldness and .... forwardness.
(a) a (b) an (c) the (d) No article

(ix) .... Pandava brothers had married Princess Draupadi and had become rulers of .... great kingdom.
(a) The, the (b) A, the (c) The, a (d) A, a

(x) This is .... urgent matter. Can we speak in .... private?"
(a) an, the (b) an, no article
(c) a, the (d) No article

2. Given below are four sentences. Choose which of them is grammatically correct.

(i) (a) Robert is a good driver for a young person.
(b) Robert is good driver for a young person.
(c) Robert is good driver for young person.
(d) Robert is a good driver for young person.

(ii) (a) Sun was bright but not glaring.
(b) The Sun was bright but not glaring.
(c) A Sun was bright but not glaring.
(d) Sun was a bright but not glaring.

(iii) (a) His lips curved into little smile.
(b) His lips curved into a little smile.
(c) His lips curved into an little smile.
(d) His lips curved into the little smile.

(iv) (a) His speech really made an impression on kids.
(b) His speech really made the impression on kids.
(c) His speech really made impression on kids.
(d) His speech really made a impression on kids.

(v) (a) He was travelling at the rate of four miles a hour.
(b) He was travelling at the rate of four miles for hour.
(c) He was travelling at the rate of four miles hour.
(d) He was travelling at the rate of four miles an hour.

(vi) (a) There was not an cloud in the sky.
(b) There was not a cloud in sky.
(c) There was not many cloud in the sky.
(d) There was not a cloud in the sky.

(vii) (a) Once away from the danger, he continued at a slower speed.
(b) Once away from danger, he continued at a slower speed.
(c) Both (a) and (b)
(d) Neither (a) nor (b)

(viii) (a) Almost immediately the water turned into ice.
(b) Almost immediately water turned into an ice.
(c) Almost immediately water turned into ice.
(d) Almost immediately the water turned into a ice.

(ix) (a) The Asia is the largest continent on the planet.
(b) Asia is the largest continent on planet.
(c) Asia is the largest continent on the planet.
(d) The Asia is largest continent on the planet.

(x) (a) After some time, he began to notice some feeling in his beaten fingers.
(b) After a time, he began to notice some feeling in his beaten fingers.
(c) After the time, he began to notice some feeling in his beaten fingers.
(d) After an time, he began to notice some feeling in his beaten fingers.

3. Correct and rewrite the sentences given below, by adding or omitting articles, as required.

(i) A village folk customarily have one meal a day of parched grains.

(ii) An country would be nothing without its people.

(iii) There is enough gold in the Earth's core to cover a whole Earth.
(iv) USA and Canada are neighbouring countries.
(v) Is the Kanchenjunga higher than the Mount Everest?
(vi) Tug of war also used to be famous Olympic game.
(vii) During 1991, French made the fake Paris to fool German bomber pilots.
(viii) The Egyptians used slabs of stone as pillows.
(xi) Ferrets were one of most popular pets in Rome.
(x) The Universal Declaration of Human Rights (UDHR) was adopted by United Nations General Assembly in December 1948.

4. Fill in the blanks with 'a', 'an' or 'the'. Write 'x' where no article is needed.

Certainly! Here are 10 sentences related to Indian history, geography, and pop culture. Fill in the blanks with 'a', 'an', 'the', or 'x':

(i) In .... ancient city of Mohenjo-daro, archaeologists discovered evidence of advanced urban planning.
(ii) Do you know if there's .... museum in Jaipur that showcases Rajasthani art?
(iii) Rani Lakshmibai was .... courageous queen who played a pivotal role in Indian history.
(iv) Mumbai is known for its vibrant film industry; Bollywood is .... significant part of Indian popular culture.
(v) The Indian Ocean is .... third-largest of .... world's oceanic divisions.
(vi) Shah Rukh Khan is .... iconic actor who has made a mark in .... Indian and international film industry.
(vii) The Himalayas are .... majestic mountain range, home to diverse flora and fauna.
(viii) Do you have .... favourite dish from .... rich and varied cuisine of India?
(ix) .... Taj Mahal, located in Agra, is considered .... masterpiece of Mughal architecture.
(x) .... Ganges River is .... sacred river in Hinduism, flowing through .... northern part of India.

ANSWERS

1. (i) (a) a (ii) (c) the
(iii) (a) the, a, an (iv) (b) A, the
(v) (d) No article (vi) (d) No article
(vii) (c) The (viii) (d) No article
(ix) (c) The, a (x) (b) an, no article

2. (i) (a) Robert is a good driver for a young person.
(ii) (b) The Sun was bright but not glaring.
(iii) (b) His lips curved into a little smile.
(iv) (a) His speech really made an impression on kids.
(v) (d) He was travelling at the rate of four miles an hour.
(vi) (d) There was not a cloud in the sky.
(vii) (c) Both (a) and (b)
(viii) (a) Almost immediately the water turned into ice.
(ix) (c) Asia is the largest continent on the planet.
(x) (a) After some time, he began to notice some feeling in his beaten fingers.

3. (i) The village folk customarily have one meal a day of parched grains.
(ii) A country would be nothing without its people.
(iii) There is enough gold in the Earth's core to cover the whole Earth.
(iv) The USA and Canada are neighbouring countries.
(v) Is Kanchenjunga higher than Mount Everest?
(vi) Tug of war also used to be a famous Olympic game.
(vii) During 1991, the French made a fake Paris to fool German bomber pilots.
(viii) Egyptians used slabs of stone as pillows.
(ix) Ferrets were one of the most popular pets in Rome.
(x) The Universal Declaration of Human Rights (UDHR) was adopted by the United Nations General Assembly in December 1948.

4. (i) the (ii) a
(iii) a (iv) a
(v) the, the (vi) an, the
(vii) a (viii) a, the
(ix) The, a (x) The, a, the

Verbs

CHAPTER 8

8.1 Definition of Verb

A verb is a word that is used to denote actions, possession or state of being.

e.g. • She **runs** every morning. (action)
• She **is** a teacher. (state of being)
• Mr. Mathur **owns/has** a Chocolate factory. (possession)

8.2 Types of Verbs

1. Main verbs
   (i) Transitive and Intransitive Verbs
   (ii) Regular and Irregular Verbs
   (iii) Finite and Non-Finite verbs
2. Linking verbs
3. Auxiliary or Helping Verbs
   (i) Primary Auxiliary Verbs
   (ii) Modal Auxiliary Verbs

Main Verbs

Main verbs are verbs that describe an action performed by the subject in the sentence.

e.g. • We **studied** for our exams.
• They **travel** a lot.
• The kids **are playing** in the park.

The action of the verbs are directed at the 'object' in the sentence.

Types of Main Verb

1. On the basis of the object of a sentence, main verbs are divided into transitive and intransitive verbs.

   (i) **Transitive Verb** A transitive verb needs an object to complete the action. Without the object, the sentence will be incomplete.

   e.g. • He **bought** a new pen.
   • Rajeev **ate** pasta for breakfast.

   (ii) **Intransitive Verb** An intransitive verb does not need an object to complete the sentence.

   e.g. • The flowers **bloomed.**
   • The baby **cried.**

2. On the basis of the change of the verb form, main verbs are divided into regular and irregular verbs.

   (i) **Regular verb** A verb that forms its past and past participle forms by adding '-d' or '-ed' to the main verb is called a regular verb.

   e.g. • She **waits** for her little brother. (Base form)
   • She **waited** for her little brother. (Past form)

   (ii) **Irregular verb** A verb that forms its past and past participle forms by changing its vowel or using different word is called an irregular verb.

   e.g. • Richie **goes** to the garden. (Base form)
   • Richie **went** to the garden. (Past form)

3. Main verbs are also divided based on the number or person of the subject.

   (i) **Finite verb** A verb that changes its form depending on the number or person of the subject in the sentence is called a finite verb.

   e.g. He **helps** the poor people.

   (ii) **Non-finite verb** A verb that doesn't change its form on the basis of number or person of the subject in the sentence is called a non –finite verb.

   e.g. Rosy wants **to adopt** a puppy.

Linking Verbs

Linking verbs are those words that connect the subject with the other words in a sentence. Some linking verbs are – is, am, are, seem, look, become, smell and touch.

e.g. The flower **smells** nice.

Auxiliary Verbs

Auxiliary Verbs or Helping Verbs are verbs that are used before the main verb to form tenses, passive forms etc. They 'help' the main verb by providing additional information about the action or state of the main verb.

Types of Auxiliary Verbs

(i) Primary/Main Auxiliary Verbs

A primary auxiliary verb is used to make a sentence grammatically complete. This verb changes its form according to the number and person of the subject as well as the time of the action.

- Be (is, am, are, was, were)
- Have (has, had)
- Do (does, did)

e.g.
- **Do you** like ice cream?
- She **did** not attend the meeting.
- They **were** standing in the queue.
- I **have** planned the outing this weekend.

(ii) Modal Auxiliary Verbs

Verbs that denote the mode of action of the main verb are called modal verbs. They are used to express ability, permission, possibility, orders etc.

Can, could, may, might, must, will, would, shall and should are modal auxiliary verbs.

PRACTICE EXERCISE

Objective and Subjective Questions

1. Fill in the blanks using appropriate primary auxiliary verbs.

(i) The museum .... closed on Mondays.
(a) will (b) has (c) is (d) were

(ii) We .... invited to the party next Saturday.
(a) am (b) were (c) have been (d) are

(iii) Despite the challenges, he .... striving for excellence in his field.
(a) has been (b) were
(c) is (d) have

(iv) The project .... set to revolutionise the industry.
(a) is (b) have been
(c) have (d) has

(v) Ali Baba and the forty thieves .... plotting to rob the treasure cave.
(a) had been (b) will have
(c) were (d) was

(vi) .... she know the answer to that question?
(a) Do (b) Does (c) Did (d) Has

(vii) The students .... excited about the upcoming school trip.
(a) are (b) have been
(c) will be (d) would be

(viii) She .... her homework before going to the party.
(a) do (b) does (c) did (d) would

(ix) .... you have any plans for the upcoming weekend?
(a) Do (b) Does
(c) Will (d) Are

(x) The old mansion .... a mysterious and eerie atmosphere.
(a) have (b) had
(c) does (d) is

2. In the given sentences, underline the action verb and identify if it is Transitive (T) or Intransitive (IT).

(i) The car sputtered and stalled on the empty highway.
(ii) The baby slept peacefully through the night.
(iii) The hikers climbed the steep mountain trail with determination.
(iv) The actor delivered an emotional monologue in the play.
(v) The old clock tick-tocked steadily on the wall, marking time.
(vi) She sewed a beautiful dress for the upcoming dance.
(vii) The river meandered through the picturesque valley.
(viii) The fire roared in the fireplace.
(ix) The artist sketched a detailed portrait.
(x) She composed a beautiful melody on the grand piano.

3. **Underline the verbs in the given sentences and state if they are finite or non-finite verbs. Use (F) for finite and (N) for non-finite verbs.**
   (i) I like to eat ice cream after dinner.
   (ii) Running is prohibited in the corridors.
   (iii) An artist is a person who creates art.
   (iv) She sang to please the audience.
   (v) She is wrapping a bandage around her arm.
   (vi) My mother cooks the best food.
   (vii) Riding a horse is a very daunting task.
   (viii) You need to know what the shape of the Earth is.
   (ix) To err is human, to forgive divine.
   (x) The doctor asked the patient to keep the sample on the counter.

4. **Read the given sentences and identify if the verb is an Action Verb, Linking Verb or a Helping verb.**
   (i) Rhea walked to the mall.
   (ii) Javed seems to be sad.
   (iii) Pallavi experimented with her paints.
   (iv) The fruit smells spoiled.
   (v) Dolly ran in the marathon.
   (vi) AR Rehman is an amazing composer.
   (vii) Priya organised the documents
   (viii) Neha looks ill.
   (ix) The first cup of coffee every morning tastes great.
   (x) Nidhi skated across the ice rink.
   (xi) Everyone was tired after the bike race.
   (xii) Prashant grew to be very tall.

ANSWERS

1. (i) (c) is (ii) (d) are
(iii) (c) is (iv) (a) is
(v) (c) were (vi) (b) does
(vii) (a) are (viii) (c) did
(ix) (a) do (x) (b) had

2. (i) sputtered, stalled; IT (ii) slept; IT
(iii) climbed; T (iv) delivered; T
(v) tick-tocked; IT (vi) sewed; T
(vii) meandered; IT (viii) roared; IT
(ix) sketched; T (x) composed; T

3.

	Finite	Non-finite
(i)	Like	To eat
(ii)	Is	Running
(iii)	Is, creates	
(iv)	Sang	To please
(v)	Is wrapping	
(vi)	Cooks	
(vii)	Is	Riding
(viii)	Need	To know
(ix)	Is	to err, to forgive
(x)	Asked	to keep

4. (i) walked action (ii) seems linking
(iii) experimented action (iv) smells linking
(v) ran action (vi) is linking
(vii) organised action (viii) looks linking
(ix) tastes linking (x) skated action
(xi) was helping, tired- action
(xii) grew action

CHAPTER 9

Adverbs

9.1 Definition of Adverbs

A word that modifies the meaning of a verb, an adjective, or another adverb is called an Adverb.

e.g.
- She ran **quickly** to catch the bus. (Modifying the verb 'ran')
- The cake was **extremely** delicious. (Modifying the adjective 'delicious')
- He speaks English **very** fluently. (Modifying the adverb 'fluently')

9.2 Kinds of Adverbs

Adverbs can be classified into the following types

Adverbs of Manner

An adverb of manner describes the way in which an action is performed.

It answers the question– 'How' or 'In what way/manner'.

e.g.
- Please speak **clearly**.
- The man drove **carelessly**.

Adverbs of Place

An adverb of place tells us where or at what place an action takes place.

It answers the question– 'Where'

e.g.
- The children are playing **downstairs**.
- It's raining. Let's go **inside**.
- They are going **abroad** to study.

Adverbs of Time

An adverb of time tells us when an action takes place. It answers the question–'When' and 'For how long'.

e.g.
- **Sometimes** I ride my bike to school.
- John's shoes were too big for him **last year**.

Adverbs of Frequency

An adverb of frequency tells us how often an action takes place. It answers the question– 'How frequently'.

e.g.
- We **usually** have pizza on Friday nights.
- I **rarely** eat fast food.

Adverbs of Degree

An adverb of degree tells us the extent or intensity of the action taking place.

It answers the question– 'To what extent or in what degree.'

e.g.
- He **completely** forgot to pick up the groceries on his way home.
- She is **pretty** good at playing the piano.

PRACTICE EXERCISE

Objective and Subjective Questions

1. Select the correct adverb to fill in the blank.

(i) She speaks English ....
(a) good (b) well (c) better (d) best

(ii) The story of 'The Panchatantra' is filled with .... tales of talking animals who impart valuable lessons.
(a) enchanting (b) musical
(c) sunny (d) green

(iii) The students listened .... to the teacher's instructions before starting the project.
(a) attentively (b) slowly
(c) happily (d) awkwardly

(iv) The comedian told the joke, and the audience laughed .... at the punchline.
(a) heartily (b) shyly (c) angrily (d) joyfully

(v) The restaurant was .... empty when we arrived.
(a) almost (b) seldom (c) always (d) nearly

(vi) The carolers sang .... as they strolled through the snow-covered neighbourhood.
(a) merely (b) heavily (c) prettily (d) merrily

(vii) The hikers reached the summit .... , equipped with the proper gear and precautions.
(a) helplessly (b) safely
(c) in the evening (d) together

(viii) The garden was .... beautiful, with a variety of vibrant flowers in full bloom.
(a) quiet (b) quietly (c) quitely (d) quite

(ix) The storm .... damaged the old barn.
(a) rapidly (b) tenderly (c) uprightly (d) severely

(x) The hot air balloon slowly drifted ....
(a) twice (b) upward
(c) ordinarily (d) now

2. Identify the type of adverb in the given sentences.

(i) He arrived at the airport a few hours ago.
(a) Adverb of Manner (b) Adverb of Place
(c) Adverb of Time (d) Adverb of frequency

(ii) The professor spoke very softly during the lecture.
(a) Adverb of Manner (b) Adverb of Place
(c) Adverb of Time (d) Adverb of Degree

(iii) He visits his grandparents every weekend, cherishing the time spent with them.
(a) Adverb of Manner (b) Adverb of Place
(c) Adverb of Time (d) Adverb of Frequency

(iv) The children are playing outside.
(a) Adverb of Manner (b) Adverb of Time
(c) Adverb of Frequency (d) Adverb of Place.

(v) Are you very worried about the exam?
(a) Adverb of Place (b) Adverb of Time
(c) Adverb of Degree (d) Adverb of Manner

(vi) The train will depart soon, so please make your way to the platform.
(a) Adverb of Time (b) Adverb of Degree
(c) Adverb of Manner (d) Adverb of Place

(vii) The bride smiled radiantly as she walked down the aisle toward her groom.
(a) Adverb of Manner (b) Adverb of Place
(c) Adverb of Time (d) Adverb of Degree

(viii) The river flowed through the picturesque valley.
(a) Adverb of Manner (b) Adverb of Place
(c) Adverb of Time (d) Adverb of Degree

(ix) The team worked together seamlessly to complete the project ahead of schedule.
(a) Adverb of Manner (b) Adverb of Place
(c) Adverb of Time (d) Adverb of frequency

(x) He dressed suitably for the formal event, wearing a tailored suit and tie.
(a) Adverb of Manner (b) Adverb of Place
(c) Adverb of Time (d) Adverb of Degree

3. Form adverbs from the following adjectives. Then use them in a sentence.

(i) Late (ii) Good (iii) Gentle (iv) Happy
(v) Heroic (vi) Serious (vii) Shiny (viii) Noble
(ix) Bad (x) Systematic

4. Rewrite the sentences given below by using the adverbs given in brackets at the correct place.

(i) He handled the fragile vase. (carefully)
(ii) The children played. (noisily)
(iii) He answered the questions in class. (confidently)
(iv) She will meet her friends. (tomorrow)
(v) I treat myself to a fancy dinner at a nice restaurant. (occasionally)
(vi) The hike was exhausting, but the view from the summit was worth it. (utterly)
(vii) You have been studying this language. (there)
(viii) I am typing the e-mail. (now)
(ix) Please go and check for the document. (upstairs)
(x) We'll be leaving for vacation. (soon)

ANSWERS

1. (i) (b) well (ii) (a) enchanting
(iii) (a) attentively (iv) (a) heartily
(v) (d) nearly (vi) (d) merrily
(vii) (b) safely (viii) (d) quite
(ix) (d) severely (x) (b) Upward

2. (i) (c) Adverb of Time
(ii) (d) Adverb of Degree
(iii) (d) Adverb of Frequency
(iv) (d) Adverb of Place
(v) (c) Adverb of Degree
(vi) (a) Adverb of Time
(vii) (a) Adverb of Manner
(viii) (b) Adverb of Place
(ix) (a) Adverb of Manner
(x) (a) Adverb of Manner

3. (i) Lately; She has been too busy lately.
(ii) Well; She paints very well.
(iii) Gently; The wind blew gently.
(iv) Happily; The daffodils happily danced in the breeze.
(v) Heroically; Rani Laxmi Bai acted heroically in the face of British aggression.
(vi) Seriously; Rani was seriously upset with Shyam.
(vii) Shinily; The car gleamed shinily in the street.
(viii) Nobly; He nobly accepted the award on behalf of the team.
(ix) Badly/Poorly; Jigyasa has performed poorly in the test this time.
(x) Systematically; She analysed the data systematically to identify patterns.

4. (i) He carefully handled the fragile vase.
(ii) The children played noisily.
(iii) He answered the questions confidently in class confidently.
(iv) She will meet her friends tomorrow.
(v) I occasionally treat myself to a fancy dinner at a nice restaurant.
(vi) The hike was utterly exhausting, but the view from the summit was worth it.
(vii) You have been studying this language there.
(viii) I am typing the e-mail now.
(ix) Please go upstairs and check for the document.
(x) We'll be leaving for vacation soon.

CHAPTER 10 Prepositions

10.1 Definition of Prepositions

A preposition is a word that shows the relation between the noun or a pronoun and some other word in a sentence.

e.g. • The ball is **on** the roof.
• Samantha is sitting **beside** Aarohi.

Prepositions are placed before a noun or a pronoun.

10.2 Kinds of Preposition

1. Prepositions of Time
2. Prepositions of Place
3. Prepositions of Direction

Note it You may come across many words that are used as adverbs, and also as preposition. Thus, in order to differentiate between them, remember that

- an adverb provides information of verbs.
- A preposition provides information on nouns and pronouns.

Prepositions of Time

Prepositions of time are words that indicate when an action or event occurs. They help to establish the relationship between the subject and the time of the action.

Here are some common prepositions of time

In

(i) To state a time of the day.

e.g. • I was cleaning in **the morning**.

(ii) To state a year or season.

e.g. • Seema was born **in 1993**. (year)

• **In winter**, the nights are long and cold. (Season)

At

(i) To state a specific time.

e.g. • We will meet **at** 11 o'clock.

(ii) To refer to specific meal times.

e.g. • He talked a great deal **at** dinner.

On

(i) For a specific day or date.

e.g. • Gandhi Jayanti is celebrated **on** 2nd October.

(ii) To refer to specific time of the day.

e.g. • He left **on** the morning of 18th May.

Since

(i) To indicate that something started in the past and continues till the present time.

e.g. • I have been working on this **since** last week.

Before

(i) To show that something happened earlier than the time or event mentioned.

e.g. • She met everyone **before** she left the town.

During

(i) To denote the length of time in which something happens.

e.g. • Pay attention **during** her play.

After

(i) Next in time or place of an event or action.

e.g. • Go to play **after** finishing your homework.

Prepositions of Place

Prepositions of place are words that describe the location or position of something in relation to another object.

Here are some common prepositions of place

In

(i) To refer to an enclosed space.

e.g. • Please keep the box **in** the cupboard.

(ii) Before the name of a country.

e.g. • Raj's wedding reception is **in** Indonesia.

At

(i) To refer to a point or a place.

e.g. • You can redeem the tickets **at** the counter.

On

(i) Used to indicate to a surface.

e.g. • The pen is **on** the chair

Above

(i) To show that something is on a higher level.

e.g. • The Sun shines **above** the clouds.

Below

(i) To show that something is on a lower level.

e.g. • He lives **below** Arun.

Between

(i) To show the position of a thing in the middle of two things.

e.g. • The house is **between** the park and the school.

Under

(i) To show that something is on the lower level.

e.g. • The shoes are **under** the chair.

Over

(i) To show that something is in direct contact with or is covering another.

e.g. • They made her comfortable by putting a blanket **over** her.

Behind

(i) Indicates a position at the back of something.

e.g. • The car is **behind** the house.

Prepositions of Direction

Prepositions of direction are used to indicate the movement or direction of an action or object.

Here are some common prepositions of direction

Toward(s)

(i) Indicates movement in the direction of someone or something.

e.g. • After the movie, we went **toward** the exit.

• The dog ran **towards** the sound.

Into

(i) To show that something moves from outside to inside.

e.g. • He threw the ball **into** the dustbin.

In

(i) To show that something is located inside another thing or place.

e.g. • The pool is **in** the school building.

Down

(i) To show movement to a lower level.

e.g. • We trekked **down** a hill.

Up

(i) To show movement to a higher level.

e.g. • He sent the package **up** using a bucket and a rope.

Across

(i) Indicates movement from one side to another, typically over a surface.

e.g. • She swam **across** the river.

PRACTICE EXERCISE

Objective and Subjective Questions

1. Fill the blanks with the most appropriate preposition.

(i) It has been ten years .... we met.
(a) since (b) for (c) about (d) from

(ii) Finish your chores .... 5pm.
(a) by (b) until (c) after (d) upto

(iii) The school is .... the library.
(a) besides (b) aside (c) toward (d) next to

(iv) We celebrate Independence Day .... the fifteenth of August.
(a) at (b) in (c) by (d) on

(v) The bridge spans .... the river.
(a) along (b) across (c) through (d) over

(vi) .... those present were my friends.
(a) Amongst (b) In
(c) Of (d) Between

(vii) Himachal Pradesh is .... the north of India.
(a) inside (b) within (c) in (d) above

(viii) I know him .... kindergarten.
(a) since (b) for (c) from (d) during

(ix) He enquired .... your health.
(a) for (b) on (c) of (d) after

(x) Public opinion was .... this Bill introduced in the Parliament.
(a) of (b) against (c) after (d) anti

(xi) The letter was pushed .... the door.
(a) in (b) underneath
(c) below (d) by

(xii) Mr. Mehta lives .... his means.
(a) behind (b) beyond (c) after (d) before

2. Complete the following sentences by selecting the appropriate options given.

(i) The train is bound ....
(a) to Delhi (b) for Delhi
(c) at Delhi (d) towards Delhi

(ii) It is ten miles .... Patna.
(a) from here to (b) here to Patna
(c) from here reaching (d) to here Patna

(iii) The house is ....
(a) in repairs (b) under repairs
(c) on repairs (d) at repairs

(iv) You can enter this expense ....
(a) under miscellaneous (b) by miscellaneous
(c) to miscellaneous (d) from miscellaneous

(v) Sonia is coming ....
(a) home back by Holi.
(b) home two days before Holi.
(c) back home when it is two days to Holi.
(d) directly from Holi.

(vi) He helps him .... money for rent.
(a) by giving (b) on giving
(c) giving (d) with giving

(vii) Maria is .... Robin.
(a) engaged to (b) engaged too
(c) engaged with (d) engaged of

(viii) Hardened criminals become .... empathy and sympathy.
(a) devoid about (b) devoid of
(c) devoid with (d) devoid off

(ix) We should not .... others, and .... focus on our own selves.
(a) be envious to, instead of
(b) envy of, instead
(c) be envious of, instead
(d) envy by, instead to

(x) This is the book I told you .... yesterday.
(a) of (b) in
(c) about (d) on

3. Fill in the blank with appropriate prepositions.

(i) The bear is going to hunt .... the pack.

(ii) I am allergic .... dust and glitter.

(iii) The city is famous .... its monuments.

(iv) Leonard keeps the house keys .... the drawer.

(v) You can visit the office anytime .... 7 am and 9 pm.

(vi) She flew .... the world to meet her grandma.

(vii) The palace was hidden .... the dense forest.

(viii) The answer to all your questions is .... the pages of this book.

(ix) My school function was organised .... the day.

(x) Bury the letter .... the castle.

4. Identify the errors and correct the following sentences. If 'no errors' are present, write 'no errors'.

(i) He was ill since Monday to Friday.

(ii) Rice sells for Rs. 100/- a quintal.

(iii) I am willing to agree at your suggestion.

(iv) I do not agree to what you are saying.

(v) I sympathised to him in his sorrow.

(vi) A true friend is always faithful with you.

(vii) I was ill on fever.

(viii) What is the time on your watch?

(ix) I was annoyed by his brother.

(x) I cannot be confident with success in this exam.

5. Underline the prepositions and identify the type of preposition (of time/of place/of direction) present in the sentences below.

(i) Can you come here on Monday?

(ii) My great great grandfather was martyred during the freedom struggle.

(iii) The ice-cream shop is below the clothing store.

(iv) The hikers journeyed across the desert to reach an oasis.

(v) We will meet her beside the fountain in the mall.

(vi) The treasure is buried on an island far, far away.

(vii) The party will take place in the Grand Banquet.

(viii) The new exhibit will run through the summer.

(ix) He placed the vase on the shelf.

(x) The ball rolled down the hill.

ANSWERS

1. (i) (a) since (ii) (a) by
(iii) (d) next to (iv) (d) on
(v) (b) across (vi) (a) amongst
(vii) (c) in (viii) (a) since
(ix) (d) after (x) (b) against
(xi) (b) underneath (xii) (b) beyond

2. (i) (b) for Delhi
(ii) (b) from here to
(iii) (b) under repairs
(iv) (a) under miscellaneous
(v) (b) home two days before Holi
(vi) (a) by giving
(vii) (a) engaged to
(viii) (b) devoid of
(ix) (c) be envious of, instead
(x) (c) about

3. (i) with (ii) to
(iii) for (iv) in
(v) between (vi) around
(vii) in (viii) within
(ix) during (x) beneath

4. (i) He was ill **from** Monday to Friday.
(ii) Rice sells **at** Rs. 100/- a quintal.
(iii) I am willing to agree **to** your suggestion.
(iv) I do not agree **with** what you are saying.
(v) I sympathised **with** him in his sorrow.
(vi) A true friend is always faithful **to** you.
(vii) I was ill **with** fever.
(viii) What is the time **by** your watch?
(ix) I was annoyed **with** his brother.
(x) I cannot be confident **of** success in this exam.

5. (i) On (Preposition of time)
(ii) During (Preposition of time)
(iii) Below (Preposition of place)
(iv) Across (Preposition of direction)
(v) Beside (Preposition of place)
(vi) On (Preposition of place)
(vii) In (Preposition of place)
(viii) Through (Preposition of time)
(ix) On (Preposition of place)
(x) Down (Preposition of direction)

CHAPTER 11

Conjunction

11.1 Definition of Conjunction

A conjunction is a word that is used to join words or group of words or sentences.

e.g. • Ruhan plays the piano. He also plays the guitar.
- Ruhan plays the piano **and** the guitar.

• Priyanka won't be singing at the event. She has a sore throat.
- Priyanka won't be singing at the event **because** she has a sore throat.

In the above example, sentences are joined with conjunctions **and** and **because** respectively.

Kinds of Conjunctions

1. Coordinating Conjunctions 2. Subordinating Conjunctions 3. Correlative Conjunctions

Coordinating Conjunctions

Coordinating Conjunctions are used to join two independent sentences.

Coordinating Conjunction	Uses	Sentences	Sentences Combined using Conjunctions
For	Used when we have to express a reason or a cause	I could not attend the wedding. I had a fever.	I could not attend the wedding **for** I had a fever.
And	To join together two sentences or words with similar ideas	She called me. She told me about her situation.	She called me **and** told me about her situation.
Nor	To introduce further negative sentence	The teacher did not smile. She did not speak to the class.	The teacher did not smile, **nor** did she speak to the class.
But	To join words or sentences with opposite ideas	He put too much sugar in the dessert. The dessert turned out delicious.	He put too much sugar in the dessert **but** it turned out delicious.
Or	To join words or sentences which offer a choice	Do the chores of the house. Clean your room.	Do the chores of the house **or** clean your room.
Yet	To join words or sentences wih opposite ideas	They were poor. They were happy.	They were poor, **yet** happy.
So	To express result of an action/event	Manisha broke her arm. She won't come to school.	Manisha broke her arm **so** she won't come to school.

Subordinating Conjunctions

Subordinating Conjunctions are words that are used to join two clauses or sentences, one of which is dependent on the other. Some of these conjuctions are discussed below

Subordinating Conjunction	Uses	Sentences	Sentences Combined using Conjunctions
Although /Though	To join words or sentences that have opposite ideas	She lives far away. She always comes on time.	**Although** she lives far away, she always comes on time.
Because	Used when we have to express a reason or a cause	Lata Mangeshkar is my favourite singer. I love her voice.	Lata Mangeshkar is my favourite singer **because** I love her voice.
As		You work take an umbrella. It is going to rain today.	You should take an umbrella **as** it is going to rain today.
If	Used when there is a condition	You work hard for the prize. You will win the prize.	You will win the prize **if** you work hard for it.
Unless		It is raining outside. You have to go to school.	**Unless** it is raining outside, you have to go to school.

Correlative Conjunctions

Correlative conjunctions are pairs of words that work together to connect words of equal importance within a sentence. Some of these conjuctions are discussed below

Correlative Conjunction	Uses	Sentences	Sentences Combined using Conjunctions
Both….and	To combine two statements or qualities together	Kenneth scores well because he is hardworking. He scores well because he is intelligent.	Kenneth scores well because he is **both** hardworking **and** intelligent.
Either….or	To express a choice	I want to travel to Manali. I want to travel to Ladakh.	I want to travel to **either** Manali **or** Ladakh.
Neither…nor	To express that none of the choices can be taken	Meenal doesn't want to go into that room. Sheela doesn't want to go into that room.	**Neither** Meenal **nor** Sheela wants to go into that room.
Not only…but also	Referring to two Actions/things/people	Her dress is extraordinary. Her jewellery is extraordinary.	**Not only** her dress **but also** her jewellery is extraordinary.

PRACTICE EXERCISE

Objective and Subjective Questions

1. Choose the most appropriate conjunction from the options and fill in the blanks.

(i) The weather was cloudy, ... it was warm.
(a) yet (b) and (c) because (d) so

(ii) She was tired, ... she stayed up late to finish the project.
(a) and (b) but (c) yet (d) so

(iii) You can choose the red shirt .... the blue one.
(a) yet (b) and (c) or (d) but

(iv) The concert was rescheduled .... the lead singer fell ill.
(a) when (b) although (c) because (d) until

(v) He is not only a good musician .... also a talented painter.
(a) or (b) but (c) and (d) so

(vi) They waited patiently .... the show was about to start.
(a) and (b) since (c) for (d) but

(vii) We should leave now .... we miss the train.
(a) while (b) otherwise (c) yet (d) unless

(viii) .... you finish your vegetables, you won't get dessert.
(a) Before (b) Either...or (c) Unless (d) Although

(ix) I cannot accept anything .... perfection.
(a) yet (b) unless (c) but (d) before

(x) He is allergic to seafood ...., he enjoys sushi occasionally.
(a) however (b) unless (c) before (d) wherever

2. In the following sentences, the underlined conjunctions might or might not have been correctly used. Choose the most appropriate replacement from the options given below.

(i) We will start the meeting at 2 PM until everyone arrives.
(a) After (b) When (c) Since (d) Yet

(ii) As long as he finishes his homework, he can go out to play.
(a) When (b) If (c) Unless (d) While

(iii) I like both ice cream and cake, yet my brother prefers pie.
(a) For (b) Nor (c) But (d) Still

(iv) Even if she went to bed, she read a chapter of her favourite book.
(a) Although (b) While (c) Before (d) For

(v) She likes coffee a lot, and she prefers tea in the morning.
(a) But (b) Yet (c) Although (d) Neither

(vi) I'll finish my work early today until I can join you for lunch.
(a) While (b) So (c) Before (d) But

3. In the following sentences, conjunctions have been used incorrectly. Replace them with correct conjunctions and rewrite the sentences.

(i) It began to rain since we went indoors.
(ii) This is the school wherever I taught.
(iii) He has been studying for morning.
(iv) Work hard as well as you will fail.
(v) You can come after you like.
(vi) Ramesh is a physicist as Shyam is a politician.
(vii) He came here or gave me a postcard.
(viii) He worked so hard because his health broke down.
(ix) He made a mistake so he was pardoned.
(x) Don't talk as you are eating.

ANSWERS

1. (i) (a) yet (ii) (b) but (iii) (c) or
(iv) (c) because (v) (b) but (vi) (c) for
(vii) (b) otherwise (viii) (c) Unless
(ix) (c) but (x) (a) however

2. (i) (b) When (ii) (b) If (iii) (c) But
(iv) (c) Before (v) (b) Yet (vi) (b) So

3. (i) It began to rain so we went indoors.
(ii) This is the school where I taught.
(iii) He has been studying since morning.
(iv) Work hard otherwise you will fail.
(v) You can come whenever you like.
(vi) Ramesh is a physicist while/and Shyam is a politician.
(vii) He came here and gave me a postcard.
(viii) He worked so hard that his health broke down.
(ix) He made a mistake but/however he was pardoned.
(x) Don't talk while you are eating.

CHAPTER 12

Interjection

12.1 Definition of Interjection

Interjections are words or phrases that are used to express strong feelings or emotions. They add excitement or emphasis to sentences.

e.g.
- **Wow,** that's amazing!
- **Oh no,** I forgot my book!
- That was a close call, **phew**!
- The company achieved its quarterly targets, **remarkable**!

Interjections are used to express various emotions such as excitement, resignation, relief, frustration, and surprise etc.

(i) Interjections are often placed at the beginning or end of a sentence for emphasis.

(ii) Interjections are usually followed by an exclamation mark.

(iii) Interjections are majorly used in informal communication, and avoided in formal writing.

12.2 Kinds of Interjection

1. Interjection of Greeting
2. Interjection of Surprise
3. Interjection of Joy
4. Interjection of Sorrow
5. Interjection of Approval
6. Interjection of Attention

The following table will help us understand the different types of interjections along with examples.

Types of Interjection	Usage	Examples
Interjection of Greeting	Interjections of greeting are commonly used to initiate conversations or show courtesy in social interactions.	• Hello! How are you? • Good morning! • Thank you!
Interjection of Surprise	Interjections of surprise convey reaction to something unexpected or extraordinary.	• Wow! That was incredible! • Oh my goodness! I cannot believe you won the contest. • What! You got a pet elephant?
Interjection of Joy	Interjections of joy denotes to celebrateion of achievements, good news, or moments of happiness.	• Yay! We won the tournament. • Hooray! It is my birthday. • Woohoo! Chinu didi is coming to visit us.
Interjection of Sorrow	Interjections of sorrow convey feelings of empathy or disappointment.	• Alas! The storm was shattering. • Oh dear! I am so sorry about your loss! • Oh no! The concert got cancelled.
Interjection of Approval	Interjections of approval expresses achievements or positive actions.	• Bravo! That was an outstanding performance. • Well done! You aced the exam. • Excellent! I love your creativity.

Note it The list given above is not the complete list of interjections.

PRACTICE EXERCISE

Objective and Subjective Questions

1. Fill in the blanks with appropriate interjections.

(i) "........., I'm so excited about the news you just shared!"
(a) Wow (b) Ouch (c) Dear (d) Uh

(ii) "........., the movie was absolutely thrilling!"
(a) Well (b) Hurray
(c) Ah (d) Dear

(iii) "..........! That was a close call during the game."
(a) Ouch (b) Yippee (c) Alas (d) Wow

(iv) "........., I can't believe you solved the puzzle so quickly!"
(a) Well (b) Wow (c) Phew (d) Dear

(v) "..........! I forgot my umbrella on such a rainy day."
(a) Alas (b) Eh (c) Yikes (d) Hey

(vi) "......., I need your help with this challenging task."
(a) Yippee (b) Phew
(c) Uh (d) Hey

(vii) "That was a fantastic performance on stage, ...!"
(a) Wow (b) Hurray
(c) Eh (d) Amazing

(viii) "..........! I accidentally spilled my coffee all over my clothes."
(a) Well (b) Ouch (c) Dear (d) Hurray

(ix) "........., this surprise party is everything I could have asked for!"
(a) Wow (b) Uh (c) Dear (d) God

(x) "......., we finally reached the mountain's summit."
(a) Hurray (b) Ah (c) Dear (d) Wow

2. Identify the interjections in the following sentences.

(i) "Well, that's an unexpected turn of events!"
(a) 'events' (b) 'unexpected'
(c) 'an' (d) 'Well'

(ii) "Oh, what a beautiful sunset!"
(a) 'Oh' (b) 'a'
(c) 'beautiful' (d) 'sunset'

(iii) "Alas! I lost my keys again."
(a) 'keys' (b) 'my'
(c) 'lost' (d) 'Alas'

(iv) "Hey! Who left the window open in the rain?"
(a) 'open' (b) 'Hey'
(c) 'the' (d) 'left'

(v) "Yippee! The weekend is finally here."
(a) 'is' (b) 'here' (c) 'finally' (d) 'Yippee'

(vi) "Ouch! That was an unexpected bump in the road."
(a) 'Ouch' (b) 'unexpected'
(c) 'bump' (d) 'in'

(vii) "Phew! I thought I'd missed the last train."
(a) 'last' (b) 'I'd'
(c) 'Phew' (d) 'thought'

(viii) "Eh! Can you believe they found a treasure in the backyard?"
(a) 'Eh' (b) 'found'
(c) 'a' (d) 'backyard'

(ix) "Wow! That science experiment worked better than I thought."
(a) 'Wow' (b) 'better' (c) 'than' (d) 'worked'

(x) "Ah! I finally understood the solution to the math problem."
(a) 'to' (b) 'Ah'
(c) 'the' (d) 'understood'

3. Fill in the blanks with suitable interjections to complete the sentences.

(i) .... The team scored the winning goal in the final minute of the game.
(ii) .... Look who just arrived at the party.
(iii) .... I accidentally deleted the important email.
(iv) ...., did you see that incredible magic trick?
(v) ...., maybe we should reschedule the picnic.
(vi) ...., can I suggest something?
(vii) ...., I will have to sit for the exam again, I did not perform too well.
(viii) ...., I think somebody is coming this way.
(ix) .... We can sit with each other on the plane.
(x) .... You deserve this promotion.

4. Make sentences using the following interjections.

(i) Woohoo (ii) Ew
(iii) Agh (iv) Huh
(v) Whoops (vi) Awesome
(vii) Bravo (vii) My God
(ix) Oh well (x) Oh my

ANSWERS

1. (i) (a) Wow (ii) (a) Well
(iii) (c) Alas (iv) (b) Wow
(v) (c) Yikes (vi) (d) Hey
(vii) (d) Amazing (viii) (b) Ouch
(ix) (d) God (x) (a) Hurray

2. (i) (d) 'Well' (ii) (a) 'Oh'
(iii) (d) 'Alas' (iv) (b) 'Hey'
(v) (d) 'Yippee' (vi) (a) 'Ouch'
(vii) (c) 'Phew' (viii) (a) 'Eh'
(ix) (a) 'Wow' (x) (b) 'Ah'

3. (i) **Hurrah**! The team scored the winning goal in the final minute of the game.
(ii) **Hey**! Look who just arrived at the party.
(iii) **Oops**! I accidentally deleted the important email.
(iv) **Woah**, did you see that incredible magic trick?
(v) **Um**, maybe we should reschedule the picnic.
(vi) **Ahem**, can I suggest something?
(vii) **Oh well**, I will have to sit for the exam again, I did not perform too well.
(viii) **Shh**, I think somebody is coming this way.
(ix) **Awesome**! We can sit with each other on the plane.
(x) **Congratulations**! You deserve this promotion.

4. (i) Wohoo! I am going to Kerala.
(ii) Ew, that spoiled milk smells terrible.
(iii) Agh! I accidentally stepped on a thorn.
(iv) Huh, I didn't expect to see you here; what a surprise!
(v) Whoops, I spilled my drink on the table.
(vi) Oh, you found my jewellery, awesome!
(vii) The Indian players showed unmatched dedication in the Asian Games, bravo!
(viii) My God, the waiting line is longer than a river.
(ix) Oh-well, I guess it's time for a coffee break.
(x) Rupali looks so preety in that gown, oh my!

CHAPTER 13

Modals

13.1 Definition of Modals

Modal or modal auxiliaries are verbs that are used to express the mood or attitude of the speaker in different contexts.

They are used to express permission, ability, suggestion, possibility or necessity.

13.2 Kinds of Modal Verbs

1. Can

(i) To express ability

e.g. She **can** speak many languages.

(ii) To indicate permission

e.g. You **can** go to the market.

(iii) Suggesting a possibility

e.g. We **can** go to the park in the evening.

2. Could

(i) To express ability in the past

e.g. When I was younger, I **could** run very fast.

(ii) To express a possibility.

e.g. You **could** call customer service.

(iii) Polite request

e.g. **Could** I borrow your pen, please?

3. May

(i) To give permission

e.g. You **may** leave the classroom after you finish the work.

(ii) To suggest possibility

e.g. It **may** rain this evening.

(iii) Expressing a wish

e.g. **May** you get all the happiness in the world!

4. Might

(i) To suggest a weak possibility

e.g. I **might** go to the Taylor Swift concert.

5. Will

(i) To express future actions

e.g. I **will** meet you at the cafe at 4pm.

(ii) To express determination

e.g. I **will** finish my assignment by tonight.

(iii) To make a promise

e.g. I **will** help you with this chapter.

6. Would

(i) To ask a polite question

e.g. **Would** you mind closing the window?

7. Shall

(i) To express all future actions of the first person pronoun

e.g. We **shall** make pizza tonight.

8. Should

(i) To give advice

e.g. You **should** finish your work rather than using your mobile unnecessarily.

9. Must

(i) To indicate necessity or obligation

e.g. You **must** follow the rules of the school.

(ii) To express strong recommendation

e.g. You **must** pay attention to details to excel in any field.

PRACTICE EXERCISE

Objective and Subjective Questions

1. Choose the most appropriate modals from the options and fill in the blanks.

(i) As the magical potion bubbled in the cauldron, the witch cackled and said, "Drink it, and you .... gain unimaginable powers!"

(a) shall (b) would (c) can (d) must

(ii) The detective received an anonymous letter with a riddle that hinted at where the missing painting .... be hidden.

(a) would (b) could (c) must (d) may

(iii) The wise old owl advised the young owl that to become a great hunter, he .... be patient and observant.

(a) must (b) would (c) should (d) might

(iv) As the storm approached, the ship's captain knew they .... change course to avoid disaster.

(a) may (b) must (c) shall (d) could

(v) The superhero .... rescue the hostages from the evil villain's den.

(a) has to (b) should (c) will (d) could

(vi) The magical amulet glowed, indicating that the one who possessed it .... harness its power.

(a) can (b) must (c) may (d) will

(vii) The children .... play in the park if it doesn't rain.

(a) must (b) would (c) can (d) may

(viii) We .... visit the museum on Saturday if it's open.

(a) might (b) need to (c) can (d) would

(ix) The plane .... take off in a few minutes, so please make sure your seatbelt is fastened.

(a) will (b) may (c) should (d) must

(x) They .... have to reschedule the meeting if the client arrives late.

(a) might (b) need to (c) can (d) should

2. Indicate whether the following sentences are correct or not. If they are incorrect, rewrite them after correcting the mistake.

(i) Would I use your pen?

(ii) You might go now.

(iii) You could follow the school rules.

(iv) She will recite the Bible since she was seven.

(v) I should turn twenty-five tomorrow.

(vi) A soldier would serve their nation.

(vii) He has to like to visit Paris.

(viii) She has to speak three languages.

(ix) It could help if you started working out regularly.

(x) You should practise diligently if you want to score a 100%.

ANSWERS

1. (i) (a), (b) would/shall (ii) (b) could
   (iii) (c) should (iv) (b) must
   (v) (c) will (vi) (a) can
   (vii) (d) may (viii) (d) would
   (ix) (d) will (x) (a) might

2. (i) Could/May I use your pen?
   (ii) You may go now.
   (iii) You must follow the school rules.
   (iv) She could recite/has recited the Bible since she was seven.
   (v) I shall turn twenty-five tomorrow.
   (vi) A soldier should/must/ought to serve their nation.
   (vii) He would like to visit Paris.
   (viii) She can speak three languages.
   (ix) Correct
   (x) Correct

CHAPTER 14 Tenses

14.1 Definition of Tenses

Tenses are verb forms that are used to express the time of an action in a sentence.

e.g.
- I **am going** to the library. (Present Tense)
- They **went** to the movies. (Past Tense)
- My sister **will bake** a pizza. (Future Tense)

In the above sentences, a verb shows actions happening in three different time.

14.2 Kinds of Tense

Tenses can be classified into three basic kinds.

Present Tense

The present tense is the form of a verb that is used to show the action that takes place in the present time.

e.g.
- She **plays** the piano every morning.
- They **are playing** football in the park.
- **I have visited** Paris three times in my life.
- They **have been studying** for the exam for three hours.

Present tense can further be classified into following types

Simple Present Tense

The simple present tense is used to state an action that is happening in the present time. It is also used for an action that happens regularly or universal fact.

Structure of a Sentence in Simple Present Tense

Singular subject + V_1 (base form of verb) + -s/-es + object
Plural subject + V_1 + object

e.g.
- She **writes** with a pen.
- We **play** in the park.

Negative Sentence

Singular subject + does not + V_1 (s/es) + Object
Plural object + does not + V_1 + Object

e.g.
- She **does not write** with a pen.
- We **do not play** in the park.

Uses of Simple Present Tense

1. To state a habitual action or actions done repeatedly It talks about actions in a general way.

e.g.
- I **cycle** to school everyday.
- I **get up** at 5 am.

2. To state a planned future action

e.g. • Tom **leaves** for Oxford tomorrow.

• The college **reopens** in July.

3. To state universal truths

e.g. • Nehru **is** the architect of modern India.

• The Earth **revolves** around the Sun.

Present Continuous Tense

The present continuous tense is used for actions which are taking place at the time of speaking.

Structure of a sentence in present continuous tense

Subject + is/am/are + V_1 + '– ing' + Object

e.g. • We **are playing** badminton.

• I **am reading** a newspaper.

Negative Sentence

Subject + is/am/are + not + V_1 + ing + Object

e.g. • **I am not meeting** Mukul

• They **are not working**

Uses of Present Continuous Tense

1. When we talk about an action that is in progress in the present time.

e.g. • She **is pleading** in the court.

• They **are driving** to the mall.

2. When we talk about a planned future action.

e.g. • She **is going** to publish her book next year.

• She **is speaking** at the conference.

3. When we planned or arranged to do things in future but not necessarily at present time.

e.g. • **I am transferring** to a new location.

• We **are going** to the new Tom Hanks' movie.

Present Perfect Tense

The present perfect tense tells us about an action that has been completed in the present and whose effects are still there.

Structure of a sentence in present perfect tense

1. Singular subject + has/have + V_3 (past participle form of verb) + object

e.g. • I **have lost** my exercise book.

• She **has worked** hard for this job.

Negative Sentence

Subject + has/have + not + V_3 + Object

e.g. • Reeta **has not** answered this question

• They **have not** done the work.

Uses of Present Perfect Tense

When the action began in the past and is still continuing in the present time.

e.g. • How long **have you waited** for the bus?

• **I have lived** here for two years.

When the exact time of an action is not known.

e.g. • They **have visited** the museum many times.

• Ambika **has washed** her hair.

Present Perfect Continuous Tense

The present perfect continuous form of a verb tells that an action started in the past and is still continuing in the present.

Structure of a sentence in present perfect tense

+ has/have been + V_1 + '–ing' + object

e.g. • **I have been studying** for 5 hours.

• They **have been watching** the stars.

Negative Sentence

Subject + has/have + not + been + V_1 + '–ing' + object

e.g. • She **has not been driving** her car these days.

• **I have not been dealing** with the work pressure greatly.

Uses of Present Perfect Continuous Tense

1. It is often used with 'for', 'how long...' and 'since'.

e.g. • How long **have you been teaching** the senior secondary?

• You and **I have been coming** to this temple since childhood.

Past Tense

The past tense form of a verb shows that the action has already taken place in the past.

e.g. • Indira Gandhi **passed** away in 1984.

• I **saw** him in the morning.

• Radhika **had been** calling her.

A verb in the past tense takes four different forms. These forms are

Simple Past Tense

The simple past tense shows actions that are completed at a specified time in the past.

Structure of a sentence in simple past tense

Subject + V_2 (past form of verb) + object

e.g. • I **ate** break fast.

• We **saw** him at the market.

Negative Sentence

Subject + did not + V_1 + Object

e.g. • I **didn't see** him at the market.
- We **didn't eat** breakfast.

Uses of Simple Past Tense

1. When we want to express actions that took place at a specific time and are over now.
   e.g. • She **visited** the museum last Saturday.
   - We **visited** the Grand Canyon during our summer vacation.
2. When we want to express past habits.
   e.g. • She **played** the piano every evening when she was a child.
   - They always **went** for a walk after dinner.

Past Continuous Tense

The past continuous tense is used to describe actions or events that were ongoing or in progress at a specific point in the past.

Structure of a sentence in past continuous tense

Subject + was/were + V_1-ing + object

e.g. • **I was studying** when the phone rang.
- The children **were playing.**

Negative sentence

Subject + was/were not + V_1-ing + object

e.g. • He **was not working** on the assignment last night.
- She **was not sleeping** when I went to her room.

Uses of Past Continuous Tense

1. When we talk about an action to indicate that one action was ongoing while another action happened. (Interrupted actions)
   e.g. • As they **were discussing** the plan, the bus arrived.
   - We **were having** dinner when the power went out.
2. To indicate parallel actions happening in the past
   e.g. • While I **was cleaning** the house, he was gardening.
   - They **were chatting** while waiting for the bus.
3. To describe background events
   e.g. • The Sun **was setting** as they walked along the beach.
   - The birds **were chirping** while the Sun was setting.

Past Perfect Tense

The past perfect tense is used to describe actions that were completed in the past.

Structure of a sentence in past perfect tense

Subject + had + V_3 + object

e.g. • I realised I **had forgotten** my keys when I reached the office.
- They **had already left** by the time we arrived.
- She **had finished** her book before the movie started.

Negative Sentence

Subject + had not + V_3 + object

e.g. • He **had not completed** the assignment when the deadline arrived.
- They **hadn't seen** each other for years before the reunion.

Uses of Past Perfect Tense

1. Actions completed before another action in the past
   e.g. • They **had finished** their meal before the guests arrived.
   - He **had already read** the book before the movie was released.
2. When narrating events in the past
   e.g. • By the time we reached the airport, the flight **had already** taken off.
   - When he arrived at the party, the guests **had already left**.

Past Perfect Continuous Tense

The past perfect continuous tense is used to describe actions or events that were ongoing over a period of time and completed in the past.

Structure of a sentence in past perfect continuous tense

Subject + had been + V_1-ing + object

e.g. • She was out of breath because she **had been running** before she arrived.
- They were tired because they **had been working** on the project all day.
- He realised he was late because the meeting **had been going** on for hours.

Negative Sentence

Subject + had not been + V_1-ing + object

e.g. • I was surprised that he **had not been studying** for the exam.
- She was rested because she **hadn't been travelling** for days.

Uses of Past Perfect Continuous Tense

1. To emphasise the duration of an action

e.g. • He was sore because he **had been exercising** vigorously.

• The garden looked beautiful because she **had been planting** flowers.

2. Actions ongoing before another action

e.g. • They were in a hurry because the bus **had been waiting** for a while.

• She felt accomplished because the project **had been progressing** steadily.

3. To describe the cause of a situation in the past

e.g. • They were out of breath because they **had been running** to catch the train.

• She was well-prepared because she **had been studying** diligently.

Future Tense

A future tense form of a verb shows that an action will happen in the future or at a later point in time.

e.g. • I **shall be joining** the congregation on Sunday.

• We **will go** to the market tomorrow.

• **Will** you **come** to the library with me?

• **Will** Mansi **be performing** this year?

A verb in the future tense takes four different forms. These forms are

Simple Future Tense

The simple future tense is used to express actions or states that will occur in the future.

Structure of a sentence in simple future tense

Subject + will/shall + V_1(base form of the verb) + Object

e.g. • I **will visit** my grandparents next weekend.

• They **shall complete** the project by the end of the month.

• She **will start** her new job on Monday.

Negative Sentence

Subject + will/shall not + V_1(base form of the verb) + object

e.g. • He **will not** attend the meeting tomorrow.

• We **shall not** forget your birthday.

Uses of Simple Future Tense

1. To describe predictions and future events

e.g. • The company **will launch** a new product next year.

• I think it **will rain** later in the day.

2. To describe spontaneous decisions

e.g. • I'm cold; I **will close** the window.

• The phone is ringing; I **will answer** it.

3. To describe promises and offers

e.g. • I **will help** you with your homework.

• She **shall lend** you her umbrella.

4. To show intentions and plans

e.g. • We **will travel** to Europe next summer.

• He **will study** for the exam over the weekend.

Future Continuous Tense

The future continuous tense is used to describe actions or events that will be ongoing at a specified time in the future.

Structure of a sentence in future continuous tense

Subject + will/shall + be + V_1-ing + object

e.g. • This time tomorrow, I **will be working** on a presentation.

• By 5 pm, they **will be celebrating** their anniversary.

• She **will be studying** when you arrive.

Negative Sentence

Subject + will/shall not + be + V_1-ing + object

e.g. • He **will not be attending** the seminar at that time.

• We **shall not be travelling** during the holidays.

Uses of Future Continuous Tense

1. Predicting ongoing actions

e.g. • I'm sure **she will be studying** when we call.

• They **will be rehearsing** for the play in the evening.

2. Future interruptions

e.g. • I **will be cooking** dinner when you come home.

• They **will be discussing** the plan when the boss arrives.

3. To express politeness or courtesy

e.g. • I **will be waiting** for your call.

• She **will be hosting** the event next week.

Future Perfect Tense

The future perfect tense is used to express actions or events that will be completed before a specific point in the future.

Structure of a sentence in future perfect tense

Subject + will/shall + have + V_3 + object

e.g. • By the time you arrive, I **will have finished** my work.

• She **will have graduated** by the end of the year.

• They **will have completed** the project before the deadline.

Negative Sentence

Subject + will/shall not + have + V_3 + object

e.g. • I **will not have forgotten** your birthday by then.
• They **will not have completed** the construction by next month.

Uses of Future Perfect Tense

1. Predictions about the completion of an action

   e.g. • I'm confident that they **will have solved** the problem by tomorrow.
   • She believes she **will have learned** the language by next year.

2. Expressing hopes, expectations, or assumptions

   e.g. • I hope you **will have finished** the report by the deadline.
   • They expect that the construction **will have completed** by the scheduled date.

3. Referring to an unfinished action at a specific future time

   e.g. • By the time the movie starts, we **will have been waiting** for an hour.
   • They **will have been working** on the project for months when it's finally completed.

Future Perfect Continuous Tense

The future perfect continuous tense is used to describe actions or events that will have been ongoing for a duration before a specific point in the future.

Structure of a sentence in future perfect continuous tense

Subject + will/shall + have been + V_1-ing + object

e.g. • By next summer, I **will have been living** in this city for five years.
• By the time you arrive, we **will have been working** on the project for three hours.
• She **will have been practising** the piano for a decade by her next concert.

Negative Sentence

Subject + will/shall not + have been + V_1-ing + object

e.g. • I **will not have been waiting** for long when you get here.
• By next month, they **will not have been renovating** the house for a year.

Uses of Future Perfect Continuous Tense

1. For emphasising the duration of an ongoing action

   e.g. • By the time you arrive, I **will have been waiting for** two hours.
   • She **will have been studying for** the exam all day by tomorrow.

2. For predicting ongoing actions leading to a point in the future

   e.g. • I believe they **will have been travelling** for months by the time they reach their destination.
   • She thinks she **will have been working** at the company for five years by her next promotion.

3. For expressing assumptions or expectations about ongoing actions

   e.g. • We **will have been preparing** for the party by the time the guests arrive.
   • They expect that she **will have been training** for the marathon for several months.

PRACTICE EXERCISE

Objective and Subjective Questions

1. Select the appropriate form of the present tense (simple, continuous, perfect, or perfect continuous) to complete each sentence.

(i) She .... on this project since last month.

(a) works (b) is working
(c) has been working (d) worked

(ii) The children .... outside when it started raining.

(a) play (b) plays
(c) were playing (d) have played

(iii) By this time next week, I .... my assignment.

(a) complete (b) will have completed
(c) have completed (d) am completing

(iv) How long .... you .... for the upcoming exam?

(a) do, study (b) are, studying
(c) have, studied (d) did, study

(v) I .... sushi before today.

(a) not eat (b) do not eat
(c) have not eaten (d) am not eating

(vi) **By the time you arrive, I .... my work.**

(a) already finish (b) will have already finished

(c) am already finishing (d) already finished

(vii) **We usually .... to the gym on Mondays.**

(a) go (b) goes

(c) are going (d) have gone

(viii) **He .... a novel for the past six months.**

(a) writes (b) has been writing

(c) has written (d) wrote

(ix) **They .... in that house since they got married.**

(a) live (b) lives

(c) are living (d) have been living

(x) **Right now, she .... a book in the garden.**

(a) reads (b) is reading

(c) has read (d) read

2. Select the appropriate form of the past tense (simple, continuous, perfect, or perfect continuous) to complete each sentence.

(i) **The artist .... the beauty of the sunset in his painting.**

(a) captured (b) was capturing

(c) had captured (d) had been capturing

(ii) **She .... goodness wherever she went.**

(a) spread (b) was spreading

(c) had spread (d) had been spreading

(iii) **The soldier .... his loyalty to his country.**

(a) showed (b) was showing

(c) had shown (d) had been showing

(iv) **Time .... quickly while we were having fun.**

(a) passed (b) was passing

(c) had passed (d) had been passing

(v) **The musician .... his talent at the concert.**

(a) displayed (b) was displaying

(c) had displayed (d) had been displaying

(vi) **She .... her skills to fix the problem.**

(a) used (b) was using

(c) had used (d) had been using

(vii) **The city .... a lot over the years.**

(a) changed (b) was changing

(c) had changed (d) had been changing

(viii) **They .... the tradition every year.**

(a) followed

(b) were following

(c) had followed

(d) had been following

3. Select the appropriate form of the future tense (simple, continuous, perfect, or perfect continuous) to complete each sentence.

(i) **I .... to the market tomorrow.**

(a) will go (b) will be going

(c) will have gone (d) will have been going

(ii) **By the time you arrive, the party ....**

(a) will start (b) will be starting

(c) will have started (d) will have been starting

(iii) **This time next week, I .... on a beach in Hawaii.**

(a) will sit (b) will be sitting

(c) will have sat (d) will have been sitting

(iv) **I .... my homework by dinner time.**

(a) will finish (b) will be finishing

(c) will have finished (d) will have been finishing

(v) **Don't call me at 9pm because I .... the football match.**

(a) will watch (b) will be watching

(c) will have watched (d) will have been watching

(vi) **By the time we get to the cinema, the movie ....**

(a) will start (b) will be starting

(c) will have started (d) will have been starting

(vii) **I .... at this company for 10 years next month.**

(a) will work (b) will be working

(c) will have worked (d) will have been working

(viii) **By the time you wake up, I .... for work.**

(a) will leave (b) will be leaving

(c) will have left (d) will have been leaving

(ix) **This time tomorrow, we .... to New York.**

(a) will fly (b) will be flying

(c) will have flown (d) will have been flying

(x) **I .... (do) all the housework by the time you get home.**

(a) will do (b) will be doing

(c) will have done (d) will have been doing

4. Read the sentences and tick the option in the bracket which uses the correct future tense form.

(i) By the time we graduate, artificial intelligence will .... (transform/be transforming/have transformed) the world.

(ii) I'm sure they will .... (plant/be planting/have planted) a thousand trees by the end of this month.

(iii) This time tomorrow, the detective will .... (solve/be solving/have solved) the mystery.

(iv) Don't disturb me at 5 pm because I will .... (participate/be participating/have participated) in a social awareness campaign.

(v) By the time the clock strikes twelve, Cinderella will .... (return/be returning/have returned) to her old self.

(vi) Will .... (you argue/you be arguing/you have argued) your case by the time the jury arrives?

(vii) I will .... (not be meeting/not have been meeting) you today, let us catch up some other day.

(viii) By the time we finish our discussion, the diplomats will .... (negotiate/be negotiating/have negotiated) a peace treaty.

(ix) She (has study/studies) Economics at the University.

(x) I (have been waiting/have waiting) for the rain to come.

(xi) He (have been travelling/has been travelling) around the world for a year now.

(xii) The sun (is rising/rises) in the east every morning.

(xiii) My friend (is having/has) a party next weekend.

(xiv) We (are knowing/know) the answer to the question.

(xv) The baby (is crying/cries) because it's hungry.

(xvi) They (are discussing/discuss) the project in the conference room.

(xvii) The train (is leaving/leaves) at 8 PM tonight.

(xviii) She (have/has) a pet dog named Max.

ANSWERS

1. (i) (c) has been working
(ii) (c) were playing
(iii) (b) will have completed
(iv) (c) have, studied
(v) (c) have not eaten
(vi) (b) will have already finished
(vii) (a) go
(viii) (b) has been writing
(ix) (d) have been living
(x) (b) is reading

2. (i) (a) captured (ii) (a) spread
(iii) (c) had shown (iv) (c) had passed
(v) (a) displayed (vi) (a) used
(vii) (c) had changed (viii) (d) had been following

3. (i) (a) will go (ii) (c) will have started
(iii) (b) will be sitting (iv) (c) will have finished
(v) (b) will be watching (vi) (c) will have started
(vii) (c) will have worked (viii) (c) will have left
(ix) (b) will be flying (x) (c) will have done

4. (i) have transformed (ii) have planted
(iii) be solving (iv) be participating
(v) have returned (vi) you be arguing
(vii) not be meeting (viii) be negotiating
(ix) studies (x) have been waiting
(xi) has been travelling (xii) rises
(xiii) is having (xiv) know
(xv) is crying (xvi) are discussing
(xvii) leaves (xviii) has

Subject-Verb Agreement

CHAPTER 15

15.1 Definition of Subject-verb Agreement

In a sentence, a verb must agree with its subject in number and person. This is called subject-verb agreement.

e.g. • Ridhi and Sanvika **teach** underprivileged kids.
• Rajni **works** at a paper company.

15.2 Rules for Subject-verb Agreement

There are some rules that should be followed to ensure that a sentence is grammatically correct. These rules are

(i) If the subject is singular, it takes a singular verb and if the subject is plural, it takes a plural verb.

e.g. • Rohan **wakes** up early in the morning.
• Riya and Diya **are** friends.

(ii) When two or more nouns are joined by the conjunction 'and', a plural verb is used.

e.g. The doctors and Rani **are** going to attend the seminar.

(iii) When there are two subjects but they refer to one idea, a singular verb is used.

e.g. Peanut butter and jelly **is** my favourite breakfast.

(iv) When two or more singular nouns are joined by 'or' or 'nor', a singular verb is used.

e.g. A pen or a pencil **is** mandatory to be carried into the seminar.

(v) Two subjects connected by either/or, or neither/nor require a singular or plural verb depending on the subject that comes later.

e.g. • Either Jane or Mary **is** going to qualify for the semi finals.
• Neither the diary nor the pens **are** on the rack

(vi) Uncountable nouns take a singular verb.

e.g. The time for the inauguration of the magazine **has** come.

(vii) The words here, there, and where are not subjects. They introduce a sentence in inverted order. The verb must agree with the subject of a sentence.

e.g. Here **are** the documents you asked for. (Here, 'documents' is the subject of the sentence)

(viii) A singular verb must be used with the singular indefinite pronouns, each, neither, either, anyone, everyone, no one, someone, anybody, everybody, nobody, somebody, anything, everything, nothing, and something.

e.g. Nobody **has** brought their car.

(ix) Some subjects, although they might appear plural (eg. News, Gymnastics, Physics, Statistics etc.) are singular in meaning and take a singular verb.

e.g. Measles **is** the only childhood disease I haven't had.

(x) A singular verb is generally used after words denoting an amount (time, money, measurement, weight, volume).

e.g. 100 kgs **is** an unhealthy weight for anybody.

(xi) Titles of books, magazines and films take singular verbs, even if they contain plural nouns.

e.g. The Birds **is** a movie from 1963.

PRACTICE EXERCISE

Objective and Subjective Questions

1. Choose which of the following sentences is grammatically correct.

(i) (a) Gold and silver are precious metals.
(b) Gold or silver are precious metals.
(c) Gold and silver is precious metal.
(d) Gold and silver is precious metals.

(ii) (a) Bread and the butter is his only food.
(b) Bread and butter is his only food.
(c) Bread and butter are his only food.
(d) None of the above

(iii) (a) Neither of them wants to attends the wedding.
(b) Neither of them want to attends the wedding.
(c) Neither of them wants to attend the wedding.
(d) Neither of them want to attend the wedding.

(iv) (a) Pasta and salad go well together for a light lunch.
(b) Pasta and salad goes well together for a light lunch.
(c) Pasta and salad go well together for light lunch.
(d) None of the above

(v) (a) There is a opportunity for you to excel in this project.
(b) There is an opportunities for you to excel in this project.
(c) There is opportunities for you to excel in this project.
(d) There is an opportunity for you to excel in this project.

(vi) (a) Today's breaking news is horrible.
(b) Today's breaking news are horrible.
(c) Today's breaking new is horrible.
(d) Today's breaking news' are horrible.

(vii) (a) Tom and Jerry is good friends who often go fishing together.
(b) Tom and Jerry is good friends who often goes fishing together.
(c) Tom and Jerry are good friends who often goes fishing together.
(d) Tom and Jerry are good friends who often go fishing together.

(viii) (a) The Arabian Nights is still great favourite.
(b) The Arabian Nights is still a great favourite.
(c) The Arabian Nights are still a great favourite.
(d) The Arabian Nights are still great favourites.

2. Fill in the blanks with the correct verbs from the brackets.

(i) How many cups of coffee .... (do/does) your colleague drink every morning?

(ii) Neither the flowers nor the trees .... (needs/need) additional watering today.

(iii) There .... (was/were) a loud noise coming from the basement.

(iv) How often .... (do/does) he .... (travel/travels) for work?

(v) The team of researchers .... (is/are) conducting experiments in the lab.

(vi) Which colour .... (do/does) you .... (prefer/prefers) for the bedroom walls?

(vii) Both my brother and my sister .... (is/are) interested in photography.

(viii) There .... (is/are) a problem and a solution to be discussed at the meeting.

(ix) How many students .... (participate/participates) in the school's chess club?

(x) The concert tickets .... (has/have) already been purchased.

(xi) Either the red car or the blue car .... (needs/need) a new paint job.

(xii) There .... (was/were) a delay in the train schedule this morning.

(xiii) Which of these dishes .... (taste/tastes) the best?

(xiv) Neither the cat nor the dog .... (likes/like) to be left alone at home.

(xv) How many countries .... (do/does/did) you (visit/visits) during your last vacation?

3. Rewrite the sentences after correcting the sentences which have errors. If no error is present, write 'no error'.

(i) A centennial are a long time to revoke regressive laws.

(ii) Money be not the only factor in job satisfaction.

(iii) The choir practise every Thursday evening

(iv) The audience are eager to see the performance.

(v) Fish and chips are classic British meal.

(vi) $50 are too expensive for that item.

(vii) 'The Avengers' are blockbuster film featuring superheroes.

(viii) Both students are prepared for the exam.

(ix) Eight hours is a enough time to finish this task.

(x) News travel quickly in the age of social media

ANSWERS

1. (i) (a) Gold and silver are precious metals.

(ii) (b) Bread and butter is his only food.

(iii) (c) Neither of them wants to attend the wedding.

(iv) (a) Pasta and salad go well together for a light lunch.

(v) (d) There is an opportunity for you to excel in this project.

(vi) (a) Today's breaking news is horrible.

(vii) (d) Tom and jerry are good friends who often go fishing together.

(viii) (b) The Arabian Nights is still a great favourite.

2. (i) does (ii) need

(iii) was (iv) does, travel

(v) is (vi) do, prefer

(vii) are (viii) is

(ix) participate (x) have

(xi) needs (xii) was

(xiii) tastes (xiv) likes

(xv) did, visit

3. (i) A centennial is a long time to revoke regressive laws.

(ii) Money is not the only factor in job satisfaction.

(iii) The choir practises every Thursday evening

(iv) The audience is eager to see the performance.

(v) Fish and chips is a classic British meal.

(vi) $50 is too expensive for that item.

(vii) 'The Avengers' is a blockbuster film featuring superheroes.

(viii) No error

(ix) Eight hours is enough time to finish this task.

(x) News travels quickly in the age of social media.

CHAPTER 16 Active and Passive Voice

16.1 Voice

Voice tells us whether the subject of the sentence is doing the action, or is the receiver of the action.

The change in voice is basically a change in the form of the main verb in the sentence.

e.g. • Meera is **preparing** a delicious meal. (Active voice)

• A delicious meal is **being prepared** by Meera. (Passive Voice)

In the first sentence, 'Meera' is the subject of the sentence, and she is doing the action of 'preparing a delicious meal'.

In the second sentence, the subject is 'a delicious meal' which is receiving the action of 'being prepared'.

16.2 Kinds of Voices

1. Active Voice 2. Passive Voice

Active Voice

When the verb shows that the subject does the action, the verb is said to be in the active voice.

e.g. • Rakhi teaches little children.

• The electrician repaired the AC.

In active voice, the emphasis is on the doer.

Passive Voice

When the verb shows that the subject receives the action, the verb is said to be in the passive voice.

e.g. • Little children are taught by Rakhi.
• The AC was repaired by the electrician.

In passive voice, the emphasis is on the action done.

Therefore, sometimes the doer of the action might not be mentioned.

e.g. • I **was told** not to talk in the class.
• The thieves **have been arrested.**

Rules for Converting Active Voice into Passive Voice

(i) The subject of a sentence in active voice becomes the object of a sentence in the passive voice. In the passive form, the said subject is preceded with a 'by'.

e.g. • **The pilot flew the plane** safely. (Active)
The plane **was flown** safely **by the pilot.** (Passive)
• **She wrote** a letter to the government. (Active)
A letter to the government **was written by her.** (Passive)

(ii) The main verb in the active voice is converted into past participle form in the passive voice.

e.g. • They are **building** a new mall. (Active)
• A new mall **is being built** (by them). (Passive)
• Shreeja is **eating** an apple.
• An apple is **being eaten** by Shreeja.

(iii) If a sentence in the active voice contains a modal verb, the word 'be' is added after the modal verb in passive voice.

e.g. • Harsh **will** cook dinner tonight. (Active)
• The dinner **will be** cooked by Harsh tonight. (Passive)
• They **might** attend the environmental conference.
• The environmental conference **might be** attended by them.

(iv) If a sentence contains a preposition after the verb, it is maintained in its passive voice.

e.g. • Someone **broke into** the shop. (Active)
• The shop **was broken into.** (Passive)

(v) Personal pronouns are changed while converting a sentence from active to passive voice in the following manner.

Active Voice		Passive Voice
I	→	Me
He	→	Him
She	→	Her
They	→	Them
We	→	Us
Who	→	Whom
It	→	It
You	→	You

Change in Tense

(vi) When we convert a sentence from active to passive voice or vice versa, the tense of the verb undergoes a change as well. Study the table given below.

Present Tense			
Tense	**Active voice** Sentence Structure	**Passive voice** Sentence Structure	**Examples**
Simple Present	V_1 +s/es	is/am/are + V_3	She **cooks** dinner. (Active) Dinner **is cooked** by her (Passive)
Present Continuous	is/am/are + -ing form of verb	is/am/are + being + V_3	**I am writing** an essay. (Active) An essay **is being written** by me. (Passive)
Present Perfect	has/have + V_3	has/have + been + V_3	The team **has won** the game. (Active) The game **has been won** by the team. (Passive)

Past Tense			
Tense	**Active voice** Sentence Structure	**Passive voice** Sentence Structure	**Examples**
Simple Past	V_2	was/were + V_3	She **played** the piano. (Active) Piano **was played** by her. (Passive)

Tense	Active voice Sentence Structure	Passive voice Sentence Structure	Examples
Past Continuous	was/were + -ing form of verb	was/were + being + V_3	She **was reading** a book. (Active) A book **was being read** by her. (Passive)
Pst Perfect	had + V_3	had + been + V_3	He **had fixed** the car. (Active) The car **had been fixed** by him. (Passive)

Future Tense

Tense	Active voice Sentence Structure	Passive voice Sentence Structure	Examples
Simple Future	shall/will + verb	shall/will + be + V_3	He **will buy** a car in a few months. (Active) A car **will be bought** by him in a few months. (Passive)
Future Perfect	shall/will + have + V_3	shall/will + have been + V_3	I **will have written** the report by tonight. (Active) The report **will have been written** by tonight. (Passive)

PRACTICE EXERCISE

Objective and Subjective Questions

1. Choose which of the following sentences is in the correct passive voice.

(i) (a) The matter should be looked into more closely.
(b) They are renovating the old house.
(c) Put on your shoes before going out.

(ii) (a) An important issue was being share during the meeting.
(b) Hari is helping Ram.
(c) I was woken up by the sun.

(iii) (a) An old temple was seen.
(b) Hockey players are arriving.
(c) The wind blows strongly

(iv) (a) The book is in the box.
(b) The rules are followed by everyone.
(c) The store was went to by me.

(v) (a) The books are reading by everyone
(b) I need to pick up some food from the restaurant.
(c) The offer was turned down by her.

2. Choose which of the following sentences is in the correct active voice that can be converted into passive voice.

(i) (a) You will have started the practice.
(b) The postman has to deliver the letter.
(c) The marathon is run.

(ii) (a) Monkeys like bananas.
(b) The most consumed drink is coffee.
(c) The metal rods were corroded over time.

(iii) (a) Regulations must be respected.
(b) The rehearsal time must be abided by.
(c) She is learning to play guitar.

(iv) (a) The toys are being played by the boys.
(b) The organisers have been working hard.
(c) She wrote a heartfelt message on her friend's birthday.

(v) (a) The sunset is beautiful.
(b) The teacher can explain difficult concepts easily.
(c) Yoga class is attending by them.

3. Change the voice of the following sentences as directed.

(i) The police arrested the dacoits. (Passive voice)
(ii) Columbus discovered America about 500 years ago. (Passive voice)
(iii) The cat drank all the milk. (Passive voice)
(iv) We saw you and Seema. (Passive voice)
(v) I shall order the carriage. (Passive voice)
(vi) The fear shall be overcome by us. (Active voice)
(vii) You will be remembered by the world. (Active voice)
(viii) Your health should be taken care of. (Active voice)
(ix) The audience is enamoured by the concert. (Active voice)
(x) The grasslands are roamed by several animals. (Active voice)

Past Continuous Tense → Past Perfect Continuous Tense

e.g. • Rumi said,"**I was cooking** when the show started." (Direct Speech)
• Rumi said that she **had been cooking** when the show started. (Indirect Speech)

Note It : Past Perfect and Past Perfect Continuous Tense do not undergo any change.

Change in Future Tense

In the sentences containing Future tense, verbs in the double quotation marks, 'will' and 'shall' change to 'would' and 'should', respectively.

e.g. • Rajesh said, "I will go to the store after work." (Direct Speech)
• Rajesh said that he would go to the store after work. (Indirect Speech)

If the words spoken by the speaker are a universal truth or habitual fact, the tense does not change.

e.g. • He said, "the Sun rises in the East." (Direct Speech)
• He said that the Sun rises in the East. (Indirect Speech)

Change in Pronouns

The pronouns are changed according to the speaker(s) and listener(s) present in the speech.

(i) First person pronouns in reported speech are changed in accordance with the subject of the reporting verb.

e.g. • She said, "I will wash the utensils." (Direct Speech)
• She said that she would wash the utensils. (Indirect Speech)

(ii) Second person pronouns in the reported speech are changed in accordance with the object of the reporting verb.

e.g. • The guard said to me, "Your package will be delivered to your flat." (Direct Speech)
• The guard informed me that my package would be delivered to my flat. (Indirect Speech)

(iii) Third person pronouns in the reported speech do not change.

e.g. • Anjali said, "He will be on leave during his exams." (Direct Speech)
• Anjali told me that he would be on leave during his exams. (Indirect Speech)

Indicators of Time

Now	→	Then
Ago	→	Before
Thus	→	So
Today	→	That day
Tonight	→	That night
Tomorrow	→	The next day
Yesterday	→	The day before /The previous day
Last Night/Week	→	The night/week before
Next Week/Year	→	The following week/year

Indicators of Place

Here	→	There
This	→	That
These	→	Those

e.g. • He said, "I will be **here tomorrow**."
• He said that he would be **there the next day**.
• She said, "I am glad to be **here tonight**."
• She said that I was glad to be **there that night**.

Change in Modals

If the reporting speech contains a modal verb, it also undergoes a change, as given below

Can changes into could

e.g. • She said, "I **can** swim across the lake." (Direct Speech)
• She said that she **could** swim across the lake. (Indirect Speech)

May changes into Might

e.g. • She asked, "**May** I use your phone?" (Direct Speech)
• She asked if she **might** use my phone. (Indirect Speech)

PRACTICE EXERCISE

Objective and Subjective Questions

1. Choose which of the verbs given in options can be used in the following sentences.

(i) The teacher said, "The Earth rotates from West to East."

The teacher said that the Earth .... from West to East.

(a) rotate (b) rotated (c) rotates (d) is rotating

(ii) Rani said that she had decided to learn Spanish. Rani said, "I .... to learn Spanish."

(a) had decided (b) have decided
(c) decided (d) am decided

(iii) He says, "I go to the temple every morning."

He says that he .... to the temple every morning.

(a) go (b) went (c) goes (d) is going

(iv) Sikander said, "I wish to climb Mount Everest one day."

Sikander said that he .... to climb Mount Everest one day.

(a) wish (b) wished (c) is wishing (d) wishes

(v) He asked, "Will you listen to me?"

He asked if I .... to him.

(a) would listen (b) will listen
(c) listened (d) will be listening

2. Choose the correct reported speech of the given sentences.

(i) "They never miss their morning jog," he observes.

(a) He observes that they never miss their morning jog.
(b) He observed that they never miss their morning jog.
(c) He observed that they don't miss their morning jog.
(d) He is observing that they don't miss their morning jog.

(ii) "She had studied for hours before taking the final exam," the teacher said.

(a) The teacher said that she has studied for hours before taking the final exam.
(b) The teacher said that she had studied for hours before taking the final exam.
(c) The teacher says that she had been studying for hours before taking the final exam.
(d) The teacher says that she has been studying for hours before taking the final exam.

(iii) "I believe in living a healthy lifestyle," she asserts.

(a) She asserts that she believes in living a healthy lifestyle.
(b) She asserts that she believes in living a healthy lifestyle.
(c) She asserted that she believed in living a healthy lifestyle.
(d) She asserts that she believed in living a healthy lifestyle.

(iv) "We were watching a movie when the storm began," she recalled.

(a) She recalled that they were watching a movie when the storm began.
(b) She recalls that we were watching a movie when the storm began.
(c) She recalled that they had been watching a movie when the storm began.
(d) She recalled that they are watching a movie when the storm began.

(v) "I'm going to a concert tonight," she said with excitement.

(a) She said that she is going to a concert that night.
(b) She said with excitement that she was going to a concert that night.
(c) She says with excitement that she is going to a concert that night.
(d) She said with excitement that she goes to a concert that night.

(vi) "Now is the perfect time to start that home renovation project," the contractor suggested.

(a) The contractor suggests that now is the perfect time to start that home renovation project.
(b) The contractor suggested that now was the perfect time to start that home renovation project.
(c) The contractor suggested that then was the perfect time to start that home renovation project.
(d) The contractor suggested that now will be the perfect time to start that home renovation project.

(vii) "I will definitely call you as soon as I arrive at the airport," she promised.

(a) She promised that she would definitely call me as soon as she arrives at the airport.
(b) She promised that she will definitely call me as soon as she arrived at the airport.
(c) She promises that she would definitely call me as soon as she arrives at the airport.
(d) She promised that she would definitely call me as soon as she arrived at the airport.

(viii) "Please pass the salt," she asked.

(a) She requested to pass the salt.
(b) She asked to pass the salt, please.

(c) She asks to pass the salt, please.
(d) She asked for passing the salt.

(ix) "I had been waiting for over an hour before the bus arrived," she complained.
(a) She complains that she has been waiting for over an hour before the bus arrives.
(b) She complained that she had been waiting for over an hour before the bus arrives.
(c) She complains that she had been waiting for over an hour before the bus arrived.
(d) She complained that she has been waiting for over an hour before the bus arrived.

(x) "I have just finished reading that book," she revealed.
(a) She revealed that she has just finished reading that book.
(b) She reveals that she had just finished reading that book.
(c) She reveals that she has just finished reading that book.
(d) She revealed that she had just finished reading that book.

3. Convert and rewrite the following sentences in Indirect Speech.

(i) "I should call my parents to let them know I have reached," he said.
(ii) "Which is the proper way to answer this question, father?" the boy enquired.
(iii) The teacher said to him, "Do not read so fast."
(iv) He said, "What a pity you did not come!"
(v) He said to him, "Is not your name Afzal?"
(vi) The traveller said, "Can you tell me the way to the nearest hotel?"
(vii) "Have you finished your homework?" he asked.
(viii) "I can assist you with your project," she offered.
(ix) "I didn't go to the party last night," he admitted.
(x) "If I were you, I would take that job offer," he suggested.

4. Convert and rewrite the following sentences in Direct Speech.

(i) I asked Mary if she would lend me a pencil.
(ii) He said that he was tired, and that he wished to go to bed.
(iii) I told him that I had not seen him for months.
(iv) He asked me if I would accompany him.
(v) He advised his sons not to quarrel amongst themselves.
(vi) He said that he would go as soon as it was possible.
(vii) She mentioned that she might consider taking a sabbatical next year.
(viii) She asked if I knew what time the movie started.
(ix) He told me to turn off the lights before leaving.
(x) They wished that the weather would be sunny for the picnic.

ANSWERS

1. (i) (c) rotates (ii) (c) decided
(iii) (c) goes (iv) (d) wishes
(v) (a) would listen

2. (i) (a) He observes that they never miss their morning jog.
(ii) (b) The teacher said that she had studied for hours before taking the final exam.
(iii) (b) She asserted that she believes in living a healthy lifestyle.
(iv) (c) She recalled that they had been watching a movie when the storm began.
(v) (b) She said with excitement that she was going to a concert that night.
(vi) (c) The contractor suggested that then was the perfect time to start that home renovation project.
(vii) (d) She promised that she would definitely call me as soon as she arrived at the airport.
(viii) (a) She requested to pass the salt.
(ix) (c) She complains that she had been waiting for over an hour before the bus arrived.
(x) (d) She revealed that she had just finished reading that book.

3. (i) He said that he should call his parents to let them know he had reached.
(ii) The boy asked his father which was the proper way to answer that question.
(iii) The teacher told/advised him not to read so fast.
(iv) He expressed his regret that the other person did not come.
(v) He inquired if the other person's name was Afzal.
(vi) The traveller asked if I could tell him the way to the nearest hotel.
(vii) He asked if I had finished my homework.
(viii) She offered to assist with my project.
(ix) He admitted that he hadn't gone to the party the previous night.

(x) He suggested that if he were me, he would take the job offer.

4. (i) I said to Mary, "Will you lend me a pencil?" /I asked Mary, "Would you lend me a pencil?"
(ii) He said, "I'm tired, and I wish to go to bed."
(iii) I said to him, "I haven't seen you for months."
(iv) He asked me, "Would you accompany me?"
(v) He said to his sons, "Don't quarrel amongst yourselves."
(vi) He said, "I'll go as soon as it's possible."
(vii) She said, "I might consider taking a sabbatical next year."
(viii) She asked me, "Do you know what time the movie starts?"
(xi) He said to me, "Turn off the lights before leaving."
(x) They said, "We wish the weather will be sunny for the picnic."

CHAPTER 18 Punctuation of Sentences

18.1 Definition of Punctuation

Punctuation refers to the symbols used in writing to separate sentences, phrases, and clauses so that their intended meaning is clear. They help us know when to pause, stop, or express something.

18.2 Kinds of Punctuation

There are many punctuation marks. We already know and use some of them regularly, these include

- full stop (.)
- comma (,)
- question mark (?)
- exclamation mark (!)
- Semicolon (;)
- Inverted Commas (' ')
- Apostrophe (,)

Here, we are focusing on following three punctuation marks.

Semicolon (;)

Connects closely related independent clauses and separates items in a list when commas are already used.

e.g. • She loves to read; her favourite genres are mystery and fantasy.
• I have lived in London, England; Paris, France; and Berlin, Germany.

Inverted Commas (' ')

Indicate direct speech, dialogue, or to highlight titles.

e.g. • He said, 'Hello.'
• I just finished reading 'To Kill a Mockingbird.'

Apostrophe (')

Shows possession or contraction of letters.

e.g. • Sarah's book (possession)
• It's (it is) a beautiful day. (contraction)

Oxford Comma

The Oxford comma, also known as the serial comma, is a comma placed after the penultimate item (second to last) in a list of three of more items.

e.g. "They sent gifts to her sons, Vishal and Sophie."

With the oxford comma, it becomes clear that gifts are being sent to her sons in addition to being sent to two other people called Vishal and Sophie.

Without it, it seems like the names of the sons are Vishal and Sophie.

Commonly Confused Punctuations

Colon vs. Semicolon

(i) Colon (:) is used to introduce a list, explanation, or elaboration.

e.g. • There are three things I love: chocolate, music, and books.

(ii) Semicolon (;) connects closely related independent clauses without a conjunction.

e.g. • She finished her work; then she went out to meet her friends.

Hyphen vs. Dash

(i) Hyphen (-) joins words in a compound word or phrase.

e.g. • well-known, high-quality product

(ii) Dash (–) used to indicate a pause or break in a sentence.

e.g. • The concert–filled with excitement–was a tremendous success.

Apostrophe vs. Quotation Marks

(i) Apostrophe (') is used to indicate possession or contraction.

e.g. • Sarah's book; It's a beautiful day.

(ii) Quotation marks (" ") are used to enclose direct speech or quotations.

e.g. • She said, "I'll be there at 3 PM."

Comma vs. Semicolon

Comma is the most commonly used punctuation mark. Therefore, it is very necessary to understand when not to use it unnecessarily.

In longer sentences, confusion arises in the use of semicolon and comma. Let us learn about it in detail.

Situation	Comma	Semicolon
1. Separating Items in a List	Used in a simple list. e.g. She bought apples, oranges, and bananas.	Used when items in the list contain commas themselves. e.g. The ingredients for the salad include lettuce, tomatoes, cucumbers, and red peppers; shredded cheese; and a variety of dressings.
2. Connecting Independent Clauses	Used with a coordinating conjunction to join independent clauses. e.g. He likes to swim, but she prefers to surf.	Used to connect closely related independent clauses without a coordinating conjunction. e.g. She finished her work; then, she went out to meet her friends.

PRACTICE EXERCISE

Objective and Subjective Questions

1. Choose the correctly punctuated sentence.

(i) (a) He can do it, (b) He can do it. (c) He can do it? (d) He can do it!

(ii) (a) I know it, I will apply it.
(b) I know it ! I will apply it
(c) I know it, I will apply it,
(d) I know it? I will apply it.

(iii) (a) He may be your friend, not mine.
(b) He may be your friend ! not mine.
(c) He may be your friend, not mine,
(d) He may be your friend. Not mine!

(iv) (a) Let us hope for the best!
(b) Let us hope for the best.
(c) Let us hope for the best,
(d) Let us? hope for the best!

(v) (a) The weather is warm, the Sun is shining. I am going for a walk in the park. I will meet my friend there.
(b) The weather is warm; the Sun is shining; I am going for a walk in the park; I will meet my friend there.
(c) The weather is warm. The Sun is shining. I am going for a walk in the park. I will meet my friend there.
(d) The weather is warm; the Sun is shining. I am going for a walk in the park; I will meet my friend there.

(vi) (a) Susan, said I can borrow her bicycle.
(b) Susan said I can borrow her bicycle.
(c) Susan, said, I can borrow her bicycle.
(d) Susan said, I can borrow her bicycle.

(vii) (a) They visited London, Paris, Rome, and Berlin during their Europe trip.
(b) They visited London Paris Rome and Berlin during their Europe trip.
(c) They visited London; Paris; Rome; and Berlin during their Europe trip.
(d) They visited London, Paris, Rome and Berlin during their Europe trip.

(viii) (a) My favourite books include Harry Potter, Pride and Prejudice, and The Great Gatsby.
(b) My favourite books include Harry Potter, Pride and Prejudice and The Great Gatsby.
(c) My favourite books include Harry Potter; Pride and Prejudice; and The Great Gatsby.
(d) My favourite books include Harry Potter, Pride and Prejudice and The Great Gatsby.

(ix) (a) We had a great time at the beach playing volleyball, building sandcastles, and swimming.
(b) We had a great time at the beach playing volleyball building sandcastles and swimming.
(c) We had a great time at the beach, playing volleyball building sandcastles and swimming.
(d) We had a great time at the beach playing volleyball, building sandcastles and swimming.

(x) (a) Mary has three pets: a cat, a dog, and a rabbit.
(b) Mary has three pets; a cat, a dog, and a rabbit.
(c) Mary has three pets: a cat, a dog and a rabbit.
(d) Mary has three pets; a cat, a dog and a rabbit.

(xi) (a) The concert starts at 7:00 pm and tickets are available at the door.
(b) The concert starts at 7:00 PM and tickets are available at the door.
(c) The concert starts at 7:00 p.m. and tickets are available at the door.
(d) The concert starts at 7:00 PM, and tickets are available at the door.

(xii) (a) Last summer, we went on a family vacation to Hawaii and had a fantastic time.
(b) Last summer, we went on a family vacation to Hawaii and had a fantastic time.
(c) Last summer we went on a family vacation to Hawaii and had a fantastic time.
(d) Last summer, we went on a family vacation to Hawaii, and had a fantastic time.

(xiii) (a) We studied the ancient civilisations of Egypt, Greece, Rome and China in history class.
(b) We studied the ancient civilisations of Egypt Greece Rome and China in history class.
(c) We studied the ancient civilisations of Egypt, Greece, Rome and China in history class.
(d) We studied the ancient civilisations of Egypt; Greece; Rome; and China in history class.

(xiv) (a) The train departs at 5:30 pm and arrives at 10:30 pm.
(b) The train departs at 5:30 PM; and arrives at 10:30 PM.
(c) The train departs at 5:30 p.m. and arrives at 10:30 p.m.
(d) The train departs at 5:30 PM, and arrives at 10:30 PM.

2. Fill in the blanks in following sentences using appropriate punctuation mark.

(i) There once was a king of Persia .... who at the beginning of his reign had distinguished himself by many glorious and successful conquests.
(ii) The King of Persia......s capital was situated in an island.
(iii) ....Sire.... replied the merchant.
(iv) God is the greatest....
(v) Who will liberate me....
(vi) May you do your best....
(vii) What is your work here....
(viii) Tabaqui is a mischief....maker.
(ix) Nobody cared to cross his path.... for he was as cunning as a fox.
(x) "Speak then...." cried twenty voices.

3. Correct the punctuation errors in the following sentences.

(i) The meeting will start at 3:00- make sure to be on time.
(ii) His essay was well-written; informative, engaging, and, thoroughly researched.
(iii) "Don't forget to bring your umbrella", she reminded him.
(iv) Sam's dog Max, is always excited to go for a walk.
(v) The concert was incredible, The band played all our favourite songs.
(vi) Can you believe it! We won the lottery!
(vii) The students completed their exams: now they eagerly await the results.
(viii) The long..awaited day finally arrived; bringing joy to everyone.
(ix) Is she? your daughter
(x) Raj is the winner; of the chess match!

ANSWERS

1. (i) (b) He can do it.
   (ii) (a) I know it, I will apply it.
   (iiii) (a) He may be your friend, not mine.
   (iv) (a) Let us hope for the best!
   (v) (c) The weather is warm. The Sun is shining. I am going for a walk in the park. I will meet my friend there.
   (vi) (b) Susan said I can borrow her bicycle.
   (vii) (d) They visited London, Paris, Rome and Berlin during their Europe trip.
   (viii) (a) My favourite books include Harry Potter, Pride and Prejudice, and The Great Gatsby.
   (ix) (c) We had a great time at the beach, playing volleyball, building sandcastles, and swimming.
   (x) (a) Mary has three pets: a cat, a dog, and a rabbit.
   (xi) (c) The concert starts at 7:00 p.m. and tickets are available at the door.
   (xii) (a) Last summer, we went on a family vacation to Hawaii and had a fantastic time.
   (xiii) (a) We studied the ancient civilisations of Egypt, Greece, Rome, and China in history class.
   (xiv) (c) The train departs at 5:30 p.m. and arrives at 10:30 p.m.

2. (i) ,
   (ii) ’ (apostrophe)
   (iii) “Sire,”
   (iv) !
   (v) ?
   (vi) !
   (vii) ?
   (viii) - (hyphen)
   (ix) ,
   (x) ,

3. (i) The meeting will start at 3:00; make sure to be on time.
   (ii) His essay was well-written: informative, engaging, and thoroughly researched.
   (iii) “Don’t forget to bring your umbrella,” she reminded him.
   (iv) Sam’s dog, Max, is always excited to go for a walk.
   (v) The concert was incredible! The band played all our favourite songs.
   (vi) Can you believe it? We won the lottery!
   (vii) The students completed their exams—now they eagerly await the results.
   (viii) The long-awaited day finally arrived, bringing joy to everyone.
   (ix) Is she your daughter?
   (x) Raj is the winner of the chess match.

Word Power

CHAPTER 19

This chapter will give you a tool to develop your vocabulary and also a revision of the word power you have developed so far. We will see antonyms, one word substitution, homophones and homonyms.

19.1 Antonyms

Antonyms are the words that have opposite meanings.

List of Some Antonyms

Words	Antonyms
Absent	present
Admit	deny
Advantage	disadvantage
Agree	disagree
Ancient	modern

Words	Antonyms
Bright	dull
Bold	meek
Build	destroy
Bitter	sweet
Capable	incapable
Careful	careless
Cheap	expensive
Cruel	kind
Dangerous	safe
Deep	shallow
Discourage	encourage
Dusk	dawn
Early	late
Empty	full
Export	import
Fade	brighten
Float	sink
Foolish	wise
Fresh	stale
Glad	sad
Gloomy	cheerful
Harsh	mild
Heaven	hell
Honest	dishonest
Hope	despair
Humble	proud
Include	exclude
Inferior	superior
Inhale	exhale
Join	separate
Just	unjust
Known	unknown
Lenient	Strict
Lend	Borrow

Words	Antonyms
Loud	quiet
Maximum	minimum
Minor	major
Odd	even
Outer	inner
Peace	noise
Patriot	traitor
Quiet	loud
Rapid	slow
Rare	common
Strong	weak
Safety	danger
Sufficient	insufficient
Tough	easy
Transparent	opaque
Victory	defeat
Wild	tame
Wide	narrow
Young	old

19.2 Synonyms

Antonyms are the words that have similar meaning.

List of Some Synonyms

Words	Synonyms
Admire	praise, appreciate
Assistance	help, support
Bear	tolerate, suffer
Below	beneath, underneath
Calm	peaceful, relaxed
Charm	fascinate, mesmerise
Definite	specific, exact
Disaster	tragedy, calamity
Enemy	opponent, competitor
Eager	enthusiastic, impatient
Famous	renowned, well-known
False	incorrect, wrong
Glory	fame, honour

Words	Synonyms
Grudge	bitterness, hatred
Gloomy	bleak, cloudy
Hate	detest, dislike
Hope	optimism, confidence
Important	necessary, essential
Idea	thought, plan
Just	immediately, presently
Jovial	cheerful, jolly
Keen	sharp, enthusiastic
Kind	caring, helpful
Look	gaze, stare
Mandatory	compulsory, required
Modest	humble, unpretentious
Need	require, necessity
Nomad	wanderer, migrant
Obstruct	shut off, block
Omnipresent	universal, worldwide
Persuade	convince, encourage
Progress	advance, develop
Quarantine	isolation, seclusion
Quest	journey, adventure
Rude	impolite, disrespectful
Rapid	fast, quick
Sacred	holy, divine
Sympathy	empathy, understanding
Trivial	insignificant, small
Think	contemplate, reflect
Urge	compel, prompt
Ugly	unattractive, hideous
Vast	immense, widespread
Vacant	empty, unoccupied
Weak	feeble, delicate
Wages	salary, income
Zeal	enthusiasm, passion
Zest	spirited, liveliness,

19.3 Homophones (Sound-alike words)

The words that pronounce the same, but have different meanings are called homophones.

Homophones may have same spellings or different spellings.

e.g. rose - a flower

rose - the past tense of rise

1. **Accept** Rahil accepted Ritu's invitation.

   Except I like all colours except blue.

2. **Access** They do not have access to the internet in the village.

   Excess We have excess of furniture. You can borrow from us.

3. **Allowed** You are not allowed to leave the exam hall before 2 pm.

   Aloud He spoke aloud.

4. **Bail** The actor was released on bail from jail.

   Bale A large tight bundle. (of hay etc)

   The women in the farm lifted the bales of hay.

5. **Bare** You should not walk bare footed on the road.

   Bear Bear can be seen in the forests.

6. **Born** He was born in Nainital.

   Borne Madhur has borne great pains to reach this position.

7. **Cell** (a small unit) The biologist studied the plant cell under a microscope.

   Sell (to transfer goods or services in exchange for money) The artist decided to sell her paintings at the local art fair.

8. **Check** (to inspect or examine something) Please check the document for any errors before submitting it.

   Cheque (a method of paying money by bank account) In some countries, people prefer to pay by cheque rather than using electronic methods.

9. **Coma** (a state of prolonged unconsciousness) After the accident, the patient remained in a coma for several days.

   Comma (a punctuation mark indicating a pause in a) Make sure to use a comma to separate items in a list.

10. **Desert** (a dry, barren area of land with little or no vegetation) The camel is well-adapted to survive in the harsh conditions of the desert.

    Dessert (a sweet course typically served at the end of a meal) We enjoyed a delicious chocolate cake for dessert after dinner.

11. **Dose** (a quantity of medicine prescribed to be taken at one time) The doctor recommended a daily dose of the medication.

    Doze (to sleep lightly or take a short nap) After a tiring day, he decided to doze off on the couch.

12. **Dear** (regarded with affection or deep fondness) She wrote a heartfelt letter to her dear friend on their birthday.

    Deer (a graceful, hoofed mammal with antlers) We spotted a group of deer grazing in the meadow.

13. **Effect** (a change that is a result or consequence of an action or other cause) The new law had a positive effect on the community.

    Affect (to have an influence on or produce a change in something) The economic downturn began to affect businesses across the country.

14. **Eminent** (standing out, renowned, distinguished) The professor is an eminent scholar in the field of physics.

    Imminent (about to happen, impending) The storm clouds gathered, and it felt like rain was imminent.

15. **Fair** She has a fair complexion.

    Fair Children like to go to the fair.

    Fare How much is the fare of the bus to Moti Nagar?

16. **Feat** (an achievement that requires great courage of skill) He performed a great feat.

    Feet (the power extremity of the leg on which a person stands or walk). His bare feet projected from this trousers.

17. **Grate** (a framework of metal bars used for cooking or heating) She used a cheese grater to grate the Parmesan for the pasta.

    Great (of an extent, amount, or intensity considerably above average) Climbing Mount Everest is a great challenge.

18. **Groan** (a low sound expressing pain or disapproval) The old chair let out a groan as he sat down.

    Grown (past participle of grow, to increase in size or develop) The once small sapling had grown into a mighty oak tree.

19. **Hair** His hair is black and silky.

    Hare There is a hare playing in the lawn.

20. **Heel** (the back part of the foot) Her new shoes were stylish but uncomfortable around the heel.

    Heal (to become healthy again, or to treat and cure a wound) With proper care, the wound began to heal.

21. **Idle** Don't sit idle.

    Idol They have a big idol of lord Ganesh in their hall.

22. **In** (inside or within a location) The keys are in the drawer.

    Inn (a small hotel or lodging house) They decided to stay at an inn for the night.

23. **Jealous** (feeling envy or resentment) She couldn't help but feel jealous of her friend's success.

    Zealous (enthusiastically devoted to a cause or pursuit) The young artist was zealous about perfecting her craft.

24. **Knight** (a warrior) The knight rode into battle, carrying a lance and shield.

    Night (the period of darkness between sunset and sunrise) They went for a stroll in the park at night.

25. **Lesson** (a period of learning or teaching) The maths lesson covered the principles of algebra.

    Lessen (to make or become less in degree, intensity, or extent) The medication helped lessen the pain.

26. **Made** The salesman made them a fool.

    Maid We don't have any maid-servant at our home.

27. **Mail** (letters and parcels sent or delivered by postal system) She received an important document in the mail.

    Male (masculine gender) The males are directed to board the plane from the right door.

28. **Nose** (a sense organ) His glasses perched on the bridge of his nose.

    Knows (third person singular of know) She knows the answer to the riddle.

29. **Not** (used to express negation or denial) I'm sorry, but I do not have any information on that topic.

    Knot (a tying made by looping a piece of string or rope) The sailor expertly tied a secure knot to keep the boat in place.

30. **One** (the number 1) There is only one apple left in the basket.

    Won (past tense of win) They won the championship after a hard-fought match.

31. **Off** (away from a place or position) Please stay off the grass; it's just been seeded.

    Of (expressing the relationship between a part and a whole) The cup is made of ceramic.

32. **Our** This is our home.

    Hour It will take an hour to get there.

33. **Pale** (light in colour) Her face turned pale when she heard the unexpected news.

Pail (a bucket, typically with a handle) The gardener used a pail to water the plants.

34. **Plain** Write all the details on a plain sheet of paper.

Plane Their plane will land in Dubai at around 6 am.

35. **Quite** Rohit is quite busy in his work.

Quiet Please, keep quiet.

36. **Rain** (water falling in drops from the atmosphere) We decided to stay indoors due to the heavy rain.

Rein (a strap used to control a horse) The rider pulled gently on the rein to guide the horse.

Reign (the period of rule of a monarch) The queen's reign was marked by prosperity and cultural growth.

37. **Raise** (to lift or move to a higher position) She decided to raise the curtains to let in more sunlight.

Rays (beams of light) The morning rays of the Sun illuminated the landscape.

38. **Sun** The Sun is shining brightly today.

Son His son studies in Singapore.

39. **See** Can you see what is there?

Sea The Arabian sea is at the West of India.

40. **Stationary** I like to keep watching the stationary water of lake.

Stationery There is a stationery store at the corner.

41. **Tail** (the hindmost part of an animal, especially when extended beyond the rest of the body) The dog wagged its tail happily.

Tale (a narrative of real or imaginary events) She enjoyed reading fairy tales before bedtime.

42. **Throne** (a ceremonial chair for a sovereign or monarch) The king sat on his ornate throne during the coronation ceremony.

Thrown (past participle of throw) He had thrown the ball so far that it landed outside the field.

43. **Umpire** (an official who oversees and enforces the rules in sports) The umpire made a fair decision despite the challenging situation.

Empire (a group of nations or territories under a single authority) The Roman Empire was a vast and powerful civilisation.

44. **Wander** They are wandering around that area.

Wonder I wonder if it rains today.

45. **Weight** His weight is 65 kg.

Wait She waited for 30 minutes.

19.4 Homonyms

Homonyms are the words that have the same spelling, but different meaning.

1. **Address**

(to refer to someone) Napoleon addressed the crowd.

(the postal address) Has she changed her address?

2. **Bat**

(Sports Equipment) He swung the bat and hit a home run in the baseball game.

(Nocturnal Animal) Bats are nocturnal creatures that fly at night.

3. **Can**

(Container) She opened a can of soda and took a sip.

(Ability) With hard work, you can achieve your goals.

4. **Date**

(Calendar Day) Today's date is the 15th of December.

(We have a dinner date on Friday night.)

5. **Fly**

(Insect) A fly buzzed around the room.

(Travel through the air) Birds fly south for the winter.

6. **Kite**

(Toy) Children love to fly kites on windy days.

(Bird) The majestic eagle soared high like a kite.

7. **Left**

(Direction) Turn left at the traffic light.

(Remained) He left his jacket at the party.

8. **Mean**

(Signify) What does this symbol mean?

(Unkind) Don't be mean; share your toys with your sister.

9. **Nail**

(Material) Hammer the nail into the wooden board.

(Body Part) She painted her nails with bright red polish.

10. **Palm**

(Tree) The palm tree swayed in the tropical breeze.

(Hand) He held the small object in the palm of his hand.

11. **Right**

(Direction) Go right at the intersection.

(Correct) She chose the right answer on the test.

12. **Rose**
(Flower) He gave her a bouquet of red roses.
(Past Tense of Rise) The Sun rose early in the morning.

13. **Saw**
(Tool) He used a saw to cut the wood.
(Past Tense of See) I saw her at the store yesterday.

14. **Trip**
(Journey) We're planning a road trip across the country.
(Stumble) Be careful not to trip over the uneven pavement.

15. **Tie**
(Fasten) He had to tie his shoelaces before going for a run.
(Equality) The game ended in a tie; neither team won.

16. **Well**
(Water Source) The village relies on the well for drinking water.
(In Good Health) Despite her age, she is still quite well and active.

19.5 One Word Substitutions

One word substitutions are defined as single words that are used in place of a group of words to denote a person, an object and a place etc.

abbreviation	a shortened form of a word or phrase.
accessible	which can be approached.
amateur	one who does something as past-time.
anonymous	of an unknown name
aquatic	animals which live in water.
audible	the sound which can be heard.
autobiography	a book on one's life written by oneself.
bankrupt	one who cannot pay back his debt.
biography	a book on one's life written by somebody else.
cemetery	a place where dead bodies are buried.
century	one hundred years.
curable	that which can be cured.
deaf	one who cannot hear anything.
democracy	the government formed for the people, by the people and of the people.
desert	a place where there is no water or plantation.
edible	suitable to be eaten
extrovert	a person who enjoys being with other people.
incurable	that which cannot be cured.
indoor	something carried on within or inside a building.
inflammable	something that is quickly and easily burnt.
insomnia	loss of sleep.
ignorant	person who doesn't know anything.
jail	a place where prisoners are kept.
kidnap	to carry away a person forcibly.
kindergarten	a place for small children.
legal	that which is lawful.
linguist	one who knows many languages.
logic	the science of reasoning.
lunar	eclipse of Moon.
notorious	that which is ill famous.
orphan	one who does not have father and mother.
orphanage	a place where orphans live.
patriot	one who loves one's own country.
pessimist	one who looks on darker side of things.
pioneer	one who leads others.
polygon	a figure with many angles or sides.
postmortem	a study of dead bodies.
robot	an intelligent and obedient machine like man.
sculpture	the art of making statues
secular	one who does not favour any religion.
simultaneous	happening at the same time.
solo	a piece of music by one person.
spokesman	one who speaks on behalf of others.
suicide	killing of oneself.
theist	one who believes in God.
thermometer	an instrument for measuring temperature.
tragedy	the story that ends in death or sorrow.
wardrobe	an almirah where clothes are kept.
zoo	a place where animals and birds are kept.
zoology	study of animals.

19.6 Idioms and Phrases

The expression that have a different meaning from its literal meaning.

off hand	The team came into the match off hand.
In spite of	In spite of poverty, she managed to get education.
In the long run	All my effort had been wasted in the long run.
For good	I am planning to quit the job for good.
At the eleventh hour	She burst up at the eleventh hour.
At a stretch	I can work upto sixteen hours at a stretch.
In black and white	I want all your information in black and white.
A man of letters	Mr. Sharma is a man of letters.
An apple of discord	Kashmir has always been an apple of discord between India and Pakistan.
To and fro	Why are you walking to and fro?
Ups and downs	I have always walking ups and downs in my life.
Kith and kin	I always wanted to avoid my kith and kin for their suggestions.
Bread and butter	I write to earn my bread and butter.
Bag and baggage	British left India bag and baggage in 1947.
All in all	President is all in all of any country.
A white elephant	Keeping an SUV in village is a white elephant.
Red lettered day	15th August is a red lettered day in the country.
Crocodile tears	I know you well, so stop shedding crocodile tears.
A child's play	Cooking is a child's play for me.
To catch red-handed	I saw a man who claimed to catch a thief red handed.
To turn a deaf ear	I could not make it out why she turned a deaf ear.
To take to task	My mother took me to task for ignoring my health.
To rain cats and dogs	It was raining cats and dogs yesterday.
To make both ends meet	I have to work hard to make my both ends meet.
Lose heart	I will not lose my heart even if I fail many a times.
To keep in dark	Children should not keep their parents is dark.
To got to the dogs	A lot of food items go to the dogs in a wedding party.
To end in smoke	All my efforts ended in smoke and it made me unhappy.
To burn midnight oil	I have seen students burning midnight oil during the exams.
To add fuel to the fire	His obscene remarks added fuel to the fire.

Integrated Exercise

Type I : Gap Filling

I. Complete the following paragraphs by filling in the blanks with the help of the given options:

1. Dr. Diesel was (i) .... gifted engineer. He (ii) .... highly practical and persevering in giving shape (iii) .... his ideas.

(i) (a) an (b) the (c) a (d) some

(ii) (a) is (b) was (c) been (d) were

(iii) (a) over (b) towards (c) on (d) to

2. When wet waste is mixed (i) .... dry waste, it is called garbage. For zero garbage, the two (ii) .... be kept separate. Dry waste can be recycled. Wet waste can be (iii) .... into compost and used for gardening in place of fertilisers.

(i) (a) in (b) on (c) into (d) with

(ii) (a) could (b) would (c) should (d) shall

(iii) (a) make (b) turned (c) mixed (d) stirred

3. During (i) .... hottest part of the year, many of our city streets seem to be on fire (ii) .... masses of Gulmohar flowers. This (iii) .... one of the most beautiful trees.

(i) (a) a (b) the (c) an (d) some

(ii) (a) from (b) by (c) with (d) over

(iii) (a) is (b) was (c) are (d) be

4. Gauri was only eight years old, but (i) .... mountain of family responsibilities had already (ii) .... (iii) .... her head.

(i) (a) a (b) the (c) an (d) some

(ii) (a) descend (b) descending (c) descended (d) descends

(iii) (a) over (b) on (c) above (d) in

5. The mere mention of the Nobel Prize (i) .... visions (ii) .... world famous scientists and economists. It is (iii) .... most coveted individual award in the world.

(i) (a) creates (b) create (c) created (d) creating

(ii) (a) for (b) of (c) from (d) over

(iii) (a) a (b) an (c) some (d) the

II. Complete the following sentences by choosing the correct options.

1. According to the doctor, this time next week, I .... around as normal and the cut on my foot .... completely.

(a) am walking / healed
(b) will be walking / will have healed
(c) walked / was healing
(d) have been walking / heal

2. .... we climbed, ... the air became, which made it difficult for us to proceed.

(a) The higher / the colder (b) The highest / the coldest
(c) To high / too cold (d) As high / so cold

3. They could easily afford to stay at the best hotels, ... they preferred to stay at small family-run guesthouses.

(a) as (b) yet (c) for (d) therefore

4. The photographer rolled a machine .... the middle .... the room.

(a) above, from (b) in, off
(c) by, across (d) into, of

5. **There's a cinema near the station, ... ?**
(a) aren't it (b) isn't there
(c) weren't it (d) isn't it

6. **The cat and the dog have a ...... enemy in the rat.**
(a) same (b) common (c) mutual (d) similar

7. **There was .... huge hole in .... napkin she took out from ...... her bag.**
(a) the, a, a (b) a, the, no article
(c) no article, the, no article (d) a, the, an

8. **The .... of cotton is very heavy.**
(a) bald (b) bail (c) bale (d) band

9. **Hypocrites try to .... appearances.**
(a) keep upon (b) keep over
(c) keep up (d) keep away

10. **Our new digital photo-print machine, the manual .... is lost awaits to be set-up properly.**
(a) of what (b) where (c) by whom (d) of which

III. Fill in the blank with most suitable word.

1. The Kohli family are very energetic and hardworking people. ..... (i) weekdays, they get up very early and ..... (ii) breakfast. Then, they go to school and work. When their office and school get over, they attend swimming classes. They have dinner at 7 pm and by 7.30 they are ready for a walk ..... (iii) their neighbourhood.

2. Monuments are objects .... (i) buildings that have been created to ...... (ii) an important person or a historic event that happened. People ..... (iii) built monuments for thousands of years.

3. An educated man is not only self-reliant ...... (i) can assist others in getting proper education. He ...... (ii) supposed to be well-mannered, kind and sympathetic. So a man who ..... (iii) acquired knowledge and skill only for his material development, cannot be called truly an educated man.

4. On a sunny spring day, Tania ran ..... (i) a bus and shouted at it to stop. She got on with her money. She ..... (ii) the conductor that she had to go to town and handed the ..... (iii) money to the conductor.

5. Once upon a time, there was a king ..... (i) central India. He was good-looking ...... (ii) very proud. He admired himself all the time, in mirrors, in water, and even in people's eyes. He called himself the .... (iii) handsome king in the world.

Type II : Editing

I. The following paragraphs have not been edited. There is one error in each line. Identify the error and write its correction against the correct blank number. Remember to underline the correction. The first one has been done for you.

1.

		Error	Correction
Enid Blyton books are, of course, of primary	e.g.	of	for
school children. Many were suitable for old	(a)	....	....
primary school children, but any are	(b)	....	....
especially write for new readers	(c)	....	....
in the early primary school years.			

2.

		Error	Correction
God like qualities are planted with us at birth.	e.g.	with	in
They grow amid the thorns of our fault. Many of us	(a)	....	....
look at ourselves and see only the thorn, the defects	(b)	....	....
We despair, thinking such we cannot do anything good	(c)	....	....
We neglect to water a good within us,	(d)	....	....
and eventually it dies.			

3.

		Error	Correction
Any people came to the site where the	(a)	....	....
revolutionary general were to be hanged. When asked if	(b)	....	....
he had any desire, the smile ran	(c)	....	....
on him dry lips and he nodded his head.	(d)	....	....

4.

		Error	Correction
Walt Disney was our hero. He	e.g.	was	is
left me a legacy that can	(a)	....	....
be enjoy time and again. He	(b)	....	....
knew who to entertain us so well.	(c)	....	....
he developed a process in creating animated films.	(d)	....	....

5.

		Error	Correction
The Gir National Park, also known by Gir Wildlife	e.g.	by	as
Sanctuary, is situated in the state of Gujarat. It was	(a)	....	....
one among the major wildlife sanctuaries to North India.	(b)	....	....
It was establishment on 18th September, 1965	(c)	....	....
as a forest reserve primary to conserve the Asiatic Lion.	(d)	....	....

6.

		Error	Correction
According to tradition, Gautama Buddha sit	e.g.	sit	sat
in meditation in the Bodhi tree at	(a)	....	....
Bodh Gaya. Unfortunately, an original tree	(b)	....	....
has disappeared and is replace	(c)	....	....
through a successor - the Peepal tree.	(d)	....	....

Type III : Omitting

In the passage that follows, one word has been omitted in each line. Write the missing word along with the word that comes before and the word that comes after it in your answer sheets.

1.

		Before	Missing	After
Buddha taught people many	e.g.	people	in	many
different ways. He taught children telling	(a)	....	....	....
stories. He gave detailed explanations the	(b)	....	....	....
path to the wise. To others, taught without	(c)	....	....	....
speaking any words all. He always	(d)	....	....	....
talked with kindness and love.				

2.

		Before	Missing	After
The Theory of Evolution states that the plants and animals				
in the world today developed a natural way from earlier	(a)	....	....	....
forms that simpler. These earlier forms developed from	(b)	....	....	....
still simpler ancestors and process goes back through millions of	(c)	....	....	....
years to the very beginning, when life was in simplest form,	(d)	....	....	....
merely a tiny mass of jelly-like protoplasm.				

3.

		Before	Missing	After
Gone the days when wedding	(a)	....	....	....
gifts meant anything was readily available. Today	(b)	....	....	....
people tend to spend effort to choose the right gift–a gift	(c)	....	....	....
that only has aesthetic appeal but also has a high usability.	(d)	....	....	....

4.

The Supreme Court made it
compulsory cinema theatres
to play national anthem with
the image of the national flag prior screening.

	Before	Missing	After
(a)	....	....	....
(b)	....	....	....
(c)	....	....	....
(d)	....	....	....

5.

A man getting very impatient.
Again and again he would peep the
doctor's room to see many patients
were left. After a long time his turn came,
he heaved a sigh of relief.

	Before	Missing	After
(a)	....	....	....
(b)	....	....	....
(c)	....	....	....
(d)	....	....	....

6.

All living things to breathe
to survive, each species has
its peculiar way. Some
breathe lungs while others through skin.

	Before	Missing	After
(a)	....	....	....
(b)	....	....	....
(c)	....	....	....
(d)	....	....	....

Type IV : Sentence Reordering

1. Rearrange the following words to form meaningful sentences.

(i) child/ the/ and/ thunder/ scared/ the/ lightning

(ii) that/ scar/ may/ leave/ wound/ a

(iii) all/ a/ noise/ the/ loud/ pigeons/ scattered

2. Rearrange the following words to form meaningful sentences.

(i) Route/ shortest/ the/ is/ to/ Noida/ what

(ii) He/ phone/ and/ reached/ dialled/ for/ the/ a/ number

(iii) Know/ what/ do/ this/ is/ you

3. Rearrange the following words to make meaningful sentences.

(i) easy/ very/ it/to /close /was/ the/ door

(ii) wear/ these/ digital/ people/ majority/ of/ days/ watches/ a

(iii) democracy/ very / important / of/ press/ in/ freedom/ is

4. Rearrange the following words to form meaningful sentences.

(i) that/ life/ began/ centuries ago/ on/ scientists think/ twenty million/ Earth/ about

(ii) brother/ instinct/ my/ first/ my/ was/ younger/ to/ignore

(iii) book/ care/ must/ with/ borrowed/ treated/ a/ be

5. Rearrange the following words to form meaningful sentences.

(i) not/ have/ when/ should/ decided/ I/ go/ on/ I

(ii) the/ habitats/ regeneration/ rate/ is/ very slow/ of/ the

(iii) mankind/ is/ one of/ the/ inventions/ greatest/ of/ Computer

6. Rearrange the following words to make meaningful sentences.

(i) adored/ she/ be/ to/ loves

(ii) sunset/ it/ is/ a/ beautiful/ what/

(iii) see/ and/ play/ things/ two / different/ parents/ as/ work

7. Rearrange the following words to form meaningful sentences.

(i) did/ succeed/ tried/ not/ but/ Charlie

(ii) beautiful/ my/ dress/ sewed/ mother/ a

(iii) a student/ to/ proper/ should/ attention/ pay/ his/ studies

8. Rearrange the following words to make meaningful sentences.

(i) dogs/ like/ the /used/ humans/ their/ showed/ that/ brains/ study

(ii) policemen/ group/ works/ of/ with/ she/ a

(iii) hands/ sound/ hear/ of/ you/ two/ the/ can

9. Rearrange the following words to make meaningful sentences.

(i) important/ games/ studies/ area/ as/ as

(ii) book/ own/ on/ afraid of/ you/ writing notes/ not be/ your/ should

(iii) people/ lakhs of/ every year/ visit/ the/ Taj Mahal

10. Rearrange the following words to make meaningful sentences.

(i) have become/ part/ developing/ airports/ essential/ an/ a/ of/ city

(ii) our/ animals/ of/ all/ environment/ the/ are/ part

(iii) sculptures/ famous/ is/ for/ temple/ the/ its

Type V : Reported Speech

Report the dialogues to complete the paragraphs that follow.

1. Mother — You seem so tired. Take some rest.

Suraj — I can't even think of relaxing. I have lots of homework to do.

Mother — You should not take so much of stress.

Suraj — Don't worry. Please give me a hot cup of tea.

Mother said to Suraj that ....(i).... Suraj replied that .....(ii)..... The mother advised him not to take so much of stress. Suraj told his mother not to worry and requested her to give him a hot cup of tea.

2. Charlie — Dear Santa, here is a list of what I want.

Patty — How do you suppose Santa Claus can afford to give away all those toys?

Charlie — Promotion! Don't kid yourself .... Everything these days is promotion! I will bet if the truth were brought about, you will find that he's being financed by some big eastern chain!

While making the list of what Charlie wanted from Santa Claus, he asked Patty how ....(i)......... all those toys? She said that ....(ii)......... and that it was possible as Santa was being financed by some big eastern chain.

3. Yashvi — How did you spend your holidays?

Saksham — I went for cricket coaching. What did you do?

Yashvi — I went for the NTSC coaching classes.

Saksham — At least during the holidays you could have enjoyed yourself.

Yashvi asked Saksham ......(i)...... his holidays. Saksham said that ....(ii)........ for Cricket coaching and wanted to know what she had doen, during holidays. When Yashvi told him that she had gone for the NTSC coaching classes, Saksham told her that she could have enjoyed herself during the holidays.

4. Himanshu — The landlord has come. Take out the money you have set aside.

Anu — But there are only three hundred rupees. If you give them to him, where is the blanket going to come from?

Himanshu — Don't worry. I will figure out some other plan.

Himanshu told his wife that the landlord had come, she should take out ....(i)... His wife, Anu said that .....(ii)..... and asked him if he gave them to him then where the blanket was going to come from.

5. Marie — Did you see my new umbrella? Isn't it fine?

Tony — Yes, it is! Did you buy it from the mall?

Marie — No, your father has brought it for me.

Marie asked her son Tony ....(i)......... umbrella and she wanted to know whether it was a fine one. Tony agreed and asked his mother ....(ii)......... the mall. His mother replied in the negative and added that his father had brought it for her

6. Customer — Why is the meal so sour?

Waiter — Nobody has complained for five days sir, about the meal.

Customer — What! Where is the Manager?

Waiter — He has gone to some other hotel to take dinner, sir.

One day a customer was taking dinner in a hotel. He asked the waiter why ....(i)............. The waiter told him ....(ii).............. At this, the customer was shocked and wanted to know where the Manager was. The waiter replied that he had gone to some other hotel to take dinner.

7. Mother — Why are you looking so worried?

Daughter — My exams are approaching.

Mother — When will they start?

Daughter — Next month, Mother.

Mother asked her daughter (i) .... The daughter replied that her exams were approaching. Mother further asked (ii) .... The daughter told her mother that they would start in the following month.

8. Mother — Rita, finish your food.

Rita — I don't want to have this food. You never give me a pizza or burger.

Mother told Rita (i) .... Rita replied that (ii) .... and told her mother that she never gave her a pizza or burger.

9. Saurav — I heard you were very sick last week. How do you feel now?

Kritika — Yes, it was a tough week. I feel better now. Thank you for asking.

Saurav told Kritika that he had heard that she was very sick the previous week. He further asked how (i) .... Kritika answered in affirmative that (ii) .... week. She further added that she felt better then and thanked Saurav for asking.

10. Rahul — Do you know that Ranjit met with an accident and is in hospital ?

Samar — Oh! I don't. Is he badly hurt? Which hospital is he in?

Rahul — The doctors say that there is nothing to worry. He is admitted to Beach Hospital.

Rahul asked Samarif he knew that Ranjit had met with an accident and was hospitalized. Samar expressed his ignorance and enquired (i) ..... He also asked (ii) .... Rahul told him that according to the doctors there was nothing to worry and said that he was admitted to the Beach Hospital.

ANSWERS

Type I : Gap Filling

I. 1. (i) (c) a (ii) (b) was (iii) (d) to
2. (i) (d) with (ii) (c) should (iii) (b) turned
3. (i) (b) the (ii) (c) with (iii) (a) is
4. (i) (a) a (ii) (c) descended (iii) (b) on
5. (i) (a) creates (ii) (b) of (iii) (d) the

II. 1. (b) will be walking/will have healed
2. (a) The higher/the colder
3. (b) yet
4. (d) into, of
5. (b) isn't there
6. (b) common
7. (b) a, the, no article
8. (c) bale
9. (c) keep up
10. (d) of which

III. 1. (i) On (ii) have (iii) around
2. (i) or (ii) honour or remember, (iii) have
3. (i) but also (ii) is (iii) has
4. (i) after (ii) told (iii) fare
5. (i) in (ii) but (iii) most

Type II : Editing

I. 1.

Error	Correction
(a) were	are
(b) any	some
(c) write	written

2.

Error	Correction
(a) fault	faults
(b) thorn	thorns
(c) such	that
(d) a	the

3.

Error	Correction
(a) Any	Many
(b) were	was
(c) the	a
(d) him	his

4.

Error	Correction
(a) me	us
(b) enjoy	enjoyed
(c) who	how
(d) in	of

5.

Error	Correction
(a) was	is
(b) to	in/of
(c) establishment	established
(d) primary	primarily

6.

Error	Correction
(a) in	under
(b) an	the
(c) replace	replaced
(d) through	by

Type III : Omitting

1.

Before	Missing	After
(a) children	by	telling
(b) explanations	of	the
(c) others	he	taught
(d) words	at	all

2.

Before	Missing	After
(a) developed	in	a
(b) that	were	simpler
(c) and	this	process
(d) in	the	simplest

3.

Before	Missing	After
(a) Gone	are	the
(b) anything	that	was
(c) spend	more	effort
(d) that	not	only

4.

Before	Missing	After
(a) Court	has	made
(b) compulsory	for	cinema
(c) play	the	national
(d) prior	to	screening

5.

Before	Missing	After
(a) man	was	getting
(b) peep	into	the
(c) see	how	many
(d) time	when	his

6.

Before	Missing	After
(a) things	have	to
(b) survive	but	each
(c) its	own	peculiar
(d) breathe	through	lungs

Type IV : Sentence reordering

1. (i) The lightning and thunder scared the child.
   (ii) That wound may leave a scar.
   (iii) A loud noise scattered all the pigeons.
2. (i) What is the shortest route to Noida?
   (ii) He reached for the phone and dialled a number.
   (iii) Do you know what is this?
3. (i) It was very easy to close the door.
   (ii) A majority of people wear digital watches these days
   (iii) Freedom of press is very important in democracy.
4. (i) Scientists think that life began on Earth about twenty million centuries ago.
   (ii) My first instinct was to ignore my younger brother.
   (iii) A borrowed book must be treated with care.
5. (i) I have not decided on when I should go.
   (ii) The regeneration rate of the habitats is very slow.
   (iii) Computer is one of the greatest inventions of mankind.
6. (i) She loves to be adored.
   (ii) What a beautiful sunset it is!
   (iii) Parents see work and play as two different things.
7. (i) Charlie tried but did not succeed.
   (ii) My mother sewed a beautiful dress.
   (iii) A student should pay proper attention to his studies.
8. (i) The study showed that dogs used their brains like humans.
   (ii) She works with a group of policemen.
   (iii) You can hear the sound of two hands.
9. (i) Studies are as important as games.
   (ii) You should not be afraid of writing notes on your own book.
   (iii) Every year, lakhs of people visit the Taj Mahal.
10. (i) Airports have become an essential part of a developing city.
    (ii) All the animals are part of our environment.
    (iii) The temple is famous for its sculptures

Type V : Reported Speech

1. (i) he seemed so tired and advised him to take some rest.
   (ii) he could not even think of relaxing as he had lots of homework to do.
2. (i) Santa Claus could afford to give away
   (ii) everything those days was promotion
3. (i) How he had spent
   (ii) he had gone
4. (i) the money she had set aside.
   (ii) there were only three hundred rupees.
5. (i) if he had seen her new
   (ii) if she had bought it from
6. (i) the meal was so sour.
   (ii) that nobody had complained for five days about the meal.
7. (i) why she was looking very worried.
   (ii) when they would start.
8. (i) to finish her food.
   (ii) she did not want to have that food
9. (i) she felt then
   (ii) it had been a tough
10. (i) if he was badly hurt.
    (ii) which hospital he was in

1 Sentences

- **Assertive/Declarative Sentences** Make general statements, end with full stop (.)
- **Interrogative Sentences** Ask questions, end with question mark (?)
- **Imperative Sentences** Give commands, request, advice etc., generally end with full stop (.)
- **Exclamatory Sentences** Present extreme emotions, end with exclamation mark (!)

2 Nouns

1 Types

1. **Proper Noun** Unique name, begin with capital letters e.g. Parth, XYZ cafe, London, etc.
2. **Common Noun** General name of people place or thing e.g. boy, cafe, bird etc.
3. **Collective Noun** Name given to a group e.g. herd, choir, etc.
4. **Abstract Noun** Name given to a feeling, state, idea, quality e.g. anger, childhood, freedom, beauty etc.
5. **Material Noun** From which, things, are made e.g. gold, silk, wood etc.
6. **Compound Noun** Noun made from two words e.g. black board, X-ray, etc.

2 Number Noun

- **Countable Noun** can be counted e.g. pens, cap.
  - **Singular** Refer one noun e.g. pen, boy, ant. etc.
  - **Plural** Refer more than one noun e.g. pens, boys, ants, etc.
- **Uncountable Noun** cannot be counted e.g. milk, hair, etc.

3 Gender Noun

1. **Masculine Gender** Refer to a male noun e.g. boy, king, lion etc.
2. **Feminine Gender** Refer to a female noun e.g. girl, queen, lioness, etc.
3. **Common Gender** Refer to a both male and female noun e.g. child, doctor, etc.
4. **Neuter Gender** Refer to a non-living things e.g. chair, ring, etc.

3 Pronouns

- **Personal Pronouns** Used in place of person or thing (He, she, I, you, we, him, her, they, then, it and us)
- **Possessive Pronouns** Shows ownership (Mine, his, hers, ours, yours and theirs)
- **Demonstrative Pronouns** Points to a particular noun (This, that, these and those)
- **Distributive Pronouns** Refers to each noun (Each, either, and neither)
- **Indefinite Pronouns** Does not refer to specific nouns e.g. any body, something, etc.
- **Relative Pronouns** Refers to noun mentioned before it (Who, whom, that, which and where)
- **Interrogative Pronouns** Ask questions (Who, whom, what, which and whose)
- **Reciprocal Pronoun** Expresses mutual action between two or more people (Each-other and one-another)
- **Reflexive Pronoun** Use to refer back to the noun (Himself, herself, yourself, myself, ourselves, themselves)
- **Emphatic Pronoun** Emphasise the noun (Same as reflexive pronoun)

4 Adverbs

- **Adverbs of Time** Indicates when action performed e.g. now, yesterday, still, yet, later etc.
- **Adverbs of Frequency** Indicates how often an action takes place e.g. regularly, rarely etc.
- **Adverb of Place** Indicates where an action is performed e.g. here, outside, near, away etc.
- **Adverb of Manner** Indicates how an action performed e.g. gracefully, angrily, fast, happily etc.
- **Adverb of Degree** Indicates intensity of an action e.g. completely, entirely, perfectly etc.
- **Interrogative Adverbs** Used to ask questions e.g. why, when, where, why, how

10 Determiners

- **Articles** Placed before noun to indicate whether is specific or general (A, an, the)
- **Possessive** Use to indicate ownership (My, your, his, her, our, their)
- **Demonstrative** Use to point to a specific noun (This, that, these, those)
- **Quantifiers** Denote the amount or quantity of a countable noun. (Enough, much, many, some, few, a few, the few, etc.)

Conjunctions

Sentences

Ver

Adjectives

9 Modals

- **Can** Expresses ability, request, possibility, suggestion
- **Could** Expresses polite request, past ability, future possibility
- **Will** Expresses request, future action, assumption, prediction
- **Would** Expresses future possibility, future action
- **Shall** Expresses future action, advice, request
- **Should** Expresses duty, obligation, possibility
- **May** Expresses polite request, wish, formal permission, present possibility
- **Might** Expresses less possibility, guess, ask permission
- **Must** Expresses necessity, prohibition, strong probability
- **Ought to** Expresses obligation, duty
- **Dare** Expresses warning, used in negative and in interrogative sense
- **Need to** Expresses absence of necessity in negative and interrogative sense

Modals

repositions

Adverbs

Grammar at a Glance

5 Verbs

- **Main Verbs or Action Words** Denote an action
  - **Transitive Verbs** Requires an object
  - **Intransitive Verbs** Does not require object
- **Linking Verbs** Serves as a connectors e.g. is, am, are, has, have, had, do, does and did
- **Helping Verbs** Used with main verbs
  - Primary (Same as linking verbs)
  - Modals
- **Finite Verbs** Changes forms with numbers and tenses
- **Non-finite Verbs** Do not change forms
  - **Gerunds** (Used as nouns)
  - **Infinitives** (Used as nouns, adjectives or adverb)
  - **Participles** (Used as adjectives)

8 Conjunctions

- **Coordinating Conjunctions** Join two or more clause of equal importance. e.g. for, and, nor, but, or, yet and so.
- **Subordinating Conjunctions** Join dependent clause to main clause e.g. as, because since, while, until etc.
- **Correlative Conjunctions** Used in pairs to join two independent clause. e.g. either....or, neither ....nor, not only....but also.

7 Prepositions

- **Prepositions of Time** Denote when person or thing performs action e.g. by, on, at, in, from, to, for, since, ago, before, till.
- **Preposition of Place** Denote the location e.g. on, at, in, between, among, behind, above, under, below.
- **Preposition of Movement** Denote movement or direction e.g. to, towards, into, from, up, down, over, across, through.

6 Adjectives

- **Adjectives of Quality** Describes the quality of noun or pronoun e.g. beautiful, tall etc.
- **Adjective of Quantity** Describes the quantity of noun or pronoun e.g. lot of, much, enough
- **Adjective of Number** Shows how many or how much quantity of nouns or pronouns e.g. one, two, first, second, etc.
- **Demonstrative Adjectives** point out the specific nouns/pronouns being refer to e.g. this, that, these and those.
- **Possessive Adjectives** shows ownership e.g. my, our, his, her, their and your.
- **Interrogative Adjectives** asks question about noun e.g. which, whose and what.
- **Proper Adjectives** formed by proper noun e.g. Indian, Spanish etc.
- **Degree of Comparison Used to Compare Noun**
  - **Positive Degree of Adjective** No comparison made e.g. good, clever, etc.
  - **Comparative Degree of Adjective** Comparison between two nouns e.g. Better, cleverer, etc.
  - **Superlative Degree of Adjective** Comparison between more than two nouns e.g. best, cleverest, etc.

SECTION D : LITERATURE

POORVI

A Bottle of Dew

by Sudha Murty

CHAPTER 1

About the Chapter The given chapter by Sudha Murty presents the importance of hard work. The chapter has two parts wherein the son of a Rich landlord, Ram Natha, believes that there is a magic potion that turns things to gold. The story presents how a sage named Mahipati taught him a lesson about hard work.

Important Characters

Rama Natha He is the son of a wealthy landowner. He believes that there is a potion that could turn anything into gold. So, he does not work in his parents' fields and spends a lot of money to get the potion. He works hard to get the potion.

The Sage, Mahipati He is a wise sage who decides to teach Ram Natha, the value of hard work.

Madhumati She is Rama Natha's wife. She is a sensible woman who knows that her husband's obsession with the potion would make them poor. However, she supports her husband and in the end helps the sage in making Rama Natha realise the value of hard work.

Chapter Summary

Part I

Introducing Rama Natha

Rama Natha was the son of a rich landlord who had left him large areas of land when he died. But Rama Natha did not look after his land. This was because he believed that there was a magic potion that could turn any object into gold. So, he spent all his time learning more about this potion. As a result, he was often tricked by people who promised to tell him about it. However, he did not give up. His wife, Madhumati, was worried about the large amount of money Rama Natha was spending on it. She was sure that soon they would become poor.

Mahipati- The Sage

Once, a famous sage called Mahipati came to their town. Rama Natha became his follower and asked him about the potion. He was surprised when the sage told him that in his travels in the Himalayas, he had heard the process to make the potion. He also told Rama Natha that making the potion was very difficult. Hearing this, Rama Natha asked the sage to tell him how to make the potion. He felt that he was very lucky.

The Process to Make the Potion

The sage told Rama Natha that he had to plant a banana plant and water it regularly. In winters, Rama Natha had to collect the dew present on the leaves in the morning and store it in a bottle. Further, when he had the five litres of dew, the sage told Rama Natha to bring the dew to him. The sage added that he would say some magic words, which will turn it into the magic potion. A single drop of the potion could turn any object into gold.

Rama Natha's Worry

After hearing the process of making the potion, Rama Natha was worried. He told the sage that it would take him many years to collect the five litres of dew.

So, the sage replied that he could plant as many banana plants as he wanted. However, the sage warned that Rama Natha must look after the plant himself and collect the dew with his own hands.

Part II

Collecting the Dew

After talking to the sage, Rama Natha went home and talked to his wife. Then, he along with his wife started to clean his large fields. He planted many banana plants, cared for them and during the winter months, collected the dew carefully. His wife, Madhumati, gathered the banana crop, took it to the market and sold it. As years passed, Rama Natha planted more plants and converted the field into a huge banana plantation. At the end of six years, Rama Natha finally had his five litres of dew.

Rama Natha's Goes to the Sage

Rama Natha took the bottle to the sage. The sage said something over the water. Then he returned the bottle and asked Rama Natha to try it. So, Rama Natha sprinkled a few drops on a copper vessel and waited for it to turn to gold. However, nothing happened and Rama Natha accused the sage of cheating. He told the sage that he had wasted six precious years of his life on nothing. The sage only smiled at Rama Natha and called Madhumati. She came with a big box containing gold coins.

The Sage's Wisdom

Rama Natha was surprised to see the gold. The sage told Rama Natha that there was no such magic potion. He added that Rama Natha had worked hard and created the plantation. He looked after the trees and his wife sold the fruits in the market. As a result, he got the money. It was his hard work that created the wealth, not magic. The sage also added that if he had told Rama Natha about this earlier, he would have not listened. So, the sage had to play a trick on him.

Rama Natha understood the wisdom behind the sage's words and worked even harder on his plantation.

Values Extracted from this Chapter

The chapter presents how an individual starts believing in shortcuts to get early and easy success. It points out that there is no such shortcut as it leads to disappointment and wasted efforts. One has to work hard and with perseverance to gain true success. The chapter also presents how wisdom comes with experience.

Word Meaning

Word	Meaning
Landlord	A person who rents out land, a building, or accommodation.
Large tracts of land	Large areas of land
Potion	A liquid with magical properties
Give up	Stop trying
Dew	Small drops of water on leaves that form during night
Plant	To sow
Chant	To repeat or sing a word or phrase
Look after them	To take something or someone
Tended	Looked after
Muttered	Spoke in a low voice
Sprinkled	To throw a little water on something
Wisdom	Deep understanding

NCERT FOLDER

NCERT Intext and Exercise Questions

LET US DISCUSS (NCERT PAGE 03)

Answer the following questions. [Refer to that part of the text whose number is given against the question. This applies to the comprehension questions throughtout the book.]

Q.1 What did Rama Natha believe?

Ans. Rama Natha believed that there is a magic potion which could turn any object into gold.

Q.2 How did the sage help Rama Natha?

Ans. The sage helped Rama Natha by telling him the process of making the magic potion. The sage told Rama Natha that he knew the recipe for the magic potion. He said that to make the magic potion he would need to plant a banana plant, water it, and take care of it himself, then, in winters, gather five litres of morning dew drops from its leaves and bring it to the sage, who would then chant some magic words and turn it into a magic potion.

Q.3 Do you think Rama Natha will be able to collect the dew? Give reason.

Ans. Yes, I think that Rama Natha would be able to collect the dew over the period of some years if he plants many banana plants. I believe so because Rama Natha was sincere and dedicated towards his belief regarding the magic potion. As a result, he did everything he could to get the potion.

No, I don't think Rama Natha will be able to collect the dew because it would take a very long time and a lot of hard work to collect five litres of dew drops from the leaves of the banana plants. Since, Rama Natha has a lazy attitude and does not want to work hard in his life, it will be impossible for him to do it.

LET US DISCUSS (NCERT PAGE 05)

Q.1 Why was Rama Natha angry?

Ans. Rama Natha was angry because he felt cheated by the sage. The sage had made him plant banana trees and collect dew for six years to get the magic potion. However, after Rama Natha had worked hard, he did not get the potion he wanted.

Q.2 How did Rama Natha and Madhumati create wealth?

Ans. Rama Natha and Madhumati create wealth by working hard in their fields. Rama Natha diligently planted the banana trees and took care of them. His wife, Madhumati, collected the fruits and sold them in the market to earn the money.

LET US THINK AND REFLECT (NCERT PAGE 06)

1. Read the following lines and answer the questions that follow.

(a) He spent all his time to learn about the magic potion. People cheated him often, promising to tell him about it, but he did not give up. His wife, Madhumati, was tired of this and also worried because she saw how much money Rama Natha was spending. She was sure that soon they would be without money.

(i) Complete the sentence with a suitable reason.

Rama Natha did not 'give up' because ....

Ans. He was sure of his belief that there was a magic potion that could change anything to gold.

(ii) Read the column which shows 'what happened' and write the correct outcome in the next column.

	What happened	Outcome
(a)	People promised to tell Rama Natha about the magic potion.	
(b)	Rama Natha was spending a lot of money.	

Ans.

	What happened	Outcome
(a)	People promised to tell Rama Natha about the magic potion.	Rama Natha was cheated out of money.
(b)	Rama Natha was spending a lot of money.	His wife, Madhumati, was sure that they would become poor.

(iii) Write whether the following statements are True or False.

(a) Madhumati was troubled about what her husband did.

(b) Rama Natha was very happy digging his fields.

(c) The sage wanted to show the right path to Rama Natha.

Ans. (a) True (b) False

(c) True

(b) Carefully, he took the bottle to the sage. The sage smiled and muttered something over the water. Then he returned the bottle and said, "Try it out". Rama Natha sprinkled a few drops on a copper vessel and waited for it to turn to gold. To his surprise nothing happened!

(i) Choose the option that lists the events given below in the correct order.

a. The sage smiled.

b. Rama Natha gave the bottle to the sage.

c. Rama Natha dropped a few drops of water on a copper vessel.

d. He said something in a low voice over the water.

e. Rama Natha waited to see if the magic worked.

(a) a, e, d, b, c (b) b, a, d, c, e

(c) c, d, a, b, e (d) a, d, b, e, c

Ans. (b) b, a, d, c, e

(ii) Fill in the blank with the correct word from the lines given above.

Seeing that the plant had dried up, the gardener .... some water on it.

Ans. sprinkled

(iii) How might Rama Natha have felt when nothing happened to the copper vessel?

Ans. Rama Natha might have felt shocked and disappointed when nothing happening to the copper vessel. He had worked hard to collect the dew drops for the magic potion for six years but the potion did not turn the copper vessel into gold when he tried to test it. So, he might have also been very angry.

2. Answer the following questions.

(a) What did the sage ask Rama Natha to do to make the magic potion?

Ans. The sage asked Rama Natha to plant banana plants, water them regularly and gather the morning dew from the leaves during the winter months. He needed him to collect five litres of dew in a bottle himself and bring it back to him. The sage, then, would then chant some magic words to turn the dew into the magic potion.

(b) Why did the sage ask Rama Natha to do everything himself?

Ans. The sage asked Rama Natha to do everything himself so that he would learn the value of hard work and patience. By making him plant the banana plants, care for them and collect the dew, the sage made sure that Rama Natha would invest his time and effort into something productive. This would ultimately lead him to the realisation that wealth is created through hard work and not through magic.

(c) How could Rama Natha have a big banana plantation after six years?

Ans. Rama Natha could have a big banana plantation after six years because over the years, he had planted many banana plants on his large tracts of land. He took great care of them, increasing their number over time. His wife, Madhumati, also helped him by selling the bananas in the market, generating income which allowed them to expand their plantation.

(d) How did the sage make Rama Natha believe that there is no magic potion?

Ans. The sage made Rama Natha believe that there is no magic potion by first having him complete the long and tough task of collecting five litres of dew from the banana leaves. When Rama Natha brought the dew to the sage, the sage muttered some magic words but nothing happened when Rama Natha sprinkled the dew on a copper vessel. The sage then revealed that the true source of wealth was actually the hard work and dedication that Rama Natha and his wife had put in the banana plantation. They had created, maintained, and then, sold the banana fruits in the market, showing that there was no need for a magic potion.

(e) Fill in the 'before' and 'after' table about Rama Natha.

What he did before meeting the sage	What he did after meeting the sage
1.	3.
2.	4.

Ans.

What he did before meeting the sage	What he did after meeting the sage
1. Not cared for his fields	3. Planted the fields with banana trees
2. Lost a lot of money to get the potion	4. Worked hard to collect the dew

LET US LEARN (NCERT PAGE 08)

1. Read the following words from the story.

promised, remember,	spending, huge,	cheated, difficult,	luck, market

Use the words correctly to complete the paragraph given below. There are two extra words in the box that you do not need.

There was a farmer who had a .... coconut plantation. He worked hard and did not depend on .... Every day was .... but he did not give up. One day, a man bought a bag of coconuts from him, and .... to pay him the money the next day. Days passed and the man did not pay him anything. The farmer felt .... About two months later, he met the same man and asked him about his money. the man said. Oh! I had forgotten. Now, I .... buying coconuts from you. And he paid the money.

Ans. huge, luck, difficult, promised, cheated, remember.

2. **Read the words from the story in Column A. Read the new words in Column B. Complete the meanings of the words given in Column B. Meanings of some words are given.**

Column A	Column B	Meaning of words in Column B
I	eye	
your	you're	short form of 'you are'
dew	due	happening at some time in the future
son	Sun	
one	won	past tense of win
ate	eight	
see	sea	

Ans. eye- an organ of the body that enables us to see

Sun- a star at the centre of our Solar System

eight- the number that comes after seven in the numerical series

sea- a vast body of salt water

3. **Choose four pairs of homophones from the table above, and for each pair write a sentence that uses both homophones in the same sentence. Check your answers by sharing them with your teacher and classmates. An example has been given below**

I ate eight **bananas for breakfast today.**

Ans.

(i) I hurt my eye while playing tennis.

(ii) If you don't tie your shoelaces you're going to fall.

(iii) There was dew on the grass blades due to the cold temperature.

(iv) Mr. William's son told him to go for a walk in the morning sun.

(v) Only one of the athletes won the gold medal in the competition.

(vi) I see that there are a lot of palm trees near the sea.

4. **Match the phrases in Column A with the phrases in Column B. Use the connecting words given in the middle column to make meaningful sentences.**

Column A	Connecting Words	Column B
The children submitted their work (When?)	because	the bell rang
He did not want to try rock climbing (Why?)	before	there was a traffic jam.
The children ran towards the gate (When?)	as soon as	the deadline.
Nitin was late to school today (Why?)	as	of his fear of heights.

Now, write the new sentences in your notebook.

Ans.
- The children submitted their work before the deadline.
- He did not want to try rock climbing because of his fear of heights.
- The children ran towards the gate as soon as the bell rang.
- Nitin was late to school today as there was a traffic jam.

5. **Here are two sentences with letter 'b'.**
Read them slowly the first time. As you read them a few more times, read them faster each time.

Bunty bhaiya bought a big bunch of bananas.
A big bunch of bananas was bought by Bunty bhaiya.

Now,try to create a tongue twister on your own and share it with your peers.

Ans. Tongue twisters
- How can a clam cram in a clean cream can?
- Six slippery snails slid slowly seaward.
- A big black bear sat on a big black rug.

LET US SPEAK (NCERT PAGE 10)

1. **Read aloud the following words from the story.**

sage promising wisdom trees surprise

All these words have the letter 's' in them. But the sound of letter 's' is not always the same.
- in sage and promising–the letter 's' has a/s/sound
- in wisdom-the letter 's' has a/z/sound
- in trees-the letter 's' has a/z/sound
- in surprise-the first letter 's' has a/s/ sound and the second has a/z/ sound

Now, speak each word clearly along with your teacher and classmates. Your teacher will now say some words. Listen carefully to the sound of 's'. Write the sound next to the word.

beds sand clothes sea was keys bags nose

Ans. beds-/s/
sand-/s/
clothes-/z/
sea-/s/
was-/z/
keys-/z/
bags-/z/
nose-/z/

2. Discuss the following questions with a partner. You may use the hints given in brackets while speaking.

(a) What does hard work mean to you?
(It means … / It is something … / Well, you see … /What I mean is …)

(b) Give three reasons why you think hard work is important.
(Firstly, I feel … because … / Secondly, I think … since … /Lastly, I believe … as …)

(c) Share three ideas you would give to someone who needs to work hard.
(To begin with, it is important that … /Next, you could … / Finally, I think you should …)

Ans. (a) Well, you see hard work means going an extra mile and doing something with dedication, to achieve your goals. It means engaging yourself in constant and serious effort. It is something that requires dedication and patience. What I mean is that it is absolutely essential for success.

(b) First, I feel hard work is important because it leads to personal development. You learn new skills and as you try to improve yourself. Second, I think hard work is crucial since it builds discipline and a strong work ethic, which are essential for achieving one's goals. Lastly, I believe hard work is important as it often leads to success and recognition, making you feel capable and proud of your efforts.

(c) To begin with, it is important that you are clear about your goals. This helps you stay focused and motivated. Next, you could create a plan to manage your time and ensure you are consistent in your efforts. Finally, I think you should stay positive and persistent, even when things don't go according to what you planned.

LET US WRITE (NCERT PAGE 11)

1. Work in pairs to complete the description of a banana. You may take the help of the words given in brackets. Share your answers with your classmates and teacher.

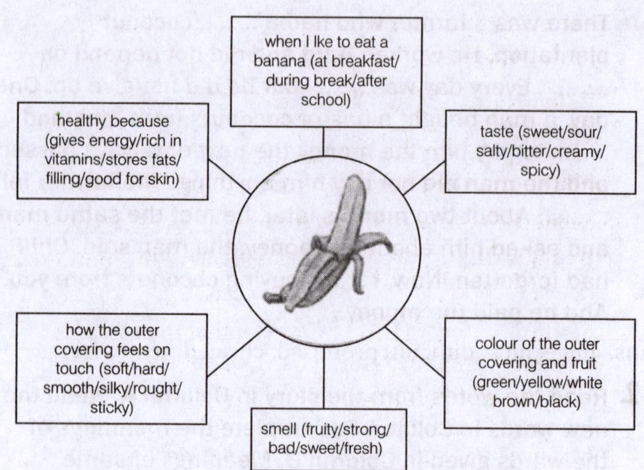

Now, use the information given in the picture to write eight sentences about a banana. Share your responses with your classmates and teacher.

Ans. Description

Banana is a sweet and soft fruit that has a refreshing fruity smell. The colour of its outer covering is yellow when it is ripe.

The outer covering of the banana feels smooth to touch. Bananas can be eaten at any time of the day and are very healthy. It is good for the skin, gives instant energy, stores good fats and is very filling.

8 Sentences

(i) I like to eat a banana during break time because it gives me a boost of energy.
(ii) Bananas are healthy because they are rich in vitamins.
(iii) The taste of a banana is sweet, which makes it a delightful fruit.
(iv) The outer covering of a banana feels smooth to the touch.
(v) Green bananas can be used to make curries as they are raw.
(vi) Bananas have a fruity and sweet smell that is quite refreshing.
(vii) Bananas taste sweet and soft, that is why it is my favourite fruit.
(viii) It is also very easy to carry with me to school and I can eat it without cutting it.

2. On the basis of the story 'A Bottle of Dew' develop a script with dialogues and enact it with expressions. Present it in the assembly or your classroom.

Ans. **Title** A Bottle of Dew

Characters

Rama Natha : Main Character

Mahipati : The wise sage

Madhumati : Rama Natha's wife, intelligent lady

Scene 1

Rama Natha : (Surprised) I can't believe this potion doesn't work!

Madhumati : (Angrily) I told you that man was just trying to get money from you. You got tricked again! When will you stop looking for that magic potion? Now, I am worried about losing all the money we have because you keep wasting it.

Scene 2

A wise sage called 'Mahipati' comes to the village and Rama Natha becomes his follower. He asks the sage about the magic potion and the sage gives him the recipe.

Mahipati : You have to plant a banana plant and water it regularly with your hands. In winter, the morning dew is on the leaves. You have to collect the dew and store it in a bottle. When you have five litres of dew, bring it to me. I will chant some magic words, which will turn it into the magic potion. A drop of the potion will change any object into gold.

Rama Natha : Really? But I'm worried that it'll take me a long time to collect five litres of dew. How will I do that?

Mahipati : You can plant as many plants as you like. But remember, you must look after them yourself and collect the dew with your own hands.

Scene 3

Six years went by and Rama Natha's lands turned into banana plantations. He takes care of each plant himself and his wife sells the crop in the market for a good price. They keep increasing the number of banana plants and finally Rama Natha succeeds in collecting five litres of dew. The sage chants some magic words and gives the bottle to Rama Natha.

Mahipati Now, try it!

The potion is ready.

Rama Natha : (Sprinkles the potion on the copper vessel…nothing happens) I have been tricked again! This potion doesn't work!

Madhumati enters with a box.

Madhumati : (Smiling) What are you talking about? Here's the gold.

Madhumati shows Rama Natha a box full of gold coins that she saved from their earnings from the plantation.

Rama Natha : (Surprised) Where did this come from?

Mahipati : There is no magic potion that can turn things into gold. You worked hard on your land and created this plantation. While you looked after the trees, your wife sold the fruits in the market. That's how you got this money. It was your hard work that created this wealth, not magic. If I had told you about this earlier, you would have not listened to me, so I have played a trick on you.

Rama Natha understood the wisdom behind these words and worked even harder on his plantation from that day on.

REVIEW EXERCISE

Including Competency Based Questions

Part I

Multiple Choice Questions

1. Rama Natha was a son of a rich landlord as

(a) he had a huge banana plantation
(b) he had a box of gold coins
(c) he had a magic potion
(d) he owned large tracts of land

Ans. (d) he owned large tracts of land

2. A liquid that has magical effects is called

(a) A magic potion (b) A fertiliser
(c) A beverage (d) None of these

Ans. (a) A magic potion

3. Which word best describes the sage?

(a) Poor (b) Kind hearted
(c) Wise (d) Proud

Ans. (c) Wise

4. Which of the following words best describes Rama Natha at the beginning of the story?

(a) Wise (b) Proud
(c) Foolhardy (d) Hardworking

Ans. (c) Foolhardy

5. **Which of the following words best describes Rama Natha's wife Madhumati?**
(a) Hardworking (b) Supportive
(c) Spendthrift (d) Both (a) and (b)

Ans. (d) Both (a) and (b)

6. **Why did the Sage Mahipati trick Rama Natha into working hard instead of telling him the truth?**
(a) Because he knew that Rama Natha would not accept his wisdom through words
(b) Because Rama Natha did not believe in the words of sages and wisemen
(c) Because Madhumati requested the sage to trick Rama Natha into working hard
(d) Because the sage was angry at Rama Natha for not giving him expensive gifts

Ans. (d) Because he knew that Rama Natha would not accept his wisdom through words

Fill in the Blanks

1. **Madhumati sold the banana crop because she wanted to .... money.**

Ans. earn

2. **Rama Natha worked hard on the banana plantation as he needed to collect .... for the magic potion.**

Ans. five litres of dew

3. **Unlike Rama Natha, Madhumati was a wise and .... woman.**

Ans. hardworking

4. **The five litres of dew collected by Rama Natha was a symbol of the hard work he had done over the course of ....**

Ans. six years

5. **The sage Mahipati wanted to teach Rama Natha that hard work is best way of achieving our ....**

Ans. goals

State True or False

1. **Madhumati was happy with Rama Natha's habits.**

Ans. False

2. **Mahipati tricked Rama Natha to teach him a lesson.**

Ans. True

3. **Rama Natha was a wise man.**

Ans. False

4. **Rama Natha punished the people who cheated him.**

Ans. False

5. **Rama Natha travelled to the Himalayas in search of the magic potion.**

Ans. False

6. **Madhumati helped Rama Natha in taking care of the banana plants.**

Ans. True

Extract Based Questions

Read the extract given below and answer the questions that follow.

A. One day, a famous sage called Mahipati came to their town. Rama Natha became his follower and asked him about the potion. To his surprise the sage answered, 'Yes, in my travels in the Himalayas, I heard how you could make such a potion. But it is difficult.' 'Tell me!' requested Rama Natha, not believing his luck.

(i) **Complete the following sentence appropriately.**
Rama Natha was looking for a magic potion that ....

Ans. could turn anything into gold.

(ii) **Why couldn't Rama Natha believe his luck?**

Ans. Rama Natha couldn't believe his luck because he had been looking for the magic potion for so many years and never got any promising answers from anyone.

(iii) **Which of the following places did the sage travel to?**
(a) Brahmaputra
(b) The Western Ghats
(c) The Thar
(d) The Himalayas

Ans. (d) The Himalayas

(iv) **State whether the following statement is True or False.**
Rama Natha became Mahipati's follower only because he wanted the magic potion.

Ans. False

B. Rama Natha went home, and after talking to his wife started cleaning his large fields, which had been lying empty all these years. There he planted rows and rows of banana plants. He tended them carefully and during the winter months collected the dew that formed on them with great care. His wife helped him too.

Madhumati gathered the banana crop, took it to the market and got a good price for it. Over the years, Rama Natha planted more and more plants and they had a huge banana plantation. At the end of six years, he finally had his five litres of dew.

(i) Place the following events in the correct order to match the story.

(a) Rama Natha talked to Madhumati.

(b) Rama Natha collected five litres of dew.

(c) Madhumati sold the bananas at the market.

(d) Rama Natha planted rows and rows of banana plants.

Ans. a-d-c-b

(ii) Why were Rama Natha's lands lying empty?

Ans. Rama Natha's lands were lying empty all these years because he did not want to work and wasted all his time looking for the magic potion.

(iii) Complete the sentence based on your understanding.

Rama Natha took care of his banana plantations with dedication, as ....

Ans. he wanted to collect five litres of dew as advised by the sage so that he could prepare a magic potion with it.

(iv) State whether the given statement is True or False.

Rama Natha failed to collect the dew and gave up.

Ans. False

C. Carefully, he took the bottle to the sage. The sage smiled and muttered something over the water. Then he returned the bottle and said, 'Try it out.' Rama Natha sprinkled a few drops on a copper vessel and waited for it to turn to gold. To his surprise nothing happened! 'This is cheating,' he told the sage. 'I have wasted six precious years of my life.'

(i) Why did the sage mutter something over the water?

Ans. The sage muttered the magical words to turn the water into a magic potion.

(ii) What happened when Rama Natha sprinkled the magic potion on the vessel?

(a) The vessel turned to stone

(b) The vessel remained unchanged

(c) The vessel turned silver

(d) The vessel turned gold

Ans. (b) The vessel remained unchanged

(iii) Do you think Rama Natha wasted six years of his life?

Ans. No. Rama Natha did not waste his time, instead he used it to be productive and became successful with his huge banana plantations.

(iv) The word that means the same as 'shower' in the given extract is ....

Ans. sprinkled

Very Short Answer Type Questions

Part II

1. What did Rama Natha's father leave him when he passed away?

Ans. Rama Natha's father left him large tracts of land when he passed away.

2. Why didn't Rama Natha look after his land?

Ans. Rama Natha did not look after his land because he wanted a magic potion and dedicated all his time looking for it.

3. Why did Rama Natha get cheated by people?

Ans. Rama Natha got cheated by people due to his belief that a magic potion that turned things to gold existed.

4. Why was Madhumati worried?

Ans. Madhumati was worried because Rama Natha did not work on his land and spent all his time and money on finding the magic potion.

5. What did Rama Natha ask the sage about?

Ans. Rama Natha asked the sage about the magic potion.

6. What did Rama Natha do after listening to the recipe of the magic potion?

Ans. Rama Natha dedicated all his time taking care of the banana plants after listening to the recipe of the magic potion.

7. Who helped Rama Natha understand the truth about the magic potion in the story?

Ans. The sage, Mahipati helped Rama Natha understand the truth about the magic potion and the value of hard work in the story.

Short Answer Type Questions

1. Why didn't Rama Natha take care of his land?

Ans. According to the story, Rama Natha believed that there existed a magic potion which could turn anything into gold and make him wealthy. Therefore, he spent all his time looking for the potion and never took care of his lands.

2. Write about Rama Natha's reaction when Mahipati said he knew the recipe of the magic potion.

Ans. When Mahipati told Rama Natha that he had heard of the recipe to make the magic potion, Rama Natha was shocked as well as excited. He could not believe his luck and excitedly asked Mahipati to tell him the recipe of the potion immediately.

3. How was Rama Natha before he met the sage and started working in his fields?

Ans. Before meeting the Sage and started working in his fields, Rama Natha was a lazy man. He spent most of his time looking for a magic potion. He believed that if he had the magic potion that could convert anything to gold, he would become wealthy.

Long Answer Type Questions

1. How did Rama Natha's wife help him in gaining wealth?

Ans. Rama Natha's wife helped him in gaining wealth. Rama Natha had planted banana plants on his large tracts of land as suggested by the sage and spent all his time tending to them. This resulted in the banana plants bearing good quality fruit. Rama Natha's wife, Madhumati, gathered the fruit crop and sold it in the market for a good price, and over the years this helped Rama Natha increase his plantation and ultimately, his earnings. This is how Rama Natha's wife helped him in gaining wealth.

2. What changes could be noted in Rama Natha's behaviour during the six years when he worked on his banana plantation? What moral do we derive from this story of Rama Natha?

Ans. Many changes could be noted in Rama Natha's behaviour during the six years when he worked on his banana plantation. During the six years when he worked on his banana plantation, Rama Natha became a very hardworking and responsible man. He took care of his plantation with dedication and stopped chasing a shortcut to get the magic potion that would turn anything into gold. The story of Rama Natha, 'A Bottle of Dew' teaches us the value of hard work through Rama Natha's example. It tells us that there is no shortcut to success or gaining wealth. We must work hard towards our goals consistently to achieve them.

3. How was Madhumati different from Rama Natha?

Ans. Madhumati was different from Rama Natha as she did not believe in the magic potion and was a responsible person.

When Rama Natha spent all his time and money looking for the magic potion, she worried that they may lose all their wealth. Also, when Rama Natha was busy collecting dew for the magic potion, she took the crop to the market and sold it for a good price to make profit.

4. Describe Rama Natha's character before his ultimate realisation by sharing some examples from the story to support your answer.

Ans. Rama Natha was the son of a wealthy landlord and inherited large tracts of land when his father passed away. However, he did not take care of his lands and was determined to find a magic potion that would turn anything into gold so that he could become rich instantly.

This suggests that he was not only lazy but also very foolish. He was easily tricked by people who claimed to know about the magic potion.

Competency Based Questions

1. If you were Rama Natha's neighbour and he came to ask you about the magic potion, how would you deal with him?

Ans. If I were Rama Natha's neighbour, I would advise him to stop looking for the magic potion. I would tell him that if such a potion existed, no one would have been poor and someone would have already claimed it. I would ask him to start working and earning money so that he could save his earnings and become rich by working hard. I would also advise him to work on the vast land that his father had left him for farming.

2. 'You can plant as many banana plants as you want. But remember, you must look after them yourself and collect the dew with your own hands.' Who is the speaker of these lines? What was his intention behind these words? Give a reason for your answer.

Ans. The speaker of these lines is the wise sage, Mahipati. By asking Rama Natha to plant banana plants and take care of them himself, Mahipati wanted him to learn the importance of hard work and stop chasing after the magic potion.

At the end of the story, when Madhumati reveals that she had been selling the banana crop and saving the earnings, Rama Natha understands why the sage had asked him to collect the dew in the first place. He realised that the wise sage wanted him to learn the importance of hard work and dedication. He learned that he had to work hard to become wealthy.

3. There is a very famous quote by Booker T. Washington-'Nothing ever comes to one, that is worth having, except as a result of hard work.' Do you think it is true? Justify the statement based on your understanding of the story 'A Bottle of Dew'.

Ans. Yes, it is true that nothing ever comes to one without putting in effort and working hard.

We can easily derive this from the story 'A Bottle of Dew' where Rama Natha spends most of his time and resources looking for a shortcut to create wealth and keeps getting cheated by people.

However, taking the wise sage's advice, when Rama Natha works hard to grow and tend to his banana plantation, he eventually becomes rich.

Grammar and Writing

1. Write the homophones of the words given in column A in column B and then form sentences making use of both the words in the same sentence.

Column A	Column B	Column A	Column B
(i) Buy	....	(ii) Break	....
(iii) Hear	....	(iv) Pear	....
(v) Site	....		

(i) ....

(ii) ....

(iii) ....

(iv) ....

(v) ....

Ans. (i) Buy-by

I like to buy fruit salad from the vendor by the river bank.

(ii) Break-brake

Ravi took a break from racing as he got his brakes checked by the mechanic.

(iii) Hear-here

(iv) I hear that Sarah is coming here for the summer break.

(v) Pear-pair

Pear is a fruit that can be paired with any dessert easily.

(vi) Site-sight

Near the construction site, there was no food vendor in sight.

2. Complete the following sentences using the appropriate connectors.

[but, however, on the other hand, otherwise, unlike]

(i) I wanted to go swimming.......I am so tired.

(ii) The film received good ratings...it was very long.

(iii) I was eager to join them for the vacation but............., my exam dates were getting closer.

(iv) Remind them beforehand..........., they might leave without taking the tickets.

(v) Zoey loved hot chocolate........John.

Ans. (i) but (ii) however (iii) on the other hand (iv) otherwise (v) unlike

3. Rama Natha had a habit of writing a diary. Imagine he had written a diary before meeting the wise sage, after meeting the wise sage and after realising the wisdom the sage wanted to give. You may start like this for all the diaries.

Diary 1

2nd August, 20XX 9:00 pm

Dear Diary

You know I am sure that ....

Diary 2

12th August, 20XX 9:00 pm

Dear Diary

I was sure that the great and wise ....

Diary 3

2nd August, 20XX 9:00 pm

Dear Diary

I could never believe in ....

Ans. Diary 1

2nd August, 20XX 9:00 pm

Dear Diary

You know I am sure that one day I would find that magic potion that could turn any object into gold. I truly believe it and when I find the potion, I will become wealthy. So, why should work in those fields, sweat to make a farm?

I will never be able to convince Madhu. She thinks I am a fool to have such a belief. I hope I find the potion soon and shut everyone's mouth.

Rama Natha

Diary 2

12th August, 20XX 9:00 pm

Dear Diary

I was sure that the great and wise sage Mahipati would help me find the potion. He has travelled far and wide, and must have learnt about the many potions that exist in the world. Hence, I have been following him religiously and finally, the sage told me the process of making the potion.

It is long and requires a lot of hard work but I will do it. At last, I would become wealthy in few years.

Rama Natha

Diary 3

2nd August, 20XX 9:00 pm

Dear Diary

I could never believe in the importance of hard work if not for sage Mahipati. In order to teach me the lesson, sage Mahipati had fooled me into cultivating a banana plantation. I had worked hard, planted the farm and collected the dew and after 6 years I thought I had the potion. However, there is no such potion. It was indeed my hard work that made me wealthy. I have learnt the lesson with difficulty and wasted many years of my life on nonsensical things. But now I will work hard in the farms.

Rama Natha

ASSESSMENT EXERCISE

Multiple Choice Questions

1. What did people do when Rama Natha asked them about the magic potion?

(a) They helped him
(b) They ignored him
(c) They took advantage of him
(d) They joined him in his quest

2. Rama Natha cleaned his lands and started planting rows and rows of banana plants because

(a) he wanted to establish a business
(b) he liked the fruit banana a lot
(c) he wanted to collect five litres of dew quickly
(d) None of the options are relevant

3. Who said the following lines and to whom?

I have wasted six precious years of my life.

(a) Mahipati to Madhumati
(b) Mahipati to Rama Natha
(c) Rama Natha to Madhumati
(d) Rama Natha to Mahipati

4. Arrange the following lines in the correct sequence based on their occurrence in the story.

(i) Rama Natha becomes a follower of Mahipati.
(ii) Madhumati gets worried.
(iii) Rama Natha tests the potion.

(a) (iii), (ii), (i) (b) (ii), (i), (iii)
(c) (i), (ii), (iii) (d) (iii), (i), (ii)

Fill in the Blanks

1. Madhumati was .... about Rama Natha.

2. Rama Natha worked hard on the ....

3. Mahipati was a .... sage.

4. The five litres of dew collected by Rama Natha was a symbol of his ....

State True or False

1. Madhumati helped Rama Natha in the fields.

2. Rama Natha was angry when the magic potion did not work.

3. Rama Natha was a lazy man.

Extract Based Questions

Read the extract given below and answer the questions that follow.

"This is cheating," he told the sage. "I have wasted six precious years of my life." But sage Mahipati only smiled and called Madhumati to come forward.

(i) Complete the following sentence appropriately.

When Rama Natha accused the sage of cheating him, Mahipati only smiled because he ....

(ii) Why did the speaker feel cheated by the Sage Mahipati?

(iii) Do you think Rama Natha could have done something better in these six years? Give reason for your answer.

(iv) Which of the following words is the opposite in meaning of the word 'precious'?

(a) Costly (b) Expensive (c) Useless (d) Treasured

Very Short Answer Type Questions

1. Why was Madhumati worried?

2. Why did Rama Natha follow the sage's advice?

3. What do we learn from Madhumati?

4. In what season did the sage ask Rama Natha to collect the dew?

Short Answer Type Questions

1. Who tricked Rama Natha and why?

2. Why didn't Rama Natha think of becoming rich by working hard?

3. Mahipati say that he had heard of the magic potion during his travels. Is it true? Give reason for your answer.

4. Why did Rama Natha plant so many trees instead of planting just one?

Long Answer Type Questions

1. Rama Natha was stubbornly set on his goal of finding the magic potion but the sage Mahipati had the perfect solution for him. How did the words of the sage end up changing Rama Natha?

2. Chanakya said that one must learn from the experience of ourselves as well as others. What lessons do you as a reader gain from the story 'A Bottle of Dew'?

The Raven and the Fox

CHAPTER 2

by Jean de La Fontaine

About the Chapter The Raven and the Fox is a classic French fable (story with a message) poem by Jean de La Fontaine. This tale of cunning and trickery presents the story of a Raven (a bird) who falls victim to the crafty fox's flattery. As a cautionary tale, it highlights the dangers of excessive pride and the false nature of flattery.

Stanzawise Explanation

Stanza 1

Mr Raven was perched upon a limb,
And Reynard the Fox looked up at him;
For the Raven held in his great big beak,
A morsel the Fox would go far to seek.

Explanation The poem begins with Mr Raven (a bird) sitting on a branch of a tree. He had some food in his great beak. Under the tree, Mr Reynard, a fox, was looking at Mr Raven. He was looking at the food that Mr Raven had. He wanted the food but knew that Mr Raven was high up on the tree and he could not reach it.

Stanza 2

Said the Fox, in admiring tones: "My word!
Sir Raven, you are a handsome bird.
Such feathers! If you would only sing,
The birds of these woods would call you King."

Explanation To get the food, the fox started admiring Mr Raven. He told Mr Raven that he was a handsome bird with beautiful feathers. He added that if Mr Raven could sing now, he would be called the ruler by the other birds who resided in the woods.

Stanza 3

The Raven, who did not see the joke,
Forgot that his voice was just a croak.
He opened his beak, in his foolish pride-
And down fell the morsel the Fox had eyed.

Explanation The Raven was an innocent bird. He forgot that his voice was not sweet or melodious but was very harsh.

So, he accepted the admiration and opened his beak to sing for the fox. As a result, the food he had in his beak fell down.

The bird, Mr Raven, is called foolish because it could not see that the clever fox was fooling him. In his pride, he opened his beak to sing and lost his food to the fox, who had wanted that food.

Stanza 4

"Ha-ha!" laughed the Fox. "And now you know,
Ignore sweet words that make you glow.
Pride, my friend, is rather unwise;
I'm sure this teaching is quite a surprise."

Explanation As soon as the food fell down, the fox took it and laughed at Mr Raven. He told the bird that now he should learn to ignore praises and flattery.

He added that pride is unwise and this teaching is a surprise for him as the Raven did not expect the situation to occur.

Values Extracted from this Chapter

The chapter presents a very simple message that one should never trust someone who praises us continuously. Such flatterers have a selfish motive which includes a loss on your part.

Word Meaning

Word	Meaning	Word	Meaning
Perched	Sitting	My word	My God
Limb	A tree branch	Croak	Harsh sound
Morsel	A small piece of food		

NCERT FOLDER

NCERT Intext and Exercise Questions

LET US DISCUSS (NCERT PAGES 14-15)

1. Fill in the blanks by choosing the correct option.

(a) Stanza 1

(i) Mr Raven is a .... (bird/frog)

Ans. bird

(ii) The name of the fox is .... (Raven/Reynard)

Ans. Reynard

(iii) Mr Raven had .... in his beak. (a piece of food/ a bunch of leaves)

Ans. a piece of food

(b) Stanza 2

(i) The Fox calls the Raven a .... bird. (foolish/good-looking)

Ans. good-looking

(ii) The Fox asks the Raven to .... (dance/sing)

Ans. sing

(iii) The Raven and the Fox live in the .... (trees/woods)

Ans. woods

(c) Stanza 3

(i) The Raven .... that he croaked. (remembered/forgot)

Ans. forgot

(ii) The Raven opened its beak to .... (eat/sing)

Ans. sing

(iii) The .... fell down. (food/Raven)

Ans. food

(d) Stanza 4

(i) The Fox .... at the Raven. (laughed/looked)

Ans. laughed

(ii) It is not .... to be too proud of oneself. (wise/unwise)

Ans. wise

(iii) The Raven learnt a .... (lesson/teaching)

Ans. lesson

2. Read the poem again and match the words in Column A with their meanings in Column B. Check your answers with your teacher and your classmates.

Column A	Column B
1. perched	(a) a small piece of food
2. morsel	(b) looked with interest at something
3. seek	(c) feeling that you are better than others
4. pride	(d) sat on a branch
5. eyed	(e) to look for something
6. limb	(f) a smaller area of forest with similar kind of trees
7. woods	(g) branch of a tree

Ans.

1. (d) 2. (a) 3. (b)
4. (c) 5. (e) 6. (g)
7. (f)

LET US THINK AND REFLECT

(NCERT PAGES 15-16)

1. Look at the pictures and number them in the order that they happen in the poem.

Ans. 2, 4, 1, 3

2. Read the following lines and answer the questions that follow.

(a) Sir Raven, you are a handsome bird.
Such feathers! If you would only sing,
The birds of these woods would call you King.

(i) 'Such feathers' refer to .... feathers.

(a) shiny and beautiful

(b) black and dull

(c) grey and long

(d) short and unattractive

Ans. (a) shiny and beautiful

(ii) Why would the birds of the woods call the Raven 'King'?

Ans. The birds would call the Raven 'King' because if he could sing in addition to having beautiful feathers, he would be considered the best bird among them.

(iii) Why does the Fox address the Raven as 'Sir'?

Ans. The Fox addresses the Raven as 'Sir' to flatter him and make him feel proud.

(b) The Raven, who did not see the joke,
Forgot that his voice was just a croak.
He opened his beak, in his foolish pride-

(i) Why did the Raven open his beak?

Ans. The Raven opened his beak to sing because he was flattered by the Fox's praise and wanted to show off his 'beautiful' voice.

(ii) Complete the following with one word from the given lines.

Fox : clever : : Raven : ....

Ans. foolish

3. Why does the Raven forget that his voice is just a croak?

Ans. The Raven forgets that his voice is just a croak because he is flattered and proud after hearing the Fox's false compliments.

4. How does Reynard make the Raven sing?

Ans. Reynard makes the Raven sing by flattering him. He tells that Raven that he is a handsome bird and would be considered a king if he could also sing beautifully.

5. Why does Reynard say that pride is not wise?

Ans. Reynard says that pride is not wise because being too proud can make you do foolish things, like the Raven opening his beak and losing his food.

6. Give one reason why the teaching is quite a surprise.

Ans. The teaching is quite a surprise for the Raven because he had not expected to be tricked by the Fox's compliments and lose his food. It makes us assume that the Raven considered itself very wise.

7. Imagine someone praises you too much. How would you react?

Ans. If someone praises me too much, I would be cautious and try to understand their intentions. I would appreciate the compliments but, I would stay humble and alert.

LET US LEARN (NCERT PAGES 16-17)

1. Write the rhyming words from the poem. One has been done for you.

Stanza 1	Stanza 2	Stanza 3	Stanza 4
(a) limb-him	(a) word-......	(a) joke-......	(a) know-......
(b)	(b)	(b)	(b) ....

Ans. Stanza 1

(a) limb - him (b) beak - seek

Ans. Stanza 2

(a) word - bird (b) sing - king

Ans. Stanza 3

(a) joke - croak (b) pride - eyed

Ans. Stanza 4

(a) know - glow (b) unwise - surprise

2. Study the underlined words in the poem.

(a) For the Raven held in his great <u>big beak</u>.

The words 'big' and 'beak' begin with the same /b/ sound.

(b) The <u>song</u> of <u>sweet</u> birds.

Now, pick another example of alliteration from Stanza 2.

Ans. woods-would

3. Choose the correct opposites form the box given below and complete the table. There are two extra words that your will not need.

wise, happy, humility, flew, remembered, notice, dim, cried, silly

	Words	Opposites
1.	perched	
2.	forgot	
3.	foolish	
4.	pride	
5.	laughed	
6.	ignore	
7.	glow	

Use any four words form the table given above to make sentences of your own.

Ans. Opposites

1. flew
2. remembered
3. wise
4. humility
5. cried
6. notice
7. dim

Sentences

1. The bird **flew** away hearing the loud noise.
2. She **remembered** his birthday and gave him a present.
3. It is **wise** to always put a lock on your luggage.
4. He accepted the honor with **humility**.
5. The child **cried** as he lost his favourite ball.
6. Please give us enough **notice** to prepare for your arrival.
7. The light is too **dim** for me to read.

LET US SPEAK (NCERT PAGE 18)

1. Narrate the poem in the form of a story. Give a different ending to the story.
You may begin like this

This is a story about a clever fox named Reynard and Mr Raven. One day...

Ans. This is a story of a clever fox named Reynard and Mr Raven. One day Mr Raven was sitting on a branch of a tree and held a delicious snack in his big beak. Reynard the fox was walking near the tree when he say Mr. Raven with the snack. Reynard was hungry and had not eaten anything since morning. So, he decided to play a trick on the bird to get the delicious looking food he had.

Reynard called Mr Raven and remarked, "Sir Raven, you really are a handsome bird. What gorgeous feathers! The birds in these forests would crown you King if you would just sing."

Mr. Raven was happy to hear the fox's praise. Reynard waited for Mr Raven to sing. He believed that that bird, in his silly arrogance, would open his beak. As a result, the snack would fall and he would have the snack all for himself. However, nothing happened. In fact, Mr Raven flew down to the fox. He divided the food into two halves and offered one to Reynard. The fox was surprised to see such an act and apologised. He told Mr Raven about his plan. Mr Raven told him that he had realised what the fox was trying to do.

He also scolded the fox for it and stated that a kind request for some food would have also gotten him the food. With this, Mr Raven held a friendship hand to the fox which he took. Since then, Mr Raven and Reynard have become good friends, sharing whatever food they could find.

LET US WRITE (NCERT PAGE 18)

1. Now, write the story you narrated in the form of a conversation.(Remember to write only the actions for the Raven as he has food in his mouth and does not speak.)
You may begin like this

Reynard Good morning, Mr Raven! You seem to be awake so early!

(Mr Raven just nods his head)

Reynard Oh, Mr Raven, you look...

Ans. Reynard Good morning, Mr Raven! You seem to be awake so early! (Mr Raven just nods his head)

Reynard Oh, Mr Raven, you look so handsome. What gorgeous feathers! The birds in these forests would crown you King if you would just sing.

(Mr Raven nods his head and flies down to Reynard. He tears the food into two halves and offers one to Reynard.)

Reynard (shocked) Uhhh....! I am so so so sorry Mr Raven. I had wanted the food just for myself. I had not eaten anything since the morning. I had been selfish and thus, tried to flatter you into singing so that the food would fell from your beak.

Mr Raven I know Reynard. But I am no fool. I knew your intentions from the very beginning. It was cruel and selfish of you to think to have all the food yourself. You had also been foolish to think that you could easily make a fool out of me.

You did not need to do anything but just request me that you are hungry and would be grateful if I could share. I would not have refused you.

Reynard (embarrassed) I am so sorry.

Mr Raven Now, don't worry. Have some food.

And hereafter, they both became friends, sharing whatever food they could find.

REVIEW EXERCISE

Including Competency Based Questions

Part I

Multiple Choice Questions

1. The Raven's voice was not sweet as described by the fox and it was just

(a) a croak (b) a chirp
(c) a coo (d) a whistle

Ans. (a) a croak

2. The Raven was .... and the fox was ....

(a) foolish, clever (b) clever, foolish
(c) wise, greedy (d) greedy, wise

Ans. (a) foolish, clever

3. The fox compliments the Raven on ....

(a) his looks
(b) his looks and voice
(c) the possibility of him being a king
(d) his big beak

Ans. (a) his looks

4. The value that we learn from the poem 'The Raven and The Fox' is

(a) we should feel proud when we receive compliments
(b) we must always share our food
(c) we must always stay humble
(d) we must not trust the words of flattery

Ans. (d) we must not trust the words of flattery

5. What was the fox's tone while complimenting the Raven?

(a) Sarcastic (b) Happy
(c) Sincere (d) Admiring

Ans. (a) Sarcastic

Fill in the Blanks

1. Reynard, the fox noticed that Mr Raven had a .... in his beak.

Ans. piece of food

2. The fox wanted the Raven to open its .... because he wanted to get the morsel from its beak.

Ans. beak

3. Mr. Raven's voice could be described as a ....

Ans. harsh and unpleasant

4. In the end, the fox is ....

Ans. happy

State True or False

1. The Raven has beautiful feathers.

Ans. False

2. The Raven is the most intelligent bird in the world.

Ans. False

3. The fox finally gets the morsel from Raven.

Ans. True

4. The Raven was sitting on a wall.

Ans. False

5. The fox starts his flattery by praising the Raven's appearance.

Ans. True

Extract Based Questions

Read the lines given below and answer the questions that follow.

A. "Such feathers! If you would only sing,
The birds of these woods would call you King."

(i) Who is the speaker here?

Ans. Reynard the fox is the speaker here.

(ii) What does he want from the listener?

Ans. Reynard wishes to flatter the listener, Mr Raven, through these words. By doing this, he would make him sing and drop his food.

(iii) Where is the conversation taking place?

(a) Woods
(b) Jungle
(c) River bank
(d) Park

Ans. (a) Woods

(iv) **State True or False for the following statement.**

The Raven was as foolish as described in the poem.

Ans. False

B. "And now you know,

Ignore sweet words that make you glow".

(i) **Who is talking to whom in the given extract?**

(a) The fox to the Raven (b) Raven to the fox

(c) The Raven to himself (d) The fox to himself

Ans. (a) The fox to the Raven

(ii) **What do these words suggest about the listener?**

Ans. From these words, it can be inferred that the listener, Mr Raven, became too proud of himself. He was foolish as he fell for Reynard's flattery and lost his food.

(iii) **State True or False for the following statement.**

The Raven fell for the fox's trick.

Ans. True

(iv) **The opposite of 'glow' is ....**

Ans. dim/dull

Part II

Very Short Answer Type Questions

1. **What did Reynard notice about Mr Raven?**

Ans. Reynard noticed that Mr Raven was holding a morsel in his big beak.

2. **Why did the fox compliment the Raven?**

Ans. The fox complimented the Raven to flatter him and make him sing. According to the fox's plan, when the Raven opened his mouth to sing, he dropped the piece of food that the fox had wanted.

3. **How did the Raven express his happiness at the compliment?**

Ans. The Raven expressed his happiness at the fox's compliment by getting ready to sing for him.

4. **What did the fox do after getting the food from the Raven?**

Ans. After getting the food from the Raven, the fox laughed at him and told him to not become foolish with pride as sweet words are not always true or sincere.

Short Answer Type Questions

1. **What should the Raven have remembered while dealing with the fox?**

Ans. While dealing with the fox, the raven should have remembered that his voice was not as sweet as the fox had described. He should also have remembered that the foxes are known for their cleverness and one should never trust their words.

2. **Why did the Raven start to sing?**

Ans. When the fox complimented the Raven and told him that he could be a king if he could sing. Listening to such words of praise from the fox, the Raven forgot that his voice was just a croak and that is why he began to sing.

Long Answer Type Question

1. **What weakness of the Raven's character made him open his mouth to sing and which characteristic of the fox made him successful in his plan?**

Ans. The Raven's weakness of giving in to flattery made him open his mouth to sing. When the fox complimented him, he became foolish with pride and forgot that his voice was melodious or pleasant. He prepared himself to sing and opened his mouth, dropping the food on the ground.

On the other hand, the fox was very clever and knew the raven's weakness. Therefore, fox's cleverness made him successful in his plan. By tricking the Raven to open his mouth to sing, the fox got himself the piece of food he wanted from the Raven.

Competency Based Questions

1. **'I' m sure the lesson is worth the price'. What was the lesson and what was the price according to the poem 'The Raven and The Fox'?**

Ans. The lesson was that we must never listen to or believe in is about flattery. The poetry teaches us that flattery is in most cases not true and done for selfish reasons. In the poem, the fox used false compliments to flatter the Raven and succeeded in tricking him.

The price paid by the Raven was that he believed in the fox's words and forgot that he was holding a morsel in his beak. As soon as he opened his mouth to sing, he dropped and lost the morsel to the fox.

2. **The famous English writer and philosopher John Ruskin once said, 'Pride is at the bottom of all great mistakes.' Explain how the poet Jean de La Fontaine uses this idea in her poem with reference to 'The Raven and The Fox'.**

Ans. John Ruskin's statement that pride is at the cause of all great mistakes is reflected in Jean de La Fontaine's poem the Raven and the Fox.

Fooled by the fox's false compliments, the Raven becomes full of pride and makes the mistake of forgetting that his voice is just a croak. He prepares to sing and opens his beak, dropping the morsel on the ground. This shows that his judgement was affected by fox's flattery which prevented him from making the right decision.

Therefore, this poem serves as a lesson to all of us. We must not let the words of others fill us with pride and forget our true personality.

Grammar and Writing

1. Has anyone ever paid you false compliments and said sweet words to take advantage of you? Describe the incident and your feelings about the same in the form of a conversation with a friend.

Ans. You : Have you ever had someone say really nice things to you, but you later realised they were just trying to get something from you?

Friend : I think so. Once that new student in our class, you know, the one with the cool pencil box, was being very friendly to me. He always said things like, "You're the best at maths!" or "You're so funny!"

You : Yes, I know what you mean.

Friend : So, one day, he asked me to lend him my favourite comic book.

I said, "Sure, no problem!" But, then he never gave it back! And after that, he even stopped talking to me.

You : That's not fair! It's like he was just pretending to be your friend to get what he wanted.

Friend : Exactly! I felt tricked and upset. It made me realise that not everyone is as nice as they seem.

You : Yes, it's important to be careful who you trust. Sometimes people say nice things just to get something from you.

2. Write three rhyming words for each of the given words.

(i) Down (ii) Glow

(iii) Unwise (iv) Sweet

Ans. (i) Town, crown, drown

(ii) Flow, blow, snow

(iii) Disguise, arise, prize

(iv) Treat, greet, meet

3. Pick out the opposites of the given words from the poem. One has been done for you as an example.

Words	**Opposites** (picked from the poem)
(i) Wise	Unwise
(ii) Humility	
(iii) Flew	
(iv) Remembered	
(v) Dim	
(vi) Cried	

Ans. (ii) Pride (iii) Perched

(iv) Forgot (v) Glow

(vi) Laughed

ASSESSMENT EXERCISE

Multiple Choice Questions

1. At the end of the poem we learn that pride is
   (a) unwise (b) important
   (c) unnecessary (d) foolish

2. According to the fox, what would the birds of the woods call the Raven if he sang?
   (a) The best singer (b) Mighty bird
   (c) The King (d) None of these

Fill in the Blanks

1. The fox flattered the Raven by telling him that the Raven was a .... bird and had a .... voice.

2. The Raven was so pleased with the .... that he opened his mouth to sing. After getting the food the fox told the Raven that he should not listen to ....

State True or False

1. The Raven's voice was melodious.
2. If the Raven would sing, the birds of the jungle would call him king.
3. The fox's real intention was to educate the Raven about not trusting the words of others.

Extract Based Questions

Read the lines given below and answer the questions that follow.

"The Raven, who did not see the joke, that his voice was just a croak"

(a) What is the 'joke' being discussed here?

(b) State whether the given statement is True or False.
The Raven laughed a lot at the joke.

(c) Which other animal makes the 'croak' sound?
(i) Frog (ii) Snake
(iii) Crocodile (iv) Fox

(d) The word that rhymes with 'croak' is ....

Very Short Answer Type Questions

1. Where was the Raven perched? What did he look like?
2. What did the fox want from the Raven?
3. Why did the fox ask the Raven to sing?

Short Answer Type Questions

1. If you were Mr Reynard, would you have advised the Raven the way the fox did after getting the morsel? Why or why not? Justify your answer by sharing evidence from the poem 'The Raven and The Fox'.
2. Why do you think the fox preached to the raven instead of just running away with the morsel?

Long Answer Type Question

1. After tricking the Raven into dropping the morsel he had in his mouth, the fox says that pride is unwise. How does the advice of the fox to "ignore sweet words that make you glow" serve to warn people about the influence of flattery and false praise on their decision-making?

Rama to the Rescue

CHAPTER 3

from Amar Chitra Katha

About the Chapter The given chapter is a folk tale taken from Amar Chitra Katha. It is in the form of a comic which describes how a couple saved themselves from being robbed with their quick thinking. The script of the comic is written by Luis M. Fernandes and the illustrations are made by Ram Waeerkar.

Important Characters

The Village Man He is a hard-working man who lived in a village. He is clever and wise as he comes up with the plan to get the thief arrested.

The Wife She is the man's wife. She is very observant as she realises that someone was trying to enter their house. She believes in her husband and acts according to their plan.

The Thief He is a smart thief who digs a hole in the wall to rob the couple.

Rama He is the village Kotwal who is very brave and observant.

Chapter Summary

A Village Man and his Wife

The comic shows that in a village, a man had returned from a hard day at work while his wife is cooking food. The man laid down on the mat stating that he was very sleepy. At that time his wife was not listening to him. Her attention is at the door of their house. As the man realises this, he asked his wife what was the matter and what was she looking at. His wife asked him to keep quiet and listen.

A Thief Tries to Enter the House

As the man listened to the voice, he realised that someone was trying to enter their house and conveyed this to his wife. Then, his wife told him that the person had entered the house as the noise had stopped. Scared, he asked his wife to lie down and to not look for the person. He, then, added that it was a thief who must have gone unnoticed by Rama, the village Kotwal.

The Thief Listens to the Couple

While the man and his wife were lying on the bed, they discussed what they should do and the man told his wife about the plan. Meanwhile, the thief had heard the voice and realised that the couple was awake. So, he decided to wait till the couple was asleep again. He also wondered where the couple kept their money. Thinking that the couple were discussing about their money, he decided to listen to their conversation carefully.

The Couple's Plan

The couple had already discussed their plan and started acting on it. They loudly talked about what they would name their child. The man replied that if they had a boy, he would name his Rama. The wife said that she liked the name and added that when the boy would be in the house, she would softy call him Rama. Then, the man asked what she would so, if the boy was in the yard. To this, his wife replied the she would call his name loudly.

The Thief Gets Angry

Hearing the couple talk about their child and not money, the thief got angry. He wished the couple stopped talking about the child and talk about their money. He thought that if they are not going to talk about money, they should go to sleep so that he could rob them.

Rama Comes to Save the Couple

While the thief is thinking, the man asked his wife what she would do if their child was not in the house or the yard but in the street.

The wife replied that she would call his name very loudly and started calling Rama very loudly. As the wife is calling Rama, the village Kotwal heard his name being called. So, he ran to the house.

Rama Catches the Thief

As Rama, the village Kotwal reached the house of the couple, he saw that a thief had dug a hole in the wall of the couple's house. He entered the house from the hole to see the thief. The thief was happily thinking that the couple had stopped talking and now he could rob them. Just then, Rama catches the thief and arrests him.

The couple was now relaxed as they heard Rama take the thief. They were happy that their plan worked and Rama had heard them.

Values Extracted from this Chapter

The chapter presents how quick thinking and cleverness saved the couple from being robbed.

NCERT FOLDER

NCERT Intext and Exercise Questions

LET US DISCUSS (NCERT PAGES 22 to 24)

Q.1 Circle the odd one

(a) The characters are-husband, wife, children

Ans. Children

(b) Who entered the house? guest, robber, Kotwal

Ans. Robber

Q.2 Write whether True or False.

(a) The man tells his plan to his wife.

Ans. True

(b) The thief wants to know where they kept their jewels.

Ans. False

LET US DISCUSS (NCERT PAGES 24 to 26)

Q.1 Along with your classmates, call out the name 'Rama'- softly, loudly and very loudly.

Ans. Do it in class.

Q.2 What do you think will happen next in the story?

Ans. According to me, Rama, the village Kotwal would come and arrest the thief.

Q.3 Work in pairs to match the words in Column A with the meanings in Column B. Check your answers by sharing them with your teacher and classmates.

	Column A		Column B
1.	wonder	(a)	In place of someone or something
2.	yard	(b)	carefully
3.	chatter	(c)	an area outside a building
4.	instead	(d)	talk for a long time about unimportant things
5.	closely	(e)	maybe
6.	perhaps	(f)	a feeling of surprise

Ans. 1-f, 2-c, 3-d, 4-a, 5-b, 6-e

Q.4 Fill in the boxes with suitable words as you read the story.

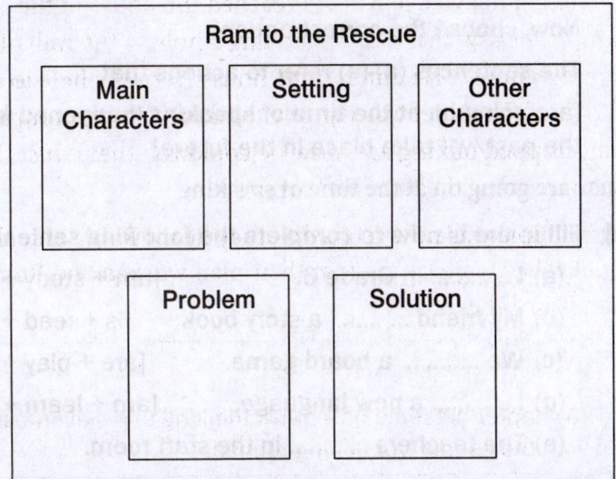

Ans. Main Characters A village man, his wife, the thief and Rama- the village Kotwal.

Setting A Village in Tamil Nadu, at night

Other Characters No side characters

Problem The thief has come to rob the couple's

Solution The village man and his wife cleverly alert the Kotwal by calling out his name loudly and the thief gets caught.

LET US THINK AND REFLECT

(NCERT PAGES 26-27)

1. Read the following lines and then answer the questions that follow.

(a) **Man** What's the matter? What are you looking at?

Wife Ssssh! Listen!

Man Somebody is trying to get in.

Wife I ... I think he has got in ... the noise has stopped.

(i) What makes the man say the first line?

Ans. The man says the first line because he finds his wife looking at something with a concerned look.

(ii) Choose the correct option.

The wife says 'Ssssh! Listen!'. What does the word 'Ssssh' mean here?

(a) Sleep (b) Help

(c) Rest (d) Be silent

Ans. (d) Be silent

(iii) How can you tell that the wife was listening carefully?

Ans. We can say that the wife was listening carefully as she noticed that the noise had stopped.

(b) Rama, the village Kotwal, ran to the house from which he heard his name being called.

Rama Oh, Oh! Some thief has dug his way into this house.

(i) Fill in the blank with the correct word from the given lines.

The villagers caught the thief and took him to the ....

Ans. village Kotwal

(ii) Choose the correct option.

What do the words "Oh, Oh!" show here?

(a) Surprise (b) Anger

(c) Pain (d) Happiness

Ans. (a) Surprise

(iii) How can you tell that the Kotwal was good at his job?

Ans. We can say that the Kotwal was good at his job because when he heard his name being called he quickly understood there was a problem and very cleverly caught the thief.

2. Give one reason why the man and his wife were not able to fall asleep.

Ans. The man and his wife were not able to fall asleep because they heard someone, a thief, trying to break into their house, which made them concerned and alert.

3. What did the thief wish would happen? Did it happen?

Ans. The thief wished that the man and his wife would stop talking about their child. He wished they would start talking about their money or just fall asleep. This did not happen because the couple continued their conversation as a clever way to call the village Kotwal.

4. How did the man and his wife get help from the Kotwal?

Ans. The man and his wife got help from the Kotwal by loudly pretending to call their child, using the Kotwal's name, Rama. This alerted the Kotwal who came to their house and caught the thief.

5. Do you think cleverness can help us solve our problems? Why do you say so?

Ans. Yes, cleverness can help us solve our problems because it allows us to think effectively and find creative solutions for difficult situations. In the story, the couple's clever idea of calling out the Kotwal's name tricked the thief and brought help, showing how quick thinking can be very effective.

LET US LEARN (NCERT PAGES 27 to 32)

1. Study the highlighted words in the following lines.

- **I'm** feeling so sleepy...
- **It's** a thief.
- **They're** awake.

The highlighted words given in the above sentences have one letter missing in each. What are they? Share them with your teacher and classmates.

Now, write the full words with the missing letter.

The missing letters are marked by an apostrophe (').

(a) .... feeling so sleepy ...

(b) .... a thief.

(c) .... awake.

Ans. (a) I am

(b) It is

(c) They are

2. Expand the following words. Two examples have been done for you. Use the contracted form of these words in sentences of your own.

S. No.	Contracted Words	Expanded Form	Sentences
(a)	what's	what is	
(b)	I'll		
(c)	I'd		
(d)	we'll		
(e)	that's		
(f)	we're		
(g)	don't		
(h)	you'll		
(i)	must've	must have	

Ans. (a) **What is** What's your favourite movie?

(b) **I will** I'll do my homework after I eat a doughnut.

(c) **I would** I'd like to sing a song.

(d) **We will** We'll go to the museum tomorrow.

(e) **That is** That's my bike.

(f) **We are** We're organising a blood donation camp.

(g) **Do not** Don't put your dirty shoes inside.

(h) **You will** You'll get a present on your birthday.

(i) **Must have** I must've left my phone at home.

3. Study the highlighted words and the words in the brackets in the following sentences from the story

(a) I am felling so sleepy. [am + feel + ing]

(b) What are you looking at? [are + look + ing]

(c) Somebody is trying to get in. [is + try + ing]

(d) They are saying something. [are + say + ing]

(e) Perhaps, they are talking about their money. [are + talk + ing]

Now, choose the correct option

The sentences (a)-(e) refer to actions that ....

[are going on at the time of speaking/happened in the past/wil take place in the future]

Ans. are going on at the time of speaking

4. Fill in the blanks to complete the following sentences.

(a) I .... in Grade 6. [am + study + ing]

(b) My friend .... a story book. [is + read + ing]

(c) We .... a board game. [are + play + ing]

(d) I .... a new language. [am + learn + ing]

(e) The teachers .... in the staff room. [are + sit + ing]

(f) My mother .... food in the kitchen. [is + cook + ing]

Ans. (a) am studying (b) is reading

(c) are playing (d) am learning

(e) are sitting (f) is cooking

5. Study the following picture and fill in the blanks with the present progressive form of verbs.

(a) Govind and Anu .... football.

(b) Pema .... flowers.

(c) Anil .... the score card.

(d) The mother .... a book.

(e) The dog .... to catch the ball.

(f) The birds .... in the sky

Ans. (a) are playing (b) is touching the

(c) is showing (d) is reading

(e) is running (f) are flying

6. Study the following sentences form the story and complete the table.

One example has been done for you.

(a) I'd better listen closely.

(b) When he's in the house, I'll can out softly to him.

(c) Then I'll call out very loudly...

S. No.	Sentence	Question	Word
1.	I'd better listen closely.	How does he listen?	(a) closely
2.	When he's in the house, I'll call you softly to him.	How does she call out?	(b)
3.	Then I'll call out very loudly.	How does she call out?	(c)

Words that give more information about the verb, such as how, when, where, etc. are called adverbs.

Ans. (b) softly (c) loudly

7. Fill in the blanks with suitable adverbs from the box given below. There are two extra words that you do not need.

warmly, gracefully, smoothly, beautifully, funnily, quickly, hurriedly

(a) He solved the mathematics problem ....

(b) The car moved .... along the highway.

(c) The musician played the guitar ....

(d) Shobha danced ....

(e) Rohit left the house ....

Ans. (a) quickly (b) smoothly

(c) beautifully (d) gracefully

(e) hurriedly

8. Fill in the blanks with suitable adverbs form the box given below. There are words that you do not need.

honestly, brightly, peacefully, sweetly, angrily, slowly, tirelessly.

Once upon a time in a small forest, animals lived (i) .... The wise old tortoise moved (ii) but always won the race against the proud rabbit. The ants worked (iii) ...., gathering food for the winter. The kind-hearted lion ruled and jungle (iv) ...., giving everyone a chance to speak. The birds sang (v) ...., making everyone in the forest happly.

Ans. (i) peacefully (ii) slowly

(iii) tirelessly (iv) honestly

(v) sweetly

9. Study the following sentences from the story and choose the correct option.

(i) Oh, hum! What a hard day it has been!

(ii) Ah, at last, they've stopped their chatter!

(iii) What should we do?

(iv) What should we name our child?

(a) Sentence (i) expresses a feeling of .... (tiredness/joy)

(b) Sentence (ii) expresses a feeling of .... (wonder/relief)

(c) Sentences (iii) and (iv) ask .... (answers /questions)

Ans. (a) tiredness (b) relief (c) questions

10. Punctuate the following sentences and write whether they are exclamatory or interrogative sentences.

(a) Wow, what an intelligent man he is

(b) Oh how big the hole is

(c) Do you like to read comic books

(d) What is your favourite story

- Sentences that express a strong feeling are called exclamatory sentences. They are marked by an exclamation mark (!).
- Sentences that ask questions are called interrogative sentences. They are marked by a question mark (?).

Ans. (a) Wow, what an intelligent man he is!

(b) Oh how big the hole is!

(c) Do you like to read comic books?

(d) What is your favourite story?

LET US SPEAK (NCERT PAGES 32-33)

1. Discuss in pairs

(a) Why do you think it's important for people to keep their house and themselves safe? Tick the suitable reasons.

(i) To be safe form injury

(ii) To keep family members and pets safe

(iii) To stop accidents from happening

(iv) To make sure they visit the doctor regularly

(v) To stop robbery

(vi) To pay the electricity bill

(vii) To save money

Ans. (i) tick (ii) tick

(iii) tick (iv) cross

(v) cross (vi) cross

(vii) tick

(b) Now, use the given hints to share your reasons in complete sentences with your teacher and classmates.

- I think it's important because ... /
- I feel it's necessary as ... /
- The reason we need to look at safety is ...

Ans.
- I think it's important because being safe from injury ensures that no one gets hurt and we get to live a healthy life.
- I feel it's necessary as keeping family members and pets safe is a priority for everyone.
- The reason why we need to look at safety is to stop accidents from happening, which can cause harm and inconvenience.

(c) Use the given hints to share three ideas on how people can keep their houses and themselves safe. Share with your classmates and teachers.

- I think they should ... /
- I suppose they could ... /
- They must ... /
- They should ... /
- How about ... /
- It might be better to ...

Ans.
- I think they should install security cameras in and around their house, and alarm systems to deter burglars and monitor their surroundings.
- I suppose they could even keep their doors and windows locked, especially when they are not at home.
- They must create an emergency plan for situations like fires, ensuring everyone knows what to do if there's an incident of fire or earthquake.
- They should regularly check and maintain smoke detectors and fire extinguishers in the house.
- How about educating family members, especially children, about safety measures and emergency contacts?
- It might be better to keep a first-aid kit and emergency supplies in an easily accessible place.

LET US WRITE (NCERT PAGE 34)

1. The next day, the neighbour asked the man in the story about what had happened. As the man, tell the neighbour what had happened in your own words. Remember to include the following.

when ....

where ....

what ....

how ....

why ....

You may begin this way

My wife and I were about to go to sleep last night when we heard someone ...

Ans. My wife and I were about to go to sleep last night when we heard someone trying to get into our house. It was quite late, around midnight. At first, we weren't sure what the noise was, but then it became clear that someone was attempting to get in our house. My wife and I listened carefully and realised that the noise had stopped, which meant the person had likely entered the house.

To handle the situation without alarming the thief, we decided to use a clever trick. We pretended to talk about naming our future child, using the name 'Rama,' which is also the name of village Kotwal. As we talked about Rama, our voices increased. Our plan worked perfectly as the Kotwal, who was nearby, heard us calling out his name and rushed to our house. The thief thought we were just discussing our future child and was caught off guard. Soon, the Kotwal arrived and arrested him on the spot.

REVIEW EXERCISE

Including Competency Based Questions

Part I

Multiple Choice Questions

1. The thief had entered the house through

(a) door (b) an open window

(c) a hole dug in the wall (d) a tunnel

Ans. (c) a hole dug in the wall

2. The couple continued to talk even when they knew there was an intruder in the house because

(a) they wanted to distract him

(b) they wanted to discuss a plan

(c) they wanted to fool him and call the Kotwal

(d) None of the above

Ans. (c) they wanted to fool him and call the Kotwal

3. The thief listened closely to their conversation because

(a) it was entertaining

(b) he wanted to know the name of their future child

(c) he wanted to know where the jewels were kept

(d) he wanted to know if they were asleep

Ans. (c) he wanted to know where the jewels were kept

4. Who said the following lines and to whom? "The plan worked! We're saved!"

(a) The man to his wife (b) Man's wife to him

(c) The thief to the Kotwal (d) The Kotwal to the couple

Ans. (b) Man's wife to him

5. Who helped the couple?

(a) The Kotwal (b) The village people

(c) The farmers (d) The priest

Ans. (a) The Kotwal

Fill in the Blanks

1. The man was .... when the thief entered the house.

Ans. preparing to sleep

2. The man asked his wife "What's the matter?" As he noticed she had a ....

Ans. concerned look on her face

3. The Kotwal was .... when he heard his name.

Ans. walking nearby

4. The thief listened to the couple ....

Ans. closely to know about where the jewels money was kept

State True or False

1. The man was frightened initially when he learned the thief had entered the house.

Ans. True

2. The wife started screaming for help as she heard someone entering the house.

Ans. False

3. The thief knew that the couple was trying to trick him.

Ans. False

4. The Kotwal entered the house through a window to save the couple.

Ans. False

5. The man caught the thief and took him to the Kotwal.

Ans. False

Extract Based Questions

Read the extracts given below and answer the questions that follow.

A.

(i) Who is not the speaker here?

(a) The thief (b) The village Kotwal

(c) The man (d) The man's wife

(ii) Why does he wish that the couple would talk about their money?

Ans. The thief wishes that the couple would talk about their money, so that it becomes easier for him to find the money and steal it.

(iii) State True or False for the following.

The man and his wife were playing a game to entertain themselves.

Ans. False

(iv) **Choose the synonym for the word 'silly' from the given options.**

(a) Cunning (b) Clever
(c) Funny (d) Foolish

B.

(i) **Who is talking here and to whom?**

(a) The man to his wife
(b) The wife to her husband
(c) The thief to the man
(d) The thief to himself

Ans. (a) The man to his wife

(ii) **What is the outcome of this conversation? How does it help the couple?**

Ans. When the wife yells "Rama, Rama" loudly, the village Kotwal Rama becomes alert. In this way, the thief gets caught and the man and his wife are able to protect themselves from the robbery.

(iii) **State True or False for the following.**

Rama is the name of the couple's son.

Ans. False

(iv) **Choose the word that is opposite of 'loudly' from the given options.**

(a) Noisily (b) Quietly
(c) Slowly (d) None of these

Ans. (b) Quietly

Part II

Very Short Answer Type Questions

1. **Who was Rama?**

Ans. Rama was the village Kotwal.

2. **Who noticed that someone was trying to get into the house?**

Ans. The man's wife first noticed that someone was trying to get into the house.

3. **How did the thief get into the house?**

Ans. The thief had dug a big hole in the wall of the house and used it to get in.

Short Answer Type Questions

1. **What was the man's reaction when he realised that there was a thief in the house?**

Ans. When the man realised that there was a thief in the house, he first became alert.

However, he remained calm and very cleverly handled the whole situation. He even asked his wife to remain calm and devised ab clever plan to get the attention of the village Kotwal, Rama.

2. **How did the man and his wife fool the thief?**

Ans. The man and his wife started talking about their future child's name loudly to deceive the thief.

By calling out the name "Rama" as if they were calling their child, they succeeded in alerting their village Kotwal Rama.

Long Answer Type Question

1. **Do you think the Kotwal was smart? Give one reason for your answer.**

Ans. Yes, I think the Kotwal was very smart. When he heard the man's wife calling his name out loudly, he immediately ran in that direction. He must have realised that there was a problem and he needed to go to the house from which the noise was coming. After reaching the house, he noticed the hole in the wall and understood the situation. He stealthily entered the house and caught the thief without giving him a chance to escape. This shows that the Kotwal was indeed smart.

Competency Based Questions

1. **In the story, what characteristics do you think the Kotwal and the couple had in common?**

Ans. In the story, 'Rama to the rescue', the couple and the Kotwal were similar. They all shared the characteristics of being smart and clever. Besides being smart, they also were calm when the thief had entered the house and handled the situation very well. The couple quickly devised a plan to alert the Kotwal and the Kotwal responded promptly by catching the thief.

2. **"Calmness is the cradle of power". Justify this statement based on your understanding of the story 'Rama to the Rescue'.**

Ans. It is true to say that calmness is the cradle of power. When one is calm, one can find solutions to every problem.

The story 'Rama to the rescue' presents the truth of the statement. The story could have taken a different turn if the man and his wife had not remained calm in the given situation. The thief could have escaped or attacked them if they had started screaming for help. However, they remained calm and did the right thing by alerting their village Kotwal and got the thief arrested. By doing this, the couple protected themselves and others in their village. Thus, we can say, calmness gives us power in any situation.

Grammar and Writing

1. Imagine you are Rama, the village Kotwal. Now, describe the incident of the attempted robbery and how you caught the thief, in your own words.

Ans. It was almost midnight and I was on night guard duty. I was making the rounds around the village as usual. I suddenly heard someone calling my name repeatedly and knew that there was something wrong. I ran in the direction where the sound was coming from and saw that someone had dug a hole in the wall of the house. I understood that someone might have entered the house from there so I quietly went in through the hole and there he was, a thief. I arrested him and put him in jail.

2. Complete the following sentences using the correct adverbs from the given options.

swiftly, neatly, slowly, loudly, properly, eagerly

swiftly, neatly, slowly, loudly, properly, eagerly

(a) My uncle walks ....
(b) Sharon does her job ....
(c) The baby is sleeping. Do not speak ....
(d) Ravi did his homework ....
(e) Cady and Ryan listened to the story ....
(f) The deer ran .... and escaped the cheetah's attack.

Ans. (a) slowly (b) neatly
(c) loudly (d) properly
(e) eagerly (f) swiftly

3. Fill in the blanks using the appropriate form of verb given in the brackets.

(a) I .... TV right now. (watch)
(b) She .... English in England. (learn)
(c) They .... for us. (wait)
(d) .... you .... with us? (come)
(e) They boys .... (sing) and the girls .... (dance)

Ans. (a) I am watching TV right now.
(b) She is learning English in England.
(c) They are waiting for us.
(d) Are you coming with us?
(e) The boys are singing and the girls are dancing.

4. Use the correct punctuation in the given paragraph.

I have a pet dog and his name is Taffy He loves to play with me in the park and he is my best friend He understands when I tell him to sit and when I tell him to turn around When I call out his name Taffy he jumps into my arms We both like to run fast but Taffy always runs faster He likes to eat meat and fish Sometimes I also give him dog biscuits as a treat I love my dog and he is like a family member to me

Ans. I have a pet dog and his name is Taffy. He loves to play with me in the park and he is my best friend. He understands when I tell him to sit and when I tell him to turn around. When I call out his name, "Taffy!" he jumps into my arms. We both like to run fast but, Taffy always runs faster. He likes to eat meat and fish. Sometimes, I also give him dog biscuits as a treat. I love my dog and he is like a family member to me.

5. Write one exclamatory and one interrogative sentence with each of the given words, using their contracted forms. One has been done for you as an example.

(a) You are

You're

- **Interrogative sentence - Are you comfortable with where you're seated?**
- **Exclamatory sentence - You're an amazing singer!**

(b) I am (c) How did (d) You have

Ans. (b) I'm
- **Interrogative Sentence** I'm Ravi and who are you?
- **Exclamatory Sentence** I can't believe that I'm selected for the finals!

(c) How'd
- **Interrogative Sentence** How'd you go to school if you missed the bus?
- **Exclamatory Sentence** How'd you make such delicious scones!

(d) You've
- **Interrogative Sentence** What you've written is correct but do you think it is good?
- **Exclamatory Sentence** Hurray! You've won the game again!

ASSESSMENT EXERCISE

Multiple Choice Questions

1. Who entered the house at night?

(i) Thief

(ii) A wild animal

(iii) The Kotwal

(iv) None of the above

2. What was the name of the Kotwal?

(i) Rama

(ii) Shyama

(iii) Mahipati

(iv) Rama Natha

3. Who said the following line and to whom?

''Ah! At last they've stopped their chatter''

(i) The man to his wife

(ii) The Kotwal to the couple

(iii) The thief to the couple

(iv) The thief to himself

Fill in the Blanks

1. The .... and his wife were in the house when they heard someone enter.

2. Rama entered the house through the .... in the wall and arrested the thief.

3. The man and his wife .... the thief by talking about their future child.

State True or False

1. Rama did not hear his name being called out.

2. The thief robbed the couple's house when they fell asleep.

3. The village Kotwal was on duty at night.

Extract Based Questions

Read the extract given below and answer the questions that follow.

''Oh, oh! some theif has dug his way into this house''

(i) Who is the speaker of this line?

(a) Rama

(b) The man

(c) The man's wife

(d) The thief

(ii) What did the speaker notice? What did he do next?

(iii) State whether the given statement is True or False.

Rama failed to catch the thief.

(iv) The past tense of 'dig' is ....

Very Short Answer Type Questions

1. What qualities of Rama are highlighted in the story?

2. What did the thief plan to do after entering the house?

Short Answer Type Questions

1. Do you think the thief was smart? Give reason for your answer.

2. ''Now soon they'll go to sleep and...'' Who is the speaker here and what is he planning?

3. What was the man's plan to save himself and his wife? Did he succeed?

Long Answer Type Questions

1. How did the couple's clever thinking help them?

2. What would have happened if the Kotwal had not heard the woman's call? How do you think the couple would have handled the situation then?

Unit-2 *(Friendship)*

The Unlikely Best Friends

CHAPTER 4

About the Chapter The given chapter by Subba Rao is a story of how each and every one of us need friends in our lives. The story focuses on the royal elephant, Gajaraj, who needed a friend to play with. The elephant finds a friend in a dog and is sad when they are separated. It ends with the friends reuniting and becoming happy again.

Important Characters

Gajaraj He is a royal elephant who is loved by the king. He needs a friend to play with.

The Dog He is a stray dog named Buntee who lives with a farmer. He becomes Gajaraj's friend.

The Mahout He is Gajaraj's caretaker. He provides food to Gajaraj and takes him for a bath.

Farmer He is the dog's owner who loves the dog very much.

Chapter Summary
Part I

Introducing Gajaraj- The Royal Elephant

Gajaraj was a royal elephant who lived in the best booth of the royal stables. The king loved Gajaraj and had ordered that the elephant should be well cared for. Hence, Gajaraj got all the royal comforts. However, Gajaraj was sad because he had no friends. The only person who interacted with him was the mahout or elephant trainer. The mahout was a kind man who served Gajaraj food and gave him a bath daily. He was a good caretaker, but not a friend.

Gajaraj Makes a Friend

Gajaraj wished to have a friend to play with. One day, in the late evening, a dog came into the stable. Gajaraj saw that the dog was tired and hungry. So, he pushed some of his food towards the dog. The dog was happy and then ate the food. As soon as he finished eating, the dog fell asleep.

The next morning, the mahout found the dog in the stable and let him stay. He noticed that Gajaraj seemed to like the company. So, he gave some food to the dog, which he accepted.

Gajaraj and the Dog Take a Bath

When Gajaraj went out for a bath, the dog went with him. In the water, Gajaraj showered using his long trunk, while the dog watched. The elephant took a trunkful of water and playfully threw the water on his friend. The dog barked as he hated taking showers. Looking at the elephant and the dog, the mahout laughed. On their way home, Gajaraj picked up the dog with his trunk and placed him on his back. The dog was very happy to get a ride.

The Dog's Owner

As the mahout was taking Gajaraj and the dog to their stable, a farmer saw the dog and called him- Buntee. As soon as the dog heard it, he ran to the farmer, who hugged him. The farmer told the mahout that he had been looking for his dog ever since he disappeared from his house. He was happy that he found him now.

The mahout allowed the farmer to take the dog home. The farmer placed a rope round the neck of the dog and took him home.

Part II

Gajaraj and the Dog are Separated

When the farmer put the rope around the dog's neck, he realised that he was being taken away from his friend. At that thought, the dog and the elephant started crying but neither the farmer nor the mahout noticed them.

Gajaraj Stopped Eating

The next day at lunch time the mahout served Gajaraj his favourite food. When the mahout came back after finishing his work, he was surprised to see that Gajaraj had not eaten anything. He asked Gajaraj if he was hungry but Gajaraj did not reply. The mahout thought that Gajaraj was suffering from indigestion and decided not to force him to eat. Gajaraj did not eat anything that night and the next day too. This worried the mahout who checked if Gajaraj was ill. He found no problem with Gajaraj and realised that Gajaraj may be missing his friend the dog.

The Dog is Sad

At the farmer's house, the dog had also not eaten anything ever since he was brought home. The farmer realised that his dog was missing his friend as he remembered how happy the dog was while sitting on the elephant's back. So, he decided to let the dog go to his friend and removed the rope with which he had tied the dog. The dog was weak as he had not eaten anything. However, he got on his feet, licked the farmer's hand and ran away.

Gajaraj and his Friend Meet Again

The dog reached the stable. As soon as Gajaraj saw the dog, he picked him up with his trunk and gave him a swing. The mahout was relieved to see the elephant happy. He quickly brought the food. By then the farmer joined him. The two men happily watched the two friends eating food. The mahout told the farmer that while Gajaraj had found a friend in the dog, he had found a friend in the farmer and hugged him.

Values Extracted from this Chapter

The chapter highlights the importance of companionship and friendship for all. It presents how all of us need friends to live a happy, joyful and fulfilling life.

Word Meaning

Word	Meaning
Booth	Rectangular space
Stables	Living spaces for animals
Interacted with	Communicated with
Strayed	Came by mistake
Munching	Chewing
Wagged	Moved from side to side
Convey	Communicate
Crumbs	Small pieces of food
Accompanied	Went with someone
Plunging	Jumping in
Trunk	Long nose
Splashed	Threw
Yelped	Cried
Delighted	Happy
Hugged	Held closely
Disappeared	Was not seen
Objection	Problem
Realise	Understand
Taken away	Separated
Winced	Shrunk back in pain or distress
Chores	Daily duties
Slight	A little
Indigestion	Upset stomach
Tummy	Stomach
Wondered	Thought
Sprang	Jumped
Joyous	Happy
Swing	Move side to side or back and forth
Relieved	Thankful
Satisfaction	Happiness

NCERT FOLDER

NCERT Intext and Exercise Questions

LET US DISCUSS (NCERT PAGE 42)

Q.1 Talk about the things that Gajaraj and Buntee did together. Now, write in the shapes given below. One has been done for you.

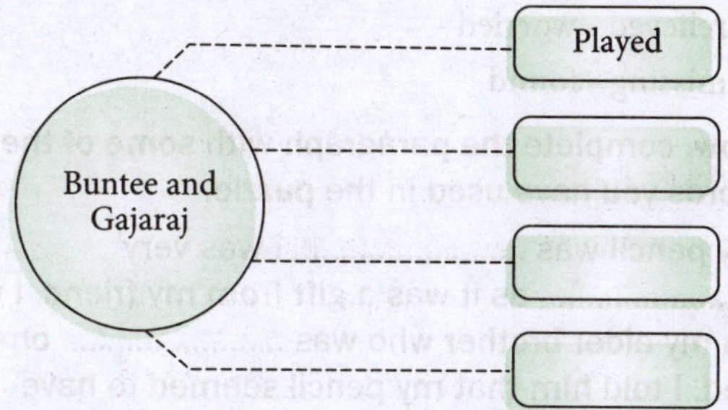

Ans. ate, bathed, slept

Q.2 Why did the farmer hug Buntee?

Ans. The farmer hugged Buntee because he was relieved to find his dog. He was worried about the dog as he had disappeared from his house.

Q.3 Do you think Buntee will leave Gajaraj and go home with the farmer?

Ans. Yes, at the moment I believe that Buntee will leave Gajaraj and go home with the farmer.

LET US DISCUSS (NCERT PAGE 45)

Q.1 Why did Gajaraj not eat his food?

Ans. Gajaraj was not eating his food because he was upset at being separated from his friend. He was missing his dog friend and so did not eat anything.

Q.2 Who were friends at the end of the story?

Ans. There are two pairs of friends at the end of the story. They are

(a) Gajaraj and Buntee (b) The mahout and the farmer

LET US THINK AND REFLECT (NCERT PAGE 45)

Q.1 Read the following lines and answer the questions that follow.

(a) In spite of royal comforts, Gajaraj was sad because he had no friends. The mahout, or elephant trainer, was the only one he ever interacted with.

The mahout was a kind man who served Gajaraj food, and gave him a bath in the elephant pond daily. He was a good caretaker, but not a friend.

(i) Complete with one word:

mahout : kind : : Gajaraj : ....

Ans. sad

(ii) The mahout was a good caretaker because he gave .... to Gajaraj and a .... in the pond.

Ans. food, bath

(iii) What do you think is the difference between a friend and a caretaker?

Ans. The difference between a friend and a caretaker is that a friend plays with you and enjoys the day with you while a caretaker makes sure that you have everything that you need to live comfortably.

(b) "Are you missing your friend?" asked the farmer remembering the happy look on Buntee's face while sitting on the elephant's back. "I cannot see you go hungry," said the farmer, "If you miss your friend so much, go to him."

The farmer removed the rope with which he had tied the dog.

(i) The farmer uses the word .... to refer to the elephant.

Ans. friend

(ii) How did the farmer know that Buntee was hungry?

Ans. The farmer knew that Buntee was hungry because he was getting weak and had not eaten anything since two days.

(iii) Why did the farmer remove the rope with which he had tied Buntee?

Ans. The farmer removed the rope with which he had tied Buntee to free him so that the dog could go to his friend.

(iv) Complete with one word.

Gajaraj : Buntee : : .... : farmer

Ans. mahout

Q.2 Give two examples to show that Gajaraj was very happy to have a friend.

Ans. We know that Gajaraj was very happy to have a friend in how he reacts with the dog. He splashed water playfully on Buntee and gave him a joyous swing with his trunk.

Q.3 How did the mahout come to know that Gajaraj was sad?

Ans. The mahout came to know that Gajaraj was sad when he realised that the elephant had not eaten anything since two days and was not reacting to the mahout.

Q.4 Why do you think Buntee licked the farmer's hand?

Ans. Buntee licked the farmer's hand because he was happy after the farmer had freed him to go to his friend. This was his way of thanking the farmer.

Q.5 What was 'unlikely' about the friendship of Gajaraj and Buntee?

Ans. 'Unlikely' means something that is not expected to happen or seems improbable. In this context, it suggests that the friendship between an elephant, Gajaraj and a dog, Buntee was very unexpected.

LET US LEARN (NCERT PAGE 46)

Q.1 Gajaraj was sad without a friend and when he met Buntee, he was filled with joy. 'Sad' and 'filled with joy' are opposites. Opposites can also be formed by adding some letters before a word. For example, un- unhappy, in- incorrect, dis- disconnect, mis- misuse. Now, take help from the words given as hints and fill up their opposites in the puzzle. (Note: All the words are from the story you have just read.)

We are opposites!

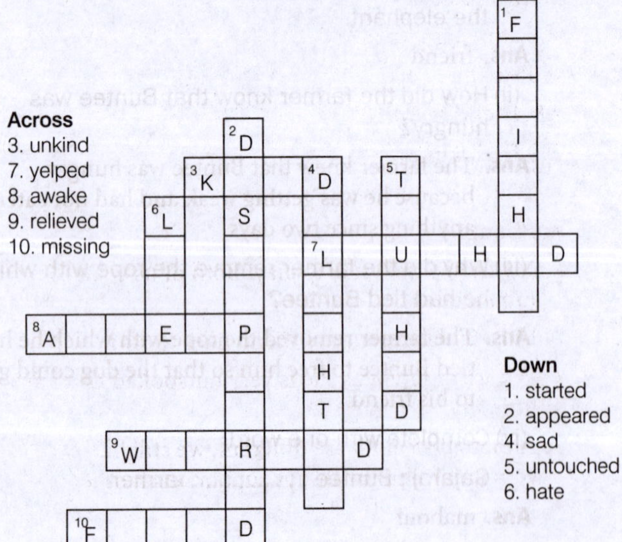

Ans. DOWN

1. started - finished
2. appeared- disappeared
4. sad - delighted
5. untouched - touched
6. hate - love

ACROSS

3. unkind - kind
7. yelped - laughed
8. awake - asleep
9. relieved - worried
10. missing - found

Q.2 Now, complete the paragraph with some of the words you have used in the puzzle.

My pencil was .... I was very .... as it was a gift from my friend. I woke up my elder brother who was .... on the bed. I told him that my pencil seemed to have .... He .... and told me to look under my pillow. I was .... when I .... the pencil there.

Ans. missing, sad, asleep, disappeared, yelped, relieved, found

Q.3 The words that tell us about an action are called verbs. In the story, the author tells us what happened before. To do that, the past form of the action word (verb) is used. Let us learn about the three forms of past tense.

Simple Past Tense	Past Progressive Tense	Past Perfect Tense
Used to show that the action had happened earlier.	Used to show that the action did not finish and was going on.	Used to show that the action was completed.
Second form of the verb + add – d or– ed to the verb	I/He/She/It + was + verb + ing We/You/They + were + verb + ing	had + third form of the verb

Given below are some verbs from the story. Put the verbs in their correct column in the table given above.

- was looking
- gave
- was missing
- had followed
- was munching
- had remained
- told
- felt
- had tied
- arrived
- looked
- had ordered
- hated
- noticed
- went
- served
- asked
- touched
- joined
- threw

Ans.

Simple Past Tense	Past Progressive Tense	Past Perfect Tense
looked	was looking	had tied
hated	was missing	had followed
went	was munching	had remained
asked		had ordered
told		
joined		
gave		
felt		
arrived		
noticed		
served		
touched		
threw		

Select the correct form of the verb to complete the passage. Check your answers with the teacher.

The farmer came back and .... (noticed/was noticing/had noticed) that Buntee was sad. He .... (tied/was tying/had tied) Buntee with a rope the day before. He .... (asked/was asking/had asked) Buntee why he was sad. Farmer .... (felt/was feeling/had felt) that Buntee .... (missed/was missing/had missed) Gajaraj and set him free.

Ans. noticed, had tied, asked, felt, was missing

Q.4 **'...neither the farmer nor the mahout noticed that the two friends were in tears.'**

The words 'neither', 'nor' are used to state that the farmer and the mahout did not notice the same thing. 'Neither, nor' connect two negative choices. For example: Neither Rohit nor I want to play football.

When you need to choose between two things that you want, you may use 'either, or'. For example: Rohit wants to play either cricket or kho-kho. It means Rohit wants to play cricket or Rohit wants to play kho-kho.

Discuss the given sentences with your teacher to practice.

- **Neither Shikha nor Anuj like to tell stories.**
- **Either Bhavesh or Abha made this painting.**

Ans. Explanation

In sentence 1, neither and nor indicate that both Shikha and Anuj do not like to tell stories. 'Neither' and 'nor' are used to connect two negative options.

In sentence 2, either and or indicate that one of the two subjects, Bhavesh and Abha, made the painting. 'Either' and 'or' indicate two choices, in which one or the other may be true/chosen.

Points to note.

- Neither/nor are used together to state two or more things are untrue or won't happen.
- Either/or is used to express a choice between two options.

LET US SPEAK (NCERT PAGE 50)

Q.1 **Gajaraj and Buntee had a wonderful time with each other even if they were 'unlikely' friends. Talk to your friends and find out your common likes and dislikes. Share your answers with the class.**

I am		My friends is ....
I like	Both of us like	My friends likes
•	•	• ....
•	•	• ....

Now, tell your classmates about your friend. You may take help of the cues given below.

- **My friend and I like to play. Both of us want ....**
- **I like to .... but my friend likes to ....**
- **We are different as she/he is .... and I am ....**

Ans. I am Radhika

I like

- Painting
- Dancing

Both of us like

- Eating tasty food
- Reading

My friend is Aditi

My friend likes

- Watching movies
- Running
- My friend and I like to play. Both of us want to have fun together.
- I like to dance, but my friend likes to sing
- We are different as she is very outspoken and I am a little shy.
- Although we both are different, we still like each other very much and we always support each other.

LET US WRITE (NCERT PAGE 51)

Q.1 Write six sentences about your friend with the help of the facts collected in the above task. Mention how you are not only similar but also different. You may take help of the words given below.

same	different	and	but
both	still	like	unlike
neither	nor	either	or

Ans. 1. Aditi and I are best friends.

2. I can talk to Aditi all day long because we have similar tastes in music, food and other things.

3. We have different personalities as I am shy and she is very outspoken. But, we are still similar in many ways and that makes our friendship stronger.

4. Neither Aditi nor I like loud music. We both like to listen to calm and upbeat songs.

5. When we both want to play different games and get confused, we pick to play either chess or ludo.

6. Sometimes, we fight, but we immediately apologise to each other and become bestfriends again.

7. I love my friend very much.

REVIEW EXERCISE

Including Competency Based Questions

Part I

Multiple Choice Questions

1. Who was very fond of Gajaraj?

(a) The king (b) The mahout
(c) The farmer (d) The soldiers

Ans. (a) The king

2. Who was the mahout?

(a) The caretaker (b) The soldier
(c) The elephant trainer (d) Both (a) and (c)

Ans. (d) Both (a) and (c)

3. What did Gajaraj feel in the stable?

(a) Happy (b) Lonely
(c) Comforted (d) Rich

Ans. (b) Lonely

4. Why did the dog bark at Gajaraj?

(a) Because it was angry
(b) Because it hated water
(c) Because it hated baths
(d) Because it was sad

Ans. (b) Because it hated baths

5. The mahout was worried that Gajaraj was ill due to ....

(a) a disease (b) indigestion
(c) loneliness (d) flu

Ans. (b) indigestion

Fill in the Blanks

1. Gajaraj, the elephant, lived in the best ....

Ans. booth of the royal stables

2. In spite of royal ...., Gajaraj was sad because he had no ....

Ans. comforts, friends

3. One morning, the mahout found a .... in the elephant's stable.

Ans. stray dog

4. When the elephant went out for a bath, the dog .... his friend.

Ans. accompanied

5. The elephant took a trunkful of water and playfully .... the water on his friend.

Ans. splashed

State True or False

1. Gajaraj stopped eating when Buntee was taken away.

Ans. True

2. The mahout understood that Gajaraj was sad because of Buntee.

Ans. True

3. Buntee licked the farmer's hand to show gratitude.

Ans. True

4. The king was unhappy about the friendship between Gajaraj and Buntee.

Ans. False

5. The story teaches us that friendship knows no boundaries.

Ans. True

Extract Based Questions

Read the extracts given below and answer the questions that follows.

A. Only when the farmer pulled the rope did the dog realise that he was being taken away from his friend. He yelped, the elephant winced, but neither the farmer nor the mahout noticed that the two friends were in tears.

(i) Why were the two friends in tears?

Ans. The two friends, dog and the elephant, were in tears because they were being separated from each other.

(ii) The simple past tense of the word 'pull' is ....

Ans. pulled

(iii) The words 'yelped' and 'winced' show that the elephant and the dog were

(a) delighted (b) content

(c) angry (d) sad

Ans. (d) sad

(iv) State whether the following sentence is True or False

The farmer and the mahout did not like Buntee and Gajaraj's friendship.

Ans. False

B. By then the farmer who had followed the dog, joined him. The two of them watched with satisfaction the two friends eating food. "It's not only Gajaraj who has found a friend," said the mahout hugging the farmer, "I've also found one."

(i) Where was the dog going when the farmer followed him?

Ans. The dog was going towards Gajaraj's stable when the farmer followed him.

(ii) Find the opposite of the word 'satisfaction' from the given options.

(a) Fulfillment

(b) Happiness

(c) Kindness

(d) Gratitude

Ans. (a) Fulfillment

(iii) State whether the statement is True or False.

The farmer became friends with Gajaraj by the end of the story.

Ans. False

(iv) Why did the farmer and the mahout feel satisfied watching the elephant and the dog eat together?

Ans. The farmer and the mahout felt satisfied watching the elephant and the dog eat together because they had not been eating anything earlier.

Part II

Very Short Answer Type Questions

1. How would you describe Gajaraj's personality?

Ans. Gajaraj was kind, gentle, and longed for a good friend.

2. How did Buntee feel when he first met Gajaraj?

Ans. Buntee felt grateful and happy to find food and shelter along with his new friend Gajaraj.

3. Why was the mahout surprised to see Gajaraj and Buntee together?

Ans. The mahout was surprised because an elephant and a dog are unlikely friends.

4. How did the farmer feel when he found Buntee with Gajaraj?

Ans. The farmer felt relieved and happy to see Buntee safe.

5. What do you think was the most important quality in the friendship between Gajaraj and Buntee?

Ans. Acceptance and kindness were important qualities in the friendship between Gajaraj and Buntee.

6. How does the story use the relationship between the mahout and the farmer to reinforce its message?

Ans. The relationship between the mahout and the farmer to reinforces the message of friendship.

It shows that bonds can form between different individuals through shared experiences.

Short Answer Type Questions

1. Why do you think the author chose the title 'The Unlikely Best-friends' for this story?

Ans. The author chose the title 'The Unlikely Best Friends' for this story as the friends the dog and the elephant, two very different animals become friends. A dog is very different from an elephant in all aspects. However, in the story we see that they play together, eat together and overcome their differences. Even though it is very 'unlikely' or unexpected, the dog and the elephant still become best-friends.

2. Describe the activities Gajaraj and Buntee do together.

Ans. Gajaraj and the Buntee spend time together, with the Buntee even accompanying Gajaraj for his bath. Gajaraj playfully splashes water on the Buntee and they enjoy each other's company. They eat together and Gajaraj even gives Buntee a ride on his back.

Long Answer Type Question

1. Describe the first meeting between Gajaraj and Buntee. How did their friendship develop?

Ans. The first meeting between Gajaraj and Buntee was nothing abnormal. Gajaraj was a royal elephant who lived in the royal stable along. One day, Buntee, a stray dog, wandered into the royal stables. Noticing that the dog was tired and hungry, Gajaraj offered him some of his food, which instantly formed a bond between him and Buntee. Despite their differences, Gajaraj was drawn to Buntee's friendliness. They both began playing together, going to the pond for the bath together, sharing food and spending time in each other's company.

This is how their bond grew stronger and they became unlikely bestfriends.

Competency Based Questions

1. Explain the role of the farmer in the story. How did his actions contribute to the development of the friendship between Gajaraj and Buntee?

Ans. The farmer is introduced to us as Buntee, the dog's owner. He initially took Buntee away from Gajaraj as the dog was his pet and he had been looking for the dog for some time.

However, when the farmer noticed that Buntee's sadness was due to the absence of his friend, the farmer showed compassion and allowed Buntee to visit Gajaraj. This act of kindness ultimately helped make the friendship between the elephant and the dog stronger.

2. The story teaches us that friendship can blossom between the most unlikely individuals. Give examples from the story to support this statement.

Ans. The story of Gajaraj and Buntee beautifully shows that friendship can blossom between the most unlikely individuals.

Despite their differences in size, species, and needs the elephant and the dog formed a deep bond of friendship. They could not speak, but only show their kindness and happiness to each other.

Gajaraj showed his kindness by sharing his food with Buntee. Buntee showed his love for Gajaraj by accompanying him everywhere. They enjoyed each other's company, played together, and cared for each other's well being. This unlikely friendship highlights the power of love and acceptance, showing that true friendship goes beyond outward appearances.

Grammar and Writing

1. Fill in the blanks with the help of the words given in the box. Note that some extra words have been provided which you may not need.

heavy	dry	withdraw	rejected
wide	forget	late	major

(i) My hair is wet but yours is ....

(ii) Raman never comes early, he is always ....

(iii) I hoped that the professor would accept my project but he .... it.

(iv) Deposit the amount at the bank and .... it whenever you need.

Ans. (i) dry (ii) late (iii) rejected (iv) withdraw

2. Write the opposite of the words given below from the story 'The Unlikely Bestfriends' and use each pair in the same sentence.

(i) Started

Ans. (i) Started - Finished

Ravi and Mark started cutting veggies for the pizza in the morning and finished baking it by afternoon.

(ii) Appeared

Ans. Appeared - Disappeared

The moon appeared briefly and disappeared as the clouds covered the night sky.

(iii) Sad

Ans. Sad - Happy

I was feeling sad that my friend could not come to my party but I was happy again when he called me.

(iv) Awake

Ans. Awake - Asleep

My dog was awake at night but I was asleep.

3. From the given extracts from the story, pick out as many verbs you can and put them in their correct column in the table below.

A farmer passing by saw the dog. 'Buntee,' he yelped. The dog ran to him. The farmer hugged the dog and told the mahout that he was looking for his dog ever since he disappeared from his house. He was glad he found him now. The mahout had no objection to the farmer taking the dog home. The farmer tossed a rope round the neck of the dog, saying, "Come Buntee, let's go home."

"Why Gajaraj, aren't you hungry?" he asked concerned. The elephant did not react. "He may have slight indigestion. Let me not force him to eat", thought the mahout. That night too, Gajaraj did not touch his food nor the next day. Now, the mahout was worried. He ran his hand on Gajaraj's tummy and felt there was nothing wrong. "Why was he not eating then? Is he missing his friend, that dog?" the mahout wondered. Meanwhile at the farmer's house, the dog had also not touched his food ever since he was brought home. "Are you missing your friend?" asked the farmer, remembering the happy look on Buntee's face while sitting on the elephant's back.

"I cannot see you go hungry," said the farmer, "If you miss your friend so much, go to him."

Simple Past Tense	Past Progressive Tense	Past Perfect Tense

Ans.

Simple Past Tense	Past Progressive Tense	Past Perfect Tense
asked	he was looking	had not touched
concerned	—	—
thought	—	—
brought		—

4. Imagine you are Buntee. Write a diary entry about your experience meeting Gajaraj and the friendship you formed.

Ans. Monday, XX/June/XXXX 09:00 pm

Dear Diary,

Today was an incredible day! I was wandering around and looking for food near the royal stables when I met the most amazing creature - a giant elephant named Gajaraj.

He was lonely, and I felt bad for him. Even though I'm small, Gajaraj did not try to scare me. We started playing together, and he shared his food with me. He gave me a ride on his back, and we had so much fun! It's amazing how an elephant and a dog can become best friends!

Buntee

ASSESSMENT EXERCISE

Multiple Choice Questions

1. The mahout laughed because
(a) Gajaraj splashed water on the dog
(b) dog fell into the pond
(c) Gajaraj gave Buntee a ride on his back
(d) Buntee scared Gajaraj

2. When the farmer found the dog to be sad, he
(a) gave him more food
(b) took him for a walk
(c) thought he was unwell
(d) let him go to the stables

3. When the mahout found that Gajaraj did not eat, he
(a) gave him bananas
(b) checked his tummy
(c) took him to the pond
(d) pushed him to eat food

Fill in the Blanks

1. The dog was .... to get a ride on the elephant's back.

2. The mahout was .... when Gajaraj did not eat his food.

3. The elephant picked up the dog with his trunk and gave him a ....

State True or False

1. Gajaraj was a happy elephant with many friends.

2. Buntee was a stray dog who wandered into the royal stables.

3. The farmer was angry when he found Buntee with Gajaraj.

Extract Based Questions

Read the extract given below and answer the questions that follow.

The next morning, the mahout found the stray dog in the stable. He did not mind the dog. He also noticed that Gajaraj seemed to like the company. So, he threw some crumbs to the dog, which the animal accepted wagging his tail.

(i) Complete with one word.
Gajaraj : kind : : Buntee : ....

(ii) Mahout did not mind the dog because .... was enjoying his company.

(iii) What does 'accepted wagging his tail' indicate?

(iv) Who found the dog in the stable?
(a) Mahout (b) Farmer (c) King (d) Gajaraj

Very Short Answer Type Questions

1. What is the main theme of the story?

2. How did Gajaraj react to the dog's absence?

3. What was the dog's reaction to being taken away?

Short Answer Type questions

1. How does the story show that friendship can overcome differences? Discuss with examples.

2. What happens when the farmer recognises the dog?

Long Answer Type Question

1. How did the mahout react to Gajaraj's sadness after Buntee was taken away? What steps did he take to help Gajaraj?

CHAPTER 5

A Friend's Prayer

About the Chapter The given poem by Jill Wolf presents a prayer about how a girl wishes to have friendships throughout her life. The poet says that her friendship makes her feel special and she wishes to do the best she can for her friends. She wants to listen to the wishes of her friends and wants to be able to make them come true. She prays that she loves her friends as they are.

Stanzawise Explanation

Stanza 1

May my friendships always be
The most important thing to me.
With special friends I feel I'm blessed,
So let me give my very best.

Explanation The speaker of the poem wishes for her friendships to be the most important thing to her throughout her life. She states that with her friends who are very special to her, she feels blessed. So, she wants to give her best to her friendships.

Stanza 2

I want to do much more than share
The hopes and plans of friends who care;
I'll try all that a friend can do
To make their wishes come true.

Explanation The speaker states that she wants to share the hopes, dreams and plans of her friends who care for her. However, she wants to do much more for her friends. She says that she would try to do everything that a friend could do to make all the wishes of her friends come true.

Stanza 3

Let me use my heart to see,
To realise what friends can be,
And make no judgements from afar,
But love my friends the way they are.

Explanation The speaker adds that she wants to use her heart to see so that she could realise what friends can be. She does not want to make judgements from a far and love her friends for the way they are. She wants her heart to understand what a true friend is. She prays that she loves her friends as they are/when they are happy. She tells us that a true friend accepts their friend for all their qualities.

Values Extracted from this Poem

The poem presents the importance of companionship and friendship for all. It highlights how we need to accept our friends for who they are. We do not need to pretend in front of our friends.

NCERT FOLDER

NCERT Intext and Exercise Questions

LET US THINK AND REFLECT (NCERT PAGE 54)

1. Complete the summary of the poem by circling the correct highlighted words.

The poet says a **prayer for/speech on** friendship and friends. She wants that friendship should always be an important part of her **complete life/school days.** She says that her friendship makes her feel **brave/special.** She wishes to do the best she can, for her friends. She wants to **clap for/listen** to the wishes of her friends. As a good friend, she **prays/imagines** that she is able to make her friend's wishes come true. She wants her **heart/mind** to understand what a true friend is. She prays that she loves her friends **as they are/when they are happy.** She tells us that a **true/correct** friend accepts their friend for all their qualities.

Ans. The poet says a (prayer for) /speech on friendship and friends. She wants that friendship should always be an important part of her (complete life) / school days. She says that her friendship makes her feel brave/ (special.) She wishes to do the best she can, for her friends. She wants to clap for/ listen to the wishes of her friends. As a good friend, she (prays) /imagines that she is able to make her friend's wishes come true. She wants her heart/mind to understand what a true friend is. She prays that she loves her friends (as they are) /when they are happy. She tells us that a (true) /correct friend accepts their friend for all their qualities.

2. Answer in one word only.

(a) How does the poet feel about special friends?

Ans. Blessed

(b) What does the poet use to realise what friends can be?

Ans. Heart

3. Read the following lines from the poem and answer the questions given below.

(a) **I want to do much more than share**
The hopes and plans of friends who care;
I'll try all that a friend can do
To make their wishes come true.

(i) Complete the sentence with the most suitable option.

These lines tell us that the speaker is ....

(a) clever (b) caring
(c) curious (d) calm

Ans. (b) caring

(ii) How will the speaker make her friends' wishes come true? (by trying hard/by working a lot)

Ans. By trying hard

(iii) Fill in the blank with a suitable word.

My friends will feel .... if their wishes come true.

Ans. happy

(b) **Let me use my heart to see,**
To realise what friends can be,
And make no judgements from afar,
But love my friends the way they are.

(i) The speaker says that feelings are important to understand friendship. Which line tells us this?

Ans. The lines that tells us that feelings are important to understand friendship is - Let me use my heart to see.

(ii) Complete the sentence with the most suitable option.

These lines tell us that the speaker is ....

(a) helpful (b) thoughtful
(c) cheerful (d) hopeful

Ans. (b) thoughtful

(iii) Fill in the blank with one word.

The speaker does not wish to make any .... She cares for them just as they are.

Ans. judgements

4. Give one reason why we can say that this poem is a prayer.

Ans. We can say that the poem is a prayer because of the first word of the poem 'May' which indicates a wish or prayer.

5. Why does the speaker 'want to do more' for her friend?

Ans. The speaker wants to do more for her friend to show how much she values her friendship and to make her friend's wishes come true.

6. Do you think that the speaker knows about the wishes of her friend? How can we say so?

Ans. Yes, the speaker knows about the wishes of her friend because she says that she wants to make those wishes come true. This implies that she knows those wishes.

7. Do you also pray for your friend? What do you wish for ? Discuss.

Ans. Yes, I pray for my friend. I wish for my friend to always be happy, healthy and successful. I pray that they achieve all their dreams and goals, and that they have the strength to overcome any challenges they face. I also wish for their well-being and hope that they always find support and love in their life.

LET US LEARN (NCERT PAGE 55)

1. The poet says, 'With special friends I feel I'm blessed'. Select the words that are similar to the meaning of being blessed, from those given below.

excited, grateful, understood, thankful, relaxed

Ans. grateful and thankful

2. Good friends have a lot of qualities. Let us list some.

loyal, h e _ _ f _ _ l, k _ _ d, c _ _ i n g, h o _ _ _ t

Ans. loyal, helpful, kind, caring, honest

Now, fill in the blanks with the words you just listed above.

(a) My friend is always .... to me even when I make a mistake.

Ans. kind

(b) My friend shares things with me. She is very ....

Ans. helpful

(c) My friend is .... because he always supports me.

Ans. loyal

(d) My friend never lies. She is an .... person.

Ans. honest

(e) My friend and I believe in .... for each other

Ans. caring

3. Think of any three of your friends. Write three sentences on why you like each one of them.

Ans. (i) I like Sunita because she always makes me smile when I'm feeling sad.

(ii) I like Deepak because he always plays with me in the park and we have lots of fun together.

(iii) I like Ria because she always has the best stories to tell and makes me laugh everytime we talk.

LET US SPEAK (NCERT PAGE 57)

1. In pairs, act the role of friends speaking to each other. Speak about the following situations

(a) A walk in the park	(b) Sharing tiffins at school
You can use the following-	You can use the following-
• Greet each other.	• Greet each other.
• Ask if your friend wishes to go with you to the park.	• Tell your friends what food items you have brought in your tiffin. Ask them what they have brought.
• If yes, make a plan about activities to do.	• Tell them you wish to share tiffins!
• If no, ask what your friend would like to do. Listen and share what you would also like to do together.	• Next, share with your friends, how it makes you feel.
• Tell your friend that you like spending time with each other.	• Appreciate your friend's food and ask what other food items they like. • Thank you friends for sharing.

2. Create a new situation and have another conversation.

Ans . Two friends Rama and Madhav talk about their upcoming summer holidays

Rama Hey Madhav, what are your plans for the summer holidays?

Madhav Hi Rama! I'm so excited. My family is planning a trip to Goa. We'll be spending time on the beaches and visiting some cool places. What about you?

Rama That sounds amazing! I'm going to my grandparents' house in the village. I love spending time there, playing in the fields and helping with the farm animals.

Madhav That sounds fun too! I remember you telling me about the mango trees there. Are they still full of ripe mangoes?

Rama Yes, they are! I can't wait to climb the trees and pick fresh mangoes. We also have a small pond where we can go fishing.

Madhav Wow, that sounds like a lot of fun. I wish I could join you. Maybe next time we can plan something together.

Rama Definitely! We should plan a trip together. It would be so much fun. Have you packed your bags yet?

Madhav Not yet, but I will soon. I need to make sure I don't forget my swimming trunks. What about you?

Rama I've started packing. I always make a list so I don't forget anything. I'm taking my favourite books and some board games too.

Madhav Great idea! We should exchange stories when we get back. Have a fantastic holiday, Rama!

Rama You too, Madhav! Enjoy the beaches and have lots of fun. See you after the holidays!

LET US WRITE (NCERT PAGE 58)

1. Describe how your friendship with your friend started.

- First list the answers for — When? Where? How?
- Then, use your sentences to write a short paragraph of about 80 words.
- Give a title to your paragraph.

Ans.

When? Where? How?

When At the beginning of 6th grade

Where In the school library

How We both reached for the same book and started talking about our favourite stories

Paragraph

A Friendship Born Over Books

At the beginning of 6th grade, I met my best friend in the school library. We both reached for the same book and started talking about our favourite stories. **This shared love for reading** quickly turned into a strong bond. We began spending our recesses discussing books and helping each other with homework. Our friendship grew from those simple conversations, and now we share many adventures and memories together.

REVIEW EXERCISE

Including Competency Based Questions

Part I

Multiple Choice Questions

1. What is the main message of the poem?

(a) Friends are not important
(b) Friendships should be valued
(c) Friends should always be judged
(d) Friends should be ignored

Ans. (b) Friendships should be valued

2. Based on the poem, friends should be

(a) Judgemental (b) Special
(c) Loving (d) Selfish

Ans. (c) Loving

3. How does the poet's use of the word 'best' in the second line contribute to the overall theme of the poem?

(a) It shows the importance of competition in friendships.
(b) It suggests that there is a difference among friends.
(c) It highlights the poet's desire to be the best.
(d) It implies the poet's commitment to her friendships.

Ans. (d) It implies the poet's commitment to her friendship.

4. The poem is a .... about friendship.

(a) song (b) story
(c) prayer (d) speech

Ans. (c) prayer

5. The lines, 'I want to do much more than share' and 'The hopes and plans of friends who care' show us that the speaker is

(a) happy
(b) delighted
(c) thoughtful
(d) brave

Ans. (c) thoughtful

Fill in the Blanks

1. The poet believes that friendships should be ....

Ans. the most important thing to her

2. The poet feels .... with her special friends.

Ans. blessed

3. The poet wants to do more than just ....

Ans. share hopes and plans with friends

4. The poet decides to love her friends ....

Ans. for the way they are

5. The overall tone of the poem can be described as ....

Ans. wishful and caring

State True or False

1. **The poet only wants to play with her friends.**

Ans. False

2. **The poet wants to make her friends the happiest.**

Ans. True

3. **The poet wants to accept her friends for who they are as a person.**

Ans. True

4. **The poet talks about the importance of changing friends according to our needs.**

Ans. False

5. **The poem suggests we should always treat our friends with kindness.**

Ans. True

Extract Based Questions

Read the lines given below and answer the questions that follow.

Let me use my heart to see,
To realise what friends can be
And make no judgements from afar,
But love my friends the way they are.

(i) **Complete the given series with the correct word.**

Logic: Mind :: Emotion: ....

Ans. Heart

(ii) **What does the line 'to realise what friends can be' mean here?**

Ans. The line 'to realise what friends can be' means that we need to be open minded and have an emotional approach towards our friends. This will help us understand our friends in a better way.

(iii) **Find the synonym for the word 'realise' from the given options.**

(a) understand (b) rationalise
(c) appreciate (d) perceive

Ans. (b) rationalise

(iv) **State true or false for the following statement.**

One should use logic to understand their friends better.

Ans. False

Part II

Very Short Answer Type Questions

1. **What does the poet wish to do for her friends?**

Ans. The poet wants to make her friends' wishes come true and go beyond sharing hopes and plans.

2. **How does the poet intend to treat her friends?**

Ans. The poet intends to love her friends the way they are and treat them with kindness. She does not wish to change them.

3. **What is the central theme of the poem?**

Ans. The central theme of the poem is the importance and value of true friendship.

3. **Explain the significance of the line 'But love my friends the way they are'.**

Ans. The line 'But love my friends the way they are' signifies that the poet does not wish to change her friends. She accepts them truly as they are, without any conditions in their friendship. She is not judgmental and loves all her friends equally.

Short Answer Type Questions

1. **What is the poet's attitude towards her friends?**

Ans. The poet's attitude towards her friends is one of love, care, and appreciation. She values them deeply and wants to be there for them. She does not want to judge her friends but love and care for them for the way they are.

2. **How does the poem make you feel about friendship?**

Ans. The poem makes me feel warm and happy about friendship. It reminds me how important it is to cherish my friends and be a good friend to others.

Long Answer Type Questions

1. **Discuss the significance of friendship as portrayed in the poem. How does the poet emphasise the importance of giving one's best in friendships?**

Ans. The poem emphasises the significance of friendship by highlighting it as the most important thing to the poet. The poet feels blessed to have special friends and expresses a strong desire to give their very best in these relationships. This emphasis on giving one's best reflects the poet's commitment to nurturing and valuing friendships. By promising to do much more than just sharing hopes and plans, the poet highlights the importance of active involvement and effort in maintaining strong bonds with friends. The poem suggests that true friendship requires dedication, kindness and a willingness to put extra efforts for each other.

2. Analyse the poet's viewpoint on making judgments in friendships. How do you think this contributes to the overall message of the poem?

Ans. The poet's viewpoint on making judgments in friendships is clear in the poem. She believes in avoiding judgments from afar and loving her friends as they are. This perspective is important to the message of the poem, which promotes unconditional acceptance and understanding in our friendships.

By talking about this approach, the poet suggests that we must have an open mind and talk to our friends about their problems instead of judging them. This approach helps in building trust and maintaining a strong bond between friends.

Competency Based Questions

1. How does the poet balance her own needs with those of her friends? What does this suggest about her character?

Ans. The poet balances her own needs with those of her friends by giving her best, while also understanding and accepting her friends. Therefore, we can say that the poet is caring, thoughtful and values her bond with her friends.

2. How does the poet's desire to make her friends' wishes come true in the poem 'A Friend's Prayer' reflect her understanding of true friendship? Discuss with reference to the poem.

Ans. The poet's desire to make her friends' wishes come true reflects a deep understanding of true friendship. Her desire goes beyond companionship and involves trying to contribute to the happiness and well being of her friends. By stating that she will 'try all that a friend can do,' the poet shows a willingness to put in the effort and support her friends. This reflects a selfless approach to friendship, where the poet prioritises her friends' needs and wishes. The poem suggests that true friendship involves support and commitment to each other's happiness.

Grammar and Writing

1. Write a paragraph of about 80 words sharing the things your best friend does for you and how it makes you feel.

Ans. My best friend is Raman. He always shares his sports with me at lunch, and we play together during the sports period at school. He helps me with my homework when I'm stuck and makes me laugh with his funny jokes. We have the best time riding our bikes and exploring new places in our neighbourhood. His kindness and support makes me feel happy and lucky to have such a great friend.

2. Choose the correct answers for the following questions.

(i) What is another word for 'friend'?

(a) Enemy (b) Buddy
(c) Stranger (d) Rival

Ans. (b) Buddy

(ii) Which word means the same as 'kind'?

(a) Mean (b) Cruel
(c) Friendly (d) Rude

Ans. (c) Friendly

(iii) What is a synonym for 'trustworthy'?

(a) Dishonest (b) Reliable
(c) Unreliable (d) Deceitful

Ans. (b) Reliable

(iv) Which word can replace 'helpful'?

(a) Useful (b) Thoughtful
(c) Supportive (d) None of these

Ans. (c) Supportive

(v) What is another word for 'loyal'?

(a) Faithful (b) Depending
(c) Truthful (d) Trustworthy

Ans. (a) Faithful

ASSESSMENT EXERCISE

Multiple Choice Questions

1. According to the poem, how do friends show care?
(a) By celebrating
(b) By acting selfless sometimes
(c) By listening to your hopes and dreams
(d) By eating together

2. In the poem, the speaker is saying good things about her
(a) Friends
(b) Family
(c) Siblings
(d) Sisters

Fill in the Blanks

1. The poet emphasises the importance of .... in a friendship, as shown by her desire to make her friends' wishes come true.

2. The poem suggests that true friendship involves .... friends for who they are, without any judgement.

3. The poet's use of the word 'blessed' implies that she views friendship as a .... and does not take it for granted.

State True or False

1. The poet believes that sharing hopes and plans is the only responsibility of a friend.

2. The poet feels that friendships are a blessing and should be cherished.

Extract Based Questions

Read the lines given below and answer the questions that follow.

So let me give my very best.
I want to do much more than share
The hopes and plans of friends who care;
I'll try all that a friend can do
To make their wishes come true.

(i) Complete the following sentence with appropriate word.
The speaker wishes to do much more than .... for her friends.

(ii) Find the synonym for the word 'wishes' from the given options.
(a) dreams (b) hopes (c) desires (d) goals

(iii) What does 'more' refer to in the line "I want to do much more than share"?

(iv) How can one try to be a better friend? Suggest three ways in which one can become a better friend based on the given extract from the poem.

Very Short Answer Type Questions

1. Identify the rhyme scheme of the poem.

2. How does the poet plan to make her friends' wishes come true?

Short Answer Type Questions

1. What message does the poet convey about judgement in friendships?

2. How does the poet's approach to friendship inspire you?

3. What emotions does the poet express in the poem?

Long Answer Type Question

1. What values does the poet's approach to friendship reflect? Discuss with examples from the poem.

The Chair

CHAPTER 6

About the Chapter The given chapter shows what true friendship is all about. The story presents Mario, a school going boy who used to show off that he had many friends. He is challenged by his grandfather to prove that he has many friends. The story shows the chair as a prop used by the grandfather to teach Mario that true friendship is about loyalty, care and affection.

Important Characters

Mario A school going boy who had many friends.

Grandfather He is Mario's grandfather who had taught Mario a lesson about true friendship.

Guneet, Asma and Deepa Mario's true friends.

Chapter Summary
Part I

Introducing Mario

There was a boy called Mario who loved to have lots of friends. He always talked about how many friends he had at school, and how he was so friendly with everyone.

One day, his grandfather placed a bet with Mario. The bet was that Mario did not have as many friends that he thought he had. He believed that most of Mario's friends were just companions or partners. He stated that if he won, Mario would have to get him a fruit chaat and if he did not, he would get Mario a fruit chaat.

Mario was Doubtful

Mario accepted the bet readily. However, he wasn't sure how he could test whether his schoolmates were real friends or not. So, he asked his grandpa for help. His grandfather suggested that he knew what Mario needed. He told Mario that the thing is kept in the attic and went to get it. When he returned, he was carrying something but Mario could not see the thing.

The grandfather told Mario that to take it. He said that it is a special chair as it is invisible. He added that it was tricky to sit on it. However, if Mario took it to school and managed to sit on it, then the magic will work and he'll be able to tell who his real friends were.

Part II

Mario Takes the Chair to School

Mario was a brave and determined boy. He took the invisible chair to school. During break time, he asked everyone to form a circle around him. He told his friends to not move as they were about to see something amazing. Then, Mario tried to sit on the chair. However, it was difficult as he could not see it. So, he missed and fell onto his backside. As a result, his classmates laughed at him.

Mario Attempts to Sit on the Chair

Mario did not want to give up. He told his friends that there was a technical problem and decided to try to sit again. But he failed, causing his classmates to laugh at him. Finally, he tried again and did not fall. He was sitting mid-air. He experienced the magic that his grandfather had told him about.

Mario looked around and saw Guneet, Asma, and Deepa-three of his friends. They were holding him up, so he wouldn't fall. Meanwhile, all the others laughed at him.

Mario Learns a Lesson

Later he told his three friends about how his grandfather had thought of a way to show him that true friends are those who care for us. A friend wouldn't be someone who takes joy in our bad luck. That evening the four children went to see Mario's grandpa as he had won the bet. They had a great time listening to stories and eating fruit chaat. From then on, the friends used the magic chair test on many occasions and whoever passed became friends for life.

Values Extracted from This Chapter

The chapter presents what true friendship is all about. It shows that genuine friendship is all about love, care, support and loyalty. Friendship should be based on respect and trust, not on mockery.

Word Meaning

Word	Meaning	Word	Meaning
Showed off	Boasted	Invisible	Impossible to see
Companions	Friends and partners	Determined	Firm in decision
Accepted	Agreed to	Set off	To go to
Readily	Without any problem	Amazing	Very surprising
Attic	A storage space in a house just under the roof	Experienced	Felt

NCERT FOLDER

NCERT Intext and Exercise Questions

LET US DISCUSS (NCERT PAGE 61)

Answer the following questions. [Refer to that part of the text whose number is given against the question. This applies to the comprehension questions throughout the book.]

Q.1 Mario was very proud of having so many friends. State whether True or False.

Ans. True

Q.2 What did the grandfather take from the attic?

Ans. The grandfather seemed to take a special invisible chair from the attic. In reality, he took nothing from the attic.

Q.3 Will Mario face any challenges?

Ans. Yes, Mario will face challenges to prove that he has as many good friends as he says he has.

Q.4 Will Mario be able to use the magic?

Ans. Yes, I think Mario will be able to use the magic as I believe that he may have some true friends.

Let Us Discuss (NCERT PAGE 64)

Q.1 Mario successfully sat on the invisible chair on his first attempt. State whether True or False.

Ans. False

Q.2 Fill in the blank with a suitable word.

Mario's grandfather challenged him to a bet of ....

Ans. Fruit Chaat

Q.3 Match the following characters with their action.

Guneet,	Asma and Deepa

Ans. held Mario up, so he wouldn't fall

Let Us Think And Reflect (NCERT PAGE 64)

1. Read the following lines and answer the questions that follow.

(a) 'Take it. It's a very special chair. As it's invisible, it's rather tricky to sit on. But if you take it to school and manage to sit on it, then the magic will work and you'll be able to tell who your real friends are.'

(i) Fill in the blanks with two words that describe the chair.

The chair is .... and ....

Ans. special, invisible

(ii) Why was it tricky to sit on the chair?

Ans. It was tricky to sit on the chair as it was invisible and Mario could not see where to sit.

(iii) Why does Mario's grandfather call the chair 'special'?

Ans. Mario's grandfather called the chair 'special' because it has the magic to reveal who Mario's true friends are by seeing who helps him when he tries to sit on it.

(b) 'Wait, wait, just a slight technical problem,' he said, trying again. But again, he missed the seat, causing more surprised looks and laughter. Mario wouldn't give up.

(i) Fill in the blank with a suitable reason.

Mario says there was a technical problem because ....

Ans. he couldn't see the invisible chair and kept missing it.

(ii) Mario's friends were very caring and helpful. State whether True or False.

Ans. False

(iii) Choose the correct option to complete the sentence.

Mario wouldn't give up. This shows he is ....

(a) strong-willed (b) loving

(c) supportive (d) hard-working

Ans. (a) strong-willed

2. Answer the following questions.

(a) What was the bet about?

Ans. The bet was about Mario proving that he had as many friends as he claimed to have. He had to prove that those people were not just partners or companions.

(b) What happened when Mario sat on the chair for the first time?

Ans. When Mario sat on the chair for the first time, he fell on his backside.

(c) How was Mario able to find his real friends?

Ans. Mario was able to find his true friends by taking the special invisible chair to his school and trying to sit on it. According to his grandfather, he would be able to sit when he finds his true friends. In school, after various attempts, Mario is able to sit and sees that three of his friends are supporting him while he was sitting.

(d) Do you think the magic chair test was good? Why do you say so?

Ans. Yes, the magic chair test was very good. It was successful in helping Mario to understand who his true friends are and what true friendship is about.

(e) What does 'friends for life' mean to you?

Ans. The expression 'friends for life' indicates a relationship involving love, care, support and loyalty. It refers to companions who will be always with me supporting and encouraging throughout the life.

(f) The grandfather's idea helped Mario find his 'real friends'. Mention any other way that would help you find out who are your 'real friends'.

Ans. Friends who always support, encourage, show the mistakes done without fear and never leave your company during misfortunes can make us understand who our real friends are.

LET US LEARN (NCERT PAGE 65)

1. Read the following words from the text.

Friendly	Suddenly	Talking	Carrying	Called	Showed

Complete the following table by dividing the words into two parts. One has been done for you.

Column A	Column B
1. Friend	ly
2.	
3.	
4.	

5.	
6.	

The words in Column A are called the root words. The sequences of letters that are in Column B which come after the root words are called suffixes.

Ans.

Column A	Column B
Sudden	ly
Talk	ing
Carry	ing
Call	ed
Show	ed

2. Match the following root words with suitable suffixes. You can use a suffix more than once as shown. Uses them to make sentences of your own. One has been done for you.

S. No.	Root word	Suffix	Word	Sentence
1.	magic	-ing	magical	The magician performed an amazing **magical** act.
2.	care	-al		
3.	celebrate	-ful		
4.	laugh	-ly		
5.	wonder	-ed		
6.	help	-tion		
7.	friend	-ous		
8.	courage	-ship		

Ans. • Careful - Be careful while cutting the vegetables with a knife.

• Celebration - Our school has a children's day celebration programme every year.

• Laughing - I started laughing when my friend cracked a joke.

• Wondering - Vishaka was wondering where her pencil was when she saw it on the floor.

• Helpful - Ravi is very helpful, he always helps me with my English homework.

• Friendly - Varun's dog Bruno is a friendly puppy.

• Courageous - We should be courageous while facing challenges in life.

3. Read the following lines from the story.

Mario, brave and determined, took the strange invisible chair...

You have already described the chair. Now, describe what kind of a person Mario is in the image given below.

[Use words from the story. You may also use words of your own.]

The words that describe the quality of a person or a thing are called adjectives.

Ans. Brave, Friendly, Curious, Adventurous, Determined

4. Match each word (adjectives) in Column A with a suitable word (noun) in Column B. You can make more than one combination. One has been done as an example.

Column A Adjectives	Column B Nouns	Column C Phrases	Column D Sentences
1. brave	friends	brave solidier	1. The brave solider marched ahead.
2. clever	rain		
3. tasty	soldier		
4. heavy	plan		
5. slight	peanuts		
6. true	cold		

Ans. • clever plan - The police made a clever plan to catch the thief.

• tasty peanuts - The squirrel filled its mouth with tasty peanuts.

• heavy rain - Our school was closed on Monday due to heavy rain in our area.

• slight cold - She is quite well now, except a slight cold.

• true friends - True friends are those who help us in need.

5. Complete the paragraph with suitable adjective-noun pairings. Use the words in the box given below.

old book magical adventures happy boy amazing stories
fantastic adventures colourful creatures old castles

Once upon a time in a little village, a/an (i) .... named Abhishek found a/an (ii) .... in the attic. He read (iii) .... about fairy lands, (iv) .... and (v) .... Abhishek's eyes got big as he imagined these (vi) .... He told his friends about the stories, and they started to have their own (vii) .... when they played together.

Ans. (i) a happy boy
(ii) an old book
(iii) amazing stories
(iv) colourful creatures
(v) old castles
(vi) magical adventures
(vii) fantastic adventures

Let us Speak (NCERT PAGE 68)

1. Work in pairs. Read the following qualities of a friend.

loving honest kind caring loyal polite respectful team-worker understanding

Discuss in pairs. Choose any four positive qualities that you would like your friend to have. Give a reason for your choice. Use the hints given below when you speak.

- **I feel my friend should be....because...**
- **I think the quality I want in my friend is being...the reason for this is....**
- **I believe my friend should be....This is in order to..**
- **If my friend is....then....**

Ans. I feel my friend should be kind, caring and loyal because these are the basic qualities of a good friend. I think the quality I want in my friend is being understanding. The reason for this is that sometimes even when we are unable to visit our friend, our connection must remain deep and unchanged.

This can happen only when your friend understands you. I believe my friend should be polite and respectful towards everyone because we become like the company we keep. Therefore, I want my friend to have good habits. If my friend is loving, then I will be the happiest person! We can build a strong friendship by sharing our love and support for each other.

LET US WRITE (NCERT PAGE 69)

1. Read the messages that Mario has written to his friends Deepa, Guneet and Asma.

Dear Deepa,

I feel so special that you are my friend. I know you will always be there for me. Before going to bed, I said a little prayer for Guneet, Asma and you. You made me realise the value of having good friends.

Best wishes,

Mario

Dear Asma,

I feel blessed to know that you are my true friend. I would have fallen again today, if it wasn't for Guneet, Deepa and you. I know I can always depend on the three of you, no matter what.

Best wishes,

Mario

(a) Now, choose the correct word given in brackets to complete Mario's message to Guneet.

Dear Guneet,

I am .... (thankful to/requesting) God to have you as a .... (lucky/real) friend for life. When everyone was .... (laughing at/talking to) me, Deepa, Asma and you showed me that you .... (will save/care for) me. You are indeed a .... (blessing/loving) in my life.

Best wishes,

Mario

Ans. thankful to, real, laughing at, care for, blessing

(b) Now, write your own message to your best friend. You may take ideas from the story, 'The Unlikely Best Friends' and the poem, 'A Friend's Prayer'.

Ans. Dear Benny,

I am thankful to God for having you as my best friend. Your presence in my life gives me immense happiness. Whenever I face any problem, I talk to you about it and feel like I can deal with it. Thank you for always supporting me and pushing me to be better.

Best wishes,

Tim

REVIEW EXERCISE

Including Competency Based Questions

Part I

Multiple Choice Questions

1. What did Mario's grandfather bring from the attic?

(a) A toy car (b) A special chair
(c) A magic wand (d) A storybook

Ans. (b) A special chair

2. What was special about the chair?

(a) It was very comfortable
(b) It was made of gold
(c) It was invisible
(d) It could fly

Ans. (c) It was invisible

3. How did Mario feel when he first saw the chair?

(a) Excited (b) Scared
(c) Bored (d) Angry

Ans. (a) Excited

4. Who helped Mario when he tried to sit on the invisible chair?

(a) His grandfather (b) His friends
(c) A magician (d) No one

Ans. (b) His friends

5. What did Mario learn from his experience with the invisible chair?

(a) To believe in magic
(b) The importance of friendship
(c) To be careful with old things
(d) To be patient

Ans. (b) The importance of friendship

Fill in the Blanks

1. There was a boy called Mario who ....

Ans. loved to have a lot of friends

2. Mario took the ....

Ans. the chair to the school

3. The magic of the .... chair revealed Mario's true friends.

Ans. strange and invisible

4. A friend wouldn't be someone who takes ....

Ans. joy in our bad luck

State True or False

1. Mario's grandfather was angry with him for not believing in the chair.

Ans. False

2. The story teaches us that it's important to believe in yourself and your friends.

Ans. True

3. Mario hoped that he would win the bet.

Ans. True

4. The chair was actually a magic chair that could grant wishes.

Ans. False

Extract Based Questions

Read the extracts given below and answer the questions that follow.

A. There was a boy called Mario who loved to have lots of friends. He showed off a lot, always talking about how many friends he had at school, and how he was so friendly with everyone. One day his grandfather said to him, "Mario, I bet you a fruit chaat. You don't have as many friends as you think you have. I'm sure many of them are nothing more than companions or partners."

(i) What does the phrase 'show off' mean?

(a) To show something to a friend
(b) To show direction
(c) To boast about something
(d) To lie about something

Ans. (c) To boast about something

(ii) If Mario won the bet he would get a ....

Ans. fruit chaat

(iii) State whether the statement is True or False.

Grandfather played a prank on Mario.

Ans. False

(iv) **Why did the grandfather make the bet?**

Ans. The grandfather made the bet to teach Mario the meaning of true friendship and to show him that not all of his friends are real friends.

B. Mario, brave and determined, took the strange invisible chair and set off for school. At break time, he asked everyone to form a circle. He put himself in the middle, with his chair. 'Nobody move. You're about to see something amazing.'

(i) **Give two adjectives that describes Mario in the extract.**

Ans. Brave and determined.

(ii) **When did Mario ask everyone to form a circle?**

(a) At break time
(b) During games period
(c) After school hours
(d) Before school started

Ans. (a) At break time

(iii) **The opposite of the word 'invisible' is ________.**

Ans. visible

(iv) **State whether the following statement is True or False.**

Everyone saw the amazing invisible chair and clapped.

Ans. False

Part II

Very Short Answer Type Questions

1. **Where did Mario take the chair before trying to sit on it?**

Ans. Mario took the chair to school before trying to sit on it.

2. **Who helped Mario when he couldn't sit on the chair and kept falling?**

Ans. Mario's friends Guneet, Asma and Deepa helped him when he could not sit on the invisible chair.

Short Answer Type Questions

1. **How did Mario feel when he first saw the invisible chair? Why do you think he felt this way?**

Ans. Mario felt excited when he first saw the invisible chair. This is because he was curious about something new and different. He probably thought it was a magical object and wanted to know more about it.

2. **Why was it important for Mario's friends to believe in him? How did their belief help him succeed?**

Ans. Mario's friends' belief in him was very important because it gave him courage. When people believe in you, it makes you feel like you can do anything. Their belief helped him to keep on trying to sit on the invisible chair even when it seemed impossible.

3. **What lesson can we learn from Mario's experience with the invisible chair? How can we apply this lesson in our own lives?**

Ans. We can learn that believing in yourself and having friends who believe in you can help you overcome challenges. Even when something seems impossible, if you keep trying and have support from others, you can achieve your goals. We can apply this lesson by being kind and supportive to our friends and by believing in ourselves when we face difficulties.

Long Answer Type Question

1. **Mario, in the story 'The Chair' experiences some challenges as he tries to sit on the invisible chair. Based on your understanding of the story, describe the challenges Mario faces and explain how he overcomes them.**

Ans. Mario faces several challenges while trying to sit on the invisible chair. First, he had to overcome his own disbelief. The concept of an invisible chair seems impossible, and Mario initially struggled to believe if it was real. Second, Mario faced the challenge of actually sitting on something he can't see. This required him to rely on his touch and balance, as well as his trust in his grandfather's words.

Finally, Mario had to ignore the reactions of his friends who were making fun of him. At first, they didn't believe him about the invisible chair, which could have been discouraging.

However, at the end, Mario overcomes these challenges with his determination to sit on the chair and his friend's support.

Competency Based Questions

1. **Do you think the story would have been different if Mario hadn't had friends to help him? Explain your answer.**

Ans. The story might have been different if Mario hadn't had friends to help him. He might have given up trying to sit on the invisible chair because it would have been too difficult on his own.

His friends' support and encouragement helped him to succeed, so it's likely that the story would have had a different ending without them.

2. Imagine you were one of Mario's friends. How would you feel if you saw Mario trying to sit on something invisible? What would you do to help him?

Ans. If I were one of Mario's friends, I would be surprised and confused to see him trying to sit on something invisible. But I would also be curious. I would want to know what he was doing. To help him, I would try to understand what he was seeing or feeling. I might ask him questions or offer to help him in some way.

Grammar and Writing

1. Write a paragraph about your bestfriend and briefly share the story about how you two became friends.

Ans. My best friend is Rohan. We met on the first day of Class 1 when I was feeling very nervous and shy. I didn't know anyone in the class, and I was worried about making new friends.

During the lunch break, I accidentally dropped my lunchbox and Rohan came over to help me pick up the food. He shared his lunch with me and we started talking. We discovered that we both love playing cricket and reading comic books. From that day on, we have been inseparable. We study together, play together, and even help each other with homework. Rohan is always there for me, and I know I can count on him no matter what.

2. Fill in the blanks with the correct synonym from the options provided.

(i) The teacher asked us to .... the essay. (Options: begin, end)
Synonym of 'start'

(ii) The room was very .... after the party. (Options: clean, messy)
Synonym of 'untidy'

(iii) She was .... to hear the good news. (Options: sad, delighted)
Synonym of 'happy'

(iv) The mountain peak was covered with .... snow. (Options: fresh, old)
Synonym of 'new'

(v) He is a very .... student. (Options: lazy, diligent)
Synonym of 'hardworking'

(vi) The movie was so .... that everyone laughed. (Options: funny, boring)
Synonym of 'humorous'

Ans. (i) begin (ii) messy
(iii) delighted (iv) fresh
(v) diligent (vi) funny

3. Match the adjectives in Column A with the appropriate nouns in Column B.

Column A (Adjectives) :	Column B (Nouns) :
(i) Bright	(a) Tree
(ii) Gentle	(b) Hero
(iii) Tall	(c) Light
(iv) Delicious	(d) Breeze
(v) Brave	(e) Cake

Ans. (i) Bright - Light (ii) Gentle - Breeze
(iii) Tall - Tree (iv) Delicious - Cake
(v) Brave - Hero

4. Describe your friends by filling in the blanks with suitable words. This is known as an acrostic poem.

F ____________
R ____________
I ____________
E ____________
N ____________
D ____________
S ____________

Ans. Friendly, Reliable, Intelligent, Energetic, Nice, Dependable, Supportive

ASSESSMENT EXERCISE

Multiple Choice Questions

1. What did Mario's friends do to help him?
   (a) They laughed at him
   (b) They ignored him
   (c) They supported him
   (d) They blamed him
2. How did Mario's grandfather react to Mario's success?
   (a) He was disappointed (b) He was angry
   (c) He was proud (d) He was indifferent
3. What was the main theme of the story?
   (a) The power of magic
   (b) The importance of friendship and belief in oneself
   (c) The dangers of old things
   (d) The need for technology

Fill in the Blanks

1. Mario's friends didn't .... him when he told them about the .... chair.
2. Mario successfully sat on the invisible chair when .... helped him.

State True or False

1. Mario's grandfather brought an old, wooden chair from the attic.
2. The chair was invisible to everyone except Mario.

Extract Based Questions

Read the extract given below and answer the questions that follow.

Leaving with his three friends, he explained to them how his grandfather had so cleverly thought of a way to show him that true friends are those who care for us. A friend wouldn't be someone who takes joy in our bad luck. That evening the four children went to see Mario's grandpa as he had won the bet. They had a great time listening to stories and eating a lot of fruit chaat.

(i) How many real friends did Mario have?

(ii) The opposite of 'clever' is ....

(iii) State whether the following statement is True or False.
A true friend laughs when you fall badly.

(iv) How many children went to see Grandpa?
(a) 2 (b) 3
(c) 4 (d) 5

Very Short Answer Type Questions

1. What kind of story is 'The Chair'?
2. Why did Grandpa challenge Mario?

Short Answer Type Questions

1. How does the story 'The Chair' reflect the importance of belief and imagination in overcoming challenges?
2. Analyse the character of Mario. How does he evolve throughout the story?

Long Answer Type Question

1. Discuss the role of friendship in Mario's journey to successfully sit on the invisible chair. How did his friends contribute to his achievement?

CHAPTER 7

Neem Baba

by S I Farooqi

About the Chapter The given chapter by S I Farooqi is in the format of a play with two scene wherein a little girl Amber is seen talking to the Neem tree. In her conversation, she asks various questions about the origin and uses of the tree. She gets to know that the Neem tree is very useful to all of us as it cures diseases, helps farmers and keeps about homes clean and healthy.

Important Characters

Amber A young girl who returns from the school and sits under the Neem tree. She asks the tree questions and feels that the tree is answering her.

Neem Tree It is the tree in the courtyard under which Amber sits. It answers Amber's questions and tells her more about itself.

Chapter Summary

Part I

Amber had come back from school and sat at a peaceful spot under the neem tree in her courtyard. She felt a connection with the tree and started talking to it.

Amber Talks to the Tree

The play begins with Amber greeting the tree. She introduces herself and asks the tree if she could ask it any question. The Neem tree replies that Amber can ask it any questions. It tells Amber that it recognises her as she played in the tree's shade in her childhood. It reminded her that she used to call it 'Neem Baba'.

Neem Tree Tells More About Itself

Amber tells the Neem tree that she had seen it almost everywhere. She also asks him to tell her more about itself. The Neem tree tells her that it was born millions of years ago somewhere in North India or Myanmar. However soon, its family spread outside India. When Amber asked where else could neem be found, the tree replied that its family could can be found in many Asian and African countries and in some parts of America.

The Name of the Tree

Amber, then, asked the tree about who named it. The Neem tree told her that the story of its name is very interesting. It told Amber that it was born in India and given Sanskrit names such as Arishta (the one who cures diseases), Nimba and Nimbaca. However, the name 'Neem' was given to it by the Iranians. The tree also told her that in Hindi, its name is Nimb but it is also called Nim, Leemba, Nimori, Nimbamond, Nimbe and Nimo in India.

Other Names of the Neem Tree

Amber's surprise increased as she got to know that the Neem tree was so well known. So, the tree added that people know about it as they find the Neem tree useful. It told Amber that scientists call the tree- 'bitter grace of God', 'nature's gift to man', and 'cleanliness-parting tree'. The tree is also called 'magic tree' and 'the tree of the twentieth century'.

Part II

The Neem Tree: Cures Diseases

After listening to the Neem tree, Amber told it that she knew that people clean teeth with its twigs and protect clothes with its leaves. She added that sometime back, when her brother had measles, the doctor told her family to put neem leaves on his bed and make him lie down on them. Amber then asked the tree about the reason why the doctor had said so.

The Neem tree replied that the doctors know that neem leaves have chemical properties that destroy germs. Measles cause itching all over the body. Neem leaves give comfort and do not allow germs to breed. It added that the leaves, bark, flowers, fruits and even roots of the Neem tree can be used to make medicines to cure many diseases.

Amber Remembers Various illnessess

Upon hearing the Neem tree's reply, Amber remembers that once she had a cough and could not breathe properly. So, her grandmother cured me with a medicine made from neem bark. She also remember that when her father had itching in the eyes, her grandmother prepared a kajal from neem flowers, which cured him.

The Neem tree was impressed that Amber knew so much about it. It advised Amber that the remedies she had mentioned are to be used only by people who are well trained and have a lot of experience.

Uses of the Neem Tree for a Farmer

Amber told the Neem tree that she would remember his advice. She then asked it if there is any use of neem for the farmers. The Neem tree replied that neem is used by farmers too. It told Amber that if the powder of neem seeds is mixed in water and sprayed on plants and trees, then locusts don't eat them. If it is used in rice fields, which is filled with water, it stops mosquito breeding and helps to increase crop yield. The Neem tree added that the mixture also saves the crop from termites, which eat roots of the crop, and it also stops breeding of other insects that eat crops.

Uses of a Neem Tree at Home

Amber then told the Neem tree that if we put the powder of neem seeds in stagnant water around our homes, mosquitoes won't breed in them. Thus, she had found a cost-effective method to stop mosquitoes from breeding. She then further asked the Neem tree to tell her the other uses of neem in daily life.

The Neem tree told her that people save their stored grains from insects by adding neem seed powder to them. Neem oil is also used to make soaps and toothpaste. Furniture made from neem wood is not eaten by termites. Neem also purifies the air. It added that many other qualities of neem had not been discovered till now. It then asked her if she would discover them when she grows up.

Amber agreed and thanked the Neem tree for its. The Neem tree blessed Amber.

Values Extracted from this Chapter

The chapter conveys the importance of nature's gifts like trees. It focuses on the various medicinal, agricultural and social value of the various aspects of trees in our daily lives. It also teaches us to respect and value our natural resources.

Word Meaning

Word	Meaning
Thought provoking Iranians	Interesting people who were born and reside in Iran
Grace	Blessing
Twigs	Small thin branches
Measles	Disease with fever and red spots on skin
Itching	Feeling the need to scratch
Breed	Grow
Cured	Recover from a diseases
Remedies	A medicine, application, or treatment that relieves or cures a disease.

Word	Meaning
Well trained	To be an expert in the field in question.
Locusts	Flying insects that damage crops
Standing	Not flowing
Crop yield	Crops produced
Termites	Insects that damage wood and buildings
Stagnant	Not flowing
Cost-effective	Good outcome in least amount of resources
Purifies	Removes harmful particles
Discovered	Found

NCERT FOLDER

NCERT Intext and Exercise Questions

LET US DISCUSS (NCERT PAGES 77-78)

Q.1 Amber found many facts about the neem tree from Neem Baba. Fill up the fact sheet based on what Neem Baba told her.

Let Us Know Our Neem		
Common name:		Given by:
Period of birth:		
Born at:		
Found in:		
Common names:		
Names given by scientists:	1.	2.
Names given by others:	1.	2.

Ans.

Let Us Know Our Neem		
Common name	Neem	Given by : Iranians
Period of birth	Millions of years ago	
Born at	North India or Myanmar	
Found in	Asian and African Countries, and some parts of America.	
Common names	Nimb, Nim, Leemba, Nimori, Nimbamond, Nimbe and Nimo.	
Names given by scientists:	1. Bitter grace of God	2. Cleanliness-parting tree
Names given by others:	1. Magic tree	2. The tree of the twentieth century

LET US DISCUSS (NCERT PAGE 80)

Q.1 How is Neem useful to farmers?

Ans. Neem is extremely useful to farmers. It helps the farmers in the following ways

- If the powder of Neem seeds is mixed in water and sprayed on plants and trees, then locusts don't eat them.
- If it is used in rice fields, where water remains standing, it stops mosquito breeding and helps to increase crop yield.
- This mixture also saves the crop from termites, which eat roots of the crop, and also stops breeding of other insects that eat crops.

Q.2 Mention some of the uses of the Neem tree.

Ans. The various uses of the Neem tree are

- Neem leaves have chemical properties that destroy germs.
- The leaves, bark, flowers, fruits and even roots of the Neem tree can be used to make medicines to cure many diseases.
- Neem seeds do not allow mosquitoes/insects to breed.
- Neem oil is used to make soaps and toothpaste.
- Furniture made from neem wood is not eaten by termites.
- Neem also purifies the air.

LET US THINK AND REFLECT (NCERT PAGE 81)

1. You just read about the Neem tree. Write any two facts that surprised you the most.

Ans. The two facts that surprised me the most about the Neem tree are

- Its various names- Arishta, Nimba, Nimbaca, Nimb, Nim, Leemba, Nimori, Nimbamond, Nimbe and Nimo. The commonly used name that was given by Iranians.
- Its use for farmer as protection from insects and termites.

2. Complete the following sentences.

(a) The old tree asked Amber to call him Neem Baba because ....

Ans. it considered itself as old and wise as a grandfather

(b) Neem seed powder protects crops from ....

Ans. locusts, mosquito breeding and termites.

(c) .... is a cost-effective method to stop mosquitoes from breeding in stagnant water.

Ans. Putting some powder of neem seeds in stagnant water around our homes

(d) One reason why doctors advise us to use neem leaves for someone suffering from measles is ....

Ans. that neem leaves have chemical properties that give comfort and do not allow germs to breed.

3. **Why can Neem Baba not remember the year when he was born?**

Ans. Neem Baba cannot remember the year he was born because he is very old and was born millions of years ago.

4. **Which parts of the neem tree are used to make medicines?**

Ans. The leaves, bark, flowers, fruits and even roots of the Neem tree can be used to make medicines to cure many diseases.

LET US LEARN (NCERT PAGES 81-83)

1. **Study these words from the text.**

- something
- neem oil
- cleanliness-parting
- well known
- grandmother
- seed powder
- childhood
- well trained
- thought-provoking

Put the compound words given above in their trees.

These words are known as compound words. There are three types of compound words, based on how the words are separated.

- **Open compound words: spaces between the words.**
- **Closed compound words: no spaces between the words.**
- **compound words: hyphens between the words.**

You may add some more words

Ans. Open compound words

- neem oil
- seed powder
- high school
- Ice cream

Closed compound words

- grandmother
- childhood
- cheesecake
- football

Hyphenated compound words

- cleanliness-parting
- thought-provoking
- editor-in-chief
- check-in

2. **Words that tell us what a person is doing are called verbs. In the table given below, match the verbs in the first column showing action in the present to verbs in the second column showing action in the past. Make a sentence with any one form of the verb. One has been done for you.**

Present	Past	Answer	Sentence
1. become	a. made	1. d	I want to become a teacher when I grow up
2. find	b. gave		
3. make	c. told		
4. discover	d. became		
5. tell	e. found		
6. give	f. discovered		

Ans.

2. (e) find-found: I find anime movies very interesting.
3. (a) make-made: Ravi's mother made lemonade for him yesterday.
4. (f) discover-discovered: ISRO has discovered a new planet near a sun-like star.
5. (c) tell-told: Radhika told the teacher that her mother was not well.
6. (b) give-gave: Mark gave a speech during the morning assembly.

3. **Neem Baba speaks to Amber as if he is a person. This figure of speech is called personification. Let us look at some more examples.**

- **The leaves whispered in the wind.**
- **The flowers danced merrily in the breeze.**

Now, discuss it with your classmates and teacher.

Ans. Some more examples of personification are

- The blanket held me close.
- The computer suffered.
- The dog scolded me.
- The camera loves her.

LET US SPEAK (NCERT PAGE 83)

Collect dry leaves of four different trees and plants around you.

1. **Make one card as given below. On the top, draw the shape of the leaf looking at the dry leaf and colour it. Inside the card, write the name of the tree/plant the leaf is taken from and one of its uses.**
2. **Now, speak about the whole process of making the card in front of the class.**
3. **Ask your classmates to identify the leaf and tell them one of its uses. After they answer, open the card, and share what you have written.**

Ans. The process of making the card in front of the class-

(i) First, I collected the leaves from the tree I had to write about and selected the best leaf out of them.

(ii) Then, I outlined and drew the leaf on a white rectangular sheet, coloured it and folded the paper to make a card.

(iii) With the help of the internet, I wrote important points about the XYZ tree.

(iv) While making this card I got to learn about the medicinal plants and trees in India and it was really fascinating!

LET US WRITE (NCERT PAGE 84)

1. You have read about Neem Baba and learnt many things about the Neem tree. Look at the trees in your neighbourhood and write a paragraph about any one tree that you like.

- **Where it is (roadside / park, etc.)**
- **How it looks (height, tree trunk, leaves, flowers, etc.)**
- **Why you like it (shade, medicinal properties, shelter, beauty, etc.)**
- **Give a title to your paragraph.**

Ans. **The Incredible Bel Patra Tree**

There is a huge Bel Patra tree in the garden of our local temple. It looks like a huge umbrella sometimes and my mother says it has many amazing medicinal properties. Bel Patra, also known as Bilva Patra, is a leaf from the Bel tree in Hinduism, offered to Lord Shiva. It symbolises his three eyes, the three main gods of Hinduism, and the three gunas of nature. It represents surrendering the ego and the three aspects of human nature to seek oneness with the divine.

REVIEW EXERCISE

Including Competency Based Questions

Part I

Multiple Choice Questions

1. What is the primary theme of the chapter "Neem Baba"?

(a) Adventure (b) Friendship
(c) Environmental awareness
(d) Historical events

Ans. (c) Environmental awareness

2. Which part of the neem tree is traditionally used as a toothbrush?

(a) Leaves (b) Bark (c) Twigs (d) Seeds

Ans. (c) Twigs

3. What is one of the key messages Neem Baba imparts to Amber?

(a) The importance of modern technology
(b) The value of traditional knowledge
(c) The need for urban development
(d) The benefits of travelling

Ans. (b) The value of traditional knowledge

4. Which of the following is not a use of Neem mentioned in the chapter?

(a) Treating skin conditions (b) Making furniture
(c) Cooking food (d) Protecting grains

Ans. (c) Cooking food

5. Neem Baba advises Amber that Neem home remedies must be used only by

(a) elders (b) teachers
(c) scientists (d) well-trained professionals

Ans. (d) well-trained professionals

Fill in the Blanks

1. Amber sat under the Neem tree in her ....

Ans. courtyard

2. The tree got her attention by ....

Ans. whispering to her

3. The tree told Amber about the ....

Ans. medicinal properties of Neem tree

4. There are many qualities of Neem that ....

Ans. are yet to be discovered.

State True or False

1. Neem Baba was an old man in the village.

Ans. False

2. Amber knew a lot about trees.

Ans. False

3. **Neem tree has many medicinal as well as other uses.**

Ans. True

4. **Neem tree purifies the air.**

Ans. True

5. **Amber was playing with her friends when she heard Neem Baba talk.**

Ans. False

Extract Based Questions

Read the extract given below and answer the questions that follow.

Dear Amber, we become well known for what we do. People find us useful and that is why they know us. Scientists call us 'bitter grace of God', 'nature's gift to man', and 'cleanliness-parting tree'. Some even call us 'magic tree' and 'the tree of the twentieth century'.

(i) Who is talking here and to whom?

Ans. Neem Baba is talking to Amber here.

(ii) According to Neem Baba, how do scientists know the Neem trees?

(a) As the magic tree
(b) As the bitter grace of God
(c) As nature's gift to man
(d) All of the above

Ans. (d) All of the above

(iii) The opposite of the word 'bitter' is ....

Ans. sweet

(iv) State whether the following statement is True or False.
Neem is a cleanliness-parting tree.

Ans. True

Part II

Very Short Answer Type Questions

(i) What is Neem Baba known for in the village?

Ans. Neem Baba is known for his extensive knowledge about the Neem tree and its benefits.

(ii) What part of the Neem tree is used as a natural pesticide?

Ans. The seeds of the neem tree are powdered and used as a natural pesticide.

(iii) How do Neem leaves help protect clothes and grains?

Ans. Neem leaves protect clothes and grains from termites.

Short Answer Type Questions

(i) What does Neem Baba teach Amber about the neem tree?

Ans. Neem Baba teaches Amber about the neem tree's uses, benefits, importance in daily life and traditional practices. By sharing this information, he also teaches Amber how important it is to protect the trees and study their properties in more detail.

(ii) How does Amber first meet Neem Baba, and what is her initial impression of him?

Ans. Amber first meets Neem Baba while sitting in her courtyard under his shade. Her initial impression of him is one of curiosity and admiration, as she is intrigued by his deep knowledge he has.

Long Answer Type Questions

(i) Describe the significance of the neem tree as explained by Neem Baba in the chapter.

Ans. Neem Baba explains that the Neem tree is highly significant due to its several benefits. It is known for its medicinal properties, with every part of the tree being useful. The leaves are used to protect clothes and grains from termites, while the seeds are powdered and used as a natural pesticide. Neem wood is resistant to termites, making it ideal for furniture.

Additionally, neem helps purify the air and is used in traditional medicine to treat various ailments. Neem Baba emphasises the tree's importance in agriculture and its role in maintaining ecological balance.

(ii) Discuss the ways in which the Neem tree is used in traditional medicine as mentioned in the chapter.

Ans. The chapter mentions several ways in which the Neem tree is used in traditional medicine. Neem leaves are used to treat skin problems due to their antibacterial properties. Neem oil is applied to wounds and used to treat infections.

The bark and roots are used in various herbal remedies to treat ailments like fever, digestive issues, and respiratory problems. Neem twigs are traditionally used as toothbrushes to maintain oral hygiene. Neem Baba explains that these traditional practices have been passed down through generations, highlighting the tree's medicinal value and its role in promoting health and well-being.

Competency Based Questions

1. What lesson do you think Amber and you as a reader learned from her interactions with Neem Baba?

Ans. Amber learns the importance of respecting and preserving nature. She gains a deeper understanding of the neem tree's value and the need to protect it for future generations.

Her interactions with Neem Baba inspire her to share this knowledge with others and promote environmental awareness.

From their interactions we learn that we must learn more about our local plants and trees and make efforts to protect them as they are beneficial for us. It is our responsibility to preserve this valuable knowledge and resource.

2. Explain the environmental benefits of the neem tree as described by Neem Baba in the chapter. What greater impact do you think it can have on our environment and health?

Ans. The chapter discusses several environmental benefits of the Neem tree. Neem trees help in purifying the air by absorbing pollutants and releasing oxygen. They also provide shade and reduce soil erosion, contributing to soil conservation. The tree's natural pesticide properties make it an eco-friendly alternative to chemical pesticides, promoting sustainable agriculture.

Neem trees support biodiversity by providing habitat and food for various species. Finally, Neem Baba emphasises that planting Neem trees can help combat climate change and improve the overall health of the environment.

Grammar and Writing

1. Imagine you are Amber. Write a diary entry noting your conversation with Neem Baba and how it made you feel.

Ans. 6th July, 20XX 8 : 00 pm

Saturday

Dear diary,

Today I had the most wonderful and magical experience. The old Neem tree in our courtyard started speaking to me when I was sitting under its shade. He told me that I could call him Neem Baba.

He also said that he had been around since I was a little kid and used to run around him while playing. With our conversation I learned that Neem tree is a very valuable tree. It has lots of medicinal and other uses. We talked for a long time today and it made me feel inspired and curious. Now, I am going to become a scientist when I grow up and learn more about Neem trees.

Amber

2. Underline the example of personification in each given sentence. If the sentence contains personification, write 'personification.' If it does not, write 'no personification.'

Example The train was impatient as it picked up its last passengers.

Ans. Personification

(i) The campfire danced in the dark as the students sat around it and sang songs.

Ans. Personification

(ii) The car's headlights winked at me and I could not see anything for a second.

Ans. Personification

(iii) My alarm clock yelled at me in the morning.

Ans. Personification

(iv) I had a very fun day at school.

Ans. No personification

(v) The wind howled in the cold winter night.

Ans. Personification

3. Rewrite the given sentences with the past forms of underlined verbs.

(i) Anant likes to draw so he bought some pencils and sheets.

Ans. Anant liked to draw so he bought some pencils and sheets.

(ii) Radhika goes to the temple with her mother.

Ans. Radhika went to the temple with her mother.

(iii) Our teacher gives us fun activities to do on weekends.

Ans. Our teacher gave us fun activities to do on weekends.

ASSESSMENT EXERCISE

Multiple Choice Questions

1. What inspires Amber to learn more about the neem tree?
(a) A school project
(b) Her mother's teaching
(c) Neem Baba's stories and explanations
(d) A television programme

2. 'Baba' in Neem indicates that Neem Baba is
(a) a sage
(b) an elder
(c) a teacher
(d) a child

3. People know about Neem trees because
(a) they find them beautiful
(b) they find them useful
(c) they are fascinated by their height
(d) they have a huge size

Fill in the blanks

1. If we put the powder of neem seeds in ....water around our homes, mosquitoes won't .... in them.

2. .... is also used to make soaps and toothpaste.

3. People save their stored grains from insects by adding .... to them.

State True or False

1. Amber's teacher taught her about the value of Neem tree.

2. The wood from Neem tree can be used to cook.

3. Neem leaves can fight away the germs.

Extract Based Questions

Read the extract given below and answer the questions that follow.

The story of my name is very thought-provoking. I was born in India and given Sanskrit names such as Arishta (the one who cures diseases), Nimba and Nimbaca. The name 'Neem' is given by the Iranians...Yes, in Hindi, my name is Nimb. In India, I have other names-Nim, Leemba, Nimori, Nimbamond, Nimbe and Nimo.

(i) List three different names given to Neem Baba.

(ii) What does the word 'thought-provoking' mean?
(a) Interesting (b) Intriguing
(c) Captivating (d) All of these

(iii) Neem Baba was born in ....

(iv) State whether the given statement is True or False.
Neem trees are found only in India.

Very Short Answer Type Questions

1. Why is neem wood preferred for making furniture?

2. How does Amber feel after learning from Neem Baba?

Short Answer Type Questions

1. What do scientists call the Neem tree? Why?

2. How did Amber's family make use of Neem Baba's medicinal properties? Give examples from the chapter.

Long Answer Type Question

1. What role does Neem Baba play in educating Amber about the neem tree, and how does this impact her understanding?

What a Bird Thought

CHAPTER 8

About the Chapter The given poem by an unknown poet talks about the growth and development of an individual with experiences of life. It presents a journey from innocence to maturity through a bird who lived a simple life and was innocent. It, however, comes out of the safety and security of its home and realises that the world is very different. It has to come out of the comfort zone to know more about the world as it is.

Stanzawise Explanation

Stanza 1

I lived first in a little house,
And lived there very well,
I thought the world was small and round,
And made of pale, blue shell.

Explanation The poem starts with the speaker, a bird, describing that it has lived happily in a very small house (preferably an egg). It thought that the world was a small and round in shape. It believed that the world was made of a delicate shell of pale blue colour.

This stanza presents the speaker's sentence of safety. It lived a simple life and believed in simple thing. It felt that everything around it was beautiful and delicate.

Stanza 2

I lived next in a little nest,
Nor needed any other,
I thought the world was made of straw,
And nestled by my mother.

Explanation In these lines, the bird moves from living in a small house to living in a nest. It was very satisfied in the nest and felt that it did not need anything else. At this stage, the bird felt that the world is made of straw from which its nest is made. The bird found comfort in its mother.

This stanza also presents the bird's simplicity. The presence of the 'mother' indicates a comfortable, protected and satisfying life.

Stanza 3

One day, I fluttered from my nest,
To see what I could find,
I said the world is made of leaves,
I have been very blind.

Explanation In these lines, the bird comes out of his/her nest to explore the world. When it sees the world, it realises that the world is not made of straw. In fact, the world is made of leaves as when the bird comes out of its nest, it sees many leaves around it. Therefore, the bird accepts that it had been blind.

This stanza shows growth and knowledge. It highlights that the bird was initially very innocent and not aware of the reality of the world. Now, it is undergoing a transformation as it realises the truth of the world around it.

Stanza 4

At length I flew beyond the tree,
Quite fit for grown-up labours,
I don't know how the world is made,
And neither do my neighbours.

Explanation This stanza states that the bird flew away from its home. It wants to be more mature and responsible. It accepts that it does not know how the world is made. It also accepts that even its neighbours do not know about the reality of the world.

The desire to explore the world shows that the bird is curious to know more about the uncertainties of the world.

Values Extracted from this Poem

The poem conveys the fact that life is journey wherein one gains knowledge and growth. It highlights that our understanding of the world is based on our experiences wherein each stage offers new viewpoints. Further, it also teaches us that we need to go beyond out comfort zones to grow and develop as better humans.

Word Meaning

Word	Meaning	Word	Meaning
Pale	Light in colour or shade	Nestled	Settle or lie comfortable within or against something
Shell	The hard outer covering of something	Fluttered	Flapping the wings quickly and lightly
Straw	Dried leaves of grain	Grown up labours	Mature and responsible adults

NCERT FOLDER

NCERT Intext and Exercise Questions

LET US DISCUSS (NCERT PAGE 87)

Q.1 Read the poem again. Identify the main idea of each stanza. There are two extra given.

(a) The bird steps out into the world.
(b) The bird lived happily in a small world.
(c) The bird becomes blind due to leaves.
(d) The bird flies away as an adult.
(e) The bird is unhappy with the straw nest.
(f) The bird lived in a cosy nest with its mother.

Ans. (a) Stanza 3 (b) Stanza 1
(c) - (d) Stanza 4
(e) - (f) Stanza 2

Q.2 Look at the pictures (a)-(d) and write the matching line form the poem for each.

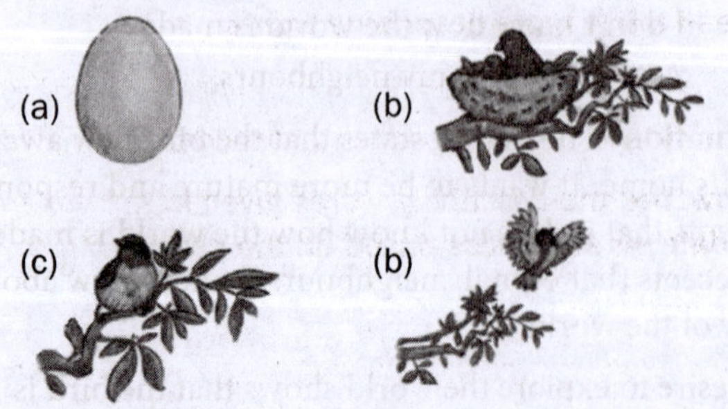

Ans. (a) I lived first in a little house..
(b) I lived next in a little nest…
(c) One day, I fluttered from my nest,…
(d) At length I flew beyond the tree,…

Q.3 Answer the following with a word from the poem and check the answers with your partner.

(a) What was the shape of the bird's first house?
_ O _ _ _
(b) What was the bird's second nest made of ?
_ _ R _ _
(c) What did the bird see when it came out of its nest?
L _ _ _ E _
(d) What did the bird do at the end ?
_ _ _ W

Ans. (a) Round (b) Straw
(c) Leaves (d) Flew

LET US THINK AND REFLECT (NCERT PAGES 88-89)

Q.1 Write whether the following sentences are True or False.

(a) The bird changed its house two times.
(b) The neighbours tell the bird about the world.

Ans. (a) True (b) False

Q.2 Read the following lines from the poem and answer the questions given below.

(a) I thought the world was made of straw,
And nestled by my mother.

(i) Who lived in the nest along with the baby bird?

Ans. The baby bird lived in the nest with its mother.

(ii) Complete the following by choosing the correct option.
The bird thought the world was made of straw because ....

(a) it lived in a straw hut

(b) its nest was made of straw

(c) its mother fed straw to it

(d) there was straw all around

Ans. (b) its nest was made of straw

(iii) Which word tells us that the baby bird was warm and comfortable?

Ans. The word 'nestled' tells us that the baby bird was warm and comfortable.

(b) I said the world is made of leaves,
I have been very blind.

(i) Why did the bird think the world was made of leaves?

Ans. The bird thought that the world was made of leaves because when it came out of its nest, it saw many leaves around it.

(ii) What does the set of words 'I said' mean?

(a) Flew

(b) Shouted

(c) Spoke

(d) Cried

Ans. (c) Spoke

(iii) Fill in the blanks to complete the sentence.
The bird felt that it had been very blind because it could not __ __ __ the leaves from __ n __ __ __ e the nest.

Ans. see, inside

Q.3 Why did the baby bird think that its first world was small, round and blue?

Ans. The baby bird thought that its first world was small, round and blue because it was in an egg which is small, round and blue.

Q.4 Where did the bird go when it fluttered from its straw nest?

Ans. When the bird fluttered from its straw nest, it went beyond the tree.

Q.5 What quality did the bird say it had, when it flew away?

Ans. When the bird flew away, it was mature and responsible as stated by 'quite fit for grown up labours'.

Q.6 Who do you think were the bird's neighbours? Why do you think so? Discuss.

Ans. The bird's neighbours were the other birds and animals that live on a tree like squirrels. Just like bird, they have not left their small world. They do not know how the world is made because they have a limited perspective and they live amongst themselves in unison.

LET US LEARN (NCERT PAGES 89-90)

Q.1 Let us write some rhyming words. One has been done for you.

Word from the poem			
Stanza -1	Stanza -2	Stanza -3	Stanza -4
well			
shell			
New rhyming words			
fell			

Ans.

Word from the poem			
Stanza -1	Stanza -2	Stanza -3	Stanza -4
well	Other	Find	Labours
shell	Mother	Blind	Neighbours
New rhyming words			
fell	Brother	Kind	Saber

Now, complete a new stanza with rhyming words at the end of each line.

I fly high and I fly low,
But one thing I surely k __ __ __,
Whenever I wish to rest,
My little nest is the __ __ __t.

Ans. know, best

Q.2 The poet uses words like 'pale', 'blue', 'round', 'straw' and 'little' to describe the bird's nest. Read a few more describing words.

pointed	green	thin	brown
small	wooden	hanging	rounf

Now, use the describing words given in the box to create six sentences based on the given picture.

(a) ....

(b) ....

(c) ....

(d) ....

(e) ....

(f) ....

Ans. (a) The wooden bird house is hanging on the pointed tree branch.

(b) There are green leaves on the branch where the bird house is hanging.

(c) The house has a small round entrance and a round window.

(d) There is a thin stick at the entrance where the bird can easily sit.

(e) The top of the bird house is red.

(f) The house is naturally brown in colour.

LET US SPEAK (NCERT PAGE 90)

Q.1 Speak with your classmates about which bird you would like to be.

Include the following points.

- Which bird are you? [I am ....]
- What do you look like? [I am .... in colour. I am a big/small bird. I have ....].
- Where do you live? [I live in .... It is (where) ....]
- What do you do during the day? [I .... I also ....]
- Do you have any message for humans? [I want to tell the humans ....]

Ans.
- I am a parrot.
- I am green in colour. I am a small bird. I have green feathers and a red beak.
- I live in the hollows of big trees. It is where I sleep and build my nest.
- I fly around and explore the area that I live in. I also like to taste mangoes on the trees during summers.
- I want to tell humans that us birds like to fly high up in the sky. We do not like to stay inside cages. So, please don't try to catch us when you see us sitting on the trees.

LET US WRITE (NCERT PAGE 91)

Q.1 Read how the bird perceived its world.

My world was small, round and light blue at first. After that my world was warm and comfortable. It was made of straw. In this world I could only see leaves whenever I stepped out. In the end, my world became big. It had the sky and the Earth as a part of it.

Q.2 Now, discuss with your teacher and classmates how you think the world would look to the following.

(a) A baby

(b) A fish

Q.3 Now, write five sentences each, for both (a) and (b), in your notebooks. You can take help from the example given in 1.

Ans. 2. (a) A baby

Big, bright colours everywhere! People make funny sounds and move in weird ways. Their faces change when they talk to me, sometimes happy, sometimes grumpy.

Everything is so big! The ceiling is like a sky, and the floor tickles my hands. Smells are strong, like sweet milk and yummy food. I like to watch the shiny things that hang above my head.

(b) A fish

The world is a watery wonderland. Sunlight filters through water like a magical glittery curtain. Plants move in graceful underwater dance around me. Tiny creatures quickly move about playing a never-ending game of hide-and-seek.

The big fish are scary, but fascinating. And then, there is a strange, flat thing above which is always moving and making ripples. I wonder what it's like to be up there.

REVIEW EXERCISE

Including Competency Based Questions

Part I

Multiple Choice Questions

1. What is the shape of the bird's first home?

(a) Oval (b) Square
(c) Round (d) Triangular

Ans. (c) Round

2. What material is the bird's second nest made of?

(a) Leaves (b) Straw
(c) Twigs (d) Feathers

Ans. (b) Straw

3. **What does the bird see when it first leaves the nest?**

(a) Flowers (b) Leaves
(c) Other birds (d) The sky

Ans. (b) Leaves

4. **What does the bird do at the end of the poem?**

(a) Returns to the nest (b) Flies beyond the tree
(c) Builds a new nest (d) Finds food

Ans. (b) Flies beyond the tree

5. **What does the bird realise about the world by the end of the poem?**

(a) It is small and confined
(b) It is made of straw
(c) It is vast and full of possibilities
(d) It is dangerous

Ans. (c) It is vast and full of possibilities

Fill in the Blanks

1. **The .... initially thought the world was made of a small, round, blue shell.**

Ans. baby bird

2. **The bird's .... made of straw.**

Ans. second home was a cosy nest

3. **When the bird left the nest, it saw ....**

Ans. leaves all around

4. **The bird felt .... in the straw nest with its mother.**

Ans. safe and nurtured

State True or False

1. **The bird flies away to another village to find its home.**

Ans. False

2. **The bird's mother tells it about how the world is made.**

Ans. False

3. **The bird changes its home three times.**

Ans. False

4. **The neighbours know about the world around them.**

Ans. False

Extract Based Questions

Read the lines given below extracts and answer the questions that follow.

A. At length I flew beyond the tree,
Quite fit for grown-up labours,
I don't know how the world is made,
And neither do my neighbours.

(i) What action is the bird talking about in the first two lines?

Ans. The bird is talking about flying for a long distance as the older birds do.

(ii) The word 'grown-up' refers to the ....

Ans. elders

(iii) Choose the word that has similar meaning as 'quite'.

(a) silently
(b) slowly
(c) completely
(d) noisily

Ans. (c) completely

(iv) State whether the following statement is True or False.
The bird thinks it knows how the world is made.

Ans. False

B. One day, I fluttered from my nest,
To see what I could find,
I said the world is made of leaves,
I have been very blind.

(i) The word 'fluttered' indicates ....

Ans. a movement outside the nest

(ii) What is the nest representative of ?

(a) Love
(b) Safety
(c) Talent
(d) Instinct

Ans. (b) Safety

(iii) Is the bird really blind? Give reason for your Ans.

Ans. No, the bird is not really blind. It calls itself blind because it had realised that it had no knowledge of the world.

(iv) State whether the following statement is True or False.
The bird is representative of all humans.

Ans. True

Part II

Very Short Answer Type Questions

1. What does not know how the world is made?

Ans. The baby bird and its neighbours do not know how the world is made.

2. How does the bird's perception of the world change after it leaves the nest?

Ans. After leaving the nest, the bird perceives the world as being made of leaves, as it is surrounded by them.

3. Where does the bird goes in the end?

Ans. In the end, the bird flies beyond the tree.

4. How does the bird feel when it is nestled by its mother in the straw nest?

Ans. The bird feels safe, cosy, and nurtured when it is nestled by its mother in the straw nest.

Short Answer Type Question

1. Why does the bird say 'I have been very blind'?

Ans. The bird says I have been very blind because it initially sees only leaves around it and thinks the world is made of leaves, but when it flies beyond the tree, it realises the world is too big and made up of many things that the bird doesn't know about yet.

Long Answer Type Question

1. Describe the journey of the baby bird as it discovers the world around it. How does its perception of the world change?

Ans. The baby bird's journey begins in a small, round, blue shell, which it initially believes to be its entire world. As it grows, it breaks out of the shell and finds itself in a cosy nest made of straw, nestled by its mother. The bird then thinks the world is made of straw. As it becomes more curious, it goes out of the nest and sees leaves all around. This leads the bird to believe the world is made of leaves.

Finally, the bird flies beyond the tree and realises the world is very big and seems endless. This journey reflects the bird's expanding understanding and the realisation that the world is much larger than it initially thought.

Competency Based Questions

1. Explain the significance of the different environments the bird encounters in the poem. How do these environments contribute to the bird's understanding of the world?

Ans. The different environments the bird sees in the poem are significant as they represent stages of its growth and learning. The shell or egg symbolises the bird's initial and limited understanding of the world. The nest is made of straw and represents a slightly bigger area, where the bird feels safe and nurtured. The leaves around the nest introduce the bird to other natural surroundings, expanding its view.

Finally, flying beyond the tree signifies the bird's realisation of the true size of the world. Each environment contributes to the bird's understanding by slowly revealing more of the world and encouraging exploration and curiosity.

2. What quality of the bird makes it explore the world around it and how does it drive its actions in the poem? Explain with examples.

Ans. 'Curiosity' is the quality that plays a crucial role in the bird's journey as depicted in the poem. It is the bird's curiosity that drives it to break out of the shell and explore the world beyond its nest.

Each new discovery, from the straw nest to the leaves and the wider world, is pushed by the bird's desire to understand its world better.

The poem highlights how curiosity is a powerful motivator for growth and learning, encouraging the bird to go beyond its initial limits and explore the unknown.

Grammar and Writing

1. Write four sentences describing your room using at least 5 words from the given box

Little	pink	blue	massive	beautiful
Colourful	round	small	excited	fluffy

Ans. (i) My personal room has pink walls with blue patterns made on one of them.

(ii) On one corner, there is a little shelf on which my round fluffy ball is kept. It is truly a beautiful.

(iii) It is a beautiful room full of colourful things.

(iv) I get very excited whenever I enter my room.

2. Find the pairs of rhyming words from the given poem.

My cat knows karate.
My frog knows kung fu.
My poodle knows judo.
My turtle does too.
They practised their punches,
their blocks, and their kicks
until they were masters
of martial arts tricks.
You'd think they'd be good now
at guarding our house,
but, yesterday morning,
they ran from my mouse. - Kenn Nesbitt

Ans. kung fu - too
kicks - tricks
house - mouse

ASSESSMENT EXERCISE

Multiple Choice Questions

1. In the line "I lived first in a little house", what does 'little house' indicate?
   (a) The nest
   (b) Bird house
   (c) The egg
   (d) None of the above
2. We can say the bird's second home was comfortable as the bird says
   (a) it was cosy
   (b) it was all it needed
   (c) it had a large space
   (d) it had a fluffy bed

Fill in the Blanks

1. The bird fluttered from its nest to see what it could ....
2. In his second home, the bird thought the world was .... by its mother.
3. At the end, the bird .... know how the world was made.

State True or False

1. The bird's neighbours knew what the world was made up of.
2. The bird's mother knew what the world was made up of.
3. The bird was curious about its surroundings.

Very Short Answer Type Questions

1. Which line in the poem shows that nobody knew what the world was made of?
2. What quality of the bird does the line 'To see what I could find' highlight?
3. What does the bird mean by 'Quite fit for grown-up labours'?

Short Answer Type Question

1. What lesson does the bird learn by the end of the poem?

Long Answer Type Question

1. How does the poem 'What a Bird Thought' talk about growth and discovery? Give examples.

Spices that Heal Us

About the Chapter The given chapter is basically a letter written by a grandmother to her grandchildren-Vikram and Vaibhavi. The letter tells the children the various medicinal uses of the spices that can be easily found in our homes. A spice is any seed, fruit, root, bark, leaf or any other part of a plant used to give taste and colour to our food. The letter points out the various remedies that can be made using these spices.

Chapter Summary

The given chapter is a letter by grandmother called Daadi to Vikram and Vaibhavi.

Introduction in the Letter

The letter starts with a greeting and stated that the grandmother received that message that the children are better now. She stated that she is very happy to know that the natural cure helped them. She tells them to try to remember the cures and share them with their friends. She adds that when she was a child, she learnt the remedies from her grandmother. Her grandmother used to find home remedies for most of the weather-related common illnesses.

Different Spices, their Benefits and Home Remedies

The grandmother, then, shares some of the benefits of the spices that most of us have in our kitchen.

- **Haldi** It is called turmeric in English. It helps in improving our energy level and digestion. It helps in reducing body pain too.
- **Methi** It is called fenugreek in English. It helps in keeping her sugar level and body weight in control. The grandmother here states that she need to soak the methi seeds overnight and drink the water in the morning to gain its benefits.
- **Jeera** It is called Cumin seeds. When they are soaked in water overnight, they can improve digestion and help cure sleeplessness.
- **Heeng** The grandmother states that when Vikram and Vaibhavi were babies and had gas in their tummy, she used to give heeng (asafoetida) water which brought them some relief. She added that Heeng can also help in controlling cough and cold.
- **Dalchini** (cinnamon) and **laung** (clove) give relief when we have toothache till we can consult a dentist.
- **Adrak** According to the grandmother, Ginger is another herb that can help us when we have cough and cold. It also gives relief from pain. She adds that ginger has been used for cooking for more than 4000 years and even today, it is extensively used in cooking Indian food.
- **Kali mirch** Black pepper is also helpful in digestion and can give us relief from body pain.
- The grandmother stated that the children may have seen that at the end of a meal, saunf (fennel seeds) and ajwain (carom seeds) are served. It is because they help in the digestion of food.
- **Elaichi** Cardamom also helps us with digestion and respiratory troubles in addition to curing bad breath.

Ending of the Letter

After giving these remedies, the grandmother asked the children to go into the kitchen and try to identify these herbs and spices. She also reminded that they must consult an elder before they use them. Then, she ended the letter by blessing them.

Values Extracted from this Chapter

The chapter conveys the importance of spices and how these natural herbs and spices can help us treat some diseases and act as remedies by following some simple steps.

Word Meaning

Word	Meaning
Cures/Remedies	A medicine, application, or treatment that relieves or cures a disease.
Relief	Reduction of pain
Consult	To take advice or suggestion from

NCERT FOLDER

NCERT Intext and Exercise Questions

LET US THINK AND REFLECT (NCERT PAGE 95)

Q.1 Read the given lines and answer the following questions.

'When I was a child, I learnt them from my grandmother. She used to find cures for most of the weather-related common illnesses in the kitchen.'

(a) Where exactly in the kitchen did her grandmother find the cures?

Ans. The grandmother found the cures in the spice box and herb jars found in the kitchen.

(b) Give one example of weather-related common illnesses.

Ans. A weather related common illness is cough and cold.

(c) What kind of relationship did the speaker have with her grandmother?

Ans. The speaker had a close and affectionate relationship with the grandmother.

Q.2 Fill in the blanks to complete the sentence.

Daadi soaked methi seeds overnight and drank the water in the morning to manage .... and ....

Ans. blood sugar levels, body weight.

Q.3 Circle the spice that is not useful for body pain according to Daadi's letter.

(a) Turmeric
(b) Fennel seeds
(c) Ginger
(d) Black pepper

Ans. Fennel seeds

Q.4 Why did Daadi ask Vikram and Vaibhavi to share the natural cures with their friends?

Ans. Daadi asked Vikram and Vaibhavi to share the natural cures with their friends so that they can also be benefited from this knowledge. Further, she wanted to pass this knowledge to the new genetaion.

Q.5 What was Daadi's final advice to Vikram and Vaibhavi?

Ans. Daadi's final advice to Vikram and Vaibhavi was to always consult an elder before using any natural cures.

Q.6 How do we know that natural cures are passed from one generation to another?

Ans. We know that natural cures are passed from one generation to another from Daadi's letter which states that she got to know about the remedies from her grandmother and now, she is teaching this to Vikram and Vaibhavi, her grandchildren.

Q.7 Why do you think we should know about the healing properties of spices?

Ans. We all should know about the healing properties of spices because they are natural and effective in curing the disease while maintaining the overall-wellbeing of an individual.

LET US LEARN (NCERT PAGES 96-97)

Q.1 You have read the uses of spices in the letter. Complete the following table with the help of your teacher. You may use the words from the box given below.

Part of the plant: root/bark/leaves/flower buds/fruit/seeds
Texture: rough/soft/silky
Taste: bitter/sweet/sour/salty/spicy

Spice	Name	Part of the plant	Colour	Texture	Taste
	Turmeric				
	Fenugreek				
	Cinnamon				
	Clove				
	Black pepper				
	Cardamom				

Ans.

Name	Part of the plant	Colour	Texture	Taste
Turmeric	Root	Yellow	Soft/silky	Bitter
Fenugreek	Seeds	Yellow/Brown	Rough	Bitter
Cinnamon	Bark	Brown	Rough	Sweet
Clove	Flower buds	Brown	Rough	Spicy
Black pepper	Fruit	Black	Rough	Spicy
Cardamom	Seeds	Green	Soft	Sweet

Q.2 Read the sentences given below.

You may share them with your friends.

You should try to remember these cures.

It can help to control cough and cold.

You must consult an elder before you use them.

I need to soak the methi seeds overnight.

I used to put heeng water on your tummy.

(a) The words given in Column A are helping verbs. Match the helping verbs in Column A with their functions in Column B.

Column A (Helping verbs)	Column B (Functions)
1. may	a. past habit
2. should	b. suggestion
3. can	c. compulsion
4. must	d. advice
5. need to	e. ability
6. used to	f. necessity

Ans. 1-b 2-d 3-e 4-c 5-f 6-a

The helping verbs in Column A are called modal verbs or modals. Each modal verb has a different function.

(b) Complete the following dialogues with any four modals from the table given above. (Use a modal only once.)

Ajay: Anand had fever last week. He (i) .... take good rest.

Suman: Yes, he (ii) .... or he will fall ill again.

Ajay: He (iii) .... take grandmother's natural cures.

Suman: Yes, we (iv) .... remember how effective they are.

Ans. (i) should (ii) needs to (iii) can (iv) must

LET US SPEAK (NCERT PAGES 98-99)

1. Daadi told Vikram and Vaibhavi about many spices. Choose one spice and introduce yourself as that spice to the class.

2. Before you speak, make a spicy headband for the spice you chose. Follow the steps given below.

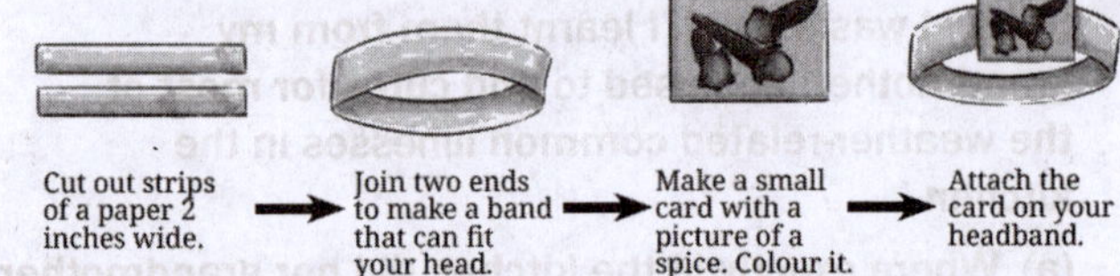

Use the headband while introducing yourself as the spice.

3. Mention the following while speaking.

- your name
- part of the plant
- colour
- texture
- taste
- benefits
- Answer
- Hello!

I am turmeric. I am the root of the plant. I am bright yellow in colour and my texture is oily and silky soft. I taste bitter but I have many antibacterial properties. I can improve your heart and skin health, keep your blood clean and save you from pains and aches in the body.

LET US WRITE (NCERT PAGES 99-100)

1. Vikram's grandmother shared two natural cures to cure his cough in her earlier letter. It was kept outside and a few drops of rain fell on it. Some of the words got washed away by the rain. Help Vikram complete the natural cures. Use the phrases given in the box below.

There are two phrases that you do not need.

Some leaves of basil	for cough	amount of honey
the mixture	for high fever	a piece of fresh ginger
you can have it	grind to get	home remedy

Natural Cures for Cough

(a) To prepare this home remedy, you just need ginger and honey. First, take .... , grate it and take the juice from it. Take about two teaspoons of this juice and add about two and half teaspoons of honey to it. Mix it properly. Warm .... slightly on very low heat for a minute. Then .... about three to four times a day to get relief from cough. Have patience to see the effect as natural cures .... with ginger and honey might take some time to show results.

(b) To prepare the second .... for cough, take about 10 grams of each long pepper, dried ginger and basil leaves. Add four to six small cardamoms and .... a fine powder. If you take this powder with an equal .... , it will give you relief from cough.

Ans. (a) a piece of fresh ginger, the mixture, you can have it, for cough

(b) home remedy, grind to get, amount of honey

2. Now, write a short paragraph on Tulsi based on the completed factsheet in 'Let us listen'.

Ans. Tulsi, also known as Holy Basil, belongs to the Lamiaceae family. First found in India, this wonder herb is now found everywhere in India and is known as the Queen of herbs. Tulsi can decrease levels of stress and cholesterol, making it beneficial for heart health.

It is used to treat disorders of breathing and digestion, and is an ingredient in products like mouthwash and medicinal tea. Tulsi leaves can be consumed by eating them raw or by adding them to tea. This herb is highly valued for its numerous health benefits and is a common remedy in traditional Indian medicine.

REVIEW EXERCISE

Including Competency Based Questions

Part I

Multiple Choice Questions

1. Which spice is known for its antiseptic properties and is used to treat wounds?

(a) Cumin (b) Turmeric
(c) Fennel (d) Cardamom

Ans. (b) Turmeric

2. From where did Daadi learn to use spices as home remedies?

(a) From her grandmother (b) From her father
(c) From her doctor (d) From various books

Ans. (a) From her grandmother

3. Which spice is commonly chewed after meals to aid digestion?

(a) Cloves (b) Cinnamon
(c) Fennel (d) Coriander

Ans. (c) Fennel

4. Which spice is known for its ability to regulate blood sugar levels?

(a) Ginger (b) Turmeric
(c) Cinnamon (d) Cloves

Ans. (c) Cinnamon

Fill in the Blanks

1. Daadi soaked methi seeds overnight and drank the water in the morning to manage ....

Ans. sugar levels and body weight

2. .... is used to relieve toothache and gum infections due to its antiseptic properties.

Ans. Clove

3. .... contains curcumin, which has anti-inflammatory and antioxidant properties.

Ans. Turmeric

4. Fennel seeds can be consumed after meals to ....

Ans. aid digestion and relieve bloating

State True or False

1. Black pepper is known for its ability to improve digestion and relieve respiratory issues.

Ans. True

2. Cardamom is used to treat toothaches and gum infections.

Ans. False

3. **Fenugreek seeds are soaked overnight and consumed to manage blood sugar levels.**

Ans. True

4. **Cinnamon is primarily used for its flavour and has no medicinal benefits.**

Ans. False

Extract Based Question

Read the given extract and answer the questions that follow.

I was a child, I learnt them from my grandmother. She used to find home remedies for most of the weather-related common illnesses. Let me share some of the benefits of the spices that most of us have in our kitchen.

(i) Who is the speaker in these lines?

Ans. Grandmother (Daadi) is the speaker of these lines.

(ii) Which one of the following is a weather-related common illness?

(a) Fever
(b) Cough
(c) Headache
(d) All of the above

Ans. (d) All of the above

(iii) Grandmother shared remedies using the .... that can be found in our kitchen.

Ans. spices

(iv) What is another word for 'benefits'?

Ans. Advantages

Part II

Very Short Answer Type Questions

1. **What did Daadi say that the children must remember before using the spices as remedies?**

Ans. Daadi said that the children must remember to consult an elder before using the spices as remedies.

2. **How does the chapter describe the use of cloves for dental health?**

Ans. Cloves are used for dental health due to their antiseptic properties, helping to relieve toothache and gum infections.

3. **What are the benefits of using Methi for blood sugar regulation mentioned in the chapter?**

Ans. Methi helps regulate blood sugar levels and reduces blood glucose levels.

Short Answer Type Questions

1. **Write the uses of Methi or Fenugreek. How does Daadi use it?**

Ans. Fenugreek is a spice that helps in keeping her sugar level and body weight in control. The grandmother here states that she need to soak the methi seeds overnight and drink the water in the morning to gain its benefits.

2. **When did Daadi use Heeng and for what?**

Ans. Daadi used heeng when Vikram and Vaibhavi were babies.

She used the spice when the children felt gaseous their tummy. She used to give heeng (asafoetida) water which brought them some relief.

Long Answer Type Question

1. **What was the purpose of Daadi's letter to Vikram and Vaibhavi?**

Ans. The purpose of Daadi's letter to Vikram and Vaibhavi was to teach them cures to weather-related illnesses using spices. She had learnt it from her own grandmother and wanted to pass it on to her grandchildren. She also told them about other benefits of the spices that we use for cooking. Through her letter, she shared her love and knowledge with her grandchildren and asked them to share it with their friends too.

Competency Based Questions

1. **Imagine you are a health expert. How would you advise someone to introduce spices into their daily diet for better health?**

Ans. As a health expert, I would advise including spices like turmeric, ginger, and cinnamon into daily meals. Turmeric can be added to curries and soups for its anti-inflammatory benefits. Ginger can be used in teas and soups to aid digestion and reduce body pain. Cinnamon can be sprinkled on oatmeal or added to smoothies to help regulate blood sugar levels. Using these spices regularly can enhance the flavour of food while providing great health benefits.

2. **How can traditional knowledge of spices be preserved and passed onto future generations?**

Ans. Traditional knowledge of spices can be preserved by noting down recipes and remedies in written or video formats.

Educational programs and workshops can be organised to teach children and elders about the benefits and uses of spices. Encouraging family members to share their knowledge and experiences with younger generations can also help. Also, promoting the use of spices in daily cooking and highlighting their health benefits through social media and community events can ensure this valuable knowledge is passed on.

Grammar and Writing

1. Imagine you are Vikram. Based on what you learnt from your Daadi's letter, write a short paragraph about any one spice.

Ans. Ajwain, also known as carom seeds, is a common spice used in Indian kitchens. It has a strong, pungent taste and is often added to dishes like parathas and curries to enhance their flavour.

Ajwain is not just a spice but also a natural remedy for various ailments. It helps in digestion and can relieve stomach aches. My grandmother always tells me to chew a few ajwain seeds if I have a tummy ache. This spice is truly a small wonder in our kitchen.

2. Fill in the blanks using the correct modals.

(i) You .... (should/shall) always listen to your parents.

(ii) .... (Can/May) I borrow your pencil for a moment?

(iii) She .... (could/will) finish her homework by evening.

(iv) We .... (must/might) wear our uniforms to school every day.

(v) He .... (could/should) swim very well when he was younger.

Ans. (i) should (ii) May (iii) will (iv) must (v) could

ASSESSMENT EXERCISE

Multiple Choice Questions

1. Daadi's letter helped the children learn to use the spices as

(a) Home remedies for common illnesses

(b) Skincare remedies

(c) Supplements for their recipes

(d) Medicine

2. Which herb can be taken after meals for good digestion?

(a) Fennel

(b) Carom seeds

(c) Both (a) and (c)

(d) None of the above

Fill in the Blanks

1. Daadi wrote a letter to .... and ....

2. The chapter talks about the use of .... as cures for common illnesses.

3. Daadi advised the children to use her recipes and .... them with others.

State True or False

1. Jeera helps in curing sleeplessness.

2. Turmeric is bad for the immune system.

3. Fennel is added to food to cure gum problems.

Very Short Answer Type Questions

1. For what conditions can home remedies be used as per Daadi's letter?

2. What did Daadi do for the children when they had stomach issues as babies?

Short Answer Type Questions

1. What are the anti-inflammatory properties of ginger mentioned in the chapter?

2. What is the role of cumin in improving our health as described in the chapter?

Long Answer Type Question

1. Describe the process of preparing a home remedy using spices as mentioned in the chapter.

Change of Heart

About the Chapter The given chapter presents the importance of participation over the focusing on victory. The story comprises of Prabhat, a school going boy, obsessed with winning. He learns the importance of enjoying the journey of the game and participation as he observes a new boy, Surya.

Important Characters

Prabhat A young school going boy who is obsessed with winning. He plays the games in which he would win. He also cheats to win a game.

Surya He is the new boy in Prabhat's school. He is very good at badminton and very bad at basketball. However, he enjoys doing everything.

Chapter Summary

Part I

Introducing Prabhat

Prabhat was a school going boy who always won. His parents, teachers and friends knew that he did not know how to accept that he had lost. He used to feel so happy at winning that he never wanted to give it up. He also felt very bad at loosing and that it was the worst thing that could happen to anyone. So, Prabhat would only play a game if he was good at it and he knew that he would win. One such game was badminton.

Surya and the Friday Badminton Game

A new student named Surya joined Prabhat's school. Surya was an excellent badminton player. Prabhat waited for the last Friday of the month when the coach conducted friendly matches in the games period. The teams for this game were decided on Monday and Prabhat and Surya were chosen to play a round against each other. Prabhat was given the responsibility of maintaining score for their match.

Preparations and the Match

Prabhat prepared for the match with great seriousness. In contrast, Surya was relaxed and spent his time, smiling and cracking jokes. However, during the match which took place at the badminton court, Surya was a real phenomenon. He won many points while laughing and joking. He was paying so little attention to the match that Prabhat managed to change the scoreboard. As a result, Prabhat cheated and managed to win. He made a big thing of his win. This loss did not matter anything to Surya who said that the game was fun and that they should play again.

Part II

Prabhat is Sad

After the game, everyone discussed how Prabhat had played so well. However, surprisingly, Prabhat could not sleep well that night. He had won the game but he did not feel as happy as he usually did. Everyone was surprised that Surya did not feel bad about losing.

Surya Enjoys Everything

The next day Prabhat was surprised to see that Surya playing basketball. Surya was so bad at the game that he could not score a basket for ten minutes. Yet, he enjoyed playing the game and his happy smile never left his face.

Prabhat had been observing Surya for some days. He noticed that Surya was very good at some things, bad at others. However, he enjoyed all the things irrespective of how he was at it.

Prabhat's Realisation

As Prabhat observed Surya, he realised that to enjoy a game, he did not need to keep a tally of his scores. He also did not need to worry about winning or losing the game. He understood that he needed to enjoy the game for its own sake. What matters is trying to do well, and enjoying every moment of it.

As Prabhat kept on observing Surya, he learnt something new every day. Soon, he realised that he was undergoing a change.

He had begun playing hide and seek and felt sad whenever it was about to end. He also started joking while playing badminton. As a result, the other students started talking amongst themselves. They discussed how Prabhat had a good sporting spirit.

Values Extracted from this Chapter

The chapter conveys the importance of enjoying everything for the sake of it and not what it brings to you.

It presents how we should not focus only on winning but should enjoy the joy of participation. It teaches us to recognise the true value of sportsmanship and fair play.

Words Meaning

Word	Meaning
Defeat	Loss
Marbles	A game played with marbles
On the contrary	Just the opposite
Terrible	Unhappy
Sensed	Had known
Significant	Important
Conducted	Organised

Word	Meaning
Cracking	Making
Phenomenon	Someone who has special qualities
Opponent	Enemy
Hopeless	Having no skill in something kept a close
Watch on	Observed
Fellow	A person
A great sporting spirit	To have a positive attitude and give your best effort in anything

NCERT FOLDER

NCERT Intext and Exercise Questions

LET US DISCUSS (NCERT PAGE 106)

Q.1 State whether the following is True or False.
Prabhat would accept losing to anyone easily.

Ans. False.

Q.2 What was special about the last Friday of each month?

Ans. The last Friday of each month was special because on that day their coach organised friendly badminton matches in the games period.

Q.3 Who was responsible for maintaining the score for the match?

Ans. Prabhat was responsible for maintaining the score for the match.

Q.4 Do you think Prabhat wished to play another match with Surya? Why do you think so?

Ans. I think Prabhat wished to play another match with Surya because after winning the match by cheating, Prabhat was not happy at all. He wanted a rematch so that he could enjoy winning the match fairly.

LET US DISCUSS (NCERT PAGE 107)

Q.1 How did Surya feel about playing?

Ans. Surya enjoyed playing. It did not matter whether he was good at the game or not, he enjoyed his participation in the game.

Q.2 What was it about Surya that Prabhat observed?

Ans. Prabhat observed that Surya enjoyed the game and did not care much about losing or winning.

LET US THINK AND REFLECT (NCERT PAGE 108)

Q.1 Read the lines given below and answer the questions.

(a) If Prabhat sensed that he would lose a game, he would not play it. He would take part only when he was sure of winning, even if the game lasted only for a minute. You could not stop him from playing the kind of games he was really good at, like badminton.

(i) Complete the sentence suitably.

Prabhat would play a game only if ....

Ans. knew he would win it

(ii) Which game was Prabhat good at playing?

Ans. Prabhat was good at playing Badminton.

(iii) Select the most suitable option to complete the sentence.

This behaviour of Prabhat tells us that he was ....

(a) good at the game (b) sure to win
(c) afraid of losing

Ans. (c) afraid of losing

(b) Surprisingly, Prabhat could not sleep well that night. He had won the game but he did not feel as happy as he usually did. What was surprising was that Surya did not feel bad about losing. What was more surprising was that Prabhat saw Surya playing basketball the next day.

(i) Select the one option that tells us about the way Prabhat was feeling that night.

(a) hurt (b) unhappy (c) afraid (d) focused

Ans. (b) unhappy

(ii) Why does Prabhat find Surya's behaviour 'surprising'?

Ans. Prabhat found Surya's behaviour to be 'surprising' because Surya did not care about losing the game. In fact, he kept on laughing and joking. Further, he also played basketball, which he was very bad at, without any care that he had not goaled.

(iii) Fill in the blank by choosing the most suitable option given in the bracket.

We can say that Surya's reaction to not winning was .... (similar to/as serious as/different from) Prabhat's.

Ans. different from

Q.2 Answer the following questions.

(a) How did Prabhat's attitude towards winning and losing affect his enjoyment of games in the beginning?

Ans. Prabhat's attitude towards winning and losing affected his enjoyment of games adversely. It affected his enjoyment of a game as he was solely focused on winning. He did not play any game if he knew he could lose in it.

(b) Why do you think Prabhat cheated in the beginning to win the badminton match against Surya?

Ans. According to me, Prabhat cheated in the beginning to win the badminton match against Surya he knew he would lose the game against Surya who was playing phenomenally. He did not want to lose and so cheated.

(c) How did Surya's attitude differ from Prabhat's?

Ans. Surya's attitude was very different from Prabhat. Before the game, Prabhat was worried but Surya was relaxed. During the match, Prabhat was keeping the scores and even cheated to win. In contrast, Surya was joking and enjoying the game. Even after the match, Surya did not show any sorrow or disappointment on losing.

(d) Do you think Prabhat's approach to games was healthy? Why or why not?

Ans. I do not think that Prabhat's approach to the games was healthy. It showed that he was not a good sportsman as he was only concerned with winning. He could not accept loss and even cheated to win.

(e) Why do you think sporting spirit is important?

Ans. A good sporting spirit is important because it teaches us the value of participation over any victory. It promotes fairness, respect and enjoyment of the game. It also teaches all of us to develop a positive attitude, build characters, and team skills.

(f) Explain how the title of the story, 'Change of Heart', is suitable.

Ans. The title of the story 'Change of Heart' is apt because the story focuses on the change in the mindset of a young school going boy, Prabhat. It presents the transformation of Prabhat, who was obsessed with winning. Now, Prabhat was a boy who understood the importance of enjoying a game for the sake of it.

LET US LEARN (NCERT PAGE 109)

1. Make as many words as possible using consecutive letters, without changing the order of the letters, from the words in the boxes. One has been done for you.

(a) BADMINTON	**Bad**	**Admin**	**Mint**	**In**	**Ton**	**On**
(b) PHENOMENON						
(c) BASKETBALL						

Now, you can choose words of your own and create your own such puzzles. Share them with your class and try solving others'.

Ans.

(a) BADMINTON	Bad	Admin	Mint	In	Ton	On
(b) PHENOMENON	No	Men	On	One	Pen	Home
(c) BASKETBALL	Basket	Ball	Tall	All	Ask	Sake

2. Read the following sentences and circle the verbs.

(a) Everyone was discussing their game and how Prabhat had played so well.

(b) He had won the game but he did not feel as happy as he usually did.

(c) What was more surprising was that Surya had not felt bad about losing.

Ans. (a) was discussing, had played

(b) had won, did not feel

(c) was, had not felt

3. Arrange the circled verbs as the first action (old action) or second action (new action). One has been done for you.

S. No.	Column A FIRST ACTION (OLD)	Column B SECOND ACTION (NEW)
1.	had played	was discussing
2.		
3.		

The verbs in Column A that refer to the first action or the old action are past perfect.

Ans.

S. No.	Column A FIRST ACTION (OLD)	Column B SECOND ACTION (NEW)
1.	had played	was discussing
2.	had won	did not feel
3.	had not felt	was

4. Fill in the blanks with the past perfect form of verbs given within the brackets.

(a) Prabhat .... already .... his homework before going to the badminton match. (finish)

(b) Surya .... basketball for years before joining the school's badminton team. (play)

(c) By the time Prabhat arrived, Surya .... already .... several matches. (win)

(d) The new student, Surya, ... Prabhat before coming to the school. (never meet)

(e) Before the games period, Prabhat .... badminton extensively. (practice)

Ans. (a) had, finished (b) had played (c) had won

(d) had never met (e) had practiced

LET US SPEAK (NCERT PAGES 111-112)

Look at the situations given below. In pairs, take turns to use the three magic words—'please', 'thank you' and 'sorry'—for the situations given below. Use the prompts given in the table to learn how to thank and apologise properly.

1. **You are Vani— You want to request your friends to take you in their team during games period.**
2. **You are Somiwon— You want to tell Hitesh to help you with the cleaning of the classroom cupboard.**
3. **You are Sumit— You accidently spilled water on Nupur's desk.**
4. **You are Hitesh— You forgot to get Simran's Art file to school.**
5. **You are Kriti— You spoke rudely to Nupur.**
6. **You are Mohan— You wish to thank Hitesh for helping you practice for the Inter-House Speech competition.**
7. **You are Meher— You are grateful that Simran helped you understand a chapter taught at school when you were absent.**
8. **You are Rima— You are thankful to Gita for helping you collect the notebooks from the staff-room.**

Request	
• Could you please ...	
• Please can you help me with ...	
• Kindly .... , please.	
For rude behaviour	**For a mistake**
• I'm very sorry for the way I behaved.	I'm sorry, that was my fault.
• I apologise. I was out of line.	
For being grateful/thankful	
• Thank you. It means so much to me that you ...	
• I truly appreciate your help with ... Thank you.	
• I wish to thank you from the bottom of my heart because you ..	

Ans. 1. Could you please take me in your team during the games period?

2. Please can you help me with the cleaning of your classroom cupboard?
3. I'm sorry, that was my fault.
4. I'm sorry, that was my fault. I forgot your Art file.
5. I am sorry for the way I behaved.
6. Thank you. It means so much to me that helped with the preparation for the Inter-House Speech competition. Thank you.
7. I wish to thank you from the bottom of my heart because you helped me understand a chapter taught at school when you were absent.
8. Thank you. It means so much to me that you helped with the collection of the notebooks from the staff-room.

LET US WRITE (NCERT PAGES 111-112)

Prabhat managed to change the scoreboard while Surya was looking elsewhere. Yet, he did not feel so happy that night. Unable to sleep, he decided to write down his feelings in his diary.

Given below is the page where he wrote his feelings that night. Complete it with the help of the phrases given in the box below.

some leaves of basil	for cough	amount of honey
the mixture	for high fever	a piece of fresh ging
you can have it	grind to get	home remedy

Saturday

17th August, 20XX 8:00 pm

1. **Today, I defeated Surya in a badminton match but (i) .... He was playing very well and was getting the points easily. I was sure that (ii) .... So, when everyone was laughing at a joke he cracked, (iii) .... No one noticed the change and (iv) .... What surprised me the most was that he said (v) .... and we should play again. How could he be so relaxed after losing a match? He should have been sad if not crying over his loss!**

   Though (vi) ...., I did not enjoy as I usually do. It really disturbed me that (vii) .... about losing the match.

   It is still bothering me. Is it because I changed the score? I do not understand myself.

   Let me sleep now. I feel that it may make me feel better. Goodnight!

Ans. (i) I do not feel happy about it

(ii) I would lose the match

(ii) I managed to change the scoreboard

(iv) everyone congratulated me after my win.

(v) he had fun playing with me

(vi) I won the match

(vii) Surya did not feel bad

REVIEW EXERCISE

Including Competency Based Questions

Part I

Multiple Choice Questions

1. What did Prabhat feel when he lost?

(a) Angry
(b) Disappointed
(c) Sad
(d) Indifferent

Ans. (c) Sad

2. Why would Prabhat refuse to play a game?

(a) When he did not want to play
(b) When he knew he would lose
(c) When he was not good at the game
(d) When he did not know the rules of the game

Ans. (b) When he knew he would lose

3. Which characteristic could be used to describe Surya?

(a) Broody (b) Irritating
(c) Handsome (d) Easy going

Ans. (d) Easy going

4. What did Prabhat feel for Surya after the match?

(a) Envious (b) Surprise
(c) Disgusted (d) Irritated

Ans. (b) Surprise

5. Surya did not know how to play ....

(a) Basketball (b) Badminton
(c) Table Tennis (d) Football

Ans. (a) Basketball

6. Prabhat's change could be characterised as......... .

(a) sudden (b) rapid
(c) gradual (d) surprising

Ans. (c) gradual

Fill in the Blanks

1. The teams for the Friday friendly match were decided on ....

Ans. Monday

2. .... was given the opportunity to keep the score.

Ans. Prabhat

3. Surya played the games .... while........... .

Ans. phenomenally, laughing and joking with everyone

4. Prabhat was unhappy because ....

Ans. he had won by cheating

5. Prabhat changed by ....

Ans. observing Surya's behaviour

State True or False

1. Everyone was worried about Prabhat's behaviour.

Ans. True

2. Prabhat did not want Surya to win.

Ans. True

3. His classmates praised Prabhat for winning.

Ans. True

4. Surya was envious of Prabhat's seriousness.

Ans. False

5. Prabhat had learned the meaning of enjoying a game properly.

Ans. True

Extract Based Questions

Read the extracts given below and answer the questions that follow.

A. On one hand, Prabhat prepared for the match with great seriousness. Surya, on the other hand, seemed relaxed, not taking the things seriously at all. He walked about the whole time, smiling and cracking jokes about all sorts of things. But on Friday, at the badminton court, Surya was a real phenomenon. He won points again and again, laughing and joking all the time.

(i) The match referred to in the extract is ....

(a) a competitive match to see who is better
(b) an audition
(c) a friendly weekly match
(d) a challenged between Prabhat and Surya

Ans. (c) a friendly weekly match

(ii) **'He won points again and again.' What does the given line tell us about 'he'?**

Ans. The given line tells us that 'he'- Surya, is a very good player of badminton.

(iii) **Do you think Prabhat's behaviour is correct in the extract?**

Ans. I think that Prabhat's behaviour in the situation presented in the extract is incorrect. The match is a friendly match in which win or loss is not little importance. Therefore, Prabhat's seriousness is not required.

(iv) **State whether the following statement is True or False.**

Surya was deliberately trying to get Prabhat jealous in the game.

Ans. False

B. Prabhat kept a close watch on Surya for some days. He was great at some things, terrible at others but what was common was the enjoyment. He enjoyed everything equally. As Prabhat went on with his observation, he realised that to enjoy a game, you did not need a scoreboard to keep a tally of your scores. Neither did you have to worry about winning and losing. You needed to enjoy the game for its own sake. What matters is trying to do well, and enjoying every moment of it.

(i) **What did Prabhat learn from Surya?**

(a) How to relax

(b) Good sportsmanship

(c) Team playing

(d) Importance of honesty

Ans. (c) Team playing

(ii) **The expression 'kept a close watch' means ....**

Ans. to observe carefully

(iii) **What did Prabhat observe about Surya?**

Ans. Prabhat observed that Surya did not care for winning. He enjoyed playing everything even if he was bad at it.

(iv) **Identify the lines which defines the lesson learnt by Prabhat.**

Ans. The lines which defines good sportsmanship as learnt by Prabhat is "Neither did you have to worry about winning and losing. You needed to enjoy the game for its own sake. What matters is trying to do well, and enjoying every moment of it."

Part II

Very Short Answer Type Questions

Answer the following questions in one sentence.

1. **According to his family, what did Prabhat not know?**

Ans. According to his family, Prabhat did not know how to accept defeat.

2. **What kinds of games did Prabhat play?**

Ans. Prabhat only played the games in which he was good and it was sure that he would win.

3. **Surya was a real phenomenon. Explain.**

Ans. The given statement indicates that Surya was a very good badminton player.

4. **Why was Prabhat surprised at Surya playing basketball?**

Ans. Prabhat was surprised at Surya playing basketball because he was playing happily inspite of the fact that he was not scored any goal.

Short Answer Type Questions

1. **Why do you think Prabhat cheated in a friendly game?**

Ans. I think that Prabhat cheated in the friendly game because he could not accept losing any game. He knew that with Surya scoring points in the game, he would definitely lose. So, to avoid losing and feeling sad, he cheated in the game.

2. **"It's been fun. We should play again some other time," said Surya. What does this tell you about Surya?**

Ans. The given lines tell us that Surya was an easy-going and happy child who enjoyed doing things for the sake of it. He understood that it was a friendly game played for fun as well as practice. Hence, his reaction shows his good sportsman spirit.

3. **What was Prabhat keeping a close watch on Surya?**

Ans. Prabhat was keeping a close watch on Surya because he was surprised at Surya's reaction to the friendly game. He found it strange that even if losing the game Surya was not sad and was even playing basketball- a game he was really bad at.

4. How did Prabhat change after observing Surya?

Ans. Prabhat changed slowly but gradually after observing Surya's nature. He realised that winning was not as important as enjoying the game. He understood that the true value of playing was enjoyment rather than victory.

Long Answer Type Questions

1. Compare and contrast the characters of Prabhat and Surya.

Ans. Both Prabhat and Surya are school going boys with very different perspectives. Prabhat was a boy obsessed with winning.

He would only play a game if he was good at it and knew that he would win.

Further, he did not know how to accept defeat and even prepared for a friendly game with complete seriousness. When he realised that he would not win the friendly game, he cheated to win.

In contrast, Surya was joyous boy who did not care for winning or losing. While preparing for the friendly match, he was relaxed and joked with everybody. Even during the game, he was not paying his complete attention and lost. However, he was not sad about it. He in fact told Prabhat that he would like to play with Prabhat.

Concluding, Surya displays true sportsmanship that is lacking in Prabhat.

2. It is self-reflection that leads Prabhat to learn the importance of enjoying the game. Justify with reference to the chapter.

Ans. It is true that self-reflection that leads Prabhat to learn the importance of enjoying the game. Mere observation without understanding one's faults and realising the need to change.

This is want happened with Prabhat. It can be said that Prabhat's parents and teachers might have told him about his obsession with victory. However, it did not change Prabhat's thinking and he continued to play the games in which he would win.

All the change that came in Prabhat was after he observed Surya.

His classmate's reaction to losing and his joyful nature surprised Prabhat. He could not understand how Surya could be so relaxed even after losing or play a game that he was bad at. Hence, Prabhat started observing Surya which made him understand his own flaws. As a result, he transformed.

Competency Based Questions

1. "Surya was paying so little attention to the match...". Do you think such an act is wise on Surya's part? Give reason for your answer.

Ans. I do not think that paying less attention to any match whether friendly or competitive is justified. Given that it was a friendly match, one could accept Surya's behaviour but cannot justify it as good. In a long run, such an act can lead to the loss of an important match.

2. Imagine the friendly weekly game was a proper competition. Do you think Surya would have been careless in it or Prabhat would have the courage to cheat?

Ans. If the friendly weekly match was a proper competition, I do not think that Surya would have been that careless.He would have no doubt enjoyed the game and not become sad even if he had lost. However, he would have given his best with complete attention.

Prabhat would also not have changed the scoreboard realising that if he were caught cheating in an important game, he could be banned from playing in competitive matches for some time as punishment.

3. Surprisingly, Prabhat could not sleep well that night. He had won the game but he did not feel as happy as he usually did.

These lines indicate that Prabhat had a conscience (an understanding of what is morally wrong or right). Do you agree? Justify.

Ans. Conscience is the understanding of what is right or wrong. Such an understanding helps us realise the importance and impact of our actions. It teaches us that we should not cheat and if we do, it prevents us from being happy or satisfied with the victory. The truth of our conscience can be seen in Prabhat's reaction after winning the game.

In the story, 'Change of Heart', Prabhat cheats in a friendly game after realising and that he would lose. So, when no one is paying attention, he changes the score board. He wins and everyone praises him. However, he is unhappy because his morality tells that his winning is not justified because he had cheated. It shows him that he is not the true winner of the game.

Grammar and Writing

1. Imagine a conversation between Prabhat and Surya after Prabhat changes his perspective. Write a dialogue about a conversation that took place between them and include Prabhat's gratitude to Surya.

Ans. **Prabhat** Hey Surya! Can I talk to you for a minute?

Surya Hey Prabhat. Sure! Everything okay?

Prabhat Yes, I just wanted to thank you for showing me the true joy of the playing.

Surya Ummmm... You are welcome, I guess.

Prabhat I know you are surprised but let me tell you all about it. I was obsessed with winning. I do not play a game in which I knew I would lose. Hell, I even cheated in that Friday friendly game to win the match. I thought you would be upset but no that was not the case. You were not sad and even told me that you wanted to play with me again. I was shocked. My shock increased when I saw you playing basketball which, by the way, you are really bad at. But you did not care.

Surya Yes, I believe that we should enjoy a game without worrying about winning or losing.

Prabhat Yes, I learned that from you. I observed you for week to come to that understanding. So, Thanks.

Surya Well, You must heard about this dialogue 'There is no sorry or thank you between friends'.

Prabhat Yes, friends?

Surya Definitely friends.

2. Write a diary entry from Surya's perspective about the day of the friendly match.

Ans. Saturday

17th August, 20XX 8:00 pm

Today was very interesting. I lost a friendly badminton match but that was not something to worry about. But what was interesting that this classmate of mine- Prabhat- was acting weird. I had heard about Prabhat from all of my friends. He was obsessed with winning and only played when he knew he would win. I mean, who does that? That just takes away the fun playing. Initially, I did not believe my friends but I saw it first hand when we were selected to play against each other. He was so serious about the game. It was just a friendly match. During the game, I was enjoying while he was worried about the score. Somehow, he won and he made a big deal about it. Everyone was praising him but he was not as happy as he showed. I think he was upset that I was not sad or worried about losing. I think if I get a chance, I would talk to him about it or I do not know what to do now. I would see what I would so. Now, good night!

Surya

3. Look at the given lines from the story.

Prabhat kept a close watch on Surya for some days. He was great at some things, terrible at others but what was common was the enjoyment. He enjoyed everything equally. As Prabhat went on with his observation, he realised that to enjoy a game, you did not need a scoreboard to keep a tally of your scores. Neither did you have to worry about winning and losing. You needed to enjoy the game for its own sake. What matters is trying to do well, and enjoying every moment of it.

(i) The passage contains any forms of the word 'enjoy'. Point out these forms and write the name of their forms.

Ans. Enjoyment-Noun

Enjoyed- Past form of verb

To enjoy- Infinitive

Enjoying- Continuous form of verb

(ii) The given passage may contain pairs of antonyms. Identify them.

Ans. Great-terrible, Winning-losing,

ASSESSMENT EXERCISE

Multiple Choice Questions

1. Prabhat wanted to keep winning because ....

(a) he loved the appreciation he received

(b) he hated losing

(c) he felt that he was the best

(d) he hated Surya

2. Surya was............ at badminton.

(a) better than Prabhat (b) phenomenal

(c) very bad (d) Both (a) and (b)

Fill in the blanks

1. Prabhat .... after the match.

2. Surya was different from Prabhat because he was ....

3. In the end, Prabhat .... while playing badminton.

State True or False

1. Prabhat wanted to taunt Surya.

2. Surya wanted a rematch to show Prabhat that he was better at badminton.

3. Prabhat and Surya loved playing with each other.

Extract Based Question

Read the extract given below and answer the questions that follow.

On that day, everyone was discussing their game and how Prabhat had played so well. Surprisingly, Prabhat could not sleep well that night. He had won the game but he did not feel as happy as he usually did. What was surprising was that Surya did not feel bad about losing. What was more surprising was that Prabhat saw Surya playing basketball the next day.

(i) The 'game' referred to the extract ended with ....

(ii) How did Prabhat prepare from the game?

(iii) Why do you think Prabhat was not happy that night?

(iv) Prabhat was surprised because ....

(a) Surya was not sad

(b) Surya was good at basketball

(c) Surya was not talking to him

(d) his cheating was discovered

Very Short Answer Type Questions

1. Prabhat was selected for keeping the scoreboard. What does this tell us about Prabhat?

2. How is Surya introduced in the story?

3. What is the most important thing in a game?

4. State one thing that depicts that Prabhat had changed.

Short Answer Type Questions

1. Why was it not surprising that Prabhat and Surya were selected to play against each other?

2. Surya was a real phenomenon. Prove in the context of the story.

3. Prabhat made a big thing of his win. Explain.

4. How did Surya react to losing the game?

Long Answer Type Questions

1. Prabhat was surprised at Surya. List the things that surprised him.

2. Prabhat changed because of Surya. Do you agree? Justify your answer.

The Winner

by Georgia Heard

CHAPTER 11

About the Chapter The given poem by Georgia Heard presents the joys in playing that we had as children. The poem shows young children including the speaker playing from evening to night without any worry in the world.

Stanzawise Explanation

STANZA 1

Evenings, we play ball
next to the creek
in our neighbour's field.
We run so fast
I can't even catch my breath.
When blue dark turns to black,
cold grass aches our feet,
trees creep close— game's over.
Night wins!

Explanation The given poem presents the views of young children who are playing games in the evening. The lines state that the children used to play with ball near the small river in their neighbours' field. The children used to run so fast that the speaker couldn't breathe comfortably or regularly. They used to stop playing only during the night when the blue colour of the sky became black. By that time, the children's feet used to hurt due to the cold grass and the trees seem to the moving closer. This indicated the end of the game.

Values Extracted From This Chapter

The chapter conveys the joys of childhood in playing and enjoying the childhood days with friends.

Word Meaning

Word	Meaning
Creek	A stream or minor tributary of a river.
Catch my breath	To pause or rest for a short time until you can breathe comfortably or regularly again
Aches	Pains
Creep	To move quietly and carefully

NCERT FOLDER

NCERT Intext and Exercise Questions

LET US DISCUSS (NCERT PAGES 116-117)

Q.1 Read the given lines from the poem. Write the meaning of the lines by identifying the words/expressions in them.

	Lines from the poem	Meaning
1.	next to the creek Clue: a small body of water.	
2.	I can't even catch my breath Clue: the child has been running.	
3.	When blue dark turns to black Clue: the colour of the sky changes from blue to black. What does it mean?	
4.	trees creep close Clue: it is evening time. Why do you think the trees seem close?	

Ans.

	Lines from the poem	Meaning
1.	next to the creek Clue: a small body of water.	near a small body of water.
2.	I can't even catch my breath Clue: the child has been running.	The children did not have time to rest or breathe properly. So, they were breathless
3.	When blue dark turns to black Clue: the colour of the sky changes from blue to black. What does it mean?	The colour of the sky changes from dark blue to black indicating that it is night.
4.	trees creep close Clue: it is evening time. Why do you think the trees seem close?	The trees seem to be getting closer as the evening has ended.

Q.2 Read the poem. Complete the following based on the poem.

The children play .... in the .... in the neighbour's .... They run so .... that they run out of breath. They continue to play till the evening when the blue sky turns .... , and the trees are not clearly visible. They can feel their feet .... , now that it is cold. Finally, they stop .... and go home as it is night.

Ans. The children play ball in the evening in the neighbour's field. They run so fast that they run out of breath. They continue to play till the evening when the blue sky turns black, and the trees are not clearly visible. They can feel their feet aching, now that it is cold. Finally, they stop playing and go home as it is night.

LET US THINK AND REFLECT (NCERT PAGES 117-118)

Q.1 Read the given lines and answer the questions that follow.

(a) *We run so fast*
I
can't
even
catch
my
breath.

(i) Complete the sentence given below with the correct option.

The speaker needs to catch her breath because

....

(a) everyone decides to walk

(b) all the friends wish to go home

(c) running fast results in being breathless

(d) they need to do breathing exercises

Ans. (c) running fast results in being breathless

(ii) Is the speaker alone? Why do you say so?

Ans. No, the speaker is not alone. We can say so because the lines used the word 'we'.

(iii) What does the pattern in the lines tell us?

Ans. The pattern of the lines tells us the speed and intensity of the game because of which the speaker is breathless.

(b) *When blue dark turns to black,*
cold grass aches our feet,
trees creep close—
game's over.
Night wins!

(i) Give one reason why the grass is cold.

Ans. The grass is cold because it is night and the temperature has become cold.

(ii) Complete the sentence suitably.

The children's feet are aching because.................... .

Ans. they have been running on the cold grass for a long time

(iii) Why does 'Night' win?

Night wins because the ....

(a) time for play has ended
(b) children are tired
(c) time to play at home begins
(d) night follows day

Ans. (a) time for play has ended

LET US LEARN (NCERT PAGES 118-119)

Q.1 Read the information given in the table and see what the poet has done in the poem 'The Winner'.

Lines from the poem	What the poet has done	Other examples
I can't even catch my breath	This tells us that the children are really out of breath. The pattern is used to highlight them being out of breath.	The leaves are falling, falling, falling.
Night wins!	The poet has used human qualities for inanimate things. Here, **night** has been shown as winning. This is called **personification.**	The sun played hide-and-seek with the clouds.

Now, try to wirte some examples of your own for both. Use your imagination when creating these examples.

Ans. 1. The water flowed rapidly

2. The stars twinkled mischievously at night

Q.2 The poet has talked about a creek in the poem. You now know that creek is a water body. Complete the word web given below by writing which other water bodies you can think of. Discuss with your teacher.

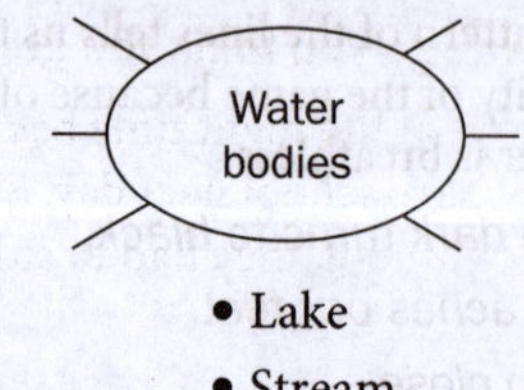

Ans.
- Pond
- River
- Ocean
- Lake
- Stream
- Sea

LET US SPEAK (NCERT PAGES 118-119)

Q.1 Enact the roles of a parent and a child.

Situation 1 Coming home late after play. (Parent upset/Child explaining)

Situation 2 Sharing details of the games you played. (Child excited/Parent asking details with interest)

Situation 3 Bring a new friend home after playtime. (Child introducing/Parent welcoming)

Ans. Situation 1

Parent Why are so late? Where were you and what were you doing? You know that you have to get home before 12 pm.

Child Sorry. I was in a group study session with my friends and lost track of time. It won't happen again.

Situation 2

Child excited Yay. Today was a wonderful day. We played so many fun games everyday. We played badminton, volleyball and even kho-kho.

Parent Really. Were you divided into teams? Who were in your team and what was your role?

Situation 3

Child Hey Maa, meet Abhinav. He is my new classmate. He recently joined our school and is an excellent cricketer.

Parent Hii Abhinav. It is so nice to meet you. Welcome to our home.

LET US WRITE (NCERT PAGE 121)

Q.1 Write a paragraph about your playtime, using the clues given below

- **What time do I go out to play?**
- **Who do I play with?**
- **What games do we play?**
- **Which is my favourite game?**
- **What do we gain from playing together?**
- **When do we finish playing and go home?**

Now, give a title to your paragraph.

Ans. My Playtime

I love playing with my friends in the evening. I usually go out to play with my friends in the evening at around 5 pm after doing my homework. I generally play with my friends who live in the same apartment complex as me. We play many games including dodgeball, football, cricket, pithoo, etc. Every day is a new game for us. We also cycle every day during our play time. I especially love dodgeball as it shows how attentive I am. It teaches me to be a team player. It builds our character and true sportsmanship among all of us. We only return home after 7 pm when we are all tired and need to have dinner to go to sleep early.

REVIEW EXERCISE

Including Competency Based Questions

Part I

Multiple Choice Questions

1. The poem is from the perspective of ....

(a) the young child (b) all children
(c) adults (d) animals

Ans. (b) all children

2. The setting of the poem is ....

(a) a park (b) a village
(c) river bank (d) a garden

Ans. (c) river bank

3. What is the speaker of the poem feeling?

(a) Regret (b) Nostalgia
(c) Sad (d) Blissful

Ans. (d) Blissful

4. Why can't the speaker catch her breath?

(a) She was running
(b) She was ill
(c) She had not rested
(d) Both (a) and (c)

Ans. (d) Both (a) and (c)

5. The image that shows the movement of time is ....

(a) smell (b) sound
(c) colour (d) None of these

Ans. (c) colour

Fill in the Blanks

1. The children were playing ....

Ans. with a ball

2. The change of the colour of the sky indicates that ....

Ans. play time is over

3. The tone of the poem is ....

Ans. playful and innocent

4. The speaker's feet .... by the end of the game.

Ans. Ache

State True or False

1. The children are playing a friendly game.

Ans. True

2. The children play till their parents call them home.

Ans. False

3. The grass is warm at night.

Ans. False

Extract Based Questions

Read the lines given below and answer the questions that follow.

I can't even catch my breath.
When blue dark turns to black,
cold grass aches our feet,

(i) The usual play time of children is ....

(a) night (b) afternoon
(c) evening (d) morning

Ans. (c) evening

(ii) State True or False

The grass is cold because of the low temperature of the night.

Ans. True

(iii) Complete the sentence appropriately:

In the given lines, the speaker is ....

Ans. out of breath because of continuously running

(iv) When and why do you think the game stops?

Ans. The game stops at the night time because the children may have school next day. So, to prepare themselves for school, they had to stop their game.

Part II

Very Short Answer Type Questions

1. Where are the children playing?

Ans. The children are playing near the river in their neighbour's field.

2. Can you think of the games they are playing?

Ans. As the children are playing with a ball and running, we can state that they may be playing- football, basketball or dodgeball.

3. Why do you think the speaker is out of breath?

Ans. The speaker is out of breath because she is running fast without stopping to take a rest or breathe properly.

Short Answer Type Questions

1. Do you think that the title of the poem 'The Winner' is apt? Give reason for your answer.

Ans. I think that the title of the poem 'The Winner' is justified. Initially, the title seems injustified as the poem is about the children playing innocently from evening till night. However, the title seems apt with the last line which indicates that the children ended the game at night, making night time the winner of their game.

2. 'Night wins!' Explain.

Ans. The given expression indicates that the night time won the game that the children had been playing continuously.

This statement indicates that there was no loser or winner in the game the children were playing. They would have continued playing if night had not come. Thus, the winner of game was night as any games ends when there is a clear winner.

Long Answer Type Question

1. The poem 'The Winner' reminds us of the childhood innocence wherein we played without any worry in the world. Comment.

Ans. It is true that the poem 'The Winner' reminds us of the childhood innocence wherein we played without any worry in the world. During our childhood, we played for many hours without any serious competition while enjoying the game for fun. We would continue playing till it was time for us to go home. In the poem also, the children started playing in the evening with a ball. They continue playing till night arrives. When their game ends their feet are aching and they cannot see anything clearly. Their game is innocent and fun. They do not care for the winner or loser and are not worried about anything.

Competency Based Questions

1. Can you suggest another title for the poem? Justify it.

Ans. Another suitable title for the poem can be 'Playtime' as the poem presents how the children play without any care in the world during their playtime. It also highlights that the children play till their playtime ends which is at night.

2. The poet has used senses to indicate the intensity of the game and the change of time. Do you agree? Give reason.

Ans. It is true to say that the poet has used senses to indicate the intensity of the game and the change of time. The sense of breath and the pattern of the lines in the poem indicates that the game that the children were playing was so intense that the children were breathless. Further, the change of the time and temperature is indicated by the cold grass and the change of the colour of the sky from dark blue to black.

ASSESSMENT EXERCISE

Multiple Choice Questions

1. The children are playing in ....
   (a) their neighbour's field (b) their school's park
   (c) a water park (d) their garden
2. The children's feet are aching because ....
   (a) they were injured
   (b) they were running
   (c) they were playing on cold grass
   (d) Both (b) and (c)

Fill in the Blanks

1. The speaker needs to catch her breath because ....
2. The children lose because ....

State True or False

1. The children played till late at night.
2. One of the children was the winner.

Extract Based Questions

Read the lines given below and answer the questions that follow.

Evenings,
we play ball
next to the creek
in our neighbour's field.
We run so fast
I can't even catch my breath.
When blue dark turns to black,
cold grass aches our feet,
trees creep close—
game's over.
Night wins!

(i) Can you tell who could 'we' be?
(ii) Complete the sentence appropriately. .... has been given the quality of a human in the poem.
(iii) The grass gets cold when ....
   (a) it is winter time
   (b) blue dark turns to black
   (c) someone has thrown cold water on it
   (d) there is a water on the grass
(iv) What can you say about the setting of the poem?

Very Short Answer Type Questions

1. Who wins in the poem in the end?
2. What are the children playing?

Short Answer Type Questions

1. How do we know it is night time?
2. Why does night win?

Long Answer Type Question

1. Write the sum and substance of the poem

CHAPTER 12

Yoga-A Way of Life

About the Chapter The given chapter presents the origin, various benefits and international recognition received by Yoga.

Chapter Summary

Origination of the Word 'Yoga'

Yoga is a physical, mental, and spiritual practice that originated in ancient India. The word 'Yoga' comes from the Sanskrit word 'yuj', which means 'to join' or 'to unite'. Hence, the word symbolises the unity of mind and body; thought and action- harmony between human and nature. It is an approach to health and well-being.

Defining Yoga

The ancient tradition of yoga was presented in a systematic way by Sage Patanjali in 'Yoga Sutras of Patanjali'. He described yoga as the means to make the mind quiet and free from all problems that may distract us. Today, yoga has become increasingly popular due to the many health benefits it offers.

Benefits of Yoga

Some of the benefits of yoga are

- Yoga postures (asanas) help to stretch and strengthen the muscles, increase flexibility, endurance (capacity to continue without giving up) and balance. This can reduce our body pain such as lower back pain and improve our overall physical fitness.
- Yoga involves breathing techniques and meditation. These help to calm the mind and reduce stress as well as anxiety. It relaxes the mind, improves the quality of sleep and increases concentration.
- Yoga boosts the immune system. It can improve heart health by lowering blood pressure and improving circulation.
- Yoga can help in losing weight in weight loss by burning calories, and maintaining health. It promotes a sense of overall well-being.

Yoga-Internationally Recognised

Because of these benefits, Yoga has been internationally recognised. The World Health Organisation (WHO) on 20th June, 2021, launched an App called WHO mYoga. The app contains a collection of videos and audio files to teach and support yoga practice. The aim of the app was to have an easy-to-use and free tool for people across the world to encourage them to practise yoga.

Practising Yoga

Anyone can start practising yoga at any given moment of time. One must remember that when one practises yoga asanas (postures), one does not just stretch the body. The mind has to be with the body. This is the reason why it should be practised without disturbances. If each stretch is coordinated with the breath and awareness, our practice will become a yogic practice.

> *hathasya prathamangatvadasanam purvamuchyate*
> *kuryattadasanam sthairyamarogyam changalaghavam*
>
> Being the first accessory of Hatha-Yoga, asana is described first. It should be practised for ganining steady posture, health and weightlessness of body.

Values Extracted from this Chapter

The chapter conveys the importance of yoga in maintaining the physical and mental health of all.

Word Meaning

Word	Meaning
Spiritual	Relating to soul
Originated	Started
Symbolises	Represents
Harmony	Balance
Holistic	Organised
Distractions	Disturbances
Flexibility	Ability to bend without difficulty
Endurance	Capacity to continue without giving up
Anxiety	Worry
Boost	Increase
Coordinated	In a ordered manner

NCERT FOLDER

NCERT Intext and Exercise Questions

LET US DISCUSS (NCERT PAGE 124)

Q.1 Read the passage again and fill in the blanks with words from the box.

sleep	lifestyle	health	strength	calm	stress	balance

Yoga is a practice that not only improves physical flexibility but also improves mental (i) .... and leads to a healthier (ii) .... It involves a series of asanas, which increase muscular (iii) .... Practicing yoga also leads to a better body and mind (iv) .... and reduces body pain such as the lower back. Moreover, the focus on breathing techniques and meditation makes the mind (v) .... , lessens (vi) .... , and improves the quality of (vii) .... This helps to adopt a more positive lifestyle.

Ans. (i) health (ii) lifestyle
(iii) strength (iv) balance
(v) calm (vi) stress
(vii) sleep

LET US THINK AND REFLECT

(NCERT PAGE 125)

Q.1 What is the aim of yoga?

Ans. The aim of yoga is to create a balance between body and mind, thought and action while boosting harmony between human and nature. It also promotes health and well-being of individuals while freeing it from distractions.

Q.2 Explain the idea of unity in yoga.

Ans. The idea of unity in yoga involves the integration of mind and body unity of thought and action and harmony between human and nature. It symbolises the joining of physical mental and spiritual practises to create a holistic approach to health.

Q.3 What does the launch of the WHO mYoga app tell us about the importance of yoga?

Ans. The launch of the WHO mYoga app highlights the global recognition of the benefits of yoga. It indicates that yoga is valued for its ablity to improve physical and mental health and that there is an international effort to make yoga accessible to people worldwide.

Q.4 Describe one long-term effect that the practise of yoga can have on a person's qualities.

Ans. One of the many long-term effects of yoga is the boost in mindfulness.

It helps in creating a distraction free mind. Regular practice of yoga can enhance a person's awareness leading to better focus and inner peace.

LET US LEARN (NCERT PAGES 125-126)

1. Let us play the game of *Antakshari*. The first word is 'yoga'. The next word must then begin with the letter 'a'. This activity will go on and the whole class will participate and will write the words on the blackboard. How many new words have you learnt?

Ans. Do it yourself .

2. Make as many words as you can using the letters shown. Use the letter 'A' in all the words that you make.

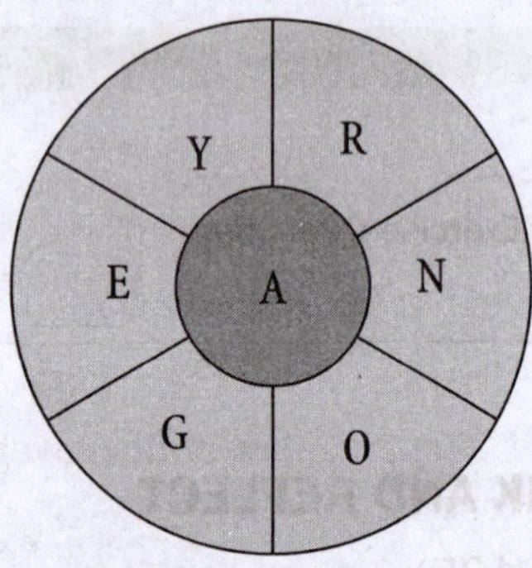

Ans. Are, ran, rang, ray, rayon, gay, rag, arrange

LET US SPEAK (NCERT PAGE 126)

1. Participate in groups of four to share your 'yoga thoughts'.

If you have tried yoga	If you have not tried yoga, yet
I practise yoga because	I wish to practise yoga because ....
My favourite thing about yoga is	I hope that once I begin practising yoga, I ....
I feel .... after a yoga session because	The kind of exercise I want to try in yoga is .... because ....
The one thing in yoga that I want to practise is .... because	

Ans.

If you have tried yoga	If you have not tried yoga
I practise yoga because it helps me relax and stay fit.	I wish to practise yoga because I want to improve my focus and build endurance.
My favourite thing about yoga is that it calms my mind and frees me from any anxiety.	I hope that once I begin practising yoga, I will become fit and have greater peace of mind.
I feel relaxed after a yoga session as removes all stresses or disturbances from my mind.	The kind of exercise I want to try in yoga is breathing techniques as they build my endurance.
The one thing in yoga that I want to practise is meditation because it helps me to boost my mental faculties.	

2. Take turns to speak and listen to others when they share their thoughts.

Ans. Do it yourself.

LET US WRITE (NCERT PAGE 127)

1. Write a short paragraph on 'The Benefits of Yoga'. You may use the following sentence starters along with your own ideas to create the paragraph.

Opening line	Yoga is important because
Supporing ideas	One benefit of yoga that interests me is
	Practising yoga can help people ....
	A popular yoga pose is .... because ....
	Yoga is not just physical exercise, it also ....
Concluding line	Finally, yoga can be a great way to , ...

Ans. Opening line: Yoga is important because it promotes our physical and mental health and well-being.

Supporting ideas:

- One benefit of yoga that interests me is that reduces stress.
- Practising yoga can help people by boosting their mental capabilities and improving their physical health.
- A popular yoga pose is Sukhasana or the Easy pose because it relaxes our mind and body.
- Yoga is not just physical exercise; it also includes mental and spiritual practices.

Concluding Line: Finally, yoga can be a great way to maintain a healthy lifestyle and boost mental peace.

REVIEW EXERCISE

Including Competency Based Questions

Part I

Multiple Choice Questions

1. The word 'yoga' is derived from ....

(a) An Arabic word (b) A Tamil word
(c) A Sanskrit word (d) An Urdu word

Ans. (c) A Sanskrit word

2. Yoga is understood as a/an ....

(a) experimental approach (b) time tested approach
(c) holistic approach (d) recognised approach

Ans. (c) holistic approach

3. Yoga was systemitised in ....

(a) Geeta (b) Ramayana
(c) Yoga Sutra of Patanjali (d) Yoga- A Way of Life

Ans. (c) Yoga Sutra of Patanjali

4. Why is Yoga internationally recognised?

(a) It had no side effects
(b) It is ancient culture
(c) It calms the mind
(d) It promotes sense of well-being

Ans. (d) It promotes sense of well-being

5. Myoga can be described as ....

(a) a video about yoga asanas
(b) an easy to use application
(c) a poster advertising yoga
(d) an easy to use application

Ans. (b) an easy to use application

Fill in the Blanks

1. Yoga indicates a .... between mind and body .

Ans. unity

2. Sage Patanjali presented Yoga as ....

Ans. the means to make the mind quiet and free from all distractions

3. .... calms the mind and reduces stress.

Ans. Meditation

4. International Yoga day is celebrated on ....

Ans. 21st June

State True or False

State whether the given statements are True or False.

1. Yoga is only about breathing techniques.

Ans. False

2. Yoga is about harmony between you and the nature.

Ans. True

3. Yoga does not have any side effects.

Ans. True

4. Yoga does not help in weight loss.

Ans. False

5. Yoga boosts our immune system.

Ans. True

Extract Based Questions

Read the extract given below and answer the questions that follow.

Yoga is a physical, mental, and spiritual practise that originated in ancient India. The word 'Yoga' comes from the Sanskrit root 'yuj', which means 'to join' or 'to unite'. This symbolises the unity of mind and body; thought and action; harmony between human and nature. It is a holistic approach to health and well-being.

(i) On the basis of the extract, can you call yoga to be a part of the Indian cultural heritage? Give reason.

Ans. Yes, on the basis of the extract, we can call yoga to be a part of the Indian cultural Heritage. This is so because the word 'yoga' itself is derived from a Sanskrit word 'yuj'.

(ii) Define Yoga in your own words on the basis of the given lines.

Ans. Yoga can be defined as the practice which promotes a balance between our minds, body and soul.

(iii) Which of the following is an antonym of 'ancient'?

(a) Outdated (b) Unity (c) Traditional (d) Modern

Ans. (d) Modern

(iv) State True or False:

Yoga does not pay attention to mental health.

Ans. False

Part II

Very Short Answer Type Questions

1. At what age or time can one do yoga?

Ans. Everyone irrespective of age can do yoga at any time of the day.

2. Who presented the ancient system of yoga?

Ans. Sage Patanjali presented the ancient system of yoga.

3. Why has yoga become popular all around the world?

Ans. Yoga has become increasingly popular around the world due to its many health benefits.

4. State one benefit of Yoga Asanas.

Ans. Yoga postures (asanas) help to stretch and strengthen the muscles, increase flexibility, endurance and balance.

Short Answer Type Questions

1. Explain the origin of the word 'Yoga'.

Ans. The word 'Yoga' comes from the Sanskrit root 'yuj' which means 'to join' or 'to unite'. The word, thus, symbolises the unity of mind and body; thought and action; harmony between human and nature.

2. How does yoga improve concentration?

Ans. Yoga improves concentration with the help of its various breathing techniques and meditation. These activities help to calm the mind and reduce stress and anxiety. It relaxes the mind which increases concentration.

3. Write a short note on mYoga?

Ans. mYoga is an application launched by the World Health Organisation (WHO) on 20th June, 2021. The app contains a collection of videos and audio files to teach yoga practise. The application is an easy-to-use and free tool for people across the world to encourage them to practise yoga.

4. When does our practise become yogic practise?

Ans. Our practise becomes yogic practise when each stretch in a yoga practise is coordinated with the breath and awareness.

Long Answer Type Question

1. List the various benefits of yoga.

Ans. Yoga offers various benefits to people irrespective of age, race and gender. These benefits are listed below:

- Yoga asanas help to stretch and strengthen the muscles, increase flexibility, endurance and balance. It can reduce body pain and improve our overall physical fitness.
- Breathing techniques and meditation in yoga help to calm the mind. It reduces stress and anxiety which relaxes the mind, improves the quality of sleep and increases concentration.
- Yoga boosts the immune system.
- Yoga improves heart health by lowering blood pressure and improving circulation.
- Yoga helps in weight loss by burning calories, and maintaining health.

Competency Based Question

1. The modern world is full of stress and worry wherein everyone is suffering from some or the other diseases. Do you think yoga is the appropriate solution for all in this lifestyle? Give reasons for your answer.

Ans. It is true to say that the modern world is full of stress and worry wherein everyone is suffering from some or the other diseases. In this world, everyone lives a hectic and busy life with no time for good food or exercise. To maintain health in such a lifestyle, yoga can be the best solution. It essentially promotes a balanced living. It not only maintains our physical fitness but also ensures that we are at peace and happy.

Yoga can act as a preventive measure and even help us cure the diseases we already suffer from. There are asanas which target certain diseases and help us get relief. The breathing techniques and meditation can help everyone relax bring a peace of mind which is missing in the highly hustling world. Hence, doing yoga for even 10 minutes is extremely beneficial for all in the modern world.

Grammar and Writing

1. You are a big yoga enthusiast. On the International Yoga day, you have been asked to give a speech on the importance of yoga for students. Write a speech with reference to the chapter.

You can start as

The modern lifestyle, the incorrect eating habits, and competition.......

Ans. The modern lifestyle, the incorrect eating habits, and competition have filled each one of us with stress and anxiety. For students, it is much more than that. From scoring well, to choosing a career and becoming successful all of these things fill the minds of students at an early age. As a result, students fill up their entire schedule as they are told that they have to start preparing early to succeed.

Such a situation makes the life of students not only stressful but also unhealthy. They do not get any time for relaxation which is as essential as other goals. Many people believe that a physically healthy body has a clear mind, better focus and low level of stress. And the best way to relax rejuvenated is to practice yoga every day. Yoga not only keeps one physically fit, but it also improves concentration as it calms the mind and keeps it healthy. Practising yoga every day reduces physical ailments, purifies the body and distresses the mind. It not only improves the body posture, but also strengthens the muscles and improves the immune system.

So, let us take small steps to keep ourselves healthy-mentally, physically and spiritually.

2. Read the given lines presented in the Let us Explore section.

A few seals of the Sindhu-Sarasvati Civilisation, dating back to 2700 BC, indicate that yoga was prevalent in ancient India. Many people contributed to its development and now, yoga has spread all over the world.

On 11th December, 2014, the United Nations General Assembly (UNGA) with 193 members accepted the proposal to celebrate '21st June' as 'International Yoga Day'.

(a) Circle the verbs and identify the tense of the verbs.

Ans.
- was , contributed, accepted- Past tense
- has spread- Present Perfect tense.

(b) Write the meanings of the following words.

(i) Prevalent **(ii) Spread**

Ans. (i) popular

(ii) to reach or expand in

ASSESSMENT EXERCISE

Multiple Choice Questions

1. Yoga includes

(a) asanas (b) breathing techniques
(c) meditation (d) All of these

2. Yuj means ....

(a) balance (b) unity
(c) harmony (d) mix

3. mYoga was launched on ....

(a) 20th June (b) 21st June
(c) 21st December (d) 19th June

Fill in the blanks

1. Yoga involves .... and ....

2. .... is essential to attain the level of yogic practice.

State True or False

1. Yoga was found in ancient India.

2. The aim of yoga is to create a balance between body and mind.

Extract Based Questions

Read the extract given below and answer the questions that follow.

Yoga postures (asanas) help to stretch and strengthen the muscles, increase flexibility, endurance and balance. This can improve overall physical fitness. This can also help to reduce body pains, such as lower back pain. Yoga involves breathing techniques and meditation, which can help to calm the mind and reduce stress and anxiety. It relaxes the mind, improves the quality of sleep and increases concentration.

(i) What is Yoga?

(ii) Yoga maintains overall well-being of students. Explain with reference to the extract.

(iii) Which of the following is a pair of antonyms present in the extract?

(a) Improve and stress
(b) Calm and anxiety
(c) Stretch and relax
(d) Both (b) and (c)

(iv) Complete the following appropriately.

Yoga can help to reduce ....

Very Short Answer Type Questions

1. What indicates that yoga is internationally recognised?

2. Who launched mYoga?

Short Answer Type Questions

1. How is mYoga helpful?

2. Why should yoga be practiced without distractions?

3. Yoga can improve heart health. Explain.

Long Answer Type Question

1. Write a short note on Yoga with reference to the chapter.

Unit-5 *(Culture and Tradition)*

Hamara Bharat -Incredible India!

CHAPTER 13

About the Chapter The given chapter presents the cultural and traditional heritage of the nation through the various art forms present in the country. The chapter presents a presentation wherein students are shown a video by their teacher. The presentation covers different traditional art forms from different states of India.

Chapter Summary

Part I

The chapter presents a scene of a classroom (a big hall) wherein the teacher has organised an event. She excitedly asked her students if they were ready to meet their friends from all over the country. The students reply yes loudly. The teacher then asked the students if anyone could tell her the programme for which all of them were there. The students answered '*Ek Bharat, Shreshtha Bharat*' together. The teacher further asked if one of the students to tell what '*Ek Bharat, Shreshtha Bharat*' is all about.

Many students wanted to answer and so raised their hands. The teacher chose Renu who was happy to get the chance. She told the class the '*Ek Bharat, Shreshtha Bharat*' means to know that we all belong to one nation and that is the bond we share. And our unity in diversity makes us the most wonderful country in the world.

Part II

The teacher smiled at Renu as everyone clapped. Just then, Bala pointed out that the video has started. The big screen showed little windows each with a smiling child. Each child had something to share.

Child 1: Akanksha

Akanksha greeted everyone and then, introduced herself. She told the class that she belonged to Uttarakhand and was going to tell them about Aipan- their folk art. She informed that the women of a family draw the Aipan on family functions and festivals. It is made with white rice flour paste on brick-red walls coloured with red clay (geru). It is made on floors and walls of puja rooms, and outside the main door of the home. She added that the designs of Aipan are very beautiful and mathematical. They are based on our cultural traditions and observations of nature.

Child 2: Priyaranjan

The second child is Priyaranjan from Odisha. He informed all that his tribe practises a 4000-year-old metal craft named Dhokra. The figure is made with clay which is dried and covered with a layer of wax. Then, the fine detailings are carved on the wax. After that, the figure is covered in clay, and put it in the fire. The wax melts and comes out of small openings. Next, the brass scrap is melted and poured into the empty space. The liquid metal takes the shape of the wax. Finally, the outer layer of clay is removed and the metal figure is made.

Child 3 Chitra

The third child is Chitra from Kerala. She told the children about the coconut shell craft. To make it, clean the outside and inside of a brown coconut shell. After that, make the inside and outside of the shell smooth by using sandpaper or a machine. Then, give the shell the shape we want, and make it stable by fixing a base under it. At last, polish it using wood polish to make it shine. She informed that people in Kerala make household things like bowls and jewellery from the coconut shells. It is a biodegradable craft.

Child 4: Balamurali

The last child is Balamurali from Andhra Pradesh. He wanted to tell the children about the 400-year-old art of making toys in his village, Kondapalli. He stated that to make the toys, they take soft wood from the nearby hills. After that, they carve each part of the toy separately.

Then, they use makku—a paste of tamarind seed powder and sawdust to join the pieces together. Next, they add the details and finish the toys. Finally, they use oil and water-colours or vegetable dyes and enamel paints to colour them. He informed the children that the toys are based on folk stories, animals, birds, bullock carts, rural life, etc.

Values Extracted From this Chapter

The chapter conveys the importance of cultural diversity and unity in the nation. It points out that unity in diversity makes India a beautiful and unique country.

Word Meaning

Word	Meaning	Word	Meaning
Geru	Red clay used as colour	Tamarind	An edible sour fruit
Carve	To make a design with a sharp tool	Sawdust	Dust of wood
Scrap	Small unwanted pieces	Dyes	Colours
Stable	Not able to move	Enamel	Paints that form a protective layer
Biodegradable	Something that will not harm the environment		

NCERT FOLDER

NCERT Intext and Exercise Questions

LET US DISCUSS (NCERT PAGE 133)

Q.1 What is the *Ek Bharat, Shreshtha Bharat* programme all about?

Ans. *Ek Bharat, Shreshtha Bharat* is all about knowing that we all belong to one nation and that is the bond we share. Our unity in diversity makes us the most wonderful country in the world.

Q.2 Why is this programme being conducted?

Ans. The programme is being conducted to make the students aware of the diversity in India. It aims at celebrating this diversity while stating that in spite of this diversity, the nation is fundamentally united.

LET US DISCUSS (NCERT PAGE 136)

On the basis of what the speakers said about the art forms, complete the table given below.

Name of the child	State	Art form	Things needed
Akanksha		Aipan	
Priyaranjan			clay, brass scrap, wax, fire
Chitra			
Balamurali	Andhra Pradesh	Kondapalli	

Ans.

Name of the child	State	Art form	Things needed
Akanksha	Uttarakhand	Aipan	white rice flour paste, geru
Priyaranjan	Odisha	Dhokra	clay, brass scrap, wax, fire
Chitra	Kerala	Coconut shell craft	Coconut shell, sand paper, base and polish
Balamurali	Andhra Pradesh	Kondapalli	Soft wood, makku—a paste of tamarind seed powder and sawdust, oil and water-colours or vegetable dyes and enamel paints

LET US THINK AND REFLECT (NCERT PAGE 136)

Q.1 Fill in the blanks to complete the following sentences.

(a) The designs for Aipan are taken from .... and ....

(b) Dhokra metal craft is very old because it is .... old.

(c) A base is needed for coconut shell craft to make it ....

(d) Soft wood, ... and colours are used to make Kondapalli toys.

Ans. (a) cultural tradition, observation from nature

(b) 4000 year

(c) stable

(d) makku (a paste of tamarind seed powder and sawdust)

Q.2 Why does Akanksha's family make Aipan?

Ans. Akanksha's family makes Aipan to decorate their house during festivals or family functions.

Q.3 In Dhokra, why does wax come out of the small openings?

Ans. In Dhokra, the wax comes out of the small openings as it melts in the fire.

Q.4 What is common in the toys made in Balamurali's village and coconut shell craft in Kerala?

Ans. Both the toys made in Balamurali's village and coconut shell craft in Kerala are biodegradable as they are made using natural ingredients.

LET US LEARN (NCERT PAGE 137)

Q.1 Priyaranjan, Chitra and Balamurali share how art works of their states are made. They use some words to show the order of making it. Those words are given in the box below.

to begin	first	then	after	that	next	finally	at last

Now, use some of these words to complete the paragraph given below. Use one word only once.

How I Get Ready for School

(i) .... I get up and go to take a shower. (ii) ...., I wear my school dress. (iii) ...., I eat my food. (iv) ...., I wear my shoes. (v) ...., I pick up my bag and go out of my home.

Ans. (i) To begin (ii) Then

(iii) Next (iv) Finally

(v) At last

Q.2 The children from different states each speak about one art form from their state.

When they speak, they use the first form of the verb. It shows something that happens regularly. It is called the present tense. With he, she and it, -s/-es is used with the verb to show the present tense. Make five sentences with the help of the words given in the table below. Use -s/-es wherever necessary. Two examples are given.

	Pronous	Verbs	Part of a sentence	Complete Sentences
(i)	**I**	ask	**how to dance.**	I know how to dance.
(ii)	You	**know**	questions to understand.	We
(iii)	**He**	tell	beautiful flowers.	You
(iv)	She	draw	a story every day.	He speaks very loudly.
(v)	It	make	**very loudly.**	She
(vi)	We	practise	paintings in free periods.	They
(vii)	They	**speak**	spellings on Friday.	It

Ans. (i) I know how to dance.

(ii) We ask questions to understand.

(iii) You draw beautiful flowers.

(iv) He speaks very loudly.

(v) She makes paintings in free periods.

(vi) They practice spellings on Friday.

(vii) It tells a story every day.

LET US SPEAK (NCERT PAGE 138)

Q.1 Speak about a local art form of your region. It can be any one out of painting, rangoli, metal craft, embroidery, music, dance or drama.

Remember to include

- the name of the art form
- what things do they need for it

- how do they make/present it

You may use the words given below when you speak.

- I know about the art form called ...
- They need ...
- To make it, first ... after that ... next ... then ... at last ...

Ans. I know about the art form called Zardozi. It is a very famous embroidery found in Delhi. The people who does this usually needan embroidery needle, a golden thread, a piece of cloth and a pen. To make it, they first stretch the piece of cloth so that it does not have any creases. Then, they make the design to embroider. Next, they use the needle and the thread to make the designs.

LET US WRITE (NCERT PAGE 139)

You heard children from different states speak about the art forms from their state. Discuss in pairs which art form you liked the most.

Now, write a paragraph with five sentences giving your reasons for liking it.

Ans. **Aipan** I like Aipan the most because it is another form of rangoli made using white rice flour paste. Imagine how gorgeous the white patterns would look on the red walls. It would be so intercesting to look at art inspired from natural elements.

Dhokra I like Dhokra the most as the brass sculpture looks gorgeous and it has such an extensive process which only makes the delicate looking sculpture even more precious. I can only imagine how beautiful the finished sculptures look fitted on a decorative shelf.

Coconut shell craft I like the coconut shell craft simply because it is biodegradable. In a world where, we are constantly polluting our planet with plastic and other man-made materials, using natural material is a boon. Coconut shell craft is a unique from of art and uses natural elements. I am interested to try my hands on it.

Toys from Kondaplli I like the toys from Kondapalli because they remind me of the old days when our elders used to play with wooden toys. These simple looking toys are not only biodegradable but also user friendly and very colourful to look at.

REVIEW EXERCISE

Including Competency Based Questions

Part I

Multiple Choice Questions

1. Where is event taking place?

(a) Classroom (b) Auditorium
(c) A big hall (d) Theatre

Ans. (c) A big hall

2. Who highlighted that the video had started?

(a) Renu (b) The teacher
(c) A random student (d) Bala

Ans. (d) Bala

3. Akanksha talks about ....

(a) rangoli (b) aipan (c) geru (d) dhokra

Ans. (b) aipan

4. Where did Priyaranjan belong to?

(a) Uttarakhand (b) Odisha
(c) Punjab (d) Kerala

Ans. (b) Odisha

5. We use .... to smoothen the coconut shell.

(a) sandpaper
(b) a machine
(c) knife
(d) Both (a) and (b)

Ans. (d) Both (a) and (b)

6. What do various art forms represent?

(a) Unity (b) Diversity
(c) Fraternity (d) None of these

Ans. (b) Diversity

Fill in the Blanks

1. The children were gathered in the hall for ....

Ans. *Ek Bharat, Shreshtha Bharat*

2. Everyone .... at Renu for her ....

Ans. clapped, explanation

3. **Akanksha greets the class by saying ....**

Ans. Pranam

4. **A unique quality of coconut shell craft is ....**

Ans. that it is biodegradable

5. **Chitra is from ....**

Ans. Kerala

6. **The toy art from Andhra Pradesh is ....**

Ans. 400-year old

State True or False

1. **The teacher wanted Renu to explain *Ek Bharat, Shreshtha Bharat.***

Ans. True

2. **The teacher explained the photos of children in windows.**

Ans. False

3. **Aipan is made near the temple premises.**

Ans. True

4. **Dhokra are bronze sculptures from Odisha.**

Ans. True

5. **We use a cardboard to stabilise the cardboard shell.**

Ans. True

Extract Based Questions

Read the extracts given below and answer the questions that follow.

A. Suprabhat! I am Priyaranjan from Odisha. My tribe practises a 4000-year-old metal craft named Dhokra. To begin, we make a figure with clay, dry it, and cover it with a layer of wax. Then, we carve the fine details on the wax. After that, we cover the figure with clay, and put it in the fire. The wax melts and comes out of small openings. Next, brass scrap is melted and poured into the empty space. The liquid metal takes the same shape as the wax.

(i) What can be an apt description of Dhokra?

(a) Toy
(b) Painting
(c) Sculpture
(d) Gadget

Ans. (c) Sculpture

(ii) Complete the sentence appropriately:

After covering the clay with wax, we ....

Ans. carve the fine details on the wax

(iii) Write the various things needed to make Dhokra.

Ans. The various things needed to make Dhokra include- clay, wax, drying space with fire and brass metal.

(iv) How would you describe the given passage?

Ans. The given passage describes the culture of Odisha. Starting from the greeting to the description of the regional art form Dhokra, the paragraph is about one aspect of the culture of Odisha.

B. Subhodayam! I am Balamurali from Andhra Pradesh. I want to tell you about the 400-year-old art of making toys in my village, Kondapalli. To make the toys, we take soft wood from the nearby hills. After that, we carve each part of the toy separately. Then, we use makku—a paste of tamarind seed powder and sawdust to join the pieces together. Next, we add details and finish the toys. Finally, we use oil and water-colours or vegetable dyes and enamel paints to colour them. These toys are based on folk stories, animals, birds, bullock carts, rural life, etc.

(i) Subhodayam is a ....

(a) form of greeting
(b) friendly banter
(c) name of the child
(d) name of the art form

Ans. (a) form of greeting

(ii) State whether the following sentence is True or False.

Makku was a colour used to paint the toys.

Ans. False

(iii) What are the inspiration for the toys?

Ans. The toys are inspired by folk stories, animals, birds, bullock carts, rural life, etc.

(iv) The toys are biodegradable. How?

Ans. The toys are biodegradable because all of the things used to make them are natural. The toys are made from soft wood from the nearby hills. Different parts of the toy are joined using makku—a paste of tamarind seed powder and sawdust to join the pieces together. Finally, oil and water-colours or vegetable dyes and enamel paints are used to colour them.

Part II

Very Short Answer Type Questions

1. State in one line what *Ek Bharat, Shreshtha Bharat* is?

Ans. *Ek Bharat, Shreshtha Bharat* is about unity in diversity.

2. What did the little windows show?

Ans. The little windows showed four children with big smiles.

3. What constitute the design of Aipan?

Ans. The Aipan designs are generally based on our cultural traditions, and observations of nature.

4. What things can be made using coconut shells?

Ans. We can make cups, jewellery and bowls using coconut shells.

5. What is the name of Balamurali's village?

Ans. Balamurali's village name is Kondapalli in Andhra Pradesh.

6. How do we decorate the toys made in Balamurali's village?

Ans. The toys made in Balamurali's villager are decorated with oil and water-colours or vegetable dyes and enamel paints.

Short Answer Type Questions

1. Do you think that the students were excited for the programme and knew all about it? Give reasons for the answer.

Ans. Yes, I think that the students were excited for the programme and knew all about it. We can say so because of their reactions to answer the questions by the teacher. They answered all the questions asked by their teacher loudly. Even when the teacher asked them to explain *Ek Bharat, Shreshtha Bharat*, all of them wanted to answer the question.

2. Write a short note on Aipan.

Ans. Aipan is the folk art of Uttarakhand made by women during family functions and festivals. It is made with white rice flour paste on brick-red walls coloured with geru. It is made on floors and walls of puja rooms, and outside the main door of the home. The beautiful designs are based on our cultural traditions, and observations of nature.

3. Why do you think is there a need to smoothen the inside and outside of the coconut shells?

Ans. There is a need to smoothen the inside and outside of the coconut shells because it has rough texture which can injure anyone. To prevent this and to make the process of designing them into bowls, cups or jewellery, we need to smoothen its surface.

4. Write the process of making the toys of Andhra Pradesh.

Ans. The toys from Andhra Pradesh are made from soft wood from the nearby hills. Different parts of the toy are joined using makku—a paste of tamarind seed powder and sawdust to join the pieces together. Finally, oil and water-colours or vegetable dyes and enamel paints are used to colour them.

Long Answer Type Questions

1. How is Dhokra made?

Ans. Dhokra is a brass sculpture made in Odisha. To begin, the figure is made with clay, dried and covered with a layer of wax. Then, fine details are carved on the wax. After that, the figure is covered with clay, and put it in the fire. The wax melts and comes out of small openings.

Next, brass scrap is melted and poured into the empty space. The liquid metal takes the same shape as the wax. Finally, the outer layer of clay is removed and the metal figure is finished.

2. Traditional art is an important part of the Indian culture. The chapter celebrates the diversity of art. Comment.

Ans. It is true to say that traditional art is an important part of the Indian culture. Each region has its own culture and traditions which is reflected in the different ways of speaking, languages, food and art forms. This can be seen in the video shown to the students.

First, each of the children in the video had a different from of greetings include- Pranam, Suprabhat, Suprabhaatam and Subhodayam. Further, each of them talk about the different art form prevalent in their region. These art form range from Aipan which is a form of rangoli made using white paste on a red background, Dhokra which is a brass sculpture, coconut shell craft and wooden toys.

Competency Based Question

1. The local Indian art forms are biodegradable and generally environment friendly. Do you agree? Give reason.

Ans. It is true to say that the local Indian art forms are biodegradable and generally environment friendly. They are made from the things are found in abundance in the region and thus are natural which do not in any way harm or pollute the environment. Three out of four forms of craft are made form natural ingredients.

Aipan is a rangoli made using white rice flour paste. Coconut shell craft shows that best out of waste craft wherein the coconut shell, which is generally considered garbage, is used to create various things. Even the toys from Andhra Pradesh are made using soft wood found in the hill. They are joined and decorated using natural ingredients.

Thus, we can say that majority of the Indian handicrafts are sustainable and eco-friendly.

Grammar and Writing

1. Read the following paragraph and answer the following questions.

Bharat has been known worldwide as a land of wise and heroic individuals. Its rich and diverse culture has attracted numerous travellers since ancient times. The people here live in unison, presenting to the world unity in diversity. Bharat is a land rich with rivers, lakes, and high mountains. Its green forests are home to many plants, insects, birds, and animals. All these elements ensure that Bharat prospers and is respected globally. As its inhabitants, we need to continue working hard and make sure that it prospers.

(a) What has Bharat always been known for?

(b) What is attractive about Bharat?

(c) What is special about the fact that the people live here in unison?

(d) What geographical features does the passage mention?

(e) What is the advice given to everyone?

Ans. (a) Bharat has always been known for its wisdom, rich and diverse culture, and its heroic individuals.

(b) The rich cultural heritage of the nation where people live in unity inspite of the diversity is the attractive quality of Bharat.

(c) The special fact that the people here live in unison presents is the unity in diversity.

(d) The passage mentions rivers, lakes, high mountains and green forests.

(e) The advice that the passage gives to everyone is that we need to continue working hard and make sure that it prospers.

2. With the modernisation and globalisation of the world, our cultural and traditional values are fading. You have read about the various ways in which we can protect our culture. Write an article on the same for your school magazine.

Ans. **How to Preserve our Cultural Heritage**

By XYZ

Culture and heritage shapes human society. We all grew up on stories glorifying our past, which helped us construct the identity of a nation, region, community or a group. Human race has always relied on its past to build the present and construct its future. Generations have lived before us and have shaped the world we reside in. However, the cultural heritage sites, museums, libraries and archive collections around the world are increasingly becoming the collateral victims of natural disasters and armed conflicts. The legacy of physical artifacts and intangible attributes of a group or socities is inherited from the past generations, maintained in the present and bestowed for the benefit of future generations. It is thus, important to protect our heritage as it adds character and distinctiveness to the place, region or community and hence provides a sense of identity. We can easily preserve our cultural heritage, if we are a little more aware. We need to understand that the destruction of our cultural heritage is the destruction of our identity.

3. Complete these words with the correct vowels (a, e, i, o, u).

(a) We like to decorate our homes with our f __ l k __ r t.

(b) Our c __ l t __ r e consists of our ideas, customs, traditions, values, arts, and languages.

(c) All of us celebrate our f __ s t __ v __ l s together.

(d) We tell stories to our children to teach them about our c __ l t __ r e, h __ s t __ r y, and l __ g __ n d s.

(e) We have our own l __ n g __ a g __ s to talk to each other.

Ans. (a) folkart (b) culture

(c) festivals (d) culture, history, legends

(e) languages

4. Read the paragraph given below.

Bharat has diverse languages, cuisines, music, dance, theatre, movies and films, handicrafts, sports, literature, festivals, paintings, sculptures, etc. The Ek Bharat, Shreshtha Bharat programme aims to enhance interaction and promote mutual understanding between people of different states/UTs through the concept of state/UT pairing. This is to celebrate the unity in diversity and strengthen the emotional bonds between its citizens. The vision is to enable people to develop a sense of common identity by sharing best practices and experiences. The programme aims to contribute to nation building by highlighting the inter-connectedness between various cultures and traditions.

Find out the antonyms of the following words from the passage.

(a) oneness

(b) diminish

(c) disable

Ans. (a) diversity

(b) enhance

(c) enable

ASSESSMENT EXERCISE

Multiple Choice Questions

1. Aipan is made during ....
   (a) festivals (b) marriages
   (c) birthdays (d) All of these
2. In Dhokra, the metal takes the shape of ....
   (a) the clay (b) the wax
   (c) the mould (d) None of these
3. Balamurali belongs to ....
   (a) Kerala (b) Odisha
   (c) Andhra Pradesh (d) Uttarakhand

Fill in the Blanks

1. We all belong to ....
2. The different words used by children for the greeting are ....
3. Aipan is made on ....

State True or False

1. The little children in the video were smiling.
2. Dhokra is made with aluminum alloy.
3. Kerala is famous for its banana art.

Extract Based Question

Read the extract given below and answer the question that follow.

I want to tell you about coconut shell craft. First, we clean the outside and inside of a brown coconut shell. After that, we make it smooth by using sandpaper or a machine. Then we give it the shape we want, and make it stable by fixing a base under it. At last, we polish it using wood polish to make it shine. We make household things like bowls and even jewellery from the coconut shells.

(i) Who is I?
(a) Renu (b) Chitra
(c) Priyaranjan (d) Akanksha

(ii) The speaker is from ....

(iii) Why do we need a base for the coconut shell?

(iv) What special quality can be identify of the craft from the passage?

Very Short Answer Type Questions

1. State a title for the programme that the children are attending.
2. Write a short note of Dhokra.
3. Define the word 'geru'.
4. How are coconut shell toys made?

Short Answer Type Questions

1. Briefly describe the content of the video shown to the students.
2. Which forms of art are biodegradable and why?
3. Write a short note on the toy craft of Andhra Pradesh.

Long Answer Type Question

1. You have been asked to write the script of the video in your own words for your class presentation. Write the script.

CHAPTER 14

The Kites

by Daphne Lister

About the Chapter The given poem by Daphne Lister is a simple representation of a child's imagination. In the poem, a young child wished to sit on the kite and enjoy looking at the different place. The child imagines the songs he/she would hear and the things that he/she would see. He/She knows that other people also want to fly a kite like him.

Stanzawise Explanation

Stanza 1

Up in the air
See the kites fly,
Like coloured birds
In the wind-whipped sky.

Explanation The given lines present a speaker who is young child who sees kites flying in the sky. To him/her the kites look like coloured birds flying in the windy sky.

Stanza 2

I wish I were small
And light as air,
I would climb on a kite
And sail up there.

Explanation In these lines, the young child wishes he were small in size and as light in weight as air. He/She wishes to be small and light so that he/she could climb on the kite and fly high up in the air.

Stanza 3

Then I would drift upon
The paper wings,
And hear the songs
That the wild wind sings.

Explanation These lines present what the young child would do when he/she is sitting on the kite which is flying in the air. The child would move in the direction of the wind on the kite made of paper. He/She would hear the sounds of the flowing wind.

Stanza 4

What fun it would be
To look right down,
Over the park
And the rooftops of town.

Explanation Now, the child states that while flying in the kite he would have a lot of fun. He would fly over the park and roofs of the building of his town. He would enjoy looking at the park and his town.

Stanza 5

The people below
Would stand and stare,
And wish they were me
High, high in the air.

Explanation The child now states that while he is flying up in the sky on the kite, the people below him on the land would look at him. They would stare at him and wish that they were the child. The people would wish to fly high up in the air on the kite.

NCERT FOLDER

NCERT Intext and Exercise Questions

LET US DISCUSS (NCERT PAGES 143-144)

Q.1 Read the poem silently. As you read, mark the given statements as True or False.

(a) The child is looking at the kites.
(b) The kites look like birds of different colours.
(c) It was a rainy day.
(d) The child wants to be like a kite.
(e) The child wishes to climb on a kite.
(f) The kite is made of cloth and plastic.
(g) The child wants to ride the kite.
(h) The child knows they would have fun.
(i) The child wants to look at the kite from a rooftop.
(j) The child would like to look at people down below.
(k) The child knows that the people would stare.

Ans. (a) True (b) True
(c) False (d) False
(e) True (f) False
(g) True (h) True
(i) False (j) True
(k) True

Q.2 Complete the following sentences.

(a) The poet says that the kites are like coloured birds ....

See the kites fly/Like coloured birds in the sky.

The kites have been compared to b _ _ _ because they ....

Ans. birds, are colourful

(b) The child wishes to be like air - I wish I were small / And as light as air.

The child wishes to be as l _ _ _ t as _ _ _. The child wishes this to be able to c_ _ _ m _ on a kite and fly.

Ans. light, air, climb

The poet uses simile in (a) and (b) to compare the kites with coloured birds and the quality of being light as air. The poet uses 'like' and 'as' to compare.

Do you think that the use of simile in this poem helps us imagine better when we read the poem? Share your thoughts with your teacher and classmates.

Ans. Yes, the use of simile in this poem helps us imagine better when we read the poem. It helps us imagine the poem very clearly.

Q.2 Find a set of words from the poem that begin with the same consonant sound.

Stanza 1

Which consonant sound do both words begin with?

Ans. The sound of 'w' in wind-whipped sky.

Stanza 3

Which consonant sound do both words begin with?

Ans. The sound of 'w' in wild wind sings.

This is called **alliteration**. For example, **big bright blue** bag, **funny fan**, etc.

Create 4 other sets of words using alliteration.

Ans.
- Sumptuous snacks
- Marvelous magazines
- Busy Bee
- Running round

Q.4 In the last stanza, the two words that the poet repeats are .... , ... to tell us that the kite is flying _ _ _ y high.

Ans. High, high, very

Q.5 Study each stanza and underline the rhyming words from the end of each line. Also, circle the end words in the stanzas that do not rhyme.

Ans.
- **Rhyming words** fly/sky, air/there, wings/sings, down/town, stare/air.
- **Non- rhyming words** air/birds, small/kite, upon/songs, be/park, below/me.

LET US THINK AND REFLECT
(NCERT PAGES 145-145)

Q.5 Read the given lines from the poem and answer the following questions.

What fun it would be
To look right down,
Over the park
And the rooftops of town.

(a) Circle the word that does not share the same feeling as 'fun': joy, excitement, care, happiness.

Ans. Care

(b) Which line tells us that the poet was somewhere above?

Ans. The line that tells us that the poet was somewhere above is to look right down

(c) Choose the scene the child saw.

Ans.

Ans. (ii)

Q.5 Answer the following questions.

(a) How does the poet describe the kites in the first two lines?

Ans. The poet describes the kites to be very colourful like the birds that fly in the sky.

(b) Why does the child say that they have to climb a tree first to get onto the kite?

Ans. The child does not state anywhere that they have to climb a tree first to get onto the kite.

(c) What are the songs that the child hears when flying atop the kite?

Ans. The child hears when flying atop the kite are the songs of the wild wind.

(d) Why did the people look up at the child and stare? If you looked up and saw that, what feelings would you have?

Ans. The people looked up at the child and stared because it was unusual and strange to see a child flying up on the kite. If I saw such a scene, I would be astonished and wished to be in the place of the child.

(e) If you were the kite carrying the child high up in the air, what would you tell them?

Ans. If I were the kite, I would tell the child to hold on tigh and enjoy the beautiful view from above, feelnig the wind and freedom of flying.

LET US LEARN (NCERT PAGES 146-148)

Q.1 Look at the picture of the kite and read what some of its parts are named.

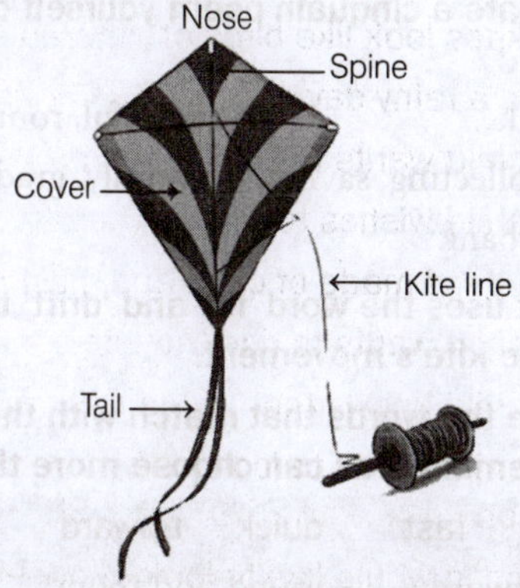

Now, complete the given conversation by filling the blanks with some 'parts of a kite' words from above.

Bina I love the long yellow t _ _ _ at the end of my kite. What colour is your kite?

Saroj My kite's c _ _ _ _ _ _ is pink. The s _ _ _ e is black.

Bina Oh wonderful! My kite l _ _ _ is red. The r _ _ l that wraps it is green. I really like it.

Saroj My kite line is red too. The tip of my kite has a blue _ _ _ e.

Bina Beautiful! Let's go and fly our pretty kite.

Ans. tail, colour, spine, line, reel, nose

Q.2 Let us create a poem using words in a kite!

The first line is the subject. Keep this to **one word**. Use a noun.	kite
The second line is **two** describing words for the noun.	pretty, colourful
Line three includes **three action** words.	flying, floating, soaring
Line four uses **two words** that describe the action words.	quickly, happily
Line five is **one word** that has the same meaning as the subject/synonym.	paper-bird

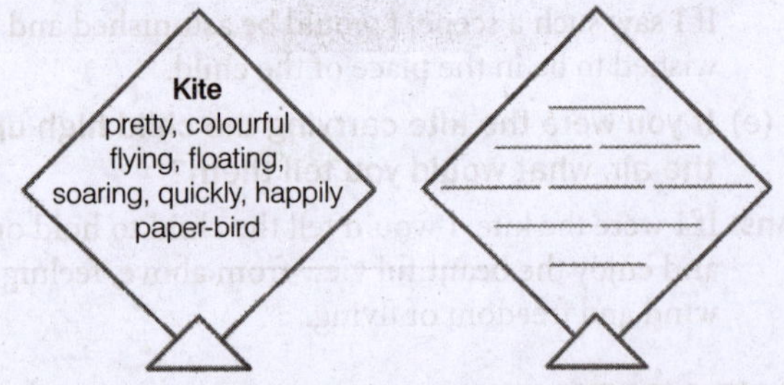

This is called a 'cinquain' poem. It is a five line poem that describes a person, a place or a thing.

Now, create a cinquain poem yourself on anything you like.

Ans. piggybank
beautiful, round
sitting, collecting, saving
carefully, gradually
personal bank

Q.3 The poet uses the word 'fly' and 'drift' to tell us about the kite's movement.

(a) Circle the words that match with the 'drift' movement. You can choose more than one word.

slow fast quick upward
downward round and round float

Ans. slow, upward, float

(b) Study some other words about the kite's movement and share what type of movement they show. You can look at (a) for the type of movement.

glide dive soar swoop circle

Ans.
- Glide means to move with a smooth, quiet continuous motion.
- Dive means to fall downwards quickly.
- Soar means to rise upwards.
- Swoop means to move rapidly downwards through the air.
- Circle means to move all the way around (someone or something), especially more than once.

Q.4 The poet has used expressions like- up in the air; look right down; stay up there; stand and stare

(a) Read how these expressions are used in the poem.

(b) In pairs, make sentences using these expressions. Discuss with your teacher and then write in your notebooks.

Ans. Do it yourself.

LET US SPEAK (NCERT PAGE 149)

Share a kite-flying experience with your classmates. If you have not flown a kite yet, share an experience of watching kites fly. Give details- Where? When? Why? How? Speak in complete sentences.

Ans. I have flown many kites in my humble years of life. The first time I saw a kite flying, I wanted to fly a kite myself and soon, my wish was fulfilled. I flew my first kite with my father when I was in grade 1. Since then, I have had many experiences to fly a kite. My most memorable experience was this years' Makar Sakranti festival in January.

All my friends had come and together we went to the safe rooftop of our locality where many elders were already flying kites.

The weather was a little hot but it had a gentle breeze which was perfect for kite flying. I took my purple tailed kite and flew it high in the sky. It was amazing to see the kite fly and also cut the lines of other's kites to scream Kai Po che. In end, we were sunburned but the day was memorable.

LET US WRITE (NCERT PAGE 149)

Q.1 Imagine yourself as a kite. In pairs, first discuss all the following hints.

- What shape of kite are you? What colours do you have? What other parts of yourself are you happy about?
- Where are you? Who do you belong to? What activities do you do? Who are your friends?
- Do you have any message for humans?

Q.2 Now, write a paragraph of about 100 words, with the title-'I am a Kite'.

Ans. Let me introduce myself. I am a kite. I am a beautiful diamond-shaped kite with vibrant red and blue colours. My long tail with small ribbons makes me look graceful as I soar in the sky. I belong to a young boy who loves flying me during the kite festivals.

I enjoy dancing with the wind competiing with other kites and touching the clouds. My friends are other colorful kites that fly with me. My message for humans is to embrace the freedom and joy that comes with flying high and to appreciate the beauty of the world from a diffrent perspective.

REVIEW EXERCISE

Including Competency Based Questions

Part I

Multiple Choice Questions

1. What does the child see in the sky?

(a) Birds (b) Kites
(c) Airplane (d) Both (a) and (b)

Ans. (b) Kites

2. The child does not want to be ....

(a) light (b) small
(c) smart (d) a kite

Ans. (c) smart

3. Which word has not been used to indicate the movement of the kite?

(a) Drift (b) Sail
(c) Fly (d) Float

Ans. (d) Float

4. The child will .... on the kite.

(a) dance to the song
(b) sing with the wind
(c) listen to the song
(d) play with the kite

Ans. (c) listen to the song

5. What is the tone of the poem?

(a) Factual (b) Nostalgic
(c) Happy (d) Innocent

Ans. (d) Innocent

Fill in the Blanks

1. The child is .... the situation in the poem.

Ans. imagining

2. The child would .... on the roofs of the houses in his town.

Ans. look down

3. The kite is made of ....

Ans. paper

Extract Based Questions

Read the lines given below and answer the questions that follow.

A.

Up in the air
See the kites fly,
Like coloured birds
In the wind-whipped sky.
I wish I were small
And light as air,
I would climb on a kite
And sail up there.

(i) The child is ....

(a) flying the kite
(b) riding on the kite
(c) looking at the kite
(d) making a kite

Ans. (c) looking at the kite

(ii) State whether the following statement True or False.

Ans. False

(iii) What does the child want to do?

Ans. The child wants to be light and small so that he/she can sit on the kite without damaging it.

(iv) Identify the word which indicates the movement of the kite.

Ans. Sail

B.

Then I would drift upon
The paper wings,
And hear the songs
That the wild wind sings.
What fun it would be
To look right down,
Over the park
And the rooftops of town.

(i) Drift indicates ....

(a) fast movement

(b) irregular movement

(c) slow movement

(d) round movement

Ans. (c) slow movement

(ii) Complete the sentence appropriately.

The child is .... to fly in the sky.

Ans. excited

(iii) Identify the expression that uses alliteration?

Ans. The expression that uses alliteration is wild wind.

(iv) Comment on the tone of the given lines.

Ans. The given lines indicates a happy and excited tone as it presents a young child enjoying his/her imagination wherein he/she is flying on the kite and looking at the various things.

Part II

Very Short Answer Type Questions

1. What kind of song does the child hear?

Ans. The child hears the sound created by the wild wind.

2. What does the child see from the kite when he/she looks down?

Ans. When the child looks down from the sky, he/she sees the miniature people in the parks and the rooftops of the houses in his town.

3. Explain wind-whipped sky.

Ans. Wind-whipped sky indicates a windy weather wherein the movement of the wings of the bird is forceful.

Short Answer Type Questions

1. Why does the child want to be light and small?

Ans. The child wants to be light and small so that he/she can climb on the kite properly without tearing it or falling from it.

2. What would people wish for? Do you think such a wish will come true?

Ans. The people would wish to climb the kite and fly in the sky like the young child. No, I do not think that such a wish can come true as our weight far exceeds the weight of the paper kite. Thus, if we sit on the kite, it will tear and become unusable.

3. List what the child would do on the kite.

Ans. On the kite, the child would slowly fly up in the sky and listen to the songs of the wind. He/she would look down to the park and the rooftops of the houses of his town.

Competency Based Question

1. What can we say about the movement of the kite? How can you say so?

Ans. The movement of the kite is slow and irregular as it moves up and down with the wind. We can say so because of the use of movement words such as sail and drift.

Grammar and Writing

1. Write a paragraph on 'If I were a Kite....

Ans. **If I were a Kite**

How beautiful it would be if we were able to fly. We would go to places. We would travel. We would fly. It feels so good to even think about it. Hence, if I were a kite, I would be very happy. I would have dressed in different colours and fly freely in the sky. I would live my life at my own will. I would not care about anything, person, idea, fame, society, etc.

I would not come down. I would just live in the sky and make my home there. There would be nobody to trouble me. Only birds would be my friend there. I would talk to them and play with them. The best part, when the rainbow is created, I would be able to touch the rainbow. Life would be fun as a kite.

ASSESSMENT EXERCISE

Multiple Choice Questions

1. What does the child feel on the kite?
   (a) Excited
   (b) Happy
   (c) Relaxed
   (d) All of the above

2. Fill in the blanks.

The people would look up to see........... .

3. State True or False

The child wants to make the other people envious of him.

Extract Based Question

Read the lines given below and answer the questions that follow.

What fun it would be
To look right down,
Over the park
And the rooftops of the town..
The people below
Would stand and stare,
And wish they were me
High, high in the air.

(a) Which word in the given extract has the same meaning "to continuously look?

(b) What would be fun for the child?

(c) Complete the following sentence.
The people below would .... and wish that they ....

(d) What do you infer from the above extract?

Very Short Answer Type Questions

1. What do people wish?
2. What kind of image does the child see from the kite?

Short Answer Type Questions

1. Do you think that the child is enjoying the kite ride? Give reasons.
2. Why does the child call kite as 'paper wings'?

Long Answer Type Question

1. Write the sum and substance of the poem.

Ila Sachani: Embroidering Dreams with her Feet

CHAPTER 15

About the Chapter The given chapter presents the story of Ila Sachani, a disabled artist. Ila with her courage, will power and determination became a successful embroidery artist. Ila Sachani was born with hanging hands which did not work. However, encouraged by her family and friends, Ila became independent and self-sufficient. Today, she has been honoured with many awards that point out that once we have the will, we can do everything.

Chapter Summary

Introducing Ila Sachani

When one enters a tiny room in Moti Vavdi village, Bhavnagar, Gujarat, one can see lots of lovely things in bright colours. One can see things such as cushions, bedcovers, pillows, etc. in beautiful designs. The creator of these designs is Ila Sachani, a wonderful lady with a big smile. She makes *Kathiawar* embroidery designs using a shiny needle. The *Kathiawar* embroidery is a style that needs a lot of skill.

Ila's Medical Condition

Ila Sachani's was born in a farmer's family in the quiet settings of Amreli, Gujarat. She was born with her hands hanging loose by her sides. This means that she could not use her hands in the usual way like other children. While other children drew figures in the sand, plucked flowers, hold a chalk or draw figures, she wanted to join them.

Ila's Family and Their Contribution

Since her childhood, Ila was encouraged to overcome her challenges by her mother and grandmother. They were skilled in *Kathiawar* embroidery and decided to teach it to Ila. They taught her how to create many beautiful patterns using her feet. Besides this, her parents also helped her learn to do things with her legs, like eating and combing her hair.

Ila's Determination

Ila found the task of threading a needle to be hard but she did not give up and became an expert in the embroidery at a young age. Over time, she learned many embroidery styles including those from outside Gujarat-*Kachhi, Kashmiri, Lucknawi*, etc.

For Ila, embroidery became a way to express herself. At first, she crafted fine designs only for her family and friends, who were awestruck by her talent. They talked about those designs to others. Soon, the people in the village discovered Ila's special skill. As a result, Ila started being admired by many.

Ila's Embroidery is Displayed

Ila's story and admiration soon reached the government office in Surat. They were so impressed by Ila's story that they decided to display some samples of her embroidery at a state exhibition. This experience opened new doors for Ila. People observed the beauty woven by her feet and readily purchased the creations. As a result, Ila became famous.

Ila's Popularity

Ila was encouraged by the popularity she received and started participating in state as well as National exhibitions. She received many awards and honours, not just for her art but also the willpower and creativity that her work showed. Ila faced a tough challenge but she worked hard and became a celebrated artist and receiver of the President's Medal.

Ila as an Inspiration

The most important change for Ila was the new independence. Through her skill, she earned a regular income and found joy in doing what she loved. She proved, through her creations, that challenges can be turned into victories with focus, hard work, positivity and never giving up.

Her embroidery, created with her feet, reminds us that art has the power to rise above physical boundaries and touch the soul.

Values Extracted from this Chapter

The chapter conveys the value of focus, hard work, positivity and a never giving up attitude. It presents the need to conserve local art and craft while promoting the values that make us successful inspite of the many challenges.

Word Meaning

Word	Meaning
Challenges	Difficulties
Plucked	To remove something from a place
Single-minded	Focused
Determination	Will power
Expert	Skillful
Awestruck	Amazed
Admiration	Praise
Popularity	Fame
Tough	Difficult

NCERT FOLDER

NCERT Intext and Exercise Questions

LET US DISCUSS (NCERT PAGE 155)

Read the paragraphs and write the main idea for each. Then, match the main idea with two supporting details.

Paragraph	Main idea	Two supporting details
1.	**Introduction to Ila Sachani's colourful embroidery**	**(i) Examples of embroidered things** **(ii) Ila's use of shiny needle**
2.	**Early challenges and family support**	(i) (ii)
3.		(i) (ii)
4.		(i) (ii)
5.		(i) (ii)
6.	Recognition at a state exhibition	(i) (ii)
7.		(i) (ii)
8-9.		(i) Financial independence and joy (ii) Challenges can be turn into victories

Ans.

Paragraph	Main idea	Two supporting details
1.	Introduction to Ila Sachani's colourful embroidery	(i) Examples of embroidered things (ii) Ila's use of shiny needle

Paragraph	Main idea	Two supporting details
2.	Early challenges and family support	(i) Early challenges and family support (ii) Hanging Hands
3.	Determination and Learning	(i) Acceptance of challenge (ii) Learnt to embroider with feet
4.	Mastering the craft	(i) Threading the needle (ii) Learnt other embroidery styles
5.	**Gaining Recognition**	(i) Praised by village (ii) Her story reached government office
6.	Recognition at a state exhibition	(i) increased sales (ii) encouraged to participate in exhibitions
7.	National Recognition	(i) received many awards and honours (ii) receiver of the President's Medals
8-9.	Financial Independence	(i) Regular income (ii) challenges can be turned into victories

LET US THINK AND REFLECT (NCERT PAGE 156)

Q.1 Read the following lines and answer the questions that follow.

Unlike other children, she could not use her hands in the usual way. While other small hands drew figures in the sand or plucked wild flowers, she wondered why she could not join them. She too wanted to hold a chalk in her hands and draw figures on a slate.

(a) Choose the correct option to fill in the blank.

'Unlike other children' means that Ila was .... (unaware/ different/simple)

Ans. different

(b) What could Ila have felt when she could not join others in things they did?

Ans. Ila could have felt sad, left out and frustrated when she could not join others in activities that required the use of hands.

(c) Complete the following with a suitable reason.

Ila could not draw figures on the slate because ....

Ans. she could not use her hands

Q.2 What creative ways did Ila and her family use to overcome the challenges she faced?

Ans. Ila and her family used various means to overcome the challenges she faced. Her grandmother and mother taught her to embroider with her feet. Her parents taught her how to do various activities with her feet. They also supported her learning of other embroidery styles.

Q.3 How did 'new independence' help Ila?

Ans. The 'new independece' helped Ila not only earn a regular income but she also found joy in doing what she loved. Further, she proved, through her creations, that challenges can be turned into victories with focus, hard work, positivity and never giving up.

Q.4 Why was the first state exhibition an important event in Ila's life?

Ans. The first state exhibition became an important event in Ila's life because it opened new doors for Ila. As people observed the beauty woven by her feet, they readily purchased the creations.

This encouraged Ila to participate in other exhibitions with brought her more opportunities and admiration.

Q.5 What does the sentence, 'art has the power to rise above physical boundaries and touch the soul', tell us about the power of art?

Ans. The given sentence indicates the fact that anyone can do art. It does not require any specific physical object or organ. It only needs a will and determination to do something.

Further, it highlight how art can affect the soul and emotions of a person which its beauty.

Q.6 How can we be helpful and encouraging like Ila's family and friends when someone faces challenges?

Ans. We can be helpful and encouraging by offering support, recognising and nurturing their talents, providing opportunitites for them to showcase their abilities, and maintaining a positive and motivating environment.

Q.7 How can Ila's story help others to overcome challenges in their lives?

Ans. Ila's story can inspire others to preserve in the face of challenges, believe in their abilities, and understand that determination and hard work can lead to success and fulfillment despite obstacles.

LET US LEARN (NCERT PAGES 156-158)

Q.1 Read the words from the text given in Column A. Then, try to understand what they mean by reading the sentences in Column B. Now, match the word to its correct synonym in Column C. There are two extra synonyms given. You may refer to the dictionary.

Column A Word	Column B Sentence	Column C Synonym
tiny	The garden was tiny but the park was really big.	silent
wonderful	The wonderful artwork made everyone clap.	work happy
quiet	The quiet library was a better place to study than the noisy classroom.	small
task	Completing the Science homework was a challenging taks as it had many questions.	difficult fantastic
tough	We know that tough times can be overcome, if we try sincerely.	dangerous

Ans.
- Tiny- small
- Wonderful- fantastic
- Quiet- silent
- Task- work
- Tough- difficult

Q.2 **Unscramble the antonyms of the words in Column A. An example has been given for you.**

Example: display - E D I H (H I D E)

(a) tiny - E G H U (H___)

(b) wonderful - R E E B L I T R (T __ R ___ B ___E)

(c) quiet - I Y N S O (N ___ ___)

(d) task - S I A E M T P (P __ S T ___ ___ ___ E)

(e) tough - SEYA (E___ ___)

Use these antonyms in sentences of your own.

Ans. (a) **Huge** There is a huge hole in the wall.

(b) **Terrible** I often have the most terrible nightmares.

(c) **Noisy** His daughter was very active and noisy in the mornings.

(d) **Postpone** The game was postponed as a mark of respect.

(e) **Easy** It's not easy to choose a career.

Q.3 **Read the sentences from the text and focus on the highlighted words.**

- You will see **lots of** bright colours.
- There are **many** lovely things like cushions and bedcovers.
- They taught her to create **many** beautiful patterns using her feet!
- She learned **many** styles.
- She received **many** awards.

(a) The highlighted words tell us about the quantity. Choose what the words show.

(i) Unmentioned quantity

(ii) Large quantity

Ans. Both. The highlighted words show an unmentioned but a huge quantity.

(b) Let us now understand what words of quantity tell us.

Fill in the blanks to complete an example for each word of quantity. Hints are given in the brackets.

(i)	We saw .... buses on the road.	(uncountable noun)
(ii)	How .... milk do you want?	(uncountable noun)
(iii)	There is .... milk needed.	(Countable noun)
(iv)	I need .... examples.	(countable noun)
(v)	I have .... energy left. She picked .... flowers.	(countable noun and uncountable noun)
(vi)	I ate .... rice.	(uncnountable noun)

Ans. (i) many (ii) much (iii) some (iv) a few (v) no, many (vi) some

Now, create two sentences for each word of quantity (i-vi), and share them with your teacher and classmates.

Ans. (i) I have many pens with me.

(ii) How much sugar is needed?

(iii) There is some water in the bottle.

(iv) He requires a few boxes.

(v) There are no pens left. You can ask Piya, she had many.

(vi) The dish needs some salt.

LET US SPEAK (NCERT PAGE 159)

In pairs, write down two questions you would like to ask Ila Sachani.

(a) Look at two examples.

- Where were you born?
- Did you go to school?
- The Yes/No questions use a rising tone at the end.

Ans. (i) Do you sometimes feel inadequate? Has someone very discriminated against you? How did you feel then?

(ii) Have you ever imagined how your life would have been if you had working hands?

(b) Speak the example questions aloud as a peer activity at least five times.

(c) Now, take turns to ask your questions to another classmate. Speak clearly and with the correct rising tone as shown in (a)

REVIEW EXERCISE

Including Competency Based Questions

Part I

Multiple Choice Questions

1. Ila Sachani was born in ....

(a) Surat (b) Amreli (c) Delhi (d) Udaipur

Ans. (b) Amreli

2. How did Ila face about her disability?

(a) Sad (b) Angry
(c) Disappointed (d) All of these

Ans. (d) All of these

3. What was the occupation was Ila's father?

(a) Farmer (b) Peon (c) Baker (d) Cleaner

Ans. (a) Farmer

4. How did Ila feel about her art?

(a) Joyful (b) Admiration
(c) Love (d) Satisfaction

Ans. (a) Joyful

Fill in the Blanks

1. Ila Sachani worked in ....
2. Ila's parents helped her to ....
3. .... was hard for Ila.
4. For Ila, embroidery was a ....
5. Ila received awards for not just .... but also ....

Answers

1. Moti Vavdi village, Bhavnagar, Gujarat.
2. learn to do things with her legs, like eating and combing her hair.
3. Threading the needle
4. way to express herself.
5. her art, the willpower and creativity that her work showed

State True or False

1. **Ila Sachani only made clothes.**
2. **Ila was indifferent to her disability.**
3. **Ila's parents did not discriminate against Ila.**
4. **Ila Sachani learned embroidery from her grandmother.**
5. **Ila Sachani's first exhibition was at the national level.**
6. **Ila Sachani's family encouraged her to overcome her challenges.**

Ans. 1. False 2. False 3. True
4. True 5. False 6. True

Extract Based Questions

Read the extracts given below and answer the questions that follows.

A. For Ila, embroidery became a way to express herself. At first, she crafted fine designs only for her family and friends, who were awestruck by her talent. They talked about those designs to others. Soon, the people in the village, too, discovered Ila's special skill and the admiration for her work began to spread.

(i) Her friends and family are .... to Ila.

(a) indifferent

(b) angry

(c) supporting

(d) demotivaters

Ans. supporting

(ii) State True or False

Ila loves to be do her embroider.

Ans. True

(iii) What was Ila's special skills?

Ans. Ila's special skill was that she worked with her feet. Her beautiful embroidery was created by her using her feet.

(iv) Write a synonym of 'awestruck'.

Ans. amazed

B. The most important change for Ila was the new independence. Through her skill, she not only earned a regular income but also found joy in doing what she loved. She proved, through her creations, that challenges can be turned into victories with focus, hard work, positivity and never giving up.

(i) What about Ila the 'new independence'?

Ans. Ila's embroidery bought her the new independence.

(ii) The given lines indicate that Ila was a/an ....

Ans. inspiration for all

(iii) Which quote fits aptly with the extract?

(a) "It is not the strength of the body that counts, but the strength of the spirit." ? J.R.R. Tolkien

(b) "It takes courage to grow up and become who you really are." - E.E. Cummings

(c) "He who is not courageous enough to take risks will accomplish nothing in life." - Muhammad Ali

(d) "Above all, be the heroine of your life, not the victim." - Nora Ephron

Ans. (a) "It is not the strength of the body that counts, but the strength of the spirit." ? J.R.R. Tolkien

(iv) What did Ila prove?

Ans. Ila proved that all challenges can be turned into victories with focus, hard work, positivity and never giving up.

Part II

Very Short Answer Type Questions

1. What was Ila Sachani's disability?

Ans. Ila Sachani's disability was that she was born with hanging hands indicating that she could not use her hands.

2. Who taught Ila Sachani embroidery?

Ans. Ila Sachani's mother and grandmother taught her embroidery.

3. How did Ila face the challenges?

Ans. Ila faced the challenges with determination, focus, hard work, positivity and never giving up.

4. Name the other embroidery styles learnt by Ila.

Ans. Ila learned many styles even ones from outside Gujarat-Kachhi, Kashmiri, Lucknawi and others.

5. How did Ila's artwork reach the government office of Surat?

Ans. Ila's artwork reached the government office of Surat because of the admiration and popularity she was receiving from her family and the people in her village.

Short Answer Type Questions

1. What problems did Ila Sachani face in her life?

Ans. Ila Sachani faced many problems in her life. She was born with hanging arms indicating that she could not use her hands. So, she had to learn how to do the basic things with the help of her parents. Further, she had to learn threading the needle which was very difficult for her. However, she overcame all the challenges with determination.

2. How did Ila react to seeing other children of her age?

Ans. As a child, Ila was sad to see other children using their hands. She wondered why she could not draw figures in the sand or pluck wild flowers. She too wanted to hold a chalk in her hands and draw figures on a slate. However, she could not do a thing.

3. *Kathiawar* was a generational art taught to Ila. Comment.

Ans. It is true that *Kathiawar* was a generational art taught to Ila. Ila's mother and grandmother were skilled in the traditional art of *Kathiawar* embroidery and shared this art with Ila.

They taught her to create many beautiful patterns using her feet. Hence, this points out that *Kathiawar* was a generational art.

4. What is the significance of ila Sachani's embroidery work?

Ans. Ila Sachani's embroidery work is significant as it showcases her unique talent and determination to pursue her passion despite facing challenges. Her creations serve as a symbol of resilience and creativity. Inspiring others to overcome their own obstacles.

Long Answer Type Question

1. Ila Sachani's story acts as an inspiration for all. Explain in 80-100 words.

Ans. It is true to sat that Ila Sachani's story acts an inspiration for all. Born as a disabled person who could not use her hands, Ila's future could have been a sad story of dependency.

However, ila with a strong support system, her determination, focus, hard work, positivity and never giving up attitude won in life. She not only learnt how to embroider with her feet, but also became an independent person with her own income.

Ila's creativity found its representation in her art which was praised by all. As a result, she not only became famous but also won many national awards and honours. Hence, her story shows how we all can overcome any challenge if we have the will to win.

Competency Based Questions

1. How can individuals support and appreciate Ila Sachani's embroidery work?

Ans. Individuals can support and appreciate Ila Sachani's embroidery work by sharing her story, attending her exhibitions, purchasing her creations, and spreading awarness about her talent.

By recognizing her efforts and achievements, we can show our admiration and encouragement for her inspiring journey.

2. How do you think Ila Sachani learned to work with her feet?

Ans. Ila Sachani learned to embroider with her feet by practicing regulary and developing her skills over time. She was inspired by the mother's embroidery work and decided to try it using her feet instead of her hands

3. Ila's work was received with admiration at the exhibition. Justify.

Ans. It is true that Ila's work received a lot of admiration at the exhibition. In the exhibition, people observed the beauty woven by her feet and readily purchased the creations.

4. Ila Sachani could succeed because she had a strong support system. Do you agree? Give reason. How does having a strong support system impact us?

Ans. It is true that Ila Sachani could succeed because she had a strong support system. A support system includes people who support you in all facets of life. They encourage you to do your best and cheer you in your success. Ila Sachani also has such a great support system. Her family, friends and the people in the village all supported and motivated Ila. Her grandmother and mother taught her the art and also to make it using her feet. They along with her siblings also supported her in her daily tasks. With such encouragement, Ila art expanded as she learnt many embroidery styles. This conviction and her beautiful designs came to be loved by everyone. Her supporters not only loved her but also spread her name everywhere. As a result, she got the opportunity and succeed in making a name for herself.

Grammar and Writing

1. Kathiawadi art is a part of what we call as the cottage industry of India. As such, with the introduction of industrialisation, the cottage industry had taken a severe hit. Think of various simple ways in which the cottage industry can be developed. Write a small paragraph on problems faced by the cottage industry and what do you think are the various ways to tackle it.

Ans. Problems

- A scarcity of funding
- Scarcity of labour
- lack of access to access to low-cost marketing

Solutions

- Efforts should be put toward the advancement of technolog.
- The government could also offer funding to help cottage industries flourish
- Aid existing and new industries with financial assistance, technical support, and direction.

2. Ila Sachani

Ans. The cottage industries in India are the most debated issue. They add to the economic value of the country but are still not given due credit for their valuable contributions.

Some of the common problems faced by cottage industries include scarcity of funding, scarcity of labour and lack of access to efficient marketing techniques which are also low cost. This elevates the difficult to survive economic pressure.

However, this can be tackled by looking at some simple solutions. Efforts can be put towards the advancement of technology.

The government could also offer funding to help cottage industries flourish. Aids can be provided to existing and new industries in the form of financial assistance, technical support and marketing access. This would ensure a bright economic future for the country.

ASSESSMENT EXERCISE

Multiple Choice Questions

1. What is the special skill of Ila Sachani?

(a) Pottery (b) Embroidery

(c) Painting (d) Sculpting

2. Where did Ila Sachani learn the art of ambroidery from her family?

(a) Amreli (b) Surat

(c) Bhavanagar (d) Anand

3. Whcih style of embroidery did Ila Sachani master?

(a) Kathiawar (b) Kachhi

(c) Kashmiri (d) Lucknawi

4. How did Ila Sachani overcome her physical challange?

(a) With her hand (b) With her legs

(c) With her mouth (d) With her eyes

Fill in the Blanks

1. At first, Ila crafted fine designs ....

2. Her friends and family were .... at Ila's art.

3. .... opened new doors for Ila.

State True or False

1. Kathiawar is an easy to do embroidery.

2. Ila's siblings did not support her.

3. Ila received appreciation at the national exhibition only.

4. Ila is a source of inspiration for all.

Extract Based Question

Read the extract given below and answer the questions that follow.

Encouraged by this popularity, Ila participated in more exhibitions, not just within the state but at the national level. She received many awards and honours, not just for her art but also the willpower and creativity that her work showed.

(i) How did Ila receive the popularity?

(ii) What does her work refer to?

(a) Painting

(b) Sculpting

(c) Embroidery

(d) Pottery

(iii) How is Ila was inspiration for all of us?

(iv) State True or False: The tone of the given lines is of astonishment.

Very Short Answer Type Questions

1. Name the things that Ila Sachani made.

2. What do people feel for Ila Sachani?

3. Name any award won by Ila Sachani.

Short Answer Type Questions

1. It was the government employees who actually changed Ila Sachani's life. Do you agree? Give reasons for your Answer.

2. How has Ila Sachani's determination and creativity been recognised?

3. Ila was no more a hidden talent, but famous! Comment.

Long Answer Type Question

1. Will power and determination can help you overcome any challenges. Explain with reference to Ila Sachani's story.

National War Memorial

CHAPTER 16

About the Chapter The given poem is about the National War Memorial located in New Delhi. The National War Memorial was established in January 2019. It is a national monument built by the Government of India in honour of our brave soldiers. The poet pays respect to these soldiers and commemorates their courage as well as sacrifice.

Stanzawise Explanation

Stanza 1 and 2

In Bharat's heartland, a grand sight to behold,
The National War Memorial, honours brave stories retold.
With respect and grace, it stands with pride,
Each name etched, each stone, each story to confide.

Explanation The lines describes the magnificent sight that can be seen at the heart of India. The poet takes us to New Delhi wherein the National War Memorial is located. The poet states that the memorial recounts and reminds us of the various heroic tales of our soldiers who have lost their lives while protecting the nation. According to the poet, the Memorial and the flame stands with grace, dignity and honour. The name of every soldier is written on each stone carefully and thoughtfully. Each of these stones preserve the heroic tale which should be shared amongst with respect.

Stanza 3 and 4

From battle fields to skies, and to oceans wide,
They stand for Bharat, side by side.
The eternal flame, in silence it glows,
Paying homage to their courage that shows.

Explanation In these lines, the poet states that thee soldiers whose names have been written on the stones of the National War Memorial have worked in different kind of areas/terrains. They have participated in wars, served in mountains and in oceans. They all stood united with India to protect their motherland.

The poet, then, talks about to mention the eternal flame that burns in the National War Memorial. This flame burns silently but brightly.

This flame symbolises the everlasting tribute to the unwavering courage displayed by the soldiers being commemorated.

Stanza 5 and 6

Their sacrifice, always in our mind,
In blessed memory, forever remind.
With pride and respect, let's always remember,
At the National War Memorial, their sacrifice forever.

Explanation In these lines, the poet emphasises that the sacrifices of the soldiers can never be forgotten. Their selfless acts will always be remembered and cherished by all. The poet, then, requests everyone to remember the brave soldiers with respect and pride forever. He wants that the soldiers should never be forgotten.

Values Extracted from this Chapter

The chapter conveys respect for the brave soldiers who have sacrificed their lives for the safety of their nation. It celebrates the patriotism and pride associated with serving the nation.

Word Meaning

Word	Meaning
Beholds	See
Etched	Written
Confide	To tell

Word	Meaning
Eternal	Permanent
Homage	Respect and honour

REVIEW EXERCISE

Including Competency Based Questions

Part I

Multiple Choice Questions

1. The tone of the given poem is ....

(a) angry
(b) regretful
(c) nostalgic
(d) reverential

Ans. (d) reverential

2. In the poem, the poet is celebrating ....

(a) soldiers
(b) leaders
(c) India
(d) Indian culture

Ans. (a) soldiers

Fill in the blanks

1. The poet takes us to ....

Ans. heart of India

2. .... is etched on the stones of the memorial.

Ans. The name of the various soldiers who died during duty

State True or False

1. The National War Memorial celebrates the freedom fighters.

Ans. False

2. The eternal flame burns silently but brightly.

Ans. True

Extract Based Questions

Read the extract given below and answer the questions that follow.

Their sacrifice, always in our mind,
In blessed memory, forever remind.
With pride and respect, let's always remember,
At the National War Memorial, their sacrifice forever.

(i) Who does the pronoun 'their' refer to?

(a) Freedom fighters (b) Public servants
(c) Brave soldiers (d) Politicians

Ans. Brave soldiers

(ii) The tone of the given lines is ....

Ans. respectful

(iii) What does the poet want us to remember?

Ans. The poet wants us to remember the sacrifices made by the brave soldiers to protect our country from any harm.

(iv) How does the National War Memorial remember 'their sacrifice'?

Ans. The National War Memorial remembers 'their sacrifice' by the means of the stones wherein the names of these soldiers are etched. Further, there is a flame that is burning to honour them.

Part II

Very Short Answer Type Questions

1. Which characteristics are attached with the National War Memorial?

Ans. The characteristics that are attached to the National War Memorial is grace, dignity, honor and respect.

2. What does the poet ask us to remember?

Ans. The poet asks us to remember the sacrifices of the brave soldiers.

Short Answer Type Questions

1. Each name etched, each stone, each story to confide. Explain.

Ans. The given lines from the poem indicate that the National War Memorial remember the name of all soldiers who sacrificed their lives. The name of each soldier is written on each stone carefully and thoughtfully. Each of these stones preserve the heroic tale which should be shared amongst with respect.

2. What does the poet wish for?

Ans. The poet wishes for all of us to remember the sacrifice, courage and heroic acts of those who have lost their lives while protecting the nation from any harm. The poet wants us to remember them with pride and respect, and never forget those people.

Sample Question Paper 1 (Unsolved)

English

Time : 3 hrs | M.M. : 80

General Instructions

1 The Question Paper contains four sections- Reading, Grammar and Writing and Literature.

2 Attempt questions based on specific instructions for each part.

Section A : Reading Skills

1. Read the given passage and answer the questions that follow. [10]

The G20 Summit was held in India from 1st December, 2022 to 30th November, 2023. But what is G20? G20, Group of Twenty is a forum for international economic cooperation. G 20 was founded in 1999 with the aim to promote economic and financial stability. India is one of the founding members of G 20. G20 comprises 19 countries and the European Union as members. The members of G20 are Argentina, Australia, Brazil, Canada, China, France, Germany, India, Indonesia, Italy, Japan, Republic of Korea, Mexico, Russia, Saudi Arabia, South Africa, Turkey, United Kingdom, United States and the European Union.

One of the themes in the G20 Agenda is the concept of LiFE (Life Style For Environment) with the aim of living in harmony with nature. We are aware that the environmental degradation is affecting all forms of life. Therefore, it is necessary to find a way of living which respects nature and other organisms that co-exist with us.

The overall summit was focused on working towards areas such as green development, climate finance, inclusive growth, digital coonomy, public infrastructure, technology transformation and reforms for women empowerment for socio-economic progress.

Did you know that G20 Logo has been inspired from the Indian National flag? It reflects the vibrant colours of India's National Flag - saffron, white and green and blue.

(i) When was the G20 Summit held?

(ii) Complete the sentence using appropriate article.

.... is a member of the G20.

(iii) Find a word from the passage which means 'global'.

(iv) State whether the statement is True or False.

LiFE was a theme of the 2023 G20 Summit.

(v) How many countries comprise the G20?

(vi) G20 Summit, 2023 focused to work on .... economy and reforms for

(vii) What is affecting all life forms?

(viii) Which of the following is not a member of the G20?

(a) North Korea (b) Indonesia

(c) Japan (d) China

(ix) The G20 logo consists of ...... colours.

(a) 3 (b) 5 (c) 4 (d) 6

(x) What reflects the vibrant colours of the Indian National Flag?

(a) Saffron, white, green and blue

(b) G20 Summit

(c) Tricolour

(d) G20 logo

2. Read the given lines and answer the following questions that follow. [10]

My name is not McGallimagoo,
Although some would have you think.
All day long they call me this,
And I really think it stinks.

McGallimagoo come here to me
McGalllimagoo sit down.
McGallimagoo is such a funny name,
But it always makes me frown.

So if you see me on the street,
Please don't call me this.
Refer to me by my proper name,
Which is Mr. Hullibajiss.

(i) What do people ask McGallimagoo to do?

(ii) Complete the sentence.
Some people called him McGallimagoo ....

(iii) Find a word from the lines which means the opposite of 'serious'.

(iv) State whether the statement is True or False.
The speaker likes to hear being called McGallimagoo.

(v) The speaker has a ...... name that is Mr. ....

(vi) Find the homophone of the word 'hear'.

(vii) Where should we refer to the speaker as Mr. Hullibajiss?

(viii) Who would think that the speaker's name is McGallimagoo?
(a) Some people (b) His family
(c) The speaker (d) Mr. Hullibajiss

(ix) What is the tone of the speaker in the above lines?
(a) Angry (b) Sad
(c) Excited (d) Annoyed

(x) What is the speaker trying to do in the above lines?
(a) Complain (b) Preach
(c) Describe (d) Sing

Section B : Writing Section

3. A. You are Ankita, Secretary of the Sports' Committee. Draft a notice notifying the students about the upcoming 'Annual Sports' festival'. **[5]**

Or

B. The following is a telephonic conversation between Rita and Asha. Rita wants to talk to her friend Arshi but she is not present at the moment so her sister Asha takes the message for her. Asha has to leave for tuition early so she decides to leave a message for Arshi. Read the conversation and write the message.

Rita : Hello! Is this 98XXXXXXXX?
Asha : Yes. May I know who's calling?
Rita : My name is Rita, a classmate of Arshi. Is she at home right now?
Asha : Actually, she has gone to aunt's place. Can I pass on any message?
Rita : Yes, please tell her that we have been selected as a team to participate in the Science Competition. It's scheduled on the 1st of next month so we have to start preparing for it.
Asha : That's good news. I'll inform her and ask her to get back to you as soon as possible.
Rita : Yes, thank you.
Asha : You're welcome. Bye.

4. A. Write a story in 120-150 words with the help of the hints given. Also give a suitable title to the story. **[5]**

An animal kingdom - shortage of food - cunning tortoise - ask birds where they got their food - heaven feast - tortoise asked for feathers from the birds - birds gave - code name to enter heaven - tortoise chose everyone of you - flown to heaven - host said feast for everyone of you - cunning tortoise ate alone as his name suggests - birds took back the feathers - bird changed - tortoise jumped and broke his shell - much later he still had one crack on his shell.

Or

B. Write a short story based on the given image. Also provide an appropriate title to the story.

5. A. **Write a letter to your friend Rakesh/Rakhi inviting him to attend your sister's marriage.** **[5]**

Or

B. **Write a letter to the Principal of your school requesting him/her to arrange painting materials for your special art class which is being held once every week.**

Section C : Grammar

6. **Fill in the blanks using suitable words given in the four options.** **[3]**

Good manners are not .... (i), nor do they come naturally. They .... (ii) learnt and practised. They are based ....(iii) the concept of consideration for others. Good manners are a necessity in every walk of life.

(i) (a) inherit (b) inherited (c) inherits (d) inheritted

(ii) (a) are (b) is (c) were (d) was

(iii) (a) in (b) on (c) at (d) for

7. **Report the given dialogue to complete the paragraph that follows.** **[3]**

Swara Hey, Ruchi! How are you? Did you enjoy during the holidays?

Ruchi Yes, I had a lot of fun with my family. We all went to Kerala for ten days and it was an amazing experience.

Swara exclaimed as she met Ruchi and asked her how she was. Further, she asked her (a)...................... Ruchi answered in affirmative and said that she (b).................... family. She added that they all had gone to Kerala for ten days and that it was an amazing experience.

8. **The following passages have not been edited. There is one error in each line. Identify the error and rectify them. Write your answer against the correct blank.** **[5]**

	Incorrect	Correction
When a leader makes a fake promise, all his actions reflect		
(i) the thought he is in and the thing	....	....
(ii) that people could does is not to	....	....
(iii) belief on any of them	....	....

9. **Rearrange the following to form meaningful sentences.** **[3]**

(i) the/is/world/wrestling/oldest/sports/in/the/one of

(ii) an/honest/boy/my/friend/is

(iii) day/I/next/shall/him/see/certainly/the

Section D : Literature

10. **Read the given extracts and answer the questions that follow.** **[5]**

A. There was a boy called Mario who loved to have lots of friends. He showed off a lot, always talking about how many friends he had at school, and how he was so friendly with everyone. One day his grandfather said to him, "Mario, I bet you a fruit chaat. You don't have as many friends as you think you have. I'm sure many of them are nothing more than companions or partners." (The Chair)

(i) What does the phrase 'show off' mean?

(a) To show something to a friend

(b) To show direction

(c) To boast about something

(d) To lie about something

(ii) If Mario won the bet he would get a ....

(iii) State True or False for the following statement.
Grandfather played a prank on Mario.

(iv) The synonym of the word companion is ....

(v) What did Mario love?

Or

B. For Ila, embroidery became a way to express herself. At first, she crafted fine designs only for her family and friends, who were awestruck by her talent. They talked about those designs to others. Soon, the people in the village, too, discovered Ila's special skill and the admiration for her work began to spread.

(Ila Sachani: Embroidering Dreams with her Feet)

(i) Her friends and family are .... to Ila

(a) indifferent (b) angry
(c) supporters (d) demotivators

(ii) State True or False for the following statement.
Ila loves to be do her embroider.

(iii) What was Ila's special skills?

(iv) Write a synonym of 'awestruck'.

(v) Why did Ila like embroidery?

11. Read the given extracts and answer the questions that follow. **[5]**

A. Their sacrifice, always in our mind, In blessed memory, forever remind.
With pride and respect, let's always remember,
At the National War Memorial, their sacrifice forever.

(National War Memorial)

(i) Who are 'their'?

(a) Freedom fighters (b) Public servants
(c) Brave soldiers (d) Politicians

(ii) The tone of the given lines is ....

(iii) What does the poet want us to remember?

(iv) How does the National War Memorial remember 'their sacrifice'?

(v) Write the synonym of the word 'pride'.

B. Let me use my heart to see,
To realise what friends can be
And make no judgements from afar,
But love my friends the way they are.

(A Friend's Prayer)

(i) Complete the given series with the correct word.

Logic: Mind :: Emotion: ....

(ii) What does the line "to realise what friends can be" mean here?

(iii) Find the synonym for the word 'realise' from the given options.

(a) Understand (b) Rationalise
(c) Appreciate (d) Perceive

(iv) State True or False for the following statement.
One should use logic to understand their friends better.

(v) Write the antonym of the word 'afar'.

12. Answer the following questions in 15-20 words. [4]

(i) Why did the fox compliment the Raven?

(ii) What did the thief plan to do after entering the house?

(iii) How did Buntee feel when he first met Gajaraj?

(iv) What part of the neem tree is used as a natural pesticide?

13. Answer any three questions in 30-40 words. [9]

(i) Why does the bird say 'I have been very blind'?

(ii) Why is the memory of the soldiers called 'blessed'?

(iii) Why does the child want to be light and small in the poem 'The Kites'?

iv) Do you think that the title of the poem 'The Winner' is apt? Give reason for your answer.

(v) Write a short note on Aipan.

14. Answer in 100-150 words. [12]

What was the purpose of Daadi's letter to Vikram and Vaibhavi?

Or

List the various benefits of yoga.

15. Answer in 100-150 words. [7]

How did Rama Natha's wife help him in gaining his wealth?

Or

Will power and determination can help you overcome any challenges. Explain with reference to Ila Sachani.

Sample Question Paper 2 (Unsolved)
English

Time : 3 hrs | M.M. : 80

General Instructions

1 The Question Paper contains four sections- Reading, Grammar and Writing and Literature.
2 Attempt questions based on specific instructions for each part.

Section A : Reading Skills

1. Read the given passage and answer the questions that follow. [10]

Patriotism is an old concept, as old perhaps as the earliest of human civilisations. But all through the history of mankind, it has been narrowly understood. Today people have begun to realise that patriotism is an essential part of human instinct. Patriotism has its negative sides particularly when it exceeds its proper bounds. People who think their own country to be the best and are blind to its weaknesses are not patriots at all.

We are the members of a large human family and so cannot neglect our duties and responsibilities towards it. Our love for the country should be conditioned by respect for the whole community. Narrow prejudice can do nothing except to bring misfortune. In trying to overlook others' interest in the modern world, we harm our own. Patriotism should be tempered with reason so that it may not be an evil.

(i) What do people recently began to realise?

(ii) Complete the following sentence

Those who are blind to a country's .... are not real patriots.

(iii) Mention a negative side of patriotism.

(iv) Find the word from the passage which means the opposite of 'strengths'.

(a) narrowly (b) essential
(c) instinct (d) bounds

(v) What is the effect of narrow prejudice?

(vi) Find the word from the passage which means 'important'.

(vii) State whether the statement is True or False.

One should respect the whole community if one truly loves his country.

(viii) What is as old as patriotism?

(a) Mankind (b) Human civilisations
(c) Human instinct (d) History

(ix) Why can't we neglect the duties towards our own country?

(a) Because we all love our country.
(b) Because we are conditioned to respect it.
(c) Because we are forced to do it.
(d) Because we are members of a large human family.

(x) Patriotism with .... won't end up turning evil.

(a) Love (b) Reason
(c) Interest (d) Prejudice

2. Read the given passage and answer the questions that follow. [10]

1. One of the greatest advances in modern technology has been the invention of computers. They are widely used in industries and in universities. Now there is hardly any sphere of human life where computers have not been pressed into service of man. We are heading fast towards the day when a computer will be as much part of man's daily life as a telephone or a calculator.

2. Computers are capable of doing extremely complicated work in all branches of learning. They can solve the most complex mathematical problems or put thousands of unrelated facts in order. These machines can be put to varied uses. For instance, they can provide information on the best way to prevent traffic jams. This whole process by which machines can be used to work for us has been called automation. In the future, automation may enable human beings to enjoy more leisure than they do today. The coming of automation is bound to have important social consequences.

3. Some years ago an expert on automation, Sir Leon Bagrit, pointed out that it was a mistake to believe that these machines could think. There is no possibility that human beings will be "controlled by machines". Though computers are capable of learning from their mistakes and improving on their performance, they need detailed instructions from human beings to operate. They can never, as it were, lead independent lives or "rule the world" by making decisions of their own.

4. Sir Leon said that in future, computers would be developed which would be small enough to carry in the pocket. Ordinary people would then be able to use them to obtain valuable information. Computers could be plugged into a national network and be used like radios. For instance, people going on holiday could be informed about weather conditions. Car drivers can be given alternative routes when there are traffic jams. It will also be possible to make tiny translating machines. This will enable people who do not share a common language to talk to each other without any difficulty or to read foreign publications.

5. It is impossible to assess the importance of a machine of this sort, for many international misunderstandings are caused simply due to our failure to understand each other. Computers will also be used in ordinary public hospitals. By providing a machine with a patient's systems, a doctor will be able to diagnose the nature of his illness. Similarly, machines could be used to keep a check on a patient's health record and keep it up to date. Doctors will, therefore, have immediate access to great many facts which will help them in their work.

(i) Computers can be used to ....

(a) Find treatment for the patient's illness
(b) Prescribe a medicine for the patient
(c) Diagnose the nature of patient's illness
(d) Keep the patient in good mood

(ii) Many international misunderstandings are caused due to our failure to understand ....

(a) ourselves (b) other nations
(c) our friends (d) each other

(iii) A computer can replace ....

(a) Telephone (b) Camera
(c) Radio (d) All of these

(iv) Computers help car drivers to ....

(v) State main capabilities of computer (any two).

(vi) What is automation?

(vii) What benefit can man derive from automation?

(viii) Why can't computers replace man?

(ix) Find the synonyms of the word 'results' from the passage.

(x) How would computer change in the future according to Sir Leon?

Section B : Writing Section

3. A. Write a paragraph on your recent trip to the Planetarium. **[5]**

Or

B. Write an email to your sister telling her about your new boarding school in Shillong. You can include details about your teachers, mode of studies, classmates, weather, etc.

4. A. Write an article on 'The Benefits of Rising Early' in about 100 words. **[5]**

Or

B. Your class is preparing for an assembly on healthy mind and body. So, you have been asked to prepare a speech on 'Eating Healthy Food' which you will speak in the aseembly. Write the speech using the following clues.

Clues

- Unhealthy eating
- Health concerns
- Junk food increasing popularity
- Need to eat balanced diet
- Include green vegetables and fruits.

5. A. Write a letter to the Principal of your school asking him/her to organise a trip to the new science museum that has opened in your locality. **[5]**

Or

B. You have noticed many stray animals on the road during the busy hours of the day. These animals cause traffic jams as well as accidents. You have already written to the concerned authorities but no action has been taken so far. Write a letter to the Editor, The Hindu, drawing attention of the Municipal Commissioner, Chennai.

Clues

- Causes traffic jams and accidents
- Concerned authorities should take strict action
- Becoming a nuisance
- Problem needs to be rectified as soon as possible

Section C : Grammar

6. Fill in the blanks appropriately by choosing the correct option. **[3]**

The mere mention of the Nobel Prize (i) .... visions (ii) .... world famous scientists and economists. It is (iii) .... most coveted individual award in the world.

(i) (a) creates (b) create (c) created (d) creating

(ii) (a) for (b) of (c) from (d) over

(iii) (a) a (b) an (c) some (d) the

7. Read the given dialogue to complete the paragraph that follows. **[3]**

Rahul : Do you know that Ranjit met with an accident and is in the hospital?

Samar : Oh! I don't. Is he badly hurt? Which hospital is he in?

Rahul : The doctors say that there is nothing to worry. He is admitted to Beach Hospital.

Rahul asked Samar if he knew that Ranjit had met with an accident and was hospitalised. Samar expressed his ignorance and enquired (a)................... He also asked (b) .... Rahul told him that according to the doctors there was nothing to worry about and said that he was admitted to the Beach Hospital.

8. The following paragraph has not been edited. There is one error in each line. Identify the error and rectify them. Write your answer against the correct blank. **[5]**

	Incorrect	Correction
Many people came to the site where the		
(i) revolutionary general were to be hanged. When asked if	....	....
(ii) he had any desire, the smile ran	....	....
(iii) on him dry lips and he nodded his head	....	....

9. Rearrange the following to form a meaningful sentence. **[3]**

(i) called/rose/the/queen/the/is/flowers/of

(ii) widely/it/grown/is/the/all/world/over

(iii) 500/there/about/are/species/roses/of

Section D : Literature

10. Read the given extracts and answer the questions that follow. **[5]**

A. Yoga is a physical, mental, and spiritual practice that originated in ancient India. The word 'Yoga' comes from the Sanskrit root 'yuj', which means 'to join' or 'to unite'. This symbolises the unity of mind and body; thought and action; harmony between human and nature. It is a holistic approach to health and well-being.

(Yoga-A Way of Life)

(i) On the basis of the extract, can you call Yoga to be a part of the Indian cultural heritage? Give reason.

(ii) Define Yoga in your own words on the basis of the given lines.

(iii) Which of the following is an antonym of 'ancient'?

(a) Outdated (b) Unity (c) Traditional (d) Modern

(iv) State True or False for the following statement.

Yoga does not pay attention to mental health.

(v) Write the antonym of the word 'Harmony'

Or

B. Subhodayam! I am Balamurali from Andhra Pradesh. I want to tell you about the 400-year-old art of making toys in my village, Kondapalli. To make the toys, we take soft wood from the nearby hills. After that, we carve each part of the toy separately. Then, we use makku–a paste of tamarind seed powder and sawdust to join the pieces together. Next, we add details and finish the toys. Finally, we use oil and water-colours or vegetable dyes and enamel paints to colour them. These toys are based on folk stories, animals, birds, bullock carts, rural life, etc.

(Hamara Bharat In Credible India)

(i) Subhodayam is a ....

(a) form of greeting (b) friendly banter (c) name of the child (d) name of the art form

(ii) State True or False for the following statement.

Makku was a colour used to paint the toys.

(iii) What are the inspirations for the toys?

(iv) The toys are biodegradable. How?

(v) What is the name of Balamurali's village?

11. Read the given extracts and answer the questions that follow. [5]

A. Then I would drift upon
The paper wings,
And hear the songs
That the wild wind sings.
What fun it would be
To look right down,
Over the park
And the rooftops of town. (The Kites)

(i) Drift indicates ....
(a) fast movement
(b) irregular movement
(c) slow movement
(d) round movement

(ii) Complete the sentence appropriately.
The child is .... to fly in the sky.

(iii) Identify the expression that uses alliteration.

(iv) Comment on the tone of the given lines.

(v) What is the antonym of the word 'fun'?

Or

B. At length I flew beyond the tree,
Quite fit for grown-up labours,
I don't know how the world is made,
And neither do my neighbours.
(What a Bird Thought)

(i) What action is the bird talking about in the first two lines?

(ii) The word 'grown-up' refers to the ....

(iii) Choose the word that has similar meaning as 'quite'.
(a) Silently (b) Slowly
(c) Completely (d) Noisily

(iv) State True or False for the follwing statement.
The bird thinks it knows how the world is made.

(v) Who are the 'neighbours' in the given lines?

12. Answer the following questions in 15-20 words. [4]

(i) Which characteristics are attached with the National War Memorial?

(ii) Can you think of the games the children are playing in 'The Winner"?

(iii) What did Daadi say that the children must remember before using the spices as remedies?

(iv) How do neem leaves help protect clothes and grains?

13. Answer any three questions in 30-40 words. [9]

(i) What should the Raven have remembered while dealing with the fox?

(ii) How did the man and his wife fool the thief?

(iii) How does the story show that friendship can overcome differences? Discuss with examples.

(iv) Explain the significance of the line "But love my friends the way they are".

(v) Explain the origin of the word 'Yoga'.

14. Answer in 100-150 words. [12]

What changes could be noted in Rama Natha's behaviour during the six years when he worked on his banana plantation? What moral do we derive from this story of Rama Natha?

Or

Mario, in the story 'The Chair' experiences some challenges as he tries to sit on the invisible chair. Based on your understanding of the story, describe the challenges Mario faces and explain how he overcomes them.

15. Answer in 100-150 words. [7]

Describe the significance of the neem tree as explained by Neem Baba.

Or

Describe the process of preparing any one home remedy using spices as mentioned in 'Spices that Heal Us'.

Sample Question Paper 3 (Unsolved)

English

Time : 3 hrs	M.M. : 80

General Instructions

1 The Question Paper contains four sections- Reading, Grammar and Writing and Literature.

2 Attempt questions based on specific instructions for each part.

Section A : Reading Skills

1. Read the given passage and answer the questions that follow. **[10]**

Newspapers are our good friends. Life without newspapers is a waste. Newspapers bring us news and views from all corners of the world. Any incident of occurrence of importance that takes place is reported by the newspapers. The word NEWS is interpreted as North, East, West and South. It means that the newspaper provides us with information and news regarding various subjects from all directions. Newspapers also give us articles on all kinds of topics such as political, social, economic, monetary, business, commerce, sports, education, health, etc.

Newspapers publish advertisements which attract the attention of the customers. They also contain book reviews of literary, historical and other books by scholars. Newspapers are of different types. Some newspapers are published daily. They are called 'Dailies'. We must cultivate the habit of reading newspapers to know what is happening around the globe. The one who reads newspapers and interprets editorial pages can only master current affairs and general knowledge. Reading newspapers helps you to find out what news is and how it is written. The one who dreams of being a journalist should not spare a day without reading the newspaper. They should be aware of the editorial and to be well-versed with vocabulary. We will get to know news from all the countries if we read newspapers regularly.

If we read the newspapers seriously, it will also help one to shine in competitive examinations.

(i) What is the full form of NEWS?

(ii) Complete the sentence.

Newspapers provide ....

(iii) Find the synonym of the word 'routine' from the passage.

(iv) What are 'Dailies'?

(v) Find the word from the passage which is a homophone of the word 'won'.

(vi) Who should be aware of the editorial and why?

(vii) Pick the word which means 'one who buys goods from a shop?'

(a) Customer (b) Editor (c) Journalist (d) Writer

(viii) Which type of book reviews do newspapers contain?

(a) Historical (b) Literary (c) Only (a) (d) Both (a) and (b)

(ix) What do newspapers bring us?

(a) Local news (b) Global news
(c) National news (d) News from specific place

(x) Journalists should be well-versed with ....

(a) editorial (b) literature (c) vocabulary (d) history

2. Read the following passage and answer the questions that follow. **[10]**

How brightly through the mist of years,
My quiet country home appears!
My father busy all the day
In plowing corn or raking hay;
My mother moving with delight
Among the milk pans, silver-bright;
We children, just from school set free,
Filling the garden with our glee.
The blood of life was flowing warm
When I was living on a farm.

(i) What are the activities that the father does?

(ii) State whether the statement is True/False.
The poet disliked his life in the country home.

(iii) Complete the sentence appropriately in context with the text given.
Among the milk pans, silver- bright, ...

(iv) Find a word from the poem which means 'delight'.

(v) Justify the following statement. The poet's life is full of happiness while living on a farm.

(vi) Provide a suitable title of the lines given.

(vii) Find the word from the given lines which means the opposite of 'dimly'.

(viii) Who were being freed from school?
(a) Father (b) Mother (c) Children (d) Speaker

(ix) What is the tone of the given lines?
(a) Angry (b) Happy (c) Nostalgic (d) Sad

(x) "The blood of life was flowing warm".
What does the above line imply?
(a) Full of energy (b) Bleeding (c) Warm blood (d) Tired from bleeding

Section B : Writing Section

3. A. Write a bio-sketch of 'Mark Zuckerberg' by using the following clues. **[5]**

- Born on May 14, 1984, New York
- Full name: Mark Elliot Zuckerberg
- Married in 2012 and has three daughters
- American computer programmer, billionaire
- Studied Computer Science at Harvard University
- Dropped out of college to focus on development of Facebook
- Co-founder and CEO of Facebook
- Re-branded all platforms to Meta in 2021
- Founded Chan Zuckerberg Initiative (CZI) with his wife Priscilla Chan
- to help in wiping out disease and improving education, to address the needs of local communities

Or

B. You have recently attended a Cartoon Art Workshop. Write a diary entry about it in 100 words.

4. **A. Write a story in about 100–120 words using the visual given. Give a suitable title to the story.** **[5]**

Or

B. Write an article on the topic 'The Need of Cleanliness in our Lives' in 100 words.

5. **A. Write a letter to your best friend narrating her the events that take place during Christmas. You are Ramesh from Bangalore.** **[5]**

Or

B. Write a letter to the editor of an English daily, making a plea to the common people to switch over to solar energy to conserve electricity and limit electricity bills.

Section C : Grammar

6. **This passage has not been edited. There is a word missing in each line and you are required to find that missing word. Choose the correct answer to fill in the blanks from the options given.** **[3]**

Family gives one all that one wants in one's life but it .... (i) often noted that people forget .... (ii) return their debt to them. There are many reasons for this but one .... (iii) the reasons is the way of thinking.

(i) (a) is	(b) be	(c) was	(d) has
(ii) (a) to	(b) on	(c) in	(d) for
(iii) (a) of	(b) for	(c) is	(d) was

7. **Read the dialogues to complete the paragraph that follows.** **[3]**

Mother	:	Why are you looking so worried?
Daughter	:	My exams are approaching.
Mother	:	When will they start?
Daughter	:	Next month, Mother.

Mother asked her daughter (a) .... The daughter replied that her exams were approaching. Mother further asked (b) .... The daughter told her mother that they would start in the following month.

8. The following passage has not been edited. There is an error in each line. Identify the error and rectify them. Write your answer against the correct blank. One has been done for you. **[5]**

	Incorrect	Correction
Once upon a time there was a		
(i) cap seller which used to sell these	which	who
(ii) caps in the villages. One day he is on	....	....
(iii) his way to selling the caps but he got	....	....
(iv) tired and so he lies down under a tree.	....	....
Soon, he fell asleep there with his caps.		

9. Rearrange the following to form meaningful sentences. **[3]**

(i) we/morning/shall/this/in/leave/village/the

(ii) know/I/a/better/teacher/for you

(iii) have/of/cup/a/often/I/tea

Section D : Literature

10. Read the given extracts and answer the questions that follow. **[5]**

A. Dear Amber, we become well known for what we do. People find us useful and that is why they know us. Scientists call us 'bitter grace of God', 'nature's gift to man', and 'cleanliness-parting tree'. Some even call us 'magic tree' and 'the tree of the twentieth century'. (Neem Baba)

(i) Who is talking here and to whom?

(ii) According to Neem Baba, how do scientists know the Neem trees?

(a) As the magic tree (b) As the bitter grace of God

(c) As nature's gift to man (d) All of these

(iii) The opposite of the word 'bitter' is ....

(iv) State True or False for the following statement.

Neem is a cleanliness parting tree.

(v) State one benefit that humans get from the neem tree.

Or

B. "I wish they would stop their silly game and talk about their money instead". (Rama to the Rescue)

(i) Who is the speaker here?

(ii) Why does he wish that the couple would talk about their money?

(iii) State True or False for the following statement.

The man and his wife were playing a game to entertain themselves.

(iv) Choose a synonym for the word 'silly'.

(a) Stupid (b) Easy

(c) Difficult (d) Intelligent

(v) Did the couple talk about their money?

11. Read the given extract and answer the questions that follow. **[5]**

A. I can't even catch my breath.
When blue dark turns to black,
cold grass aches our feet, (The Winner)

(i) The usual play time of children is ....
(a) night (b) afternoon
(c) evening (d) morning

(ii) State True or False for the following statement. The grass is cold because of the low temperature of the night.

(iii) Complete the sentence appropriately.
In the given lines, the speaker is ....

(iv) When and why do you think the game stops?

(v) Write a synonym for the word 'aches'.

Or

B. "And now you know,
Ignore sweet words that make you glow."
(The Raven and the Fox)

(i) Who is talking to whom in the given extract?
(a) The fox to the Raven (b) Raven to the fox
(c) The Raven to himself (d) The fox to himself

(ii) What do these words suggest about the listener?

(iii) State True or False for the following statement.
The Raven fell for the fox's trick.

(iv) The opposite of 'glow' is ....

(v) Why should you ignore sweet words?

12. Answer the following questions in 15-20 words[4]

(i) Who presented the ancient system of yoga?

(ii) What things can be made using coconut shells?

(iii) What kind of image does the child see from the kite?

(iv) What according to the baby bird the world is made of in the beginning?

13. Answer any three questions in 30-40 words. **[9]**

(i) How does the poem make you feel about friendship?

(ii) Why didn't Rama Natha take care of his land?

(iii) When did Daadi use Heeng and for what?

(iv) Each name etched, each stone, each story to confide. Explain based on 'National War Memorial'.

(v) What other title would you suggest for the poem 'The Winner'? Give reason for your answer.

14. Answer in 100-150 words. **[12]**

Compare and contrast the characters of Prabhat and Surya.

Or

Discuss the role of friendship in Mario's journey to successfully sit on the invisible chair. How did his friends contribute to his achievement?

15. Answer in 100-150 words. **[7]**

How did the mahout react to Gajaraj's sadness after Buntee was taken away? What steps did he take to help Gajaraj?

Or

Ila Sachani's story acts as an inspiration for all. Explain with examples from her story.